The works of Francis Bacon / collected and edited by James Spedding, Robert Leslie Ellis, and Douglas Denon Heath. Volume 10 of 14

Francis Bacon

The works of Francis Bacon / collected and edited by James Spedding, Robert Leslie Ellis, and Douglas Denon Heath.
Bacon, Francis
collection ID ocm16990544
Reproduction from Harvard Law School Library
Vols. 1-7: New ed. Imprint varies: v. 8-9: London : Longman, Green, Longman and Roberts; v. 10-14: London : Longmans, Green, Reader and Dyer.
London : Longman, 1861-1879.
14 v. : ill., ports., facsims. ; 22 cm.

The Making of Modern Law collection of legal archives constitutes a genuine revolution in historical legal research because it opens up a wealth of rare and previously inaccessible sources in legal, constitutional, administrative, political, cultural, intellectual, and social history. This unique collection consists of three extensive archives that provide insight into more than 300 years of American and British history. These collections include:

Legal Treatises, 1800-1926: over 20,000 legal treatises provide a comprehensive collection in legal history, business and economics, politics and government.

Trials, 1600-1926: nearly 10,000 titles reveal the drama of famous, infamous, and obscure courtroom cases in America and the British Empire across three centuries.

Primary Sources, 1620-1926: includes reports, statutes and regulations in American history, including early state codes, municipal ordinances, constitutional conventions and compilations, and law dictionaries.

These archives provide a unique research tool for tracking the development of our modern legal system and how it has affected our culture, government, business – nearly every aspect of our everyday life. For the first time, these high-quality digital scans of original works are available via print-on-demand, making them readily accessible to libraries, students, independent scholars, and readers of all ages.

The BiblioLife Network

This project was made possible in part by the BiblioLife Network (BLN), a project aimed at addressing some of the huge challenges facing book preservationists around the world. The BLN includes libraries, library networks, archives, subject matter experts, online communities and library service providers. We believe every book ever published should be available as a high-quality print reproduction; printed on-demand anywhere in the world. This insures the ongoing accessibility of the content and helps generate sustainable revenue for the libraries and organizations that work to preserve these important materials.

The following book is in the "public domain" and represents an authentic reproduction of the text as printed by the original publisher. While we have attempted to accurately maintain the integrity of the original work, there are sometimes problems with the original work or the micro-film from which the books were digitized. This can result in minor errors in reproduction. Possible imperfections include missing and blurred pages, poor pictures, markings and other reproduction issues beyond our control. Because this work is culturally important, we have made it available as part of our commitment to protecting, preserving, and promoting the world's literature.

GUIDE TO FOLD-OUTS MAPS and OVERSIZED IMAGES

The book you are reading was digitized from microfilm captured over the past thirty to forty years. Years after the creation of the original microfilm, the book was converted to digital files and made available in an online database.

In an online database, page images do not need to conform to the size restrictions found in a printed book. When converting these images back into a printed bound book, the page sizes are standardized in ways that maintain the detail of the original. For large images, such as fold-out maps, the original page image is split into two or more pages

Guidelines used to determine how to split the page image follows:

• Some images are split vertically; large images require vertical and horizontal splits.
• For horizontal splits, the content is split left to right.
• For vertical splits, the content is split from top to bottom.
• For both vertical and horizontal splits, the image is processed from top left to bottom right.

THE

WORKS

OF

FRANCIS BACON.

VOL. X.

THE

WORKS

OF

FRANCIS BACON

BARON OF VERULAM, VISCOUNT ST ALBAN,

AND

LORD HIGH CHANCELLOR OF ENGLAND

COLLECTED AND EDITED BY

JAMES SPEDDING, M.A.,

OF TRINITY COLLEGE, CAMBRIDGE,

ROBERT LESLIE ELLIS, M.A.,

LATE FELLOW OF TRINITY COLLEGE, CAMBRIDGE,

AND

DOUGLAS DENON HEATH,

BARRISTER AT-LAW, LATE FELLOW OF TRINITY COLLEGE, CAMBRIDGE

VOL X

THE LETTERS AND THE LIFE, VOL. III

LONDON

LONGMANS, GREEN, READER, AND DYER

1868.

PRINTED BY

J P TAYLOR AND CO , LITTLE QUEEN STREET,

LINCOLN'S INN FIELDS

THE LETTERS AND THE LIFE

OF

FRANCIS BACON

INCLUDING ALL HIS

OCCASIONAL WORKS

NAMELY

LETTERS SPEECHES TRACTS STATE PAPERS MEMORIALS DEVICES
AND ALL AUTHENTIC WRITINGS NOT ALREADY PRINTED AMONG HIS
PHILOSOPHICAL LITERARY OR PROFESSIONAL WORKS

NEWLY COLLECTED AND SET FORTH

IN CHRONOLOGICAL ORDER

WITH A

COMMENTARY BIOGRAPHICAL AND HISTORICAL

BY

JAMES SPEDDING

VOL III

LONDON:
LONGMANS, GREEN, READER, AND DYER.
1868.

TX
B129w

J. E. TAYLOR AND CO, PRINTERS,
LITTLE QUEEN STREET, LINCOLN'S INN FIELDS

PREFACE.

———◆———

THE two volumes last published included all Bacon's occasional works of the descriptions enumerated in the title-page, up to April 1601. The two which I publish now carry on the series to the end of 1613, when he had just been made Attorney General. They are set forth upon the same plan in all respects as the former, and what I have to say about each piece will be found beside it.

The chief thing to be noticed here is the engraving which accompanies this volume, but which it will probably be thought expedient to transfer to Vol. I.

In the " History and Plan of the Edition " prefixed to the Philosophical works, I told what I then knew about the portraits of Bacon, at which time (January, 1857) I had not seen any likeness of him in mature life which did not appear to be traceable to one or other of two originals,—the full-length painting at Gorhambury by Van Somer, or the old engraving by Simon Pass. But among the miniatures lent to the South Kensington museum for exhibition in 1865 there was a small one belonging to the Duke of Buccleuch, which though evidently representing not only the same man but the same *likeness* of the same man as Van Somer's picture, could not be taken for a copy of it. In all those points in which copies always agree and independent originals always differ,—the attitude, the point of view, the arrangement of the dress, the light and shadow, etc.,—the resemblance between the two was exact: in all those in which all copies fall short and only the best come near,—the physiognomical character, the drawing of the more delicate features, the living look,—the differences were considerable and the

inferiority of the large picture manifest. All that was in the
picture (as far as the head and shoulders) might easily have
been got from the miniature: but there was much in the
miniature which could not possibly have been got from the
picture. And though, if we judge from modern practice, it may
seem improbable that an artist of reputation like Van Somer
would have painted a full-length portrait of a living subject
from a miniature drawing by another man, I was told by the
late Sir Charles Eastlake that it is not so. In those times it
was the common practice (he said), when a portrait was wanted,
to have in the first instance a careful drawing done in miniature; from which various copies would afterwards be made in
any size or style that might be wished, "and therefore" (he
added) "when you meet with two portraits of that period—a
miniature and a life-size painting—of which there is reason to
believe that one has been copied from the other, the presumption always is that the miniature was the one taken from the life."
I am persuaded that there is no other way of explaining satisfactorily the peculiar relation between these two; and I now
look upon the Duke of Buccleuch's miniature as the undoubted
head of that whole family of Bacon portraits.

That it has never been engraved before, I cannot assert posi-
tively; for it is evident to me now that Houbraken's well-
known engraving was taken, not from Van Somer's painting (as
I formerly supposed), but from this,—either directly or through
some other copy. The resemblance however which convinces
me of that fact is only in the composition and the general effect.
It does not extend to the features, which are treated as usual
with so little care for the likeness that no one could guess from
the copy what the character of the face in the original really is.
Without saying therefore that it has never been engraved
before, I may at least say that another engraving was wanted,
and having by the Duke of Buccleuch's permission (for which I
hope everybody will join me in thanking him) had one made
directly from the original, I leave it to speak for itself and make
good its own title to acceptance.

Of the history and adventures of this miniature before it

came into the Duke's possession nothing, I believe, is known. It is said to be by Peter Oliver; though, if the dates be correct, he must have been a very young man when it was done. Isaac Oliver is said to have died in 1617, Peter to have been born in 1601. The picture is dated 1620. If there is no better reason for ascribing it to Peter than that his father was dead when the date was inserted, it is obvious to suggest that the date represents the time when it was *finished*. the face may have been painted some years earlier. But whether it were a very early work of the son's or a very late one of the father's, or a work left unfinished by the father and finished by the son, it is a masterly performance, and bears upon its face the evidence of its value. The letters seen round the margin, giving the year date and the age date, are in the original painted with gold on the blue background of the picture, round the inner border. In white on black it was thought they would be scarcely visible In all other respects the engraving is as exact as it could be made.

There still remains to be discovered the original of Pass's print; which is to be sought for, not (as I once thought) among pictures by Cornelius Jansen, but among miniatures by Hilliard and the Olivers A miniature undoubtedly representing the same portrait, and also ascribed to Peter Oliver, was to be seen in another part of the same exhibition at South Kensington; and though I cannot think that it was the same which Pass engraved, because the engraving has so much more life and character in it, or that it can have been the work of either Oliver's own hand at any stage in the development of their powers, it affords a fair presumption that such a miniature was once in existence.

The new matter of Bacon's own, contained in these two volumes,—reckoning as new not only what has not been printed before, but what has not been included in any former edition of Bacon's works—would fill about 150 pages, if collected together. A good deal of it however consists of notes of his speeches in Parliament, taken from the Journals of the House of Commons, which are so disjointed and fragmentary that it will be a question with many, whether they ought to have been included in a

work of this kind. It was a question with myself. But as I
believe them to be genuine fragments of his speeches, taken
down at the time as fast as a not very ready writer could follow;
and as the proceedings of Parliament were so important a part
of the business of the time, and Bacon so important an actor in
them; and as I have myself learned from these fragmentary
and disjointed notes so much about his political life which I
could not have learned either from summary accounts or ex-
tracts; I thought it better to print all that there are, and so
bring the whole of the evidence within reach of everybody. In
order to make them as intelligible as I could, I have been
obliged to enter into a history and discussion of the Parliamentary proceedings more minute than has been attempted before,
and I think it will be found that there is both novelty and interest in the matter which the investigation has brought out. To
myself at least much of it is new.

All the pieces in these, as in the preceding volumes, have
been collated with the originals referred to in the footnotes . in
most cases the proof-sheets have been corrected from them ; nor
have any alterations been admitted without notice into the text,
except in regard of spelling and punctuation. In spelling and
punctuation I have followed modern usage in all cases but one,
which is peculiar. The *Commentarius Solutus*, which will be
found near the beginning of the next volume, is copied from a
note-book of private memoranda, of which a large proportion
are set down in so abbreviated a form that the interpretation is
doubtful. To supply the full words by conjecture would be to
settle innumerable questions without authority, and at the same
time to obliterate the facts upon which the conjecture rests. In
this case therefore I have endeavoured to produce a *literatim*
copy; and having had the best assistance both in deciphering
the manuscript and correcting the proofs, I hope it will be found
to be as nearly a *fac-simile* of the original as was compatible
with the use of my type and the length of my line.[1]

J. S.

---

[1] The date however at the top of p 63 ought to be 26, instead of 25   The
error appears to have crept in after the proofs were settled, in replacing an imperfect letter. It was 26 in the last revise which I saw.

CONTENTS

OF THE THIRD VOLUME.

—◆—

BOOK III.

CHAPTER I.

A.D. 1601, APRIL—DECEMBER   ÆTAT. 40.

Page

1 Altercation between Bacon and Coke in the Exchequer . 1

LETTER TO MR SECRETARY CECIL, 29th of April, 1601 . 2

LETTER OF EXPOSTULATION TO THE ATTORNEY GENERAL . 4

2 Death of Anthony Bacon   His character and services . . 5

Story told of him by Sir Henry Wotton examined and explained . 9

3 Fines and pardons of the persons engaged in Essex's Conspiracy

Sum assigned to Bacon out of Catesby's fine . . . 14

LETTER TO MR. M. HICKES. [Aug. 1601] 14

4 The Queen and the Monopolies. Occupation of Kinsale in Ire-

land by the Spaniards. A new Parliament summoned . . 15

5 Notes of Speeches by Bacon.

SPEECH ON BRINGING IN A BILL AGAINST ABUSES IN WEIGHTS

AND MEASURES 17

SPEECH FOR REPEALING SUPERFLUOUS LAWS . . 19

6. Grant of 4 subsidies, payable in three years and a half . . 20

REPORT OF BILL TOUCHING THE EXCHEQUER . . . 21

8 Commencement of the attack upon Monopolies . . . 23

SPEECH IN THE HOUSE AGAINST A BILL FOR THE EXPLANA-

TION OF THE COMMON LAW IN CERTAIN CASES OF LETTERS

PATENTS 26

Bill committed

SPEECH IN COMMITTEE AGAINST THE SAME . . . 28

Motion for a petition to the Queen for leave to pass an Act making

monopolies of no more force than they are at the Common Law

Seconded by Bacon   but no decision taken. Cecil's inter-

ference. The Queen's message. Proclamation to suspend the

execution of Monopoly patents till tried by Common Law

Page

   Satisfaction of the House   The Queen's last speech to her people   29
9 Notes of Speeches on several occasions
   SPEECH ON BRINGING IN A BILL CONCERNING ASSURANCES
      AMONG MERCHANTS   34
   SPEECH AGAINST THE REPEAL OF THE STATUTE OF TILLAGE .   35
   SPEECH AGAINST A MOTION FOR MAKING A JUDICIAL EXPO-
      SITION OF A STATUTE PART OF THE STATUTE   .   .   .   36
   SPEECH AGAINST COMMITTING TO THE TOWER FOR AN AS-
      SAULT ON A MEMBER'S SERVANT   37
   SPEECH AGAINST THE REPEAL OF AN ACT RELATING TO CHA-
      RITABLE TRUSTS   38

CHAPTER II

A D 1601–1603, DECEMBER—APRIL   ÆTAT. 41–43.

1. Money difficulties. Mortgage of Twickenham Park   Reference
   to the Lord Treasurer.
   THE STATEMENT OF THE CAUSE BETWIXT MR. FRA. BACON
      AND MR. TROTT   40
2 Defeat of the Spanish forces in Ireland   44
   LETTER TO MR SECRETARY CECIL enclosing CONSIDERATIONS
      TOUCHING THE QUEEN'S SERVICE IN IRELAND   .   .   45
3. Submission of Tyrone   Montjoy's instructions and proceedings
   Illness and death of Elizabeth   53
4 James I. proclaimed King   55
   Bacon seeks to get himself recommended to his favour   .   56
   LETTER TO MR. MICHAEL HICKS, 19 March, 1602   .   .   57
   LETTER TO THE EARL OF NORTHUMBERLAND, A FEW DAYS
      BEFORE QUEEN ELIZABETH'S DEATH   .   .   .   58
   Letters to Gentlemen of the Scotch Court.
   A LETTER TO MR. DAVID FOULES IN SCOTLAND UPON THE
      ENTRANCE OF HIS MAJESTY'S REIGN   .   .   .   59
   A LETTER TO EDWARD BRUCE, ABBOT OF KINLOSS .   .   60
   AN OFFER OF SERVICE TO HIS MAJESTY K. JAMES UPON
      HIS FIRST COMING IN   62
   A LETTER RECOMMENDING HIS LOVE AND SERVICES TO SIR
      THOMAS CHALLONER, THEN IN SCOTLAND, UPON HIS MA-
      JESTY'S ENTRANCE   63
   A LETTER TO MR FOULES, 28TH OF MARCH, 1603   .   64
   A LETTER TO MR. DAVYS, THEN GONE TO THE KING, AT
      HIS FIRST ENTRANCE, MARCH 28, 1603   .   .   .   65
   A LETTER TO DR MORRISON, A SCOTTISH PHYSICIAN, UPON
      HIS MAJESTY'S COMING IN   66

Page

A LETTER TO MY LORD OF NORTHUMBERLAND, MENTIONING A PROCLAMATION DRAWN FOR THE KING AT HIS ENTRANCE   67

A PROCLAMATION DRAWN FOR HIS MAJESTY'S FIRST COMING IN, PREPARED BUT NOT USED 67

Proceedings of the Council during the interregnum . . . 71

A LETTER TO MR. TOBY MATTHEW, SIGNIFYING THE WISE PROCEEDING OF KING JAMES AT HIS FIRST ENTRANCE TO THIS KINGDOM 73

A LETTER TO MR. ROBERT KEMPE UPON THE DEATH OF QUEEN ELIZABETH 74

Relations between Bacon and Lord Southampton.

A LETTER TO THE EARL OF SOUTHAMPTON UPON THE KING'S COMING IN 75

Bacon's interview with the King and first impressions.

A LETTER TO THE EARL OF NORTHUMBERLAND AFTER HE HAD BEEN WITH THE KING 76

CHAPTER III

A D 1603. ÆTAT. 43.

1. Bacon's official position and prospects 78

2 State of his private affairs   Project of marriage.
   LETTER TO ROBERT, LORD CECIL, 3 July, 1603   . 79
   LETTER TO THE SAME, 16 July, 1603 81
   A NOTE OF MY DEBTS 82

3. Progress of philosophical speculations   Preface to intended treatise *De Interpretatione Naturæ* 82
   Probable occasion and object of book on the *Advancement of Learning* 88

4 A BRIEF DISCOURSE TOUCHING THE HAPPY UNION OF THE KINGDOMS OF ENGLAND AND SCOTLAND   dedicated in private to his Majesty 90

5 Dispute between the High Churchmen and the Puritans. True policy of the government 99
   CERTAIN CONSIDERATIONS TOUCHING THE BETTER PACIFICATION AND EDIFICATION OF THE CHURCH OF ENGLAND . 103

6 Conference at Hampton Court. Order of proceeding. Results. 127

CHAPTER IV.

A D. 1603 ÆTAT. 43.

1 The Priest's plot. Trial of Sir Walter Ralegh   . . . 133

Page

2. Popular impressions with regard to Bacon's conduct towards
Essex   whence derived   Convenience of the time for explanation   136

Sir Francis Bacon his Apology in certain imputations
concerning the late Earl of Essex, in a letter to Lord
Montjoy, now Earl of Devonshire   139

Reasons for believing that the explanation was not considered unsatisfactory by Bacon's contemporaries   161

CHAPTER V

A.D 1604   ÆTAT 44

1 A new Parliament summoned   Great question of Privilege   Sir
Francis Goodwin's case   Conference with the King   .   . 163

Notes of Bacon's speech on the question whether the
Commons should agree to a conference with the
Judges (March 29)   166

Committee appointed to draw up reasons against conferring—
Bacon to deliver them to the Lords   167

Notes of his report to the House (April 3)   .   . 167

Committee appointed to confer with the Judges—Bacon to be
spokesman   169

Notes of his report of the Conference (April 11)   . 169

Compromise proposed and agreed to   172

2 Arrest of Sir Thomas Shirley for debt   Dispute between the
Commons and the Warden of the Fleet   .   .   . 172

Notes of Bacon's speech (May 10)   .   .   . 175

Interference of the King   176

3 State of the law with regard to Wardship, Purveyance, Monopolies, etc, referred to a Committee   176

Resolutions of Committee reported by Bacon.   Notes of
Report (March 26)   178

Conference with the Lords concerning Wardship agreed to
Reported by Bacon   178

Notes of Report   179

4 Petition to the King touching Purveyors, presented (April 27)
A speech made by Sir Francis Bacon, Knight, chosen
by the Commons to present a petition touching
Purveyors, delivered to his Majesty in the withdrawing chamber at Whitehall in the Parliament
held 1° et 2° Jac the first session (April 27)   . 181

Notes of Bacon's report of the King's answer   . 187

Page

Conference with the Lords touching Purveyors—reported by Bacon

NOTES OF REPORT 189

Further proceeding postponed till next session . . 190

5 Proceedings with regard to the Union   Debate on the union in name 196

NOTES OF BACON'S FIRST SPEECH (April 16) . . 191

Preparations for Conference with the Lords. NOTES OF BACON'S SECOND SPEECH (April 19) . . 192

The King makes a speech to the members of the Lower House, and offers a project of an Act of Parliament . . . 193

NOTES OF BACON'S REPORT OF THE KING'S SPEECH (April 21) 195

Dissatisfaction of the Commons.   Abortive Conference with the Lords   The King's 'project' referred by him to the Judges Objections to change of name.   Committee instructed to make preparations for another Conference with the Lords . . 196

BACON'S REPORT OF THE ARRANGEMENTS MADE BY THE COMMITTEE (April 27) 197

The Judges unfavourable to the change of name by Act of Parliament   Conference with the Lords   NOTES OF BACON'S INTRODUCTORY SPEECH   Commissioners of Union to be appointed   NOTES OF BACON'S REPORT OF THE CONFERENCE (April 30) 200

OTHER CONFERENCES REPORTED BY HIM (May 1, 2, 9) . 202

Draft delivered in by Bacon, of AN ACT FOR THE BETTER GROUNDING OF A FURTHER UNION TO ENSUE BETWEEN THE KINGDOMS OF ENGLAND AND SCOTLAND (May 12) . 204

Commissioners chosen and Act passed 207

6 Dissatisfaction of the King   His letter to the Commons . 207

Conference with the Lords about a book published by a Bishop in derogation of the Lower House   NOTES OF BACON'S REPORT OF THE CONFERENCE.   The Bishop rebuked and made to acknowledge his error.   Liberty of the Press . . 208

Protest of Convocation against pretensions of the House of Commons.   Unsatisfactory conference with the Lords on Wardships and Tenures.   Another speech from the King Union Act passed with unusual expedition.   Interchange of explanations.   Apology of the Commons   Hint from the Lords that a subsidy would be welcome . . . 210

NOTES OF BACON'S REPORT OF CONFERENCE (June 22) . 214

Motion received doubtfully and withdrawn by the King's desire Parliament prorogued (July 7) . . . 215

Page
LETTER TO TOBY MATTHEW   216

CHAPTER VI

A D 1604, JULY—DECEMBER   ÆTAT 44

1. Vacation work. Preparations for the meeting of the Commissioners for the Union. LETTER TO SIR ROBERT COTTON (Sept. 8) 217

CERTAIN ARTICLES OR CONSIDERATIONS TOUCHING THE UNION OF THE KINGDOMS OF ENGLAND AND SCOTLAND .   . 218

2. DRAUGHT OF A PROCLAMATION TOUCHING HIS MAJESTY'S STILE, PREPARED NOT USED   235

3 Proceedings of the Commissioners for the Union. Notes from Journal 240

4 Resolutions digested into form by Bacon, and a preamble prepared

THE MOST HUMBLE CERTIFICATE OR RETURN OF THE COMMISSIONERS OF ENGLAND AND SCOTLAND, AUTHORISED TO TREAT OF AN UNION FOR THE WEAL OF BOTH REALMS. 2 JAC 1   PREPARED BUT ALTERED   .   .   . 242

Unanimity of the Commissioners (all but one) and prosperous despatch of their business (Dec. 6, 1604). Causes of delay in submitting their recommendations to Parliament   .   . 245

CHAPTER VII.

A D 1605-6   ÆTAT 45

1 The Solicitor-General (Fleming) made Chief Baron. Doderidge made Solicitor (Oct 28, 1604)   247

2 Interval of leisure for Bacon. Progress of the *Advancement of Learning* 248

LETTER TO THE LORD CHANCELLOR, TOUCHING THE HISTORY OF BRITAIN (April 5, 1605) 249

3. Publication of the *Advancement of Learning*. Presentation copies.

A LETTER TO THE EARL OF NORTHAMPTON, WITH REQUEST TO PRESENT HIS BOOK TO HIS MAJESTY .   .   . 252

A LETTER TO SIR THOMAS BODLEY, UPON SENDING HIM HIS BOOK OF THE ADVANCEMENT OF LEARNING   . 253

A LETTER TO THE EARL OF SALISBURY, UPON SENDING HIM ONE OF HIS BOOKS OF ADVANCEMENT OF LEARNING .   . 253

A LETTER TO THE LORD TREASURER BUCKHURST, UPON THE SAME OCCASION OF SENDING HIS BOOK OF ADVANCEMENT OF LEARNING   .   .   . 254

Page

A LETTER OF THE LIKE ARGUMENT TO MY LORD CHANCELLOR 254

4 Gunpowder Plot . . . .
  LETTER TO TOBY MATTHEW 255
  Bishop Andrewes and the *Advancement of Learning*. Death of the Chief Justice of the Common Pleas Succeeded by Sir Francis Gawdy, puisne Judge of the King's bench . 256

5 LETTER TO THE EARL OF SALISBURY Enclosing an Examination relating to the Gunpowder Plot 257
  LETTER TO SIR M HICKES (Jan 27) 259

6. Second session of James's first Parliament. The King relates the discovery of the Plot (Nov 9, 1605). Adjournment to January 21. Altered temper of the Commons. Grant of 2 subsidies agreed upon (Feb. 10) Question of Union postponed 259

7. Articles against Recusants Conference between the two Houses.
  NOTES OF BACON'S REPORT (Feb. 7) . . . 262

8 Conference on Ecclesiastical grievances Deprived Ministers . 264
  NOTES OF BACON'S REPORT (April 29) . . . 265

9. Question of Purveyance resumed Bill brought in. Conferences.
  NOTES OF BACON'S REPORT (March 1) . . . 267
  Second Conference (March 4). Coke argues against the bill Long debates in the House Bacon in favour of composition.
  NOTES OF HIS SPEECH (March 7) . . . 269
  Composition given up. Bill proceeded with, but lost in the Upper House 271
  Proclamation put forth for the prevention of future abuses in Purveyance 272

10 Progress of Subsidy Bill. Grant of 2 subsidies agreed to (Feb 10). A third to be added, and Committee instructed accordingly (March 18). Bacon to report proceedings . 273
  LETTER TO THE EARL OF SALISBURY (March 22) . 275
  Rumour that the King had been assassinated
  NOTES OF BACON'S REPORT FROM THE SUBSIDY COMMITTEE (March 25) 276
  Bill for 3 subsidies agreed on. Preamble to be drawn by Bacon.
  LETTER TO THE EARL OF SALISBURY . . . 277
  Bill passed and ready, but has to wait for the Grievances. Grievances presented May 13, answered May 14 : Subsidy bill sent up to the Lords May 15 278

11 The King and the Grievances. His public declaration to the Commons through the Speaker (March 18). Course pursued by the Commons in collecting and presenting them . 278
  NOTES OF BACON'S REPORT OF THE KING'S ANSWER (May 15) 282

Page

12 Attainder of offenders in the Gunpowder plot. Question whether those of the King's Counsel that were members of the House could be admitted to give evidence for the Crown. Notes of Bacon's speech 283

13. Bill for the regulations of fees for copies out of Courts of Record 284

Sir Francis Bacon's arguments against the Bill of Sheets 285

Parliament prorogued (May 27) 287

CHAPTER VIII.

A D. 1606-7, march—july. ætat 46.

1. Rumour of promotions in the law
Letter to the Earl of Salisbury . . . 288
No changes made 289

2 Marriage of Bacon to Alice Barnham (May 10, 1606) . . 290

3 Death of Sir Francis Gawdy. Coke succeeds him as Chief Justice of the Common Pleas (June 29, 1606) Sir Henry Hobart made Attorney General Promotion of Doderidge to the office of King's sergeant, and of Bacon to that of Solicitor, intended but not effected 292
A Letter to the King touching the Solicitor's place 293
A letter of like argument to the Lord Chancellor . 295
A letter to my Lord of Salisbury touching the Solitor's place 296

4. Death of Mr Bettenham of Gray's Inn.
Letter to Sir Thomas Posthumus Hobby (Aug. 4, 1606) 298
Memorial to Bettenham erected by Bacon . . 299

5. A letter of request to Dr Playfer to translate the Advancement of Learning into Latin . . 300
Death of Playfer (Feb. 2, 1608-9) 302
Letter to Sir Mich Hickes 302

6. Parliament meets again, Nov. 28, 1606 Answer to the petition of Grievances. Debates on the Instrument of Union.
Notes of Bacon's speech Nov 25, 1606 . . . 303
Committee appointed to prepare for Conference with the Lords. Article of Commerce disputed House adjourned from 18 December to 10 February 304
Article concerning general naturalization opposed by Fuller . 306
A speech used by Sir Francis Bacon in the Lower House of Parliament, concerning the Article of Naturalization (Feb. 17) 307

Pago

7. Question of law concerning the *Post-nati* Conference with the Lords SIR FRANCIS BACON'S REPORT OF THE FIRST DAY'S CONFERENCE TOUCHING THE QUESTION WHETHER THE SCOTCHMEN BORN SINCE THE KING CAME TO THE CROWN BE NATURALISED IN ENGLAND (imperfect) . . 327

SIR FRANCIS BACON'S REPORT THIS 2 OF MARCH OF THE CONFERENCE HAD WITH THE LORDS THE WEEK BEFORE wherein is first contained the reasons of the Lower House in point of law whether the Scots born since the King came to the Crown be naturalised in England, which they held *negative*, and the opinion of the Judges for the affirmative (imperfect) 329

8 Determination of the Commons to ignore the distinction between the cases of the *Antenati* and the *Postnati*. Motion for a perfect union (March 28) opposed by Bacon 332

A SPEECH USED BY SIR FRANCIS BACON, KNIGHT, IN THE LOWER HOUSE OF PARLIAMENT, BY OCCASION OF A MOTION CONCERNING THE UNION OF LAWS 335

The King's speech to the Commons immediately before the Easter recess (March 31) Another speech after their reassembling (May 2) Project of General Naturalisation allowed to drop 341

9. Progress of Bill for abolishing hostile laws. Difficulties in Committee Act passed 342

10 Merchants' petition to Parliament for redress of wrongs from Spain Conference between the two Houses

A REPORT MADE BY SIR FRANCIS BACON, KNIGHT, IN PARLIAMENT, OF A SPEECH DELIVERED BY THE EARL OF SALISBURY, AND ANOTHER SPEECH DELIVERED BY THE EARL OF NORTHAMPTON, AT A CONFERENCE CONCERNING THE PETITION OF THE MERCHANTS UPON THE SPANISH GRIEVANCES PARLIAMENT 5° JACOBI (June 17) . . 347

Bacon made Solicitor General at last (June 25). End of Session (July 4) 362

CHAPTER IX.

A D 1607. ÆTAT 47.

1. Enlargement and final settlement of the plan of the Great Instauration. Idols of the Theatre. *Cogitata et Visa* . . 363

A LETTER TO SIR THO. BODLEY AFTER HE HAD IMPARTED TO SIR THO. A WRITING ENTITULED COGITATA ET VISA 366

2 Dispute about the Jurisdiction of the Provincial Council in Wales 367

Page

A VIEW OF THE DIFFERENCES IN QUESTION BETWIXT THE
  KING'S BENCH AND THE COUNCIL IN THE MARCHES . 368
SUGGESTION SUBMITTED TO THE EARL OF SALISBURY FOR
  THE SETTLING OF THE DISPUTE BETWEEN THE KING'S
  BENCH AND THE COURT OF WALES .   .   . 382
4 A new President appointed with a new set of Instructions   .
PROCLAMATION TOUCHING THE MARCHES   .   .   . 385
5. Attempt to improve the constitution of petty juries by getting
  gentlemen to serve on them.
PROCLAMATION CONCERNING JURORS   . 389

Index to Volume III   .   . 393

CORRIGENDA FOR VOL. III.

— ◆ —

p.	l.	*for*	*read*
7	(*last line*)	E. Cole	R. Cole
10	28	*parlexia*	*parlerie*
11	6	worth	worth'
12	15	person	a person
21	19	collusion	collision
23	1	8	7
54	17	out	out of
218[1]	6 (*up*)	the Commons	your Commons
,,	,,	the first	their first
,,	,,	Commons	. Commissioners
222	13	virtues	virtue
223	25	cannot take it	can take
225	28	or	and
226	11	an entire	to be an entire.
227	(*margin*)	stamps	stamps of
229	20	of York	at York
230	11	they shall bear	they of Scotland shall bear
234	Marginal note 10 should be opposite l. 7		
255	2 (*up*)	your	you
265	*last line*	upon	open.
346	5	thoughful	thoughtful

[1] This and the 9 following *Corrigenda* are from a MS. which I did not see till after the sheets were worked off. Harl. MSS. 4149, fo. 114. It is only a collector's copy, of no special authority, but I cannot doubt that it supplies the true reading in these places

LETTERS AND LIFE OF FRANCIS BACON.

BOOK III.

CHAPTER I.

A.D. 1601.   APRIL TO DECEMBER.   ÆTAT. 40.

1.

It is singular that of two men so remarkable in their several ways as Bacon and Coke,—whose fortunes, objects, tastes, ideas, and dispositions crossed each other at so many points, and whose business must have brought them so continually into company and so frequently into conflict,—the personal relations should be so little known   No anecdotes have been preserved by the news writers of the day which enable us to form a clear idea of their behaviour to each other when they met,—the style of their conversation, or the temper of their courtesies   Of one or two collisions on matters of official business occurring at a later time we have Bacon's report, and of one or two passages of good-humoured repartee.   But if it were not for the two letters which come next in order, we should know nothing of the sort of personal feeling which, on one side at least, must have lain very near the surface, and been ready on provocation to break out   From the fact that Bacon on this occasion thought it expedient to set down in writing a memorandum of what passed, while it was fresh, we may infer that the case was exceptional.   But if his report be true, it must be taken to imply a great deal as to the terms upon which the two men habitually stood towards each other.

The occasion was a motion made by Bacon in the Exchequer for re-seizure of the lands of a relapsed recusant   In what way such a motion was likely to affront the Queen's attorney-general, who had never shown any tenderness for such offenders, I am not sure that I understand correctly. But I suppose that the recusant in question had been previously discharged from the penalties of recusancy upon submission and Bacon's argument for the reseizure may have reflected on the management of the case on that occasion in the Queen's behalf "*Reseiser*" (says Cowell) "is a taking again of lands into the King's hands, whereof a general livery or *ouster le main* was formerly missued by any person or persons, and not according to form and order of law" If such had been the case here, it may have been through Coke's fault

The thing is not elsewhere alluded to, so far as I know nor was this report made public at the time, or meant to be published afterwards It was addressed privately to Sir Robert Cecil, and remained among the collections at Hatfield, where Mardin finding it sent a copy to Birch, who printed it in his " Letters, Speeches, Charges," etc , in 1763 From his copy I take it, only with a slight alteration in the date, which as given by Birch (24th of April, 1601) involves a difficulty For as the letter was obviously written either on or immediately after the first day of a term, and Easter Term did not begin in 1601 till the 29th of April, there must be a mistake somewhere And the figures 4 and 9 being, in Bacon's hand, often very like each other, and the whole difficulty being removed by the correction of that figure, I have not hesitated to make it   Even if the original manuscript has been correctly copied, it is easier to suppose a slip of Bacon's own pen, than to explain the date in any other way.

To Mr Secretary Cecil.[1]

It may please your Honour,

   Because we live in an age where every man's imperfections is but another's fable ; and that there fell out an accident in the Exchequer, which I know not how nor how soon may be traduced, though I dare trust rumour in it, except it be malicious or extreme partial ; I am bold now to possess your Honour, as one that ever I found careful of my advancement and yet more jealous of my wrongs, with the truth of that which passed , deferring my farther request until I may attend your honour ; and so I continue

Your Honour's very humble
and particularly bounden,
Fr. Bacon.

Gray's Inn, this 29th[2] of April, 1601

[1] Letters, Speeches, etc , p 21
[2] 24th in Birch's copy But as Easter Term in 1601 began on the 29th of April, there can be little doubt that it is a mistake

*A true remembrance of the abuse I received of Mr. Attorney
General publicly in the Exchequer the first day of term, for
the truth whereof I refer myself to all that were present.*

I moved to have a reseizure of the lands of Geo Moore, a
relapsed recusant, a fugitive, and a practising traytor, and shewed
better matter for the Queen against the discharge by plea, which
is ever with a *salvo jure.*   And this I did in as gentle and reasonable terms as might be.

Mr. Attorney kindled at it, and said, "Mr. Bacon, if you
have any tooth against me, pluck it out; for it will do you more
hurt than all the teeth in your head will do you good"   I answered coldly in these very words; "Mr Attorney, I respect
you: I fear you not: and the less you speak of your own greatness, the more I will think of it"

He replied, "I think scorn to stand upon terms of greatness
towards you, who are less than little, less than the least," and
other such strange light terms 'he gave me, with that insulting
which cannot be expressed.

Herewith stirred, yet I said no more but this: "Mr. Attorney, do not depress me so far; for I have been your better, and
may be again, when it please the Queen"

With this he spake, neither I nor himself could tell what, as
if he had been born Attorney General; and in the end bade me
not meddle with the Queen's business, but with mine own, and
that I was unsworn, &c.   I told him, sworn or unsworn was all
one to an honest man; and that I ever set my service first, and
myself second; and wished to God, that he would do the like.

Then he said, it were good to clap a *cap. utlegatum* upon my
back!   To which I only said he could not; and that he was at
a fault; for he hunted upon an old scent.

He gave me a number of disgraceful words besides; which I
answered with silence, and shewing that I was not moved with
them.

The threat of the *capias utlegatum* was probably in reference to
the arrest of Bacon for debt in September, 1598.   See Vol. II p 106
What the "further request" may have been, or what the issue of it,
we have no information.   But it appears from an undated letter
printed by Dr Rawley in the 'Resuscitatio' from Bacon's own register, and suiting this occasion very well though usually placed later,

that Bacon thought it worth while to address some words of expostulation to Coke himself It is true that this letter, as printed in the 'Resuscitatio,' contains the words "my *master's* service," which would imply that it was written after the accession of King James. But in the manuscript collection in the British Museum (Add. 5503), which I take to be a better authority than Rawley's copies (see Vol I p 233, note 1), the word is clearly written *Mris*, and in the *Remains*, where the letter in question was first published, it is printed "Mrs" And therefore the same reason which led Birch to date it some time between March, 1603, and June, 1606,—that is, between the accession of James and the promotion of Coke to the Bench,—requires us to date it between November, 1595, and March, 1603,—that is, between the appointment of Fleming as solicitor, and the death of Elizabeth, during which period, though other occasions may have occurred to provoke it, this is the only one which we know did occur This therefore is undoubtedly its proper place in this collection, and if we suppose it to have been written on the 29th or 30th of April 1601, we shall not be far wrong

A LETTER OF EXPOSTULATION TO THE ATTORNEY-GENERAL, SIR EDWARD COKE.[1]

Mr Attorney,

I thought best, once for all, to let you know in plainness what I find of[2] you, and what you shall find of me.   You take to yourself a liberty to disgrace and disable my law, my experience, my discretion.   What it pleaseth[3] you, I pray, think of me I am one that knows both mine own wants and other men's; and it may be, perchance, that mine mend, and others stand at a stay. And surely I may not endure in public place to be wronged, without repelling the same to my best advantage to right myself You are great, and therefore have the more enviers, which would be glad to have you paid at another's cost Since the time I missed the Solicitor's place (the rather I think by your means) I cannot expect that you and I shall ever serve as Attorney and Solicitor together but either to serve with another upon your remove, or to step into some other course, so as I am more free than ever I was from any occasion of unworthy conforming myself to you, more than general good manners or your particular good usage shall provoke.   And if you had not

---

[1] Addl MSS 5503, fo 36   [2] So Res   The MS has *with*
[3] So R   The MS reads "my discretion, what it please you   I praye thinke of mee, that I am that know," etc

been shortsighted in your own fortune (as I think) you might have had more use of me But that tide is passed. I write not this to show my friends what a brave letter I have written[1] to Mr Attorney; I have none of those humours But that I have written is to a good end,[2] that is to the more decent carriage of my mistress' service, and to our particular better understanding one of another This letter, if it shall be answered by you in deed, and not in word, I suppose it will not be worse for us both. Else it is but a few lines lost, which for a much smaller matter I would have adventured. So this being but[3] to yourself, I for myself rest

Bacon had many grave objections, no doubt, to Coke's way of doing his business, and on a fit occasion would have been ready to state them; but there is no reason for thinking that he ever provoked this kind of treatment by speaking of him either publicly or privately with disrespect Among the greatest admirers of Coke in modern times there is none who has not admitted more to his disadvantage, both morally and intellectually, (out of his own particular domain) than Bacon ever alleged or insinuated, and *within* that domain Bacon never questioned his preeminence, although he hoped, in the course of time, to do something in it himself that would raise the question with posterity In the meantime the tone in which he ordinarily spoke of him as a lawyer may be inferred from a joke preserved in Dr Rawley's common-place book, which being too light to have a section to itself, I insert here; though a little before its true date. In January 1602–3, the Queen made eleven new sergeants-at-law, the last being one Barker, " for whose preferment (says Chamberlain) the world finds no other reason but that he is Mr Attorney's brother-in-law "[4] " Nay, if he be Mr. Attorney's brother in *law*, he may well be a sergeant," said Bacon, who, according to Rawley's story, was standing by [5]

2.

It was about this time that Bacon lost his brother " Anthony Bacon," says Chamberlain to Carleton, writing on the 27th of May, 1601, " died not long since, but so far in debt that I think his brother

---

[1] *wrote* MS, *writ* Remains.   [2] *end* om MS   [3] *but* om Resusc
[4] Chamberlain's Letters, temp Eliz (Camb Soc), p 177
[5] Lambeth MSS 1034 Rawley writes "Lo Coke" instead of "Mr Attorney " not knowing the date But there can be no doubt that this was the time Rawley's story begins, " When Sergeant Barker was made Sergeant, my Lo said there were 11 Biters and one Barker " Chamberlain's ends, " or else (as one said) that among so many biters there should be one barker " which sounds like the truer version

is little the better by him." He had been suffering so long and so severely from gout and stone that his early death requires no other explanation, though the shock of mind which he must have felt from the last proceedings of the Earl of Essex, and the disclosures consequent upon them, would no doubt hasten the natural work of disease.

This is not the place for an enquiry into his life and character, which would indeed involve a review of great part of the foreign policy of England during the last twenty years of the sixteenth century, for he was so entirely a man of business that to understand his life it would be necessary to understand the business first. But being one of the very few persons who have looked into the voluminous collection of his correspondence preserved at Lambeth, having examined much of it carefully and turned over the leaves of all, and come from the perusal with a tolerably clear impression of his personal character,—though that was not the immediate object of my enquiry,— I may as well record it here the rather because under Dr Birch's treatment the touches which disclose temper, humour, and character are mostly lost in the process of translation from the first person into the third, and from the living language of passion into the proprieties of historical narrative But the correspondence in its original shape is fresh and lively, contains letters from both parties, and ranges over fifteen or sixteen years It is of the most various and miscellaneous kind and though the collection (never perhaps complete) has suffered from the hand of time while it lay packed out of the way in bundles, it has evidently suffered nothing from the hand of selection Everything seems to have been kept that was not lost or mislaid Letters from his mother with directions that they should be burned immediately for fear his men should see them, letters from his steward, with details of receipt and payment, letters from intelligencers abroad full of political secrets; letters from pressing creditors, from wary purchasers, from Popish fugitives, and Protestant preachers, from attached patron, great acquaintance, familiar friends, kinsmen more or less familiar, grateful dependants, lawyers, statesmen, doctors, money-lenders,—together with his own rough drafts, written to dictation,—all appear to have been preserved and docketed, and are now bound up together, not indeed in perfect order,—for the arranger has not attended to the division of the civil year—but in such order that with a little trouble they may be read consecutively On the authority of this correspondence, in which it would be hard for any salient feature of the character to hide itself, Anthony Bacon may be confidently described as a grave, assiduous, energetic, religious man, with decided opinions, quick feelings, warm attachments, and remarkable power of attaching others, a gentleman of high strain, open handed and generous beyond his means, but sensitive and irritable, a little too apt to suspect, feel, and resent an injury, a little too hasty to speak of it, and occasionally, I dare say, driven by the perplexities of pecuniary embarrassment into unreasonableness and injustice, but generally fair, tolerant, and liberal.

How far he was justly charged with *extravagance* it is not so easy to judge He spent more than his income, but he spent it in public service, and though I dare say he spent it freely, there is no evidence to show that it was either unworthily spent or unwisely The acquaintance of many people, and of great people, was of real importance to a man who aspired to supply England with intelligence from France; but it was necessarily expensive The art of setting many instruments in motion, and gathering the fruits of many men's industry, was an art of great value, but it could not be carried on without liberal rewards And though it may be truly said that if expenses were incurred in the service of the government, the government ought to have repaid him, it may be as truly answered that that was not the fashion in Elizabeth's days Besides, his capacity for service had first to be proved He may have hoped that when the value and the cost of his work should be known the loss would be in some way made good, his future services accepted at their worth, and his fortunes established But his business at present was to show what he could do, and a determination to keep his expenditure within his income may have been a determination to forego important opportunities In a letter to his brother written in the fifth year of his residence abroad, which would be in 1584 or 1585, after speaking of a sum of £500 which he had sent for, and "which I know," he adds, "will give occasion to my mother and you of marvel, perhaps of suspicion," and after directing him to send certain jewels, he goes on to say, "How I mean to employ them you shall understand hereafter, and neither you nor any able to dislike, no more than the rest of mine expenses, if you knew as well as myself, as by God's grace one day you shall, the times, places, manner, and end of their spending"[1] And that the business in which he was engaged was really of public importance, and therefore worth risks and sacrifices, appears from the terms in which his services were acknowledged by the man who was of all others in the best position to appreciate them The following letter from Sir Francis Walsingham was written about the same time as the letter to Francis Bacon just quoted, and refers, if not to the same services, at least to services of the same kind —

[1] From a letter-book of A B's belonging to Mr E Cole

Sir,

I received your last of the 12th of February, and have not failed to acquaint her Majesty with the contents thereof, who very graciously accepteth that your so dutiful remembrance of her service, affirming that the great care and diligence you have performed in that behalf showeth whose son you are as also that her Highness is right glad to find by so good and kindly experience that she hath a gentleman of your quality so towardly and able to do her service. And for that her Majesty is given to understand that during the term of your travel hitherto you have often fallen sick, and are still subject to great indispositions, she hath willed me to signify unto you that she would have you for the time you are yet to remain abroad to have a more earnest care to preserve your health, which her Highness doth especially charge you to do chiefly when you remove from place to place, and that if not for your own safety, yet for her own sake

Touching the matter by you advertised, her Majesty conceiveth thereby your ripeness of judgment, and (the particularities concurring with the soundest advertisements she receiveth nearer hand) findeth that you have had better intelligence in that corner than hath been received from any others in those parts, whereby it is seen that your credit is good with the evil affected of that nation remaining there   And therefore, notwithstanding you remove to Paris, *I shall heartily pray you by all the best means you may devise to continue your intelligence with the parties with whom it seemeth you can prevail*, very much the rather for that the same may greatly import her Majesty's service

For myself I must pray you to hold me excused, if hitherto I have not often written unto you, which I assure you hath happened through the uncertainty of your being, occasioned as I hear by your long and often sickness And, lastly, for that I perceive how that your friends do generally hold an opinion of your weak nature and indisposition, unfit to abide the hardness you should find by travelling into other remote parts, besides many other reasons they have imparted unto you, persuading your return, for mine own part, as one that for so many good respects wish you so well as I do, I cannot but friendly advise you, *after you have remained there some time*, to think on your repair home with as convenient speed as you may, as well in respect of your outward estate of health and otherwise, as also for the particular comfort myself among other your good friends should receive now after so many years of your absence to see and enjoy you in your own country And so with hearty remembrance of you, I commit you to the Lord from my house in London, the first of March, 1581

Your assured loving friend,
Fra Walsingham.[1]

It appears plainly from this that Walsingham, though he con-

---

[1] From the same letter book p 59   A copy, in the hand (as I suppose) of A B's amanuensis

curred formally in advising him on his own account to return, would
have been glad for the sake of the country that he should stay
In a man of spirit and liberality, of conscious ability, of patriotic
impulses, and of moderate income, a position like this would be quite
enough to explain an excess of expenditure   Nor was his case much
altered in this respect, when on his return to England after Walsingham's death he was taken into the confidence of the Earl of
Essex, and trusted (not as a servant, but as friend[1]) with the management of all his political correspondence.—a very large business,
which could not be properly conducted without hospitalities, libera-
lities, servants, and means of locomotion   To account, therefore, for
his "extravagance,"—that is, for his spending more than his income,
—it is not at all necessary to suppose him a self-indulgent volup-
tuary, as he has been represented of late, upon no other ground that
I can hear of a "gay" man, of easy nature and lax morals, "roving
and mercurial," "fond of good wines and bright eyes," "everywhere
at home," "halffellow" with all classes, a lover of "finery, and show,
and pleasure," one of "a jovial crew," "running from bad to worse,"
and finally sinking into a premature grave, "the victim of his companion's riot and evil ways,"—(the companion being the Earl of
Essex) imputations no way countenanced by the correspondence
at Lambeth, in which, though it may be inferred from the tone of
affectionate regard with which he is addressed by so many correspondents of different classes and characters that there was something about him very interesting and attractive, there is no indication
of impurity or excess, or even gaiety, either in life or conversation
And indeed, if it were not for a story told by Sir Henry Wotton
nearly thirty years after his death, which is difficult to deal with
because it stands so completely by itself, his character would be clear
of all serious imputation, except on the score of insolvency : nor was
he insolvent in any other sense than this—that he had to draw
upon his capital to pay his debts for he seems always to have borrowed at interest and upon security, and there is no reason to suppose that any of his creditors were losers in the end by their dealings
with him
    Now Wotton's tale, though inconsistent with the notion that he
was a man of pleasure, implies (if true) that he was something very
much worse nor can his evidence be dismissed like that of an
anonymous storyteller or dealer in scandal for Wotton was personally acquainted with him, was in the Earl's service at the same

---

[1] Two or three years after, Lady Bacon objected to his lodging in Essex House,
on the ground that having been "hitherto esteemed a worthy friend," he would
then be accounted the Earl's "follower.' Birch, I p 278

time, and was a well known man, of many accomplishments, of good
position, and great employments   Still it carries no authority which
entitles it to over rule criticism   and when it stands quite unsup-
ported, and relates to transactions necessarily of a very secret character to which he was not himself a party, and gives no hint of the
manner in which he came by the knowledge, and is difficult to reconcile with other evidence undoubtedly authentic, and was not
published till all those who could have confirmed it if true, and
all those who would have cared to question it if false, were equally
dead,—the question may fairly be raised, whether he was a man
whose report must be accepted as conclusive—a man incapable of
believing a thing upon insufficient grounds   And upon this point
we happen to have evidence in discredit of his pretensions, quite as
respectable as his own   In the correspondence between Chamberlain and Carleton, who both knew him, he is frequently mentioned,
and always as a man upon whose words they set no value   "Touching all that I wrote you before of Signor Fabritio," (says Chamberlain, June 17, 1612—"Signor Fabritio" is the name under which
Sir Henry Wotton is usually spoken of in these letters,—I do not
know why) "I should not nor could not believe it, but that sometimes unfitness and unlikeliness makes a thing more likely." "I
agree with you in opinion" (says Carleton, speaking of some impressions to his disadvantage of which Chamberlain had warned him)
"that Fabritio hath lent me that charity   and if for satisfying his
particular malice on other occasions the King's service did not suffer,
I could easily forgive him."[1]   And again, speaking of another report
about himself, "I know not out of whose shop should come this
parleria, unless my good old friend Fabritio will never leave his old
trade of being *fabler*, or, as the Devil is, father of lies."[2]   "Hither
came yesterday Signor Fabritio," (says Chamberlain, writing from a
great house in the country, where some new building was going on)
"and stays till to-morrow, .. and as he is ignorant in nothing,
so he takes upon him to propound many new devices, and would
fain be a director where there is no need of his help   He discourseth
liberally of the matter of Savoy, and shows himself so partial,"[3] etc
And again (July 5, 1617), returning some papers which Carleton had
sent him, "a man shall understand more by one of them than by
twenty Fabritios, who still *antiquum obtinet*, and cannot leave his
old custom of posting things over to the next courier, which commonly proves Tom Long, the carrier   for I never knew him yet discharge any debt that way, though he promised round things to
somebody else besides you, which I came to see by chance, being

[1] 'Court and Times of James I,' vol 1 p 182   [2] Ib p 209   [3] Ib p 260

present at the receipt· but hitherto, for ought I can hear, they neither appear round nor square, but flat farlies and idle conceits "[1] Again (August 9), " Touching Fabritio's precious advertisement . he [Secretary Winwood] gave me this answer—'I cannot precisely say what it may come to, but as far as I can gather, never trust my judgment if it prove any matter of worth So that this *legatus peregre missus* will make good his *mentiendi causa* as well in that as he doth in his last letters (which I saw yesterday), that the Venetians had lost more than a million and a half in merchandise upon two gallies taken by the Neapolitan fleet I would scant change states with him or with all I know of his name, if I had but so much as there was lacking of that sum "[2]

Other passages might be quoted in the same tone but these are enough to show that Wotton was not a man whose uncorroborated statement was considered conclusive by all who knew him, which is all I mean to assert He is not the less, however, entitled to a hearing, and with this introduction by way of caution, he shall tell his story for himself.

" The Earl of Essex had accommodated Master Anthony Bacon in partition of his house, and had assigned him a noble entertainment This was a gentleman of impotent feet, but of a nimble head, and through his hand ran all the intelligences with Scotland, who being of a provident nature (contrary to his brother the Lord Viscount St. Alban's), and well knowing the advantage of a dangerous secret, would many times cunningly let fall some words, as if he could much amend his fortunes under the Cecilians (to whom he was near of alliance, and in blood also), and who had made (as he was t unwilling should be believed) some great proffers to win him awa ch once or twice he pressed so far, and with such tokens and sign arent discontent, to my Lord Henry Howard, afterwards Earl of 1 ampton (who was of the party, and stood himself in much umbrage with the Queen), that he flies presently to my Lord of Essex (with whom he was commonly *primæ admissionis*, by his bedside in the morning), and tells him that, unless that gentle e presently satisfied with some round sum, all would be vented ok the Earl at that time ill provided, (as indeed oftentimes his con re low), whereupon he was fain suddenly to give him Essex-house, which the good old Lady Walsingham did afterwards disengage out of her own store with 2500 pound and before he had distilled 1500 at another time by the same skill So as we may rate this one secret (as it was finely carried) at 4000 pounds in present money, besides at the least 1000 pound of annual pension to a private and bedrid gentleman What would he have gotten if he could have gone about his own business ?"[3]

---

[1] ' Court and Times of James I,' vol ii p 15   [2] Ib p 26
[3] ' Reliquiæ Wottonianæ,' p 13

Now what passed between Anthony Bacon and Lord Henry Howard on this occasion (if such an occasion ever was), or between Lord Henry and the Earl, would of course be known to very few, and therefore that no rumour of such a transaction should have got abroad for thirty years (though strange considering all the circumstances), and that Wotton should have remained the sole depository of the secret, is not conclusive against it. But when a witness is found to be ill-informed on points which lie open to observation and can be checked by other evidence, we may fairly doubt whether in matters known to few and mentioned by nobody except himself his testimony is weighty enough to override improbabilities. Now in a house so open and so well frequented as Essex House, the habits and general relations of a man of such a large and various acquaintance as Anthony Bacon, and the nature of his connexion with so popular person as the Earl, cannot have been any secret. Yet it is certain that Wotton, when he wrote this passage, had a very loose and erroneous impression regarding them. It is true that Anthony Bacon lived in Essex House from October, 1595, to March, 1600, and that much secret correspondence passed through his hands. But if he had "a noble entertainment"—that is, if he lived there at the Earl's charge—how is it that his mother had to remonstrate with him upon the amount of his bill for coals during the summer months of 1596?[1] Again if he had an annual pension of £1000, how is it that among so many letters relating to financial perplexities—letters to and from creditors pressing for payment, lenders demanding security, the brother who shared his difficulties, his liabilities, and his purse the mother who criticised and deplored his expenses—there is not somewhere or other an allusion to so large an item as this in the reckoning of his means and expectations—being more than twice as much as all his rents came to? Yet "of this pretended pension," says Birch, "there is not the least trace in all Mr Bacon's papers." Again if in cunning and policy he wanted to make Essex believe that the Cecils were "making great proffers to win him away," how is it that he so often and so openly complained of their unnatural neglect? Our evidence on these points is, of course, negative; for evidence in direct contradiction of charges which nobody made and suspicions which nobody was supposed to entertain, was not to be expected. But in supposing that Anthony Bacon was a man "of a provident nature" in money matters, it cannot be doubted that Wotton was utterly mistaken. Upon this point our evidence is positive and conclusive, proving that he was neither a getter nor a keeper of money, but altogether a borrower and spender. And it is

[1] Birch, ii. p 371

a mistake which can only be accounted for by supposing that Wotton knew nothing about his private affairs, and very little about his character and habits. If, therefore, we find the rest of the story hard to reconcile with what we know otherwise, we need not believe it merely because he did seeing that in a thing where it was so much less easy to be mistaken he could so easily make a mistake Now that if Anthony Bacon was really a man capable of extorting money from one who trusted him by threatening to betray the trust, his character could have so completely concealed itself throughout all that long and various correspondence as to leave an impression directly contrary, and that if he had been known by anybody, not an accomplice, to have abused his trust so grossly, his reputation as an attached and loyal friend to the Earl, could have remained unsullied till his death, and survived him without a shadow of suspicion for thirty years (for the suspicions which the friends of Essex were so ready to take up against his brother never reflected upon him),—these things are to me simply incredible.   And as by a slight conjectural emendation in Wotton's story the whole difficulty which it involves may be made to disappear, we can scarcely be rash in concluding that it arose out of a misreport,—a misreport credulously listened to at the time, as whispered scandal commonly is,—imperfectly recollected through the haze of thirty years,—and pieced into a smooth story by a lively imagination driving a ready pen   That Essex had important secrets with which Anthony Bacon was acquainted, that he had also extensive agencies which required money to nourish them, and that the money was not always ready at hand—this we know   That in some exigency connected with one of these secret agencies a large sum of money had to be borrowed in a hurry, that Essex House was pledged to the lender by way of security, that the money passed (as it naturally would) through Anthony Bacon's hand ; that nobody knew what was done with it, but that (some rumour of the transaction getting abroad) it was *supposed* by somebody that he had obtained it for himself—this we can easily believe and the rest followed naturally   *How* he obtained the money, as no man could know, except himself and the Earl and whatever confidential agent passed between them, every man was the more free to guess   The secret circumstances would easily be supplied, and a story made up, which seemed probable enough to Wotton and others who knew no more of the personal relations of the two men than he appears to have done, and which was accordingly believed at the time, and repeated long after,—probably with variations *ad libitum*,—as the true history of what passed   In this there would be nothing strange   But with our means of information, which are really very much more and better than theirs, it is easier to believe that Wotton was mistaken than that the story he tells was true.

3.

As soon as the depth and extent of the Essex conspiracy had been well ascertained, and the principal leaders executed, the others were allowed to purchase their pardons   "There is a commission," says Chamberlain, 27 May, 1601, " to certain of the Council to ransom and fine the Lords and gentlemen that were in the action, and have already rated Rutland at 30,000*l* Bedford at 20,000*l* Sands at 10,000*l* Mounteagle at 8000*l* and Cromwell at 6000*l* Catesby at 4000 marks," etc.[1] Money thus falling into the Treasury was usually bestowed upon deserving servants or favoured suitors in the way of reward, and Bacon on this occasion came in for a share. Out of Catesby's fine, 1200*l* was assigned to him by the Queen's order, and on the 6th of August the Attorney-General received directions from the Council to prepare an assurance accordingly- -a act of which we owe the discovery to Mr Jardine,[2] and which explains and dates the following letter The fine, it seems, was to be paid by instalments, and each instalment was to be divided *pro rata* among the several assignees But the absence of the Attorney, " busied to entertain the Queen," would cause some delay in the payments upon the first instalment, and Mr Hickes, a friendly creditor, would no doubt accept the excuse and wait.

This letter was printed by Mr Montagu from the original, which is in the British Museum, though, being written in extreme haste, he did not succeed in reading it quite correctly The date may be inferred from the fact that a few days after the letter from the Council was written, the Queen   made a step " from Windsor "to Mr Attorney's at Stoke, where she was most sumptuously entertained," etc There can be no doubt, therefore, that this was the occasion, and the date was probably the 6th or 7th of August, 1601

To Mr. Michael Hickes [4]

Sir,

The Queen hath done somewhat for me, though not in the proportion I hoped. But the order is given, only the monies

[1] Chamberlain's Letters, p 108
[2] Narrative of the Gunpowder Plot (1857), p 31   The letter from the Council is printed in Dixon's ' Personal History of Lord Bacon,' p 125
[3] Chamberlain's Letters, pp 115, 117   The Queen was at Windsor on the 13th of August
[4] Lansd MSS cvii fo 11   Original, own hand

will not in any part come to my hand this fortnight, the later by reason of Mr Attorney's absence, busied to entertain the Queen, and I am loth to borrow the meanwhile. Thus hoping to take hold of your invitation some day this vacation, I rest

Your assured friend,
Fr. Bacon.

4

I omitted to state that after the Speaker had handed in the Subsidy Bill at the close of the last Parliament, he proceeded in a set speech, drawn up for the purpose by a committee, to thank the Queen in the name of the whole House for her " most gracious care and favour in the repressing of sundry inconveniences and abuses practised by Monopolies and Patents of Privilege "[1] To which the Lord Keeper answered that " Her Majesty hoped that her dutiful and loving subjects would not take away her Prerogative, which was the chiefest flower in her garden and the principal and head-pearl in her crown and diadem, but that they would rather leave that to her disposition And as her Majesty had proceeded to trial of them already, so she promised to continue that they should all be examined, to abide the trial and true touchstone of the law "[2]

This was on the 9th of February, 1597 8, and was an answer satisfactory for the time But even if the Queen was in her own judgment fully alive to the evil and danger of these abuses, and in her own inclination really desirous to be rid of them, she was not likely to pursue the inquiry very zealously just then Postponement of decisive action as long as the matter would bear postponement, which in her youth she had deliberately practised as a politic art to keep enemies holding off and friends holding on, had grown into a habit which she could hardly overcome when it was most her interest to do so, and at this time she had businesses on hand of more pressing importance Henry IV of France was negociating a separate treaty of peace with Philip, which would increase the danger of England from Spain, and she was sending Sir Robert Cecil over to remonstrate. That treaty being, in spite of her remonstrances, soon after concluded, the great question of peace or war with Spain pressed for a resolution, and divided her council table In the meantime the condition of Ireland was becoming every day more alarming, and threatened to absorb the most liberal grant ever voted by Parliament as fast as the money came in. With one " whose nature was not to resolve but to delay,"[3] these cares and alarms would be

---

[1] D'Ewes, p 573.   [2] Ib p 547
[3] R Cecil in his conversation with Lady Bacon, i p 316

enough to keep the monopoly question in the waiting-room, without supposing any deliberate intention to evade it   Nor was the removal of the abuse quite so simple a matter perhaps as it seemed to people unacquainted with the exigencies of the Government and the state of the Exchequer   Elizabeth is charged with a dislike of spending money   Yet she kept no private hoard   what she did spend she spent all upon public objects   and in order to meet those objects, even with a regard to economy which is now thought unworthy of a Queen, she was forced to call upon her people for contributions far beyond all precedent   It should never be forgotten that during the first twenty-seven years of her reign a single subsidy had never served for less than four years   during the next ten it had never served for more than two   then came three whole subsidies payable in four years, and now three payable in three, and all likely to be less than enough.   This was not a convenient time for giving up an independent source of income   for to depend upon other people for anything which she could not do without— this she did really dislike   Now, by granting monopoly-patents she could reward servants without either spending her own money, or laying herself under obligations to Parliament, or exposing herself to complaints from anybody in particular, whereas to call in those already granted would bring a host of troublesome complainants about her   It is not to be wondered therefore, that while the struggle in Ireland, beginning as it did with a costly failure and still far from its termination, was drawing upon her resources at the rate of more than £300,000 a year,[1] the inquiry into these patents was allowed to wait until the last approaching necessity of another Parliamentary grant reminded her of her parting promise

This necessity began to be felt in October, 1600 [2] and in the beginning of Hilary Term (23 January 1600–1) she gave orders to Coke and Fleming to "take speedy and special course" for them [3] But before they were well entered on the business, they were interrupted by the insurrection of the Earl of Essex and the proceedings consequent upon it, which kept them busy till the summer vacation   And before the vacation was over, a crisis occurred which made it advisable to summon Parliament without delay   On the 23rd of September, Don Juan d'Aquila, with 1000 men, three parts of them being of the best soldiers in Spain, landed on the southern coast of Ireland, occupied Kinsale, and proclaimed the Queen deprived of her crown by the Pope's sentence, her subjects thereby

---

[1] Parliamentary Debates in 1610 (Camden Soc Publ), p 1
[2] Cecil's speech in the House of Commons
[3] Fleming's speech   D'Ewes, p 648

absolved from their allegiance, and himself come " to deliver Ireland from the jaws of the Devil "[1] a crisis well fitted to stimulate the loyalty of an English Parliament, and dispose them to vote supplies freely without standing too obstinately upon domestic differences which could wait for times of more leisure

The new Parliament met on the 27th of October, and was opened by the Queen in person with the usual formalities, and a speech from the Lord Keeper   To the Lower House (the members of which during the Lord Keeper's speech had been by some mismanagement shut out), the causes of their meeting—which were in fact nothing more than to provide means of defence against the present and threatened dangers—were set forth at large by Sir R Cecil, on the 3rd of November whereupon, immediately and without any debate, a committee was appointed to meet on the 7th, to consider the case

5

The four intervening days were occupied with bills brought in or motions made by private members among which there are two which still retain, in consideration of the mover, some little interest for us

It seems that the House was not disposed to pay much attention to the business thus brought before it   Several bills were read and rejected, some read and ordered to be engrossed, but none discussed —as if the money bill had been their only serious business.   Now in Bacon's opinion it was important to the health of the relation between Crown and Parliament, that Parliament should never seem to be called for money only, but always for some other business of estate besides   And the case being now much the same as in 1593 (concerning which see Vol I p 213), he endeavoured in the same way, by interposing a discussion on some topic of popular and legislative character, to cover the nakedness of the appeal for pecuniary help   The supply committee was to meet on Saturday, the 7th, and on Thursday, as we learn from Townshend, to whose notes we are indebted for almost all we know of the debates during Elizabeth's four last Parliaments, " Mr Bacon stood up to prefer a new bill," and spoke as follows .—[2]

SPEECH ON BRINGING IN A BILL AGAINST ABUSES IN WEIGHTS AND MEASURES

Mr. Speaker,

I am not of their minds that bring their bills into this House

[1] Camden   [2] D'Ewes, p 626   Harl MSS 2283, f 12

obscurely, by delivery only unto yourself or to the clerks, delight-
ing to have the bill to be *incerto authore*, as though they were
either ashamed of their own works, or af..id to father their own
children   But I, Mr Speaker, have a bill here, which I know
I shall be no sooner ready to offer but you will be ready to receive and approve. I liken this bill to that sentence of the poet,
who sets this as a paradox in the fore-front of his book, *first water,
then gold*, preferring necessity before pleasure; and I am of
the same opinion, that things necessary in use are better than
those things which are glorious in estimation. This, Mr. Speaker,
is no bill of state nor of novelty, like a stately gallery for
pleasure, but neither to dine in nor sleep in, but this bill is a
bill of repose, of quiet, of profit, of true and just dealing; the
title whereof is an Act for the better suppressing of abuses in
weights and measures.

We have turned out divers bills without disputation   and for
a house of wisdom and gravity, as this is, to bandy bills like balls,
and to be silent, as if nobody were of counsel with the Commonwealth, is unfitting in my understanding for the state thereof
I 'll tell you, Mr Speaker, I 'll speak out of mine own experience
that I have learned and observed, having had causes of this
nature referred to my report, that this fault of using false weights
and measures is grown so intolerable and common that, if you
would build churches, you shall not need for battlements and bells
other things than false weights of lead and brass.   And because
I would observe the advice which was given in the beginning of
this Parliament, that we should make no new laws, I have made
this bill only a confirmation of the statute of the 11 Henry 7,
with a few additions, to which I will speak at the passing of the
bill, and shew the reasons of every particular clause, the whole
being but a revival of a former statute; for I take it far better
to scour a stream than turn a stream.   And the first clause
is that it is to extend to the Principality of Wales, to constrain
them to have the like measures and weights to us in England.

The next day (Nov 6),—apparently with the same object of awak-
ening the House to a due sense of its proper business, and asserting
its position as a legislative assembly,—he made a motion like that
which he had seconded at the beginning of the last Parliament (see
Vol II p 78)—a motion for a Committee to repeal superfluous
laws   For his speech on this occasion, which is not given by D'Ewes,

we are also indebted to Townshend's collection whose note runs as follows —

SPEECH FOR REPEALING SUPERFLUOUS LAWS.

May it please you, Mr. Speaker, not out of ostentation to this House, but reverence I do speak it, that I do much wonder to see the House so continually divided, and to agree upon nothing; to see so many laws here so well framed, and offences provided against, and yet to have no better success or entertainment I do think every man in his particular bound to help the Commonwealth the best he may; and better it is to venture a man's credit by speaking than to stretch a man's conscience by silence, and to endeavour to make that which is good in nature possible in effect.[1]

Laws be like pills all gilt over, which if they be easily and well swallowed down are neither bitter in digestion nor hurtful to the body Every man knows that time is the true controller of laws, and therefore there having been a great alteration of time since the repeal of a number of laws, I know and do assure myself there are many more than I know laws both needless and dangerous.[2]

I could therefore wish that as usually at every Parliament there is a Committee selected for the continuance of divers statutes, so the house would be pleased also that there might be a Committee for the repeal of divers statutes, and of divers superfluous branches of statutes. And that every particular member of this House would give information to the Committees what statutes he thinketh fitting to be repealed, or what branch to be superfluous, lest, as he sayeth, *pluat super nos laqueos* The more laws we make the more snares we lay to entrap ourselves.[3]

I do not find that these motions had any " better success or entertainment" than the others The last raised no discussion at the time, and merged ultimately, as the similar motion in 1597 had done, in an ordinary "continuance act" The Weights and Measures Bill was read a second time the next day, and upon some objections in details summarily thrown out. Upon the question for committing,

---

[1] The original has " to make that good in nature which is possible in effect "
[2] So the paragraph stands in Townshend and in the MS also, except that it has 'any number,' instead of 'a number' evidently very much misreported or misprinted   [3] Townshend, p 194 Harl MSS 2283, fo 15 b

there were, says Townshend, "some twelve I, I, I, but not one for the engrossing, but all said No So it was rejected "[1]

The truth is, I fancy, that the House was in as great a hurry to get the necessary supplies voted, as the Queen was to receive them, and that they could not attend with spirit to anything else until they had seen that business safely through The Spaniards were besieged, it is true, in Kinsale by land, and ships had been sent to cut off their supplies by sea, and "many of our discoursers," says Chamberlain,[2] "gave them for lost, and made it a matter of ease to defeat them by sickness, famine, or the sword," but they were still there, and Tyrone was approaching from the North with a force almost as large as the besieging army It may easily be believed therefore, that to provide whatever was necessary for their speedy capture or expulsion seemed to the House the one business to which for the present all others must be postponed It is certain that they acted in the matter as if they thought so And as soon as Bacon's Weights and Measures Bill was disposed of, this was the next business that came on

6

Sir Walter Raleigh led the way, and though the discussion lasted into the dark, it appears to have turned entirely upon matters of of detail To the amount of the grant—an amount quite unprecedented—there are no traces of opposition from any quarter Opinions differed upon the mode of distribution, and in particular upon the question whether the "three-pound men" should be included But a grant of four whole subsidies, with eight fifteens and tens,— the first to be paid all at once next February, the others each in divided payments at half-yearly intervals, the whole therefore payable within three years and a half,—was agreed on in Committee that same Saturday afternoon and on Monday in the House, after some further discussion of details, "the Speaker appointed the Committees for drawing of the Subsidy Bill,—all to hasten it, and so the House arose "[3]

All this time, not a murmur of discontent is to be traced in the journals, not an allusion to monopolies, not a mention of conditions or reciprocal concessions, but all was going so rapidly and smoothly that one of the members thought it necessary to remind the House that they had as yet done nothing else, and to express a hope "that her Majesty would not dissolve the Parliament till some acts were

[1] Townshend, p 197   [2] 31 Oct 1601, p 119
[3] Townshend, p 205   The Speaker, I suppose, *read the names* of the Committees, who had already been appointed by the House p 203

passed "[1] On the part of the Government what little it was necessary to say was said by Sir R Cecil and the only observation of
Bacon's which is reported, is in favour of the non-exemption of " the
three-pound men," upon which, concurring with the majority of the
Committee, he concluded " it was *dulcis tractus pari jugo* and therefore the poor as well as the rich not to be exempted "[2]

What makes the unanimity of the House in this matter the more
remarkable is, that their hearts were all the while full of serious
discontent with the Government, on account of the still growing
grievance of monopolies, that they had come up from all parts of
the country charged with complaint and remonstrance, and that the
feeling, when it found utterance at last, was general enough and
strong enough to silence all expressions of dissent, if any dissent
existed It is curious also to observe, in an assembly so miscellaneous and not very orderly in its debates, how slow this feeling
was in finding a tongue After the subsidy-question had been settled
on the 9th of November, there was no more lack of debating Questions of various kinds,—including a point of privilege which brought
them into collision with the Lord Keeper,[3] and a Bill against Pluralities of Benefices which touched the Prerogative,—were largely and
noisily discussed But it was not till the 18th that a word seems to
have been uttered about Monopoly-Patents, nor does any action on
that subject appear to have been expected by the public outside
" The Parliament," says Chamberlain, writing on the 14th, " huddles
in high matters only they have had a cast at Osborne's office, to
correct and amend it at least, but there is no great hope of success
The Alpha and Omega is concluded already. I mean the giant of
four subsidies and eight fifteens "[4]

Now " Osborne's office " was not one of the monopoly-patents ;
but the office of Treasurer's Remembrancer in the Exchequer, in
which it seems that abuses had been found A bill on the subject
had been brought in, and was then under reference to a Committee,
whose report was brought up by Bacon on the 18th, in a speech of
which Townshend has preserved for us the following note —

[1] Townshend, p 204   [2] Ib p 204
[3] The Speaker had directed a warrant for a new writ to the Clerk of the Crown
The Lord Keeper desired to have the warrant directed to himself Some of the
members (Bacon among them) preferred that course as more honourable to the
House " It is far more honourable for this house (said Bacon) in my opinion when
our warrant shall move the principal member of Justice, than when it shall command a base, petty, or inferior servant to the Clerk of the Crown, or the Clerk of the
Petty Bag It will be said our warrant *emanavit improvide*, when we shall direct
our warrants to these base officers, when we may move the Great Seal of England
by it, even as soon as either Petty Bag or Petty officer " But upon inquiry it was
found that the precedents were the other way, and the Lord Keeper did not insist
D'Ewes, pp 636, 637, 643 And see further on, p 25
[4] Camd Soc Publ p 122

Mr Francis Bacon brought in the Bill touching the Exchequer, now thus entituled *An Act for the better observation of certain orders set down and established in the Exchequer under her Majesty's Privy Seal.*

At which time he said —

Mr Speaker This Bill hath been deliberately and judiciously considered of by the Committees, before whom Mr. Osborne came, who, I assure this house, did so discreetly demean himself, and so submissively referred the state of his whole office to the Committees, and so well answered in his own defence, that they would not ransack the heaps or sound the bottoms of former offences, but only have taken away something that was superfluous and needless to the subject.

Though the Committees have reformed some part, yet they have not so nearly eyed every particular, as if they would pare to the quick an office of her Majesty's gift and patronage.

This Bill is both public and private public, because it is to do good unto the subject, and private, because it doth no injustice to the particular officer The Committees herein have not taxed the officer by way of imputation, but removed a tax by way of imposition.

I will not tell you that we have taken away either in *quo titulo* or Chequer language, but according to the poet, who saith, *Mitte id quod scio, dic quod rogo,* I will omit that which you have known and tell you that you know not, and are to know, and that in familiar terms (And so he told the substance of the Bill)

We found that her Majesty, whose eyes are the candles of our good days, had made him an officer by Patent, in which that he might have right, her Majesty's Learned Counsel were in sentinel, to see that her Majesty's right might not be suppressed. If my memory hath failed me in delivery of the truth of the proceeding and the Committees' determination, I desire those that were there present to help and assist me Here is the Bill. So he called aloud to the Serjeant of the House, and delivered him the Bill to be delivered to the Speaker Which said Bill was read *prima vice* [1]

---

[1] 18 Nov 1601 Townshend, p 223 D'Ewes, p 642 Harl MSS 2283, fo 36 b
This Bill went through its several stages in the Commons, but appears to

8

So far, everything had been going as sweetly as possible for the
Queen   But shortly after Bacon had delivered his bill to the sergeant, symptoms of the smothered fire, the significance of which
appears to have been well understood at head quarters, found their
way to the surface

As the course of proceeding is not very clearly explained, I give
the passage in the very words of Townshend, who was no doubt an
eye and ear witness of what took place

"Mr Dyott of the Inner Temple, said —Mr Speaker, there be many
commodities within this realm, which being public for the benefit of
every particular subject, are monopolized by Patent from her Majesty,
only for the good and private gain of one man   To remedy the abuses of
those kind of Patents, which are granted for a good intent by her Majesty, I am, Mr Speaker, to offer to the consideration of yourself and
this House, an Act against Patents purporting particular power to be given
to sundry Patentees, etc   It hath a very long title

"Mr Laurence Hide, of the Middle Temple, said   I would, Mr Speaker,
only move you to have an Act read containing but twelve lines   It is an
exposition of the Common Law touching these kind of Patents, commonly
called monopolies"[1]

The move seems to have been unexpected   For, if Townshend's
note may be trusted, it was received at the time in silence, the
House proceeding at once to the discussion of another bill, on a
different subject —a bill about which there was "much dispute"
From what happened after, it may be suspected that this was contrived with the Speaker's concurrence by Cecil, in order to evade
or postpone the dangerous question   But though it had lain quiet
so long, it could not when once raised be laid again   And
(strangely enough) the member who brought it up afresh was a man
officially connected with the Government   The other bill having been,
"after much dispute," committed, and the House being engaged in
naming the Committees, "Mr Downalde"[2] (we are told), "the Lord

have been dropped at last, in consequence of the introduction of a *proviso* by the
Lords, which (though the Commons were willing to assent to it) there was not
time to insert as proposed before the dissolution   The only part taken by Bacon
in its further course, of which we have any record, is the following short speech
on the question whether the counsel of the clerks should be heard before it was
committed   "I did rather yieldingly accept than forwardly embrace this labour
imposed upon me   I wish the counsel may be heard, because we shall have the
more time of consideration what to do   There is nothing so great an impediment
to certainty of prevailing as haste and earnestness of prosecuting   I therefore
think it fit that they might have time assigned them to proceed by counsel"
(Townshend, p 237)
[1] Townshend, p 224   Harl MSS 2283, fo 39
[2] George Downhall, I presume, Member for Launceston

Keeper's secretary, stood up, and desired that the Bill which Mr Hide
called for touching Patents might be read " The Speaker desired
him to wait till the Committees were named after that, he said, he
might speak   But I suppose Cecil saw in the face of the House
that the question would have to be met, and felt that he must con-
trive to get his instructions before it came on   And therefore,
while they were proceeding with the naming of the Committees, he
" spake something in Mr Speaker's ear " who, as soon as the time
and place of commitment were named, immediately rose, " without
further hearing Mr Downalde " and so the House adjourned
Whether Cecil's whisper had anything to do with it, I do not know,
but some irregularity there clearly was   And that may be the reason
why D'Ewes (not understanding perhaps how it could have happened
according to the usages of the House) omits this whole passage, as
related in that private journal of which he otherwise makes such
large use, and gives merely the entries from the " original journal-
book of the House,"—which contain no hint of it Nevertheless,
when we read further that Mr Downalde took the Speaker's conduct
" in great disgrace, and told him he would complain of him the
next sitting, to which the Speaker answered not one word, but
looked earnestly on him, and so the press of people parted them,"
we need not doubt that the note was taken from the life

Neither need we doubt that Elizabeth knew that same evening
what had passed, and made up her mind for what was coming   For
Elizabeth, though she often seemed to venture into dangerous positions and to run great risks, knew how to measure her own forces,
and always kept some course in reserve upon which she might fall
back in an emergency   If her ministers could hold the ground for
her, it was best   If not, she could still come herself

On this occasion she had a day's respite Thursday, the 19th,
was occupied with matters in which the House always took an eager
interest, and spoke with many tongues   A burgess elect, being
stopped on his way up to London, had " sent up his solicitor to follow his causes in law," etc   The solicitor had been arrested at the
suit of a tailor, and carried prisoner to Newgate, where " after a
discharge gotten because he said he served a Parliament-man, he
was no sooner discharged, but straight he was again arrested and
carried to the Compter, and there lay all night, until he sent to
the Sergeant-at-arms, who fetched him out and kept him in his
custody "[1] The question was whether this were a breach of privilege, inasmuch as the master had not taken the oaths, and it was
not till after much examination, re-examination, discussion, and con-

[1] Townshend, p 225 Harl MSS 2283, fo 40

sultation, that the solicitor was ordered to be discharged, and the
tailor and his officer to pay all fees, and undergo three day's imprisonment   Immediately upon this came a report of proceedings
in another privilege question of higher interest,—the question
pending between the House and the Lord Keeper   Mr Secretary
Herbert had delivered their message to his Lordship, who had replied
that upon consideration of "the weightiness of divers businesses
now in hand," etc , "he would not now stand to make contention,"
but "would be most ready and willing to perform the desire of the
House "[1]

All this was satisfactory, but it consumed time, and nothing
more was said about the monopolies that day   On Friday, however,
the 20th,—though not till after a long debate on a Bill against wilful
absence from Church, and the hearing of another complaint from a
member whose man had been arrested on his way up to London,—
the great question at last forced its way into the front

" The Speaker," says Townshend, " gave the Clerk a Bill to read.
And the House called for the Checquer Bill   some said *Yea*, and
some said *No* and a great noise there was

"At last Mr Laurence Hide said —' To end this controversy,
because the time is very short, I would move the House to have a
very short bill read , entituled *An Act for Explanation of the Common
Law in certain cases of Letters Patents*   And all the House cried
I, I, I "[2]

The long silence being at length broken, the cry of grievance
found no want of tongues, and seems to have been felt from the first
to be irresistible for though some of the members must have been
personally interested in the monopolies, not a voice was raised in
defence of them   A difference of opinion no doubt there was, but
it turned wholly upon the *form* of the proposed proceeding for redress   In the *object* of the measure, namely to obtain relief from
the grievance, all parties were prepared to concur. Nor was the
disputed point of form material to that object, though very material
in other ways.   For the remedy proposed by the Bill was to declare
these Patents illegal by the Common Law. Now since they had
been granted in virtue of a prerogative which was at that time confidently assumed, asserted, and exercised, as indisputably belonging
to the Crown ; which, though not perhaps wholly undisputed, was
freely allowed by a large body of respectable opinion , and which had
not as yet been disallowed by any authority that could claim to be
decisive , it was now no longer the monopolies, but the Prerogative
itself, that was in question   It was like one of the cases of privilege

[1] Townshend, p 226   [2] Ib p 229

with which the House had just been dealing   As the arrest of a
debtor, though by a process strictly legal, was a breach of Privilege
if the debtor was servant to a member, so the taking away of Patents
by Act of Parliament was an invasion of Prerogative if they had been
granted by a right constitutionally belonging to the Crown   And
as the House would certainly have denied the right of the tailor to
dispute the legality of their Privilege, so might the Queen deny the
right of the House to dispute the constitutionality of her Prerogative
Nor indeed except by implication, was such a right now asserted
The question was not whether the House *might* meddle with the
Prerogative, but whether this Bill *did*   And it is a notable fact
that as the stoutest champions of the Prerogative disclaimed all wish
to uphold monopolies, so the most eager assailants of monopoly
disclaimed all intention of questioning the Prerogative

Cecil said nothing   He had been excused the day before from
going up with a Bill to the Lords, ' because he was troubled with a
cold "[1] and perhaps he had not recovered his voice   But after a
speech from the member for Warwick,—which was not so much
against the legality of the Patents as against the proceedings of
the Patentees' deputies and against those proceedings rather as
transgressing the commission than as taken in virtue of it—Bacon
rose to speak against the Bill   And for a note of the tenour of his
speech we are again indebted to Townshend

SPEECH IN THE HOUSE AGAINST A BILL FOR THE EXPLANA-
TIONS OF THE COMMON LAW IN CERTAIN CASES OF LETTERS
PATENTS.[2]

The gentleman that last spake coasted[3] so for and against the
Bill, that for my own part, not well hearing him, I did not well
understand him.   The Bill, as it is, is in few words, but yet
ponderous and weighty

For the prerogative royal of the Prince, for my own part I
ever allowed of it· and it is such as I hope I shall never see
discussed.   The Queen, as she is our Sovereign, hath both an
enlarging and restraining liberty of her Prerogative : that is,
she hath power by her Patents to set at liberty things restrained
by statute law or otherwise· secondly, by her Prerogative she
may restrain things that are at liberty.

[1] Townshend, p 226
[2] 20 Nov 1601   Townshend, p 231   D'Ewes, p 614   Harl MSS 2283, f 15, b
[3] *tossed*, Townshend , *costed* in MS

For the first she may grant *non obstantes* contrary to the
penal laws, which truly, in my conscience (and so struck himself on the breast), are as hateful to the subject as monopolies.

For the second if any man out of his own wit, industry, or
endeavour, find out anything beneficial to the Commonwealth,
or bring any new invention which every subject of this kingdom
may use, yet in regard of his pains and travel therein, her Majesty perhaps is pleased to grant him a privilege to use the same
only by himself or his deputies for a certain time. This is one
kind of monopoly Sometimes there is a glut of things, when
they be in excessive quantity, as perhaps of corn, and perhaps
her Majesty gives licence of transportation to one man   This is
another kind of monopoly. Sometimes there is a scarcity or
a small quantity ; and the like is granted also.

These, and divers of this nature, have been in trial, both at the
Common Pleas upon action of trespass, where, if the Judges
do find the privilege good and beneficial for the Commonwealth
they will then allow it, otherwise disallow it, and also I know
that her Majesty herself hath given commandment to her Attorney-General to bring divers of them, since the last Parliament,
to trial in her Exchequer. Since which time at least fifteen or
sixteen, of my knowledge, have been repealed ; some upon her
Majesty s own express commandment, upon complaint made
unto her Majesty by petition, and some by *Quo Warranto* in the
Exchequer

But, Mr. Speaker (said he, pointing to the Bill), this is no
stranger in this place, but a stranger in this vestment   The
use hath been ever by petition to humble ourselves to her Majesty, and by petition desire to have our grievances redressed,
especially when the remedy toucheth her so nigh in point of
Prerogative. All cannot be done at once ; neither was it possible since the last Parliament to repeal all.

If her Majesty make a patent or, as we term it, a monopoly
unto any of her servants, that must go and we cry out of it : but
if she grants it to a number of burgesses or a corporation, that
must stand, and that forsooth is no monopoly.

I say, and I say again, that we ought not to deal or judge
or meddle with her Majesty's Prerogative. I wish every man
therefore to be careful in this point, and humbly pray this
House to testify with me that I have discharged my duty in

respect of my place in speaking on her Majesty's behalf, and protest I have delivered my conscience in saying that which I have said.

The question, therefore, was reduced simply to this   Should they proceed by Bill or by Petition? In the course of the warm and very free spoken debate which followed, two or three members expressed a decided opinion for proceeding by Bill, on the ground that the proceeding by Petition had been tried last Parliament and done no good, others expressed a decided opinion against it   But the general feeling of the House seems to have been in favour of committing the Bill, "in order to devise a course" the question as to the mode of proceeding being therefore left open. So it was agreed that they should go into Committee on it the next afternoon

One point, however, this first debate had settled   It had revealed the temper of the House and the Country on the subject, and showed the Queen that if her Prerogative was to continue unquestioned she must not allow it to be approached in that temper from that side   As yet she stood personally disengaged, not having committed herself in the matter, except in professing intentions which she had neglected to carry out   She had no difficulty, therefore, in taking the position which the time required, and made her arrangements at once, I suppose, with that view   The Prerogative was not be meddled with . upon that point she was not going to make any concession   But the Patents themselves might every one, if necessary, go overboard, and that would be enough, if handsomely done

On Saturday afternoon, Nov 21, the Committee met according to appointment   Cecil was still silent, and Bacon was again the chief speaker on the side of the Government   The general objection, which he had already urged, and which would have applied to *any* bill for such a purpose, he repeated, adding a particular objection applicable to this particular bill, which nobody seems to have attempted to answer, and which was in fact, I should think, unanswerable   The note of his speech, which contains all we know about it, does not read like a very good report, but the argument is intelligible enough

SPEECH IN COMMITTEE AGAINST A BILL FOR EXPLANATION OF THE COMMON LAW IN CERTAIN CASES OF LETTERS PATENTS [1]

The Bill is very injurious and ridiculous : injurious, in that it taketh or rather sweepeth away her Majesty's Prerogative;

[1] 21 Nov, in the afternoon Townshend, p 238   D'Ewes, p 648   Harl MSS 2283, fo 51 b

and ridiculous, in that there is a proviso that this statute should
not extend to grants made to Corporations. That is a gull to
sweeten the Bill withal, it is only to make fools fain   All men
of the law know that a Bill which is only expository to expound
the Common Law doth enact nothing. neither is any proviso
good therein   And therefore the proviso in the statute of 34
Hen. VIII of Wills (which is but a statute expository of the
statute of 32 Hen VIII of Wills) touching Sir John Gains-
ford's will, was adjudged void.   Therefore I think the Bill unfit,
and our proceedings to be by Petition

Here again the true question was proposed in its simple terms;
but the Committee could not keep within it   An attempt on the
part of the Solicitor-General to make the Queen's case clearer, by
explaining what she had done in the matter since the last Parliament,
what she had intended to do, and why she had done no more, roused
one of the members for Middlesex to produce a long list of Patents
granted since the last Parliament, the reading of which provoked
the famous question 'whether *Bread* was not among them?' and
was followed by a state of excitement tending to no definite resolution,—when Townshend himself, " seeing that the Committees could
agree upon nothing," came forward with a motion   a motion which
received from Bacon an approval so emphatic that the exposition of
his policy and proceedings in this matter (which have been much
misrepresented) would not be complete without describing it
    The proposition was in effect this —That the Committee should
draw up a speech to the Queen, humbly petitioning, not only " for
the repeal of all monopolies grievous to the subject,"—with a view
to which every member of the House was to be invited to put in his
complaints in writing,—but likewise for leave to make an Act that
they might be of no more force, validity, or effect than they are at
the Common Law, without the strength of her Prerogative,"—(a
thing which, though they *might* do it now, yet, in a case so nearly
touching her Prerogative, they would not, as loyal and loving subjects, offer to do without her privity and consent),—and that as soon
as this address was drawn up the Speaker should be sent at once
(not at the end of the session, as on the last occasion) to speak it to
her, and at the same time to deliver with his own hand the lists of
monopolies complained of
    This motion, which was quite in accordance with Bacon's idea of
the proper way of proceeding, was seconded by him in "a long
speech," of which, however, all we know is, that it " concluded thus
in the end "

Why you have the readiest course that possibly can be devised. I would wish no further order to be taken but to prefer the wise and discreet speech made by the young gentleman, even the youngest in this assembly, that last spake. I'll tell you, that even *ex ore infantium et lactantium* the true and most certain course is propounded unto us.[1]

After which speech of Bacon's the Committee separated, without deciding upon anything except that they would meet again on Monday

It seems, however, that there was an obstruction somewhere For on Monday the debate fell away from the point again Nor did Cecil, who came forward at last, succeed in giving it a better direction, unless indeed his object were (as I rather suspect it was) to introduce an element of disagreement for the purpose of postponing the decision For after giving his opinion at large upon most of the topics which had been discussed, but without drawing towards any conclusion, he ended, very strangely, with recommending "a new commitment, to consider *what her Majesty might grant and what not*, and what course they should take, and upon what points,' [2] etc —a recommendation which, proceeding from him, it is difficult to understand, except as a device to keep the waters troubled, for it seemed to import a discussion of the Prerogative itself, and which was met by a counter-recommendation, coming (to make the matter stranger) from the popular side,—for it was moved by one of the members who in the first debate had spoken most decidedly in favour of proceeding by Bill, and seconded by the member who had spoken most vehemently and powerfully against the monopolies—much to the effect of Townshend's proposition of Saturday evening, namely, "that they should be suitors unto her Majesty that the Patentees should have no other remedies than by the laws of the realm they might have, and that their Act might be drawn accordingly."[3] This motion ' the House seemed greatly to applaud,'" and might, one would think, have passed at once, but that Cecil, for some reason or other, was not disposed to withdraw his own, and the conclusion was that *both* motions should be determined upon by the Committees that afternoon. Yet in the afternoon, unless Townshend's notes are strangely imperfect, neither of them was put to the question, nor indeed was any question put at all But the old ground was beaten over again lists of monopolies were handed about privately and one of these, containing nearly forty titles of

[1] Townshend, p 239   [2] Ib 243   [3] Ib 243

Patents granted within the last twenty-eight years, was read out openly by Cecil himself after which they again separated without concluding upon anything,—to meet in the afternoon of the next day.

These repeated adjournments with no result naturally excited dissatisfaction and suspicion, and on Tuesday morning, "after some loud confusion in the House touching some private murmur concerning monopolies," Cecil had to come forward again, his "zeal to extinguish monopolies making him to speak, to satisfy their opinions that thought there should be no redress of them" He said "he had been a member of the House in six or seven Parliaments, and yet never did he see the House in so great confusion . They had had speeches, and speech upon speech, without either order or discretion One would have had them proceed by Bill, and see if the Queen would have denied it Another that the Patents should be brought there before them and cancelled —and this were bravely done Others would have them proceed by way of petition," etc "But I wish," he concluded, "every man to rest satisfied until the Committees have brought in their resolutions, according to your commandments"

And what was it then that hindered the Committees from coming to a resolution—seeing that there was no difference at all among them in their ends, no material difference about the means, and a general inclination in favour of one of the two courses proposed? The answer, I think, must be that the Queen was going to lay the waves herself, and they were not to subside till she appeared The extraordinary disorder and confusion which had reigned in the Committee ever since Cecil took a prominent part in the proceedings, and which was leading to an embarrassment from which they could not extricate themselves, was a condition (whether natural or artificial) necessary to give full effect to the scene which followed, and which, as Bacon had no part in it except as a deeply interested spectator, I must be content to describe less at large than I should otherwise wish.

Such a petition from the Commons as Bacon recommended would have opened a fair passage out of the difficulty. But the Queen knew of a more excellent way The draught of the Subsidy Bill had been proceeding without any check not a murmur had escaped during all this excitement to show that anybody regretted the grant or wished to hold it back and she bethought herself (being, though not formally apprised, yet known to be aware of what had passed) that it would be no less than gracious, in a case so unusual, to make some acknowledgment Thus it came to pass that on that very afternoon, when the Committee on Hide's Bill was to have met

again for the fourth time, the Speaker was sent for to convey her
hearty thanks to the House for the care they had shown of her
state and kingdom in agreeing to so large a subsidy at the very
beginning of the session   He was to tell them from her how highly
she valued this evidence of their affection , how their love was her
dearest possession, and to repay it by defending them from all oppressions, her chief and constant care   In token of which he was
to inform them further, that having lately understood, partly from
her Council and partly by petitions delivered to her as she went
abroad, that certain Patents which she had granted had been abused
and made oppressive by the substitutes of the Patentees, she had
given order to have them reformed   some should be presently revoked, and all suspended until tried and found good according to
law , and the abusers should be punished

Such was the substance of the message which the Speaker, "to
his unspeakable comfort," had to deliver to the House the next
morning, and in which, coming to us as it does at the second reflexion—a report of a report—some image may still be traced of
that majesty of demeanour, that "art and impression of words," with
which Elizabeth so well knew how to rule the affections of a people
The Speaker having concluded his report with a congratulation upon
this happy solution of their difficulties, Cecil—now quite himself
again, and in high spirits—explained at length what was to be done
the sum of which was shortly this   It had been found that some of
the Patentees had been in the habit of extorting money from ignorant
and helpless people by threatening them with proceedings which the
patents themselves did not justify   therefore a proclamation was
to go forth immediately, suspending the execution of all these patents without exception, and referring them to the decision of the
common law.

This being all that anybody proposed either to ask for or to do
without asking, the House was overcome with delight   One of the
most vehement speakers on the popular side,[1] even he who had declared only five days before that "there was no act of the Queen's
that had been or was more derogatory to her own Majesty, or more
odious to the subject, or more dangerous to the commonwealth, than
the granting of these monopolies,"[2] was the first to express his entire
satisfaction , and immediately moved that the Speaker should be sent
to the Queen, not only to thank her for what she had done, but to
apologize for what they had said, and " humbly to crave pardon " for
" divers speeches that had been made extravagantly in that House "
And though the second clause of his motion was rejected, on the

---

[1] Francis Moore, Member for Reading   [2] Townshend, p. 233

ground that "to accuse themselves by excusing a fault with which they were not charged, were a thing inconvenient and unfitting the wisdom of that House,"[1] the first was carried unanimously   A dozen members were immediately chosen to accompany the Speaker, and the Privy Councillors were requested to obtain leave for them to attend her

But she knew how to keep her state   Cecil came back the next day with a short answer in these words   "You can give me no more thanks for that which I have promised you than I can and will give you thanks for that which you have already performed"   "You shall not need," he added, "(your good will being already known) use any actual thanks   neither will she receive any, till by a more actual consummation she hath completed this work   At that time she will be well pleased to receive your loves with thanks, and to return you her best favours "[2]

This was on Thursday   On Saturday, the promised Proclamation being published "and in every man's hand," they were informed that she would receive them on Monday in the afternoon,—40, 50, or 100 of them   But when they were proceeding to select the hundred, there rose a cry at the lower end of the House of *all, all, all*   which being reported to the Queen, she gave leave for all to come   She received them in state, and having heard the address of thanks, delivered by the Speaker in a style which reminds one of the Liturgy, replied in a style peculiar to herself   If she had known that it was her last meeting with her people and studied to appear that day as she would wish to be remembered ever after, she could not have done it better   Gracious, grateful, affectionate, familiar, seated high above the reach of injury or offence and filled with awful confidence in the authority deputed to her, yet descending to exchange courtesies, accept benefits, acknowledge and excuse errors—

> "She bowed her eminent top to their low ranks,
> Making them proud of her humility,"

and I suppose never appeared so unquestionably and unapproachably sovereign as then when she spoke to them most freely, feelingly, and touchingly, in the tone of a woman and a friend

So ended an exciting and rather critical ten days' work, to the full satisfaction of everybody   the monopoly question being effectually disposed of for the time, and the Queen seated more firmly than ever in the admiration and affection of her people [3]

[1] "Mr Francis Bacon spake to the same effect also, and in the end concluded thus   *Nescio quod peccati portet hæc purgatio* "—Townshend, p 252
[2] Townshend, p 253
[3] "The Patents for Monopolies granted to several persons are suppressed and

9.

The rest of the business of the Session has not much interest for us, but as Bacon's name appears in the journals from time to time, I am bound to give account of what he said and did

There was one Act passed, which, if not originally his own, seems to have fallen into his hands in its progress through the Committee "An Act Concerning Matters of Assurances amongst Merchants"

It seems that formerly, if any dispute arose upon a question of assurance, the practice was to settle it by arbitration, the arbitrators being appointed by the Lord Mayor   But of late it had been becoming usual to decline arbitration, and force the party assured to seek his remedy by suit in the Queen's courts   This course caused delay which was very inconvenient to the merchant, and a bill was brought in by somebody to remedy it   The particular provisions of this bill are not reported, but the Committee to which it was referred[1] seem to have thought them inadequate, and to have recommended a new bill instead, giving power to the Lord Chancellor to appoint a standing commission for the determination of such disputes "in a brief and summary course, without formality of pleadings or proceedings," their decrees being subject under certain conditions to an appeal in Chancery[2]

The report of this Committee was brought up by Bacon on the 7th of December, with the following speech —

SPEECH ON BRINGING IN A BILL CONCERNING ASSURANCES AMONG MERCHANTS

I am, Mr Speaker, to tender to this House the fruit of the Committees' labour, which tends to the comfort of the stomach of this realm , I mean the merchant , which if it quail or fall into a consumption, the State cannot choose but shortly be sick of that disease.   It is inclining already

A certainty of gain is that which this law provides for , and by Policy of Assurance the safety of goods is assured unto the merchant   This is the lodestone that draws him out to adventure, and to stretch even the very punctilio of his credit.

The Committees have drawn a new bill, far differing from the

suspended but this is done by Her Majesty's proclamation, and not by any statute, because her M mercy and grace should be the more superabundant , and you should not believe what contentment the Commons receive at it" Levinus Monck to Mr Wilson, 12 Dec 1601 S P O Domestic

[1] 13 Nov D'Ewes, p 626   [2] Statutes of the Realm, 43 Eliz c. 12

old   The first limited power to the Chancery, this to certain
Commissioners by way of Oyer and Terminer   The first that it
should only be there   this that only upon appeal from the Commissioners it should be there finally arbitrated.   But lest it may
be thought to be for vexation, the party appellant must lay *in de-
posito*, etc   And if upon hearing it goes against him, must pay
double costs and damages

We thought this course fittest for two reasons

First, because a suit in Chancery is too long a course, and the
merchant cannot endure delays

Secondly, because our courts have not the knowledge of their
terms, neither can they tell what to say upon their cases, which
be secrets in their science, proceeding out of their experience

I refer the Bills, both old and new, to your considerations,
wishing good success therein, both for comfort of the Merchant
and performance of our desires.   The Bill is entitled *An Act for
Policy of Assurance used amongst Merchants* [1]

The new Bill, having been referred in its turn to a Committee,
and brought up again by Bacon, with some amendments (14 Dec),
was passed in the end, without any observations that we hear of [2]

Another debate in which he took part was upon a motion for
repealing a favourite Act of his own   In the general Act "for the
continuance of divers statutes and the repeal of others," it was proposed to include "The Statute of Tillage," on the ground that it laid
a burden upon the husbandman which, when corn was cheap (as it
was then), he could not bear.   Bacon whose own measure it was
(see Vol. II pp 79–83), opposed the motion on the same grounds of
general policy which he had formerly urged and always continued to
hold sound ; as may be gathered from the following short note of his
speech

SPEECH AGAINST THE REPEAL OF THE STATUTE OF TILLAGE

"The old commendation of Italy by the poet is *Potens viris
atque ubere gleba*, and it stands not with the policy of the
State that the wealth of the kingdom should be engrossed into
a few pasturers' hands   And if you will put in so many provisoes as be desired, you will make so great a window out of the
law that we shall put the law out of the window, etc

---

[1] Townshend, p 789 Harl MSS 2283, fo 91   [2] D'Ewes, pp 680, 681, 685

The husbandman a strong and hardy man,—the good foot-man which is a chief observation of good warriors," etc.

So he concluded the statute not to be repealed, etc [1]

He was answered by Sir Walter Ralegh with arguments founded on good free trade principles but in the end the statute was con-tinued, only with a provision that it should not apply to Northum-berland

It was also moved to ' annex" to the ' statute of Rogues" a cer-tain "exposition" of it, which had been made, it seems, by the justices

The following note of Bacon's speech against this motion contains all that the journals tell us as to the effect and the fate of it

SPEECH AGAINST A MOTION FOR MAKING A JUDICIAL EXPO-SITION OF A STATUTE PART OF THE STATUTE

There were never yet but two *Articuli* the one *Articuli super Chartas*, when the sword stood in the Commons' hand the other *Articuli Cleri*, when the Clergy of the land bare sway and that done upon deliberation and grave advice

I beseech you remember, these are done by Judges, and privately, and perhaps in a chamber And shall we presently without scanning or view enact them? It befits not the gravity of this house

And so after a long speech, dashed it.[2]

Breaches of privilege, in the form of liberties taken with members' servants, were unusually frequent during this Session, and made the proceedings unusually lively. But the only case in which Bacon is mentioned as taking a part in the debate was the following —

Mr Fleetwood, a member of the House, had sent by his servant a sum of money in a bag to one Holland, a scrivener Holland after-wards told Fleetwood that there wanted £10 6s of the proper sum Fleetwood's man being called in and "justifying the payment," Hol-land gave him the lie whereupon he gave Holland the lie whereupon Holland with the help of his man beat him Fleetwood brought the matter before the House, and the question was whether they should be sent to the Tower, or taken into custody by the sergeant

Bacon's opinion is thus reported —

[1] Townshend, p 299 Harl MSS 2283, fo 98 b
[2] Ib p 290 Harl MSS 2283, fo 92

SPEECH AGAINST COMMITTING TO THE TOWER FOR AN ASSAULT
ON A MEMBER'S SERVANT.

I have been a member of this House these seven Parliaments,
and never yet knew above two that were committed to the
Tower   The first was Arthur Hall, for that he said the Lower
House was a new person in the Trinity, and (because these words
tended to the derogation of the state of this House, and giving
absolute power to the other) he was therefore committed   The
other was Parry, that for a seditious and contemptuous speech
made even there (pointing to the second bench) was likewise
committed.   Now this offence is not of the like nature, and
very small, not done to the person of any member of this
House   And therefore I think the Sergeant's custody is punishment sufficient [1]

The conclusion was, that Holland and his man should both be in
the Sergeant's custody for five days, and pay double fees

But the question which brought Bacon out in the mood least in
accordance with his traditional reputation, was one relating to Charitable Trusts   and it is a pity that the point in dispute is not more
fully recorded
An Act had been passed in the last Session to prevent the mis-
application of the revenues of colleges, hospitals, and other charitable
institutions   By this Act the bishops were armed with powers
which were found or thought to be dangerous; a bill ' to explain the
meaning of the Statute" was accordingly brought in,[2] and on the
second reading referred to the Committee for Repeal of Statutes [3]
In Committee it was agreed to repeal the existing Act and pass
a new one   In the course of the new bill through its stages, a
question arose whether the old Act should be repealed by the general
Act for the Repeal of Statutes, or by the new one   that is, (if I understand the point rightly), whether it should be repealed or only
amended   Bacon seems to have been, for some reason or other, extraordinarily eager *against* the repeal   The fragment of his speech
which Townshend has preserved, does not enable me to understand
the importance of the point in dispute, or the particular motives of
his opposition, but the passage has a personal interest, as giving
us a glimpse of him in a state of excitement to which he did not
often give way in public

[1] Townshend, p 260   Harl MSS 2283, fo 70 b
[2] 24 Nov   Townshend, p 216   [3] 28 Nov   D'Ewes, p 617

He said (we are told) among many other things—

That the last Parliament there were so many other bills for the relief of the Poor that he called it a Feast of Charity. And now this statute of 39° having done so much good as it was delivered to the House, and the Lord Keeper having told him that he never revoked but one decree of the Commissioners, we should do a most uncharitable action to repeal and subvert such a mount of charity, and therefore we should rather tenderly foster it than roughly cry away with it

I speak (quoth he) out of the very strings of my heart; which doth alter my ordinary form of speech, for I speak not now out of the fervency of my brain, etc

So he spake something more against the bill put in by Mr Phillips for repeal   by reason Bishops' lands were put in, and inrolments, etc, which he said was a good fetch and policy for the sole practices[1] of the Chancery.

Mr Phillips answered, That he would not speak as he had spoken, rather out of humour than out of judgment; neither had he brought to the House a market-bill or mercer's bill concerning the state, etc   And so, after many persuasions for the bill, and bitter answers to Mr Bacon, he ended with desire to put it to the question whether it should be repealed by the public act or by his private bill[2]

A long debate followed, which ended in an agreement that it should be repealed by the general Act

Without knowing what were the provisions of the new bill, as originally proposed, it is impossible to guess what should have made Bacon so vehement, for the mere form of proceeding could hardly involve anything very material   but there is no doubt about the fact Not only was it remembered and noticed in the House the next day, but it seems that the counsel of the night[3] had not restored him to his usual composure   The next morning a question of privilege was under discussion   Sir Francis Hastings—whose brother, Lord Huntington, was one of the parties interested—was going to speak a second time, when the following dialogue occurred —

"Mr Bacon interrupted him, and told him 'it was against the course' To which he answered, 'He was old enough to know when and how often to speak' To which Mr Bacon said, 'It was no

[1] Sic   qu practisers?   [2] Townshend, p 291, Harl MSS 2283, fo 92 b
[3] "In nocte consilium"   Essay of Counsels, vi p 426

matter, but he needed not to be so hot in an ill cause' To which Sir Francis replied, 'In several matters of debate a man may speak often so I take it is the order He (pointing to Mr Bacon) talks of *heat* If I be so hot as he was yesterday, then put me out of doors '"[1]

And again in the afternoon, when two bills were to be debated, and there was some dispute which should have precedence, Townshend tells us that "Mr Francis Bacon kept such a quoil to have the bill concerning Charitable Uses put to the question," that the other bill "was clean hushed up "[2]

Nothing, however, remains to show what the points in dispute were and in the end a new Act was passed for precisely the same purpose as the former—only with several new provisoes and some limitation of the power confided to the bishops—under the title of "An Act to redress the misemployment of lands, goods, and stocks of money, heretofore given to Charitable Uses," whether satisfactory to Bacon or not, I cannot say

---

[1] Townshend, p 297   Harl MSS 2283, fo 97 b   [2] Ib p 298, fo 98

CHAPTER II.

1

WHEN a man is afflicted with chronic disease of the purse his worst friend is a too liberal lender   In June, 1591, Anthony Bacon, in thanking his mother for assenting to some arrangement for the satisfaction and assurance of Mr Nicholas Trott, described him as a friend who ' had shown more real confidence and kindness " towards himself and Francis, than " all their brothers and uncles put together would have performed, if they had been constrained to have had recourse to them in the like case "[1]   But in June, 1591, Francis was in continual expectation of being made Solicitor General, and was beginning to be actually employed in business of the learned counsel   Before the end of 1596 the hope of the Solicitor-Generalship was extinct, his other prospects dim, his credit at a discount, and the kind and confident friend turned into the aggrieved and complaining creditor [2]   As it usually happens in such cases, either story taken by itself sounds reasonable : and the evidence is not complete enough to give us the means of judging between them. Abuse of confidence is complained of on both sides ; by the creditor, in the shape of promises unperformed , by the debtor, in the shape of usurious interest demanded , and on both sides, I dare say, the complaint was sincere , though in a transaction between friends the presumption is commonly against the borrower, because the lender can always behave like a gentleman if he will, whereas the borrower has not perhaps the means of doing so   Bacon, not being able to repay what he had borrowed, was forced at last to mortgage Twickenham Park , and it seems that the deed gave Trott a right of entry if the debt were not paid before November, 1601   To avoid this, Bacon,—now owner of all that his brother had left, and with

[1] Vol I , 323, note
[2] See Trott's letter to Anthony Bacon, 7 Aug 1597   Lambeth MSS 661, 170 And Anthony's to Francis, 7 Dec 1596. Add MSS Br Mu 4122, 186

some ready money from Catesby's fine to help,—resorted to his friends Maynard and Hickes, who endeavoured to negociate a settlement of Trott's claims The matters in dispute were referred to the Lord Treasurer And I suppose it was either with a view to that reference, or to some subsequent question arising out of it, that the following statement was drawn up by Bacon The original is preserved among the Lansdowne MSS , but is not in Bacon's own handwriting, and has no date The docket, written in another hand, which I take to be Hickes's, merely describes it as " The state of the cause betwixt Mr Fra Bacon and Mr Trott "

> The state of the account between Mr Trott and me, as far as I can collect it by such remembrances as I find; my trust in him being such as I did not carefully preserve papers; and my demands upon the same account [1]

About 7 or 8 years passed I borrowed of him upon bonds	200 *l.*	The monies lent in particulars
Soon after I borrowed upon bond other . .	200 *l.*	
Upon my going northward I borrowed of him by my brother's means . . .	100 *l.*	
But this was ever in doubt between my brother and me , and my brother's conceit was ever it was twice demanded, and that he had satisfied it upon reckonings between Mr Trott and him		
About a twelvemonth after, I borrowed of him, first upon communication of mortgage of land, and in conclusion upon bond	1200 *l.*	
But then upon interest and I know not what reckonings (which I ever left to his own making) and his principal sum, amounting to 1700 *l.* was wrapped up to 2000 *l* , and band given according as I remember.		
And about August xliido Rnæ I borrowed of him upon the mortgage of Twicknam p.k .	950 *l*	
So as all the monies that Mr. Trott lent at any time amount to the total of	2650 *l.*	The total of Trott's principal

[1] Lansd MSS lxxxviii. fo 50

<table>
<tr><td>Mr Trott's receipts at several times</td><td>Of this sum he hath received, about 5 years since, upon sale of certain marshes in Woolwich . . . .</td><td>300 l.</td></tr>
<tr><td></td><td>He received about 4 years since, upon sale of a lease I had of the parsonage of Red-bourne . . . .</td><td>150 l.</td></tr>
<tr><td></td><td>He received about 3 years since, upon sale of the manor of Burstone . . . .</td><td>800 l</td></tr>
<tr><td></td><td>He received about 2 years since, of Mr Johnson of Gr Inn, being my surety for 200 l principal . . . .</td><td>233 l</td></tr>
<tr><td></td><td>He received of my cousin Kemp, another of my sureties, at the least . . .</td><td>100 l.</td></tr>
<tr><td></td><td>He hath received in divers small sums of 10, 30, 10 l, upon computation of interest</td><td>210 l.</td></tr>
<tr><td>Trott's receipts</td><td>So as the sums which he hath received amount to the total of</td><td>2093 l.</td></tr>
</table>

	He hath now secured unto him, by mortgage of Twicknam Park . . .	1259 l 12ˢ
	Upon my cousin Cooke's band	210 l
	Upon Mr Ed Jones's band .	208 l
	Upon mine own band . . .	220 l
The debt depending.	Sum total	1897¹ 12ˢ

<table>
<tr><td>His further demands of interest till November.</td><td>He demandeth further for charges and interest till the first November 1601</td><td>138¹ . 4ˢ 8ᵈ</td></tr>
<tr><td>The total of his demands</td><td>So the total sum of the money he now demandeth is . . .</td><td>2035 . 16 . 8</td></tr>
<tr><td></td><td>So as the whole sum of principal and interest amounteth to . . . .</td><td>4128 . 16 . 8</td></tr>
<tr><td></td><td>Deduct out of this the principal, viz . 2650 l</td><td></td></tr>
<tr><td></td><td>Remaineth in interest grown . .</td><td>1478 16 . 8</td></tr>
</table>

Upon this account I demand the abatement of some part of the interest, considering he hath been beholding to me, and his estate good and without charge, and mine indebted. And this I demand because upon every agreement and renew of assurance he made faithful promise (as himself confessed before my Lord Treasurer) that he would submit the interest to arbitrament of

friends. And divers of my creditors that made no such promise,
and are less able and more strangers to me, have in friendly
manner made me round abatements.

But absolutely I demand the abatement of interest upon interest, which no creditor that ever I [had][1] did so much as offer to
require. And this cannot be so little as 400^{lb}: for his manner
was upon every new account to cast up interest and charges,
and to make it one principal, as appeareth by his last account
and other writings.

Thirdly, I demand the abatement of 400^{lb} which he hath no
conscience to demand, for his colour is that because my Brother
sold him land charged with a rent of 4^{lb} (as I remember by the
year) more than he sayeth he intended, therefore I should pay
the value of the inheritance of this Rent.

Fourthly, I demand the abatement of 100^{lb}, by his own agreement to be defalked upon his mother's death (as by his indenture
appeareth), and though it were conditional if I paid it by a day,
yet it is all one, for if I paid not, it is accounted for.

> So as I will make him this offer, if he will discharge
> the three bonds and the interest since, I will pay
> him down his 1259^{lb} 12^s for the redemption of
> Twicknam Park.

How far this offer was equitable it is not possible to judge without knowing what was the rate of interest agreed upon, what were
the exact dates of the payments on either side, and whether any
items in the account were disputed—points which we have no means
of ascertaining, for though there are in the same volume[2] two
letters from Trott to Hickes, dated the 18th and 19th of December,
1601, and written after the Lord Treasurer had made his award, I
do not find any counter-statement of the account on his side, or any
copy or note of the award itself Assuming however, in the absence
of all evidence to the contrary, that the sums and dates are correct
as far as they go, it may be roughly estimated as equivalent to the
repayment of the principal with compound interest at 10 per cent
For I find that if the payments on either side had been made at
Midsummer, and a fresh account opened each year, the balance
against Bacon (interest being calculated at 10 per cent) would have
amounted at Midsummer, 1601, to £1247. And though this may
not have been according to the terms of the bargain, in which a high

---

[1] 'had,' omitted in MS   [2] fo 48 and 54.

charge would probably be made to cover the risk of losing all, yet if in the end Trott did not in fact lose anything, but in the course of the eight years over which the account ran recovered the whole of his principal, with compound interest at 10 per cent, he had not (in his character of friend) much to complain of.

From his letters to Hickes of the 18th and 19th of December, I gather (though it is not distinctly stated) that the sum awarded by the Lord Treasurer's auditor was £1800, to be paid by the 22nd of December, but that, at Hickes's intercession Trott agreed to make some further abatement, and to allow another month's delay. As we hear no more of it, I conclude that the money was paid by the 22nd of January, 1601-2,—Bacon's forty-first birthday,—and Twickenham Park redeemed.

2.

The prosperous proceeding and gracious parting with her last Parliament was not the only contribution brought by the Christmas of 1601 to the felicities of Queen Elizabeth. On Christmas Eve, an attempt by Tyrone, with the largest rebel army ever brought together in Ireland, acting in combination with two or three thousand newly-landed Spaniards, to relieve the troops in Kinsale, was anticipated and defeated by Montjoy; and the relieving force so completely broken that the Spanish general, finding his enterprise hopeless,—the rather because the ships sent from Spain with fresh provisions of war had been at the same time attacked and destroyed in the harbour of Castlehaven by Sir Richard Leveson,—prepared to capitulate. The news of this decisive victory reached London on 2nd of January, 1601-2, and was followed on the 20th by a report of the terms of capitulation; the sum of which was that the Spaniards should surrender all the places they held, and be allowed to go away with all they brought with them, and help to transport it. The blow was fatal to the rebellion. Montjoy, pressing his advantage with judicious assiduity, and planting garrisons as he proceeded, gradually established himself in military possession of the whole country.

But military possession, though indispensable as a preparation for the work that had to be done, was not the work itself. How to cure the disease out of which this great rebellion—a rebellion of eight years' duration—had sprung, was the great problem of estate which now pressed for solution; and much depended upon the right treatment being adopted, and adopted immediately, at this conjuncture. Sir Robert Cecil was now the leading man at the English Council-board; and to him Bacon volunteered a memorial on the subject, which he thought worth preserving in his own collection,

and of which the interest is not yet obsolete   The exact date of the
composition I have not been able to ascertain   But the allusion to
a Spanish enterprise against Algiers, coupled with the fact that he
was writing in the ' dead vacation time," leaves little room for doubt
that it was sent to Cecil in the summer of 1602,—probably in August [1]

A LETTER TO MR SECRETARY CECIL, AFTER THE DEFEATING OF
   THE SPANISH FORCES IN IRELAND, INCITING HIM TO EM-
   BRACE THE CARE OF REDUCING THAT KINGDOM TO CIVILITY,
   WITH SOME REASONS SENT INCLOSED [2]

It may please your Honour,

   As one that wisheth you all increase of honour, and as one
that cannot leave to love the state (how little interest soever I
have, or may come to have in it), and as one that now this dead
vacation time hath some leisure *ad aliud agendum*, I will presume
to propound unto you that which though you cannot but see, yet
I know not whether you apprehend and esteem it in so high a
degree; that is, for the best action of importation to yourself of
honour and merit of her Majesty and this crown, without ven-
tosity or popularity, that the riches of any occasion, or the tide of
any opportunity, can possibly minister or offer   And that is the
causes of Ireland, if they be taken by the right handle   For if
the wound be not opened again, and come not to a recrudency
by new foreign succours, I think that no physician will go on
much with letting blood *in declinatione morbi*, but will intend
to purge and corroborate.   To which purpose I send you my
opinion, without labour of words, in the enclosed, and sure I
am that if you shall enter into the matter according to the vivacity of your own spirit, nothing can make unto you a more gain-
ful return   For you shall make the Queen's felicity complete,
which now (as it is) is incomparable, and for yourself, you shall
shew yourself as good a patriot as you are thought a politic, and
make the world perceive you have no less generous ends than
dexterous delivery of yourself towards your ends; and that you
have as well true arts and grounds of government as the facility
and felicity of practice and negotiation; and that you are as well

[1] "The soldiers and gallies which are come hither out of Italy are now to be
employed against the Turk in a second enterprise upon Algiers, wherein the King
of Fez is to become a partner with Spain, etc"   *Abstract of an advertisement
out of Spain of the 6th of August*, 1602   Lambeth MSS 604, fo 181
   "In Spain the enterprise of Algiers dissolved   the gallies returned to Italy "
Cecil to Sir G Carew, 4 Nov 1602   Ib fo 217
   Add MSS 5503, fo 12

seen in the periods and tides of estates, as in your own circle
and way than the which I suppose, nothing can be a better
addition and accumulation of honour unto you

This I hope I may in privateness write, either as a kinsman
that may be bold, or as a scholar that hath liberty of discourse,
without committing any absurdity.   But if it seem any error for
me thus to intromit myself, I pray your Lordship believe, I ever
loved her Majesty and the state, and now love yourself; and
there is never any vehement love without some absurdity, as the
Spaniard well says *desvario con la calentura.* So desiring your
Honour's pardon, I ever continue.

Considerations touching the Queen's service in Ireland [1]

The reduction of that country as well to civility and justice as
to obedience and peace (which things, as affairs now stand, I hold
to be inseparable), consisteth in four points

1 The extinguishing of the relicks of the war.
2 The recovery of the hearts of the people
3. The removing of the root and occasions of new troubles.
4. Plantations and buildings

For the first, concerning the places, times, and particularities
of further prosecution in fact, I leave it to the opinion of men of
war; only the difficulty is, to distinguish and discern the propositions which shall be according to the ends of the state here,
(that is, final and summary towards the extirpation of the
troubles), from those which, though they pretend public ends, yet
may refer indeed to the more private and compendious ends of
the council there; or the particular governors or captains [2]
But still, as I touched in my letter, I do think much letting of
blood,[3] *in declinatione morbi,* is against method of cure and
that it will but induce necessity and exasperate despair, and
percase discover the hollowness of that which is done already,
which now blazeth to the best shew.   For Taghas and proscrip-
tions of two or three of the principal rebels, they are no doubt
jure gentium lawful: in Italy usually practised upon the ban-
ditti; best in season where[4] a side goeth down, and may do

[1] Rawley's ' Resuscitatio ' R Add MSS 5503 A Lansd MSS 238 fo 89 B
[2] *or rather particular governors or captains there* A   *or other particular go
vernors or captains* B
[3] *So* B *letting blood* A   [4] *when* B

good in two kinds, the one, if they take effect, the other in the[1] distrust which may follow amongst the rebels themselves. But of all other points, to my understanding, the most effectual is the well expressing or impressing of the design of this state upon that miserable and desolate kingdom; containing the same between these two lists or boundaries, the one, that the Queen seeketh not an extirpation of that people, but a reduction, and that now she hath chastised them by her royal power and arms, according to the necessity of the[2] occasion, her Majesty taketh no pleasure in effusion of blood, or displanting of antient generations. The other that her Majesty's princely care is principally and intentionally bent upon that action of Ireland, and that she seeketh not so much the ease of charge, as the royal performance of the office of protection and reclaim of those her subjects: and in a word, that the case is altered so far as may stand with the honour of the time past: which it is easy to reconcile, as in my last note I shewed[3]. And again, I do repeat, that if her Majesty's design be *ex professo* to reduce wild and barbarous people to civility and justice, as well as to reduce[4] rebels to obedience, it makes weakness turn Christianity, and conditions graces; and so hath a fineness in turning utility upon point of honour, which is agreeable to the humour of these times. And besides, if her Majesty shall suddenly abate the lists of her forces, and shall do nothing to countervail it in point of reputation of a politic proceeding, I doubt things may too soon fall back into the state they were in. Next to this adding of reputation to the cause by imprinting an opinion of her Majesty's care and intention upon this action, is the taking away of reputation from the contrary side, by cutting off the opinion and expectation of foreign succours; to which purpose this enterprise of Algiers (if it hold according to the advertisement, and if it be not wrapped up in the period of this summer) seemeth to be an opportunity *coelitus demissa*. And to the same purpose nothing can be more fit than a treaty or a shadow of a treaty of a peace with Spain, which methinks should[5] be in our power to fasten at least *rumore tenus*, to the deluding of as wise people as the Irish. Lastly (for this point) that which the ancients called *potestas facta redeundi ad sanitatem*, and which is but a mockery when the enemy is strong or proud, but effectual in his declination, that is, a liberal pro-

---

[1] *the* om A   [2] Om A   [3] This clause is omitted in A and B
[4] *produce* A   [5] *will* A

clamation of grace and pardon to such as shall submit and come in[1] within a time prefixed, and of some further reward to such as shall bring others in, that one's[2] sword may be sharpened by another's, is a matter of good experience, and now I think will come in time   And perchance,[3] though I wish the exclusions of such a pardon to be exceeding few, yet it will not be safe to continue some of them in their strengths,[4] but to translate them and their generations into England, and give them recompence and satisfaction here for their possessions there, as the King of Spain did by divers families of Portugal.

To the effecting of all the points aforesaid, and likewise those which fall within the divisions following, nothing can be (in priority either of time or matter) better than the sending of some Commission of countenance, *ad res inspiciendas et componendas*, for it will be a very significant demonstration of her Majesty's care of that kingdom, a credence to any that shall come in and submit, a bridle to any that have their fortunes there, and shall apply their propositions to private ends, and an evidence that her Majesty, after arms laid down, speedily pursueth a politic course, without neglect or respiration   and it hath been the wisdom of the best examples of government

Towards the recovery of the hearts of the people, there be but three things *in natura rerum*

1. Religion.
2. Justice and protection
3. Obligation and reward

For Religion (to speak first of piety, and then of policy), all divines do agree, that if consciences[5] be to be enforced at all (wherein they differ), yet[6] two things must precede their enforcement; the one, means of instruction, the other, time of operation, neither of which they have yet had.   Besides, till they be more like reasonable men than they yet are, their society were rather scandalous to the true religion than otherwise, as pearls cast before swine : for till they be cleansed from their blood, incontinency, and theft (which are now not the lapses of particular persons, but the very laws of the nation) they are incompatible with religion reformed.   For policy, there is no doubt but to

[1] *in* om A, B   [2] *one* A, B   [3] *percase* B, R
[4] *strength* B, R   [5] *conscience* A   [6] (*wherein yet they differ*) R

wrastle with them now is directly opposite to their reclaim, and cannot but continue their alienation of mind from this government. Besides, one of the principal pretences whereby the heads of the rebellion have prevailed both with the people and with the foreigner, hath been the defence of the Catholic religion and it is this that likewise hath made the foreigner reciprocally more plausible with the rebel. Therefore a toleration of religion (for a time not definite) except it be in some principal towns and precincts, after the manner of some French edicts, seemeth to me to be a matter warrantable by religion, and in[1] policy of absolute necessity. And the hesitation[1] in this point I think hath been a great casting back of the affairs there. Neither if any English papist or recusant shall, for liberty of his conscience, transfer his person family and fortunes thither, do I hold it a matter of danger, but expedient to draw on undertaking, and to further population. Neither if Rome will cozen itself, by conceiving it may be some degree to the like toleration in England, do I hold it a matter of any moment, but rather a good mean[2] to take off the fierceness and eagerness of the humour of Rome, and to stay further excommunications or interdictions for Ireland But there would go hand in hand with this, some course of advancing religion indeed, where the people is capable thereof; as the sending over some good preachers, especially of that sort which are vehement and zealous persuaders, and not scholastical, to be resident in principal towns; endowing them with some stipends out of her Majesty's revenues, as her Majesty hath most religiously and graciously done in Lancashire · and the recontinuing and replenishing the college begun at Dublin; the placing of good men to be bishops in the sees there, and the taking care of the versions of bibles, catechisms, and other books of instruction, into the Irish language; and the like religious courses; both for the honour of God, and for the avoiding of scandal and insatisfaction here by the show of a[3] toleration of religion in some parts there.

For Justice, the barbarism and desolation of the country considered, it is not possible they should find any sweetness at all of justice, if it shall be (which hath been the error of times past) formal, and fetched far off from the state; because it will require running up and down for process, and give occasion for polling

---

[1] of A   [2] meanes A   [1] a, om A

and exactions by fees, and many other delays and charges.   And
therefore there must be an interim, in which the justice must be
only summary; the rather, because it is fit and safe for a time
the country do participate of martial government   And therefore I could wish in every principal town or place of habitation,
there were a captain or governor, and a judge, such as recorders
and learned stewards are here in corporations, who may[1] have a
prerogative commission to hear and determine *secundum sanam
discretionem*, and as near as may be to the laws and customs of
England ; and that by bill or plaint, without original writ, re-
serving from their sentence matter of free-hold and inheritance,
to be determined before a superior judge itinerant, and both
sentences, as well of the bayliwick judge as the itinerant, to be
reversed (if cause be) before the council of the province to be established there with fit instructions

For Obligation and Reward, it is true (no doubt) which was
anciently said, that a state is contained in two words, *præmium*
and *pœna*.   And I am persuaded, if a penny in the pound which
hath been spent in *pœna* (for this kind of war is but *pœna*, a
chastisement of rebels, without fruit or emolument to this state)
had been spent in *præmio*, that is, in rewarding, things had never
grown to this extremity.   But to speak forwards.[2]   The keeping
of the principal Irish persons in terms of contentment, and without cause of particular complaint, and generally the carrying of
an even course between the English and the Irish, whether it be
in competition, or whether it be in controversy, as if they were
one nation (without that[3] same partial course which hath been held
by the governors and counsellors there, that some have favoured
the Irish and some contrary) is one of the best medicines of[4]
state.   And as for other points of contentment, as the counte-
nancing of their nobility as well in this court as there, the imparting of knighthood ; the care of education of their children,
and the like points of comfort, they are things which fall into
every man's consideration.

For the extirping of the seeds of troubles, I suppose the main
roots are but three.   The first, the ambition and absoluteness of
the chief of the[5] families and septs.   The second, the licentious
idleness of their kernes and soldiers, that lie upon the country
by cesses and such like oppressions   And the third, their[6] bar-

[1] *may*, om. A   [2] *afterwards* A   [3] *the* A   [4] *that state* R
          [5] *chief of the*, om. A   [6] *the* A, B

barous laws, customs, their Brehen law,[1] habits of apparel, their
poets or heralds that enchant them in savage manner, and sundry other such dregs of barbarism and rebellion, which by a
number of politic statutes of Ireland, meet to be put in execution,
are already forbidden, unto which such addition may be made
as the present time requireth. But the deducing of this branch
requireth a more particular notice of the state and manners
there than falls within my compass

For Plantations and Buildings, I find[2] it strange that in the
last plot for the population of Munster, there were limitations
how much in demesne, and how much in farm, and how much
in tenancy; again, how many buildings should be erected, how
many Irish in mixture should be admitted, and other things foreseen almost to curiosity; but no restraint, that they might not
build *sparsim* at their pleasure, nor any condition that they
should make places fortified and defensible. Which omission was
a strange neglect and secureness, to my understanding. So as
for this last point of plantations and buildings, there be two considerations which I hold most material; the one for quickening,
and the other for assuring. The first is, that choice be made of
such persons for the government of towns and places, and such
undertakers be procured, as be men gracious and well beloved, and
are like to be well followed. Wherein for Munster, it may be (because it is not *res integra,* but that the former undertakers stand
interessed,) there will be some difficulty But surely in mine
opinion, either by agreeing with them, or by over-ruling them
with a parliament in Ireland, (which in this course of a politic
proceeding infinite occasions will require speedily to be held,) it
will be meet to supply fit qualified persons of undertakers The
other that it be not left (as heretofore) to the pleasure of the undertakers and adventurers, where and how to build and plant,
but that they do it according to a prescript or formulary. For
first, the places, both maritime and inland, which are fittest for
colonies or garrisons, (as well for doubt of the foreigner, as for
keeping the country in bridle,) would be found, surveyed, and resolved upon · and then that the patentees be tied to build in those
places only, and to fortify as shall be thought convenient And
lastly, it followeth of course, in countries of new populations, to
invite and provoke inhabitants by ample liberties and charters.

[1] *laws* R.   [2] *doe find* B

E 2

3.

What might have been done in this matter if Elizabeth had lived, it is vain to inquire. She lived only to see the first part of the work accomplished—the rebellion effectually subdued.

As yet indeed she showed no sign of decaying powers, and it was only the number of her days that warned her councillors to prepare for a successor. On the 7th of September, 1602, she completed her sixty-ninth year, yet her administration was never more active, vigorous, and prosperous, nor ever more her own. Reinforcements were despatched to the army in Ireland in sufficient numbers and with sufficient speed to complete the pursuit and defeat of the scattered rebels. A naval force was fitted out to keep the Spanish navy in employment or in check, and so cut off all hope of further assistance from that quarter. And besides active negociations carried on through her ambassador with Henry IV to secure common action in the immediate exigencies, she was in secret personal correspondence with him about his great design for the settlement of Europe,—an enterprise in which he and his great minister were still reckoning upon her individual co-operation as a condition almost indispensable.[1] The year was a year of plenty. Her health continued good. Every packet brought news of some head of rebellion coming in. And at last Tyrone himself, finding all overtures of *conditional* submission summarily rejected, offered " without standing upon any terms or conditions, both simply and absolutely to submit himself to her Majesty's mercy."[2]

This offer was contained in a letter to Montjoy, dated 22nd December, 1602.[3] But though, to save appearances, and to give the overture a chance of being entertained, it was made nominally unconditional, it was not to be expected that Tyrone would really give himself up without some assurance of life and liberty, and the question which Montjoy seems to have referred to the Queen was what assurance he might give. It has been said that her dealing with this question betrayed the infirmity of age, and it is true that she did not go exactly at the pace her councillors desired. In that, however, it cannot be said that she was unlike herself: and to me it seems that she was never more like herself than in the management of the whole matter. For as the time which passed before Montjoy received his answer represents the strength of her reluctance to

---

[1] " We considered the death of the King of Spain as the most favourable event that could happen to our design ; but it received so violent a shock by the death of Elizabeth as had like to have made us abandon all our hopes." *Sully's Memoirs*

[2] Goodman's History of his own times. edited by Brewer, ii. 42   [3] Ib. p 41

make any conditions with such an offender,—a reluctance which she
would have felt at any time of her life,—so the answer which he received at last represents the victory of good sense and policy over
personal inclination, in which such struggles always ended. The
exact date at which she received Tyrone's offer of submission, I have
not been able to ascertain, but, as it had to go round by Galway,[1]
it would reach her probably about the middle of January On the
2nd of March Montjoy received a packet containing three letters
two from herself, dated respectively the 16th and 17th of February, and
one from Cecil dated the 18th ; the effect of which, taken all together,
was this. As an inducement to Tyrone to come in, he might in the first
instance promise him his life, and " such other conditions as should
be honourable and reasonable for the Queen to grant him " If that
were not enough, he might promise him his liberty likewise—liberty
to " come and go safe, though in other things they did not agree "
When he came, he might pass him a pardon upon certain specified
conditions, of which it is enough to say here that they were similar
in all the main points to those which had been required in March,
1597-8. for which see Vol. II p 97. Upon these conditions, *if they
could be got* If, however, he could not be brought to accept them
all, then, " rather than send him back unpardoned to be a head still
of rebellion," Montjoy was to use his discretion, and get such " other
reasonable conditions " as he could [2]

Whatever may have been the anxiety of her councillors, the event
proved that the commission was both ample enough and speedy
enough for the occasion For Montjoy, following her own example,
showed himself in no hurry, but waited for another petition from
Tyrone, who as late as the 20th of March, which was nearly three
weeks after the letters from England had arrived, wrote once more
to remind him that he was still without answer, and to press urgently
for an interview By the time this petition reached him however
(which was on the 23rd), he had heard that the Queen was dangerously ill · and seeing the importance of getting the business concluded before the prospect of a new reign or a disputed succession
should beget new hopes, he seized the occasion at once and changed
his pace On the 24th he commissioned two gentlemen to confer
with Tyrone, and sent out at the same time the necessary letters of
protection on the 27th, received news that he had consented to
come the next day, having just heard (privately and not officially)

[1] Goodman's History of his Own Times edited by Brewer, ii p 54
[2] See the original letters, as printed by Brewer from the Tanner MSS —Goodman, ii pp 41–53 They are not given by Moryson, though referred to more
than once in Montjoy's letters, in terms which imply that they contained his final
instructions in the matter See Itinerary, part ii book 3, ch 2

that the Queen was dead, wrote to hasten him—keeping his intelligence in the mean time secret   on the 30th, gave him audience in a style as stately and imperial as Elizabeth herself could have desired   on the 31st, received his written submission upon the conditions prescribed , thereupon promised him in the Queen's name pardon, with restoration of title and (with some exception) of lands, etc. · on the 4th of April, brought him to Dublin   on the 5th, received official news of the Queen's death , and on the 6th caused him to make a new submission in the same form to the new King. So that the last act of Elizabeth's administration was as successful as any, and nothing lost by the delay.

She died on the 24th of March, after an illness of about three weeks , and as her complaint did not take any acute form, or answer to any name more definite than " melancholy," th discoursers of the time busied themselves in inventing causes to account for it. Half a dozen possible or probable causes of mental mortification were easily assigned, out which those who think that the death of a woman in her seventieth year requires any extraordinary explanation may take their choice   But the fact is that she had removed from London to Richmond on the 21st of January in very foul and wet weather, which was suddenly followed by a very severe frost [1] and if we suppose that she then caught a bad cold, which attacked some vital organ , and that, (like most people of strong minds in strong bodies, unused to illness,) she was at once impatient of the sensation of weakness, unwilling to have it seen, distrustful of remedies, intolerant of expostulation, and secretly apprehensive of the worst, we shall need no other explanation of all the incidents of her illness which rest upon good evidence   " No doubt " (says Chamberlain) " but you shall hear her Majesty's sickness and manner of death diversely related   for even here the Papists do tell strange stories, as utterly void of truth as of all civil honesty or humanity   I had good means to understand how the world went, and find her disease to be nothing but a settled and unremoveable melancholy, insomuch that she could not be won or persuaded neither by the counsel, divines, physicians, nor the women about her, once to taste or touch any physic , though ten or twelve physicians that were continually about her did assure her with all manner of asseverations of perfect and easy recovery if she would follow their advice   . Here was some whispering that her brain was somewhat distempered, but there was no such matter , only she held an obstinate silence for the most part, and because she had a persuasion that if she once lay down she should never rise, could not be gotten to bed in a whole

[1] Chamberlain to Carleton, 27 Jan 1602-3 p 174

week till three days before her death so that after three weeks' languishing, she departed the 24th of this present," etc [1]

"I dined with Dr Parry in the Privy Chamber," writes Manningham in his diary, on the 23rd of March, "and understood by him, the Bishop of Chichester, the Dean of Canterbury, the Dean of Windsor, etc, that her Majesty hath been by fits troubled with melancholy some three or four months, but for this fortnight extreme oppressed with it, insomuch that she refused to eat anything, to receive any physic, or admit any rest in bed, till within these two or three days She hath been in a manner speechless for two days. Very pensive and silent since Shrovetide [2] sitting sometimes with her eye fixed on one object many hours together Yet she always had her perfect senses and memory, and yesterday signified by the lifting up of her hands to heaven (a sign which Dr. Parry entreated of her) that she believed that faith which she hath caused to be professed, and looked faithfully to be saved by Christ's merits and mercy only, and no other means She took great delight in hearing prayers, would often at the name of Jesus lift up her hands and eyes to Heaven she would not hear the Archbishop speak of hope of her longer life, but when he prayed or spake of Heaven or those joys, she would hug his hand. It seems she might have lived if she would have used means, but she would not be persuaded, and princes must not be forced. Her physicians said she had a body of firm and perfect constitution likely to have lived many years."[3]

The next day he adds that about three o'clock in the morning she "departed this life mildly, like a lamb easily like a ripe apple from the tree cum leni quadam febre, absque gemitu"

The consciousness or apprehension that she was no longer mistress of her own powers is quite enough to account for the melancholy which oppressed her It is easy to believe that, whatever her physicians might say, she felt her faculties failing, and did not choose to outlive them.

4.

As a matter of policy, there was perhaps no part of Elizabeth's proceedings more questionable from first to last, in the judgment of her best councillors, than her refusal to let the question of succession be settled, or even discussed Yet here again, if the event be accepted as judge, it is hard to say that she was wrong Her own authority endured to the last without diminution, and her successor took her place at once, without contention or disturbance

[1] 30 March, 1603 Dom James I, vol i no 6
[2] Shrove Tuesday fell on the 5th of March in 1602-3
[3] Harl MSS 5353, fo 111

"The Proclamation," writes Manningham, on the night of the 24th, "was heard with great expectation and silent joy no great shouting I think the sorrow for her Majesty's departure was so deep in many hearts that they could not so suddenly show any great joy, though it could not be less than exceeding great for the succession of so worthy a King And at night they showed it by bonfires and ringing No tumult, no contradiction, no disorders in the city every man went about his business as readily, as peaceably, as securely, as though there had been no change, nor any news ever heard of competitors."[1]

Nor did this outward calm in any respect belie the fact And yet to statesmen the crisis was not the less an anxious one, for public as well as private reasons The danger of a competition for the Crown was indeed past, and the sensation is described by Bacon as like that of waking from a fearful dream[2] But the very absence of competition implied the existence of expectations or hopes in different parties, whose interests being opposite their hopes could not all be fulfilled No policy could prevent the growth of discontents, but whether they should grow to be dangerous would depend upon the position which the new King took up among the contending parties and conflicting interests

With such questions Bacon was familiar, and he could not but feel that he had matter in him which would be of service. His professional ambition had always aspired to employment in the business of the state and his chances of personal success in life and of recovery from the embarrassments with which he had been so long struggling, and from which he was not yet free, lay all in that direction On all accounts, therefore, it was a prime object with him to obtain the favourable regard of the new King, and he lost no time in using such opportunities as he had The most important person in England was his cousin Sir Robert Cecil, and next to him perhaps (at that time) the Earl of Northumberland, who had been engaged for some years, together with Cecil and Lord Henry Howard in a secret and confidential correspondence with James, and had within the last few days been invited by the Council to assist them[3] and who, being besides a man of letters and learning, was qualified to appreciate Bacon's value and sympathize with his tastes in that department also He was acquainted likewise, more or less, with several persons about the Scotch Court, who had been in correspondence with his brother in the service of the Earl of Essex, and were likely

[1] Harl MSS 5353, fo 111
[2] Beginning of a History of Great Britain—Works, VI. 277
[3] Corresp of K James with Cecil and others (Camd Soc), p 73

on that account to be regarded with favour   To all these, knowing that a man may be forgotten merely for want of a reminder, he now addressed himself,—directly or indirectly, as seemed most becoming or most discreet in each case,—in what style and taste the following letters (all belonging to this occasion, and written nearly at the same time, though the precise order cannot be determined) will sufficiently show

As his best chance with Cecil,—whose professions of friendship, though outwardly very frank and affectionate, did not necessarily represent any great zeal for his advancement,—he resorted to his constant friend Hickes , who had been secretary to Burghley, and seems now to have been serving his son in the same capacity, and to have been a great favourite with him [1]

To Mr. Michael Hicks.[2]

Mr Hickes,

The apprehension of this threatened judgment of God, *percutiam pastorem et dispergentur oves gregis*, if it work in other as it worketh in me, knitteth every man's heart more unto his true and approved friend   Which is the cause why I now write to you, signifying that I would be glad of the comfort of your society and familiar conference as occasion serveth   And withal, though we card-holders have nothing to do but to keep close our cards and to do as we are bidden, yet as I ever used your mean to cherish the truth of my inclination towards Mr. Secretary, so now again I pray as you find time let him know that he is the personage in this state which I love most · which containeth all that I can do, and expresseth all which I will say at this time.   And this as you may easily judge proceedeth not out of any straits of my occasions, as mought be thought in times past, but merely out of the largeness and fullness of my affections   And so for this time I commend me to you, from my chamber at Gray's Inn this 19th of March, 1602.

Your assured friend,

Fr Bacon.

To the Earl of Northumberland he addressed himself directly, and apparently about the same time   The letter (which had previously

[1] See Lansd MSS 88, *passim*
[2] Lansd MSS 88, p 107 Original own hand Addressed "To my very good friend, Mr Mich Hicks, at his howse in the Strond "

appeared in the 'Remains' as addressed to the Earl of *Northampton*
—an easy though a very considerable mistake) comes from his own
collection, and was printed by Rawley in the 'Resuscitatio' As in
other similar cases, I take the text from the manuscript copy in the
British Museum

A Letter of recommendation of his service to the Earl
    of Northumberland, a few days before Queen Eliza-
    beth's death [1]

It may please your good Lordship,

As the time of sowing of a seed is known, but the time of
coming up and disclosing is casual, or according to the season,
so I am a witness to myself, that there hath been covered in my
mind, a long time, a seed of affection and zeal towards your Lordship, sown by the estimation of your virtues, and your particular honours and favours to my brother deceased, and to myself,
which seed still springing, now bursteth forth into this profession   And to be plain with your Lordship, it is very true, (and no
winds or noises of civil matters can blow this out of my head
or heart,) that your great capacity and love towards studies and
contemplations of an higher and worthier nature than popular
(a nature rare in this world, and in a person of your Lordship's
quality almost singular,) is to me a great and chief motive to
draw my affection and admiration towards you   And therefore,
good my Lord, if I may be of any use to your Lordship, by my
head, tongue, pen, means, or friends, I humbly pray you to hold
me your own ; and herewithal, not to do so much disadvantage
to my good mind, nor partly to your own worth, as to conceive
that this commendation of my humble service proceedeth out
of any straits of my occasions, but merely out of an election,
and indeed the fulness of my heart   And so wishing your Lordship all prosperity, I continue, etc

These letters were written while the Queen was still living, but without hope of recovery.   Upon her death his first step was to recommend
himself to those of his acquaintance in the Scotch Court who were
most likely to be employed in English affairs   One of these was Mr.
David Foulis, who had been used by James in his negotiations with
England during the ten years preceding, had served as resident ambassador in London from 1594 to 1596, and had been on terms of

[1] Add MSS 5503, fo 19

great friendship and confidence with Anthony Bacon [1] Another was Mr. Edward Bruce, Abbot of Kinloss, who had been twice sent to England on particular embassies, first in April, 1594, and again (with the Earl of Mar) in 1600–1 the embassy out of which grew the secret correspondence between the King and Cecil [2]

Messengers were of course despatched as soon as possible from the Council to the King, and by one of these Bacon sent to Mr Foulis the following letter, which comes from his own register-book.

A LETTER TO MR. DAVID FOULES, IN SCOTLAND, UPON THE ENTRANCE OF HIS MAJESTY'S REIGN. [3]

Sir,

The occasion awaketh in me the remembrance of the constant and mutual good offices which passed between my good brother and yourself, whereunto (as you know) I was not altogether a stranger, though the time and design (as between brethren) made me more reserved. But well do I bear in mind the great opinion which my brother (whose judgment I much reverence) would often express to me, of the extraordinary sufficiency, dexterity, and temper, which he had found in you, in the business and service of the King our sovereign lord This latter bred in me an election, as the former gave an inducement for me, to address myself to you, and to make this signification of my desire towards a mutual entertainment of good affection and correspondence between us. hoping that both some good effect may result of it towards the King's service; and that for our particulars, though occasion give you the precedence of furthering my being known by good note unto the king, so no long time will intercede before I on my part shall have some means given to requite your favours, and to verify your commendation. And so with my loving commendations, good Mr Foules, I leave you to God's goodness. From Gray's Inn, this 25th of March.

The same day he wrote a letter of like import to Bruce, though it seems doubtful whether it was sent For it is not given by Dr. Rawley in the 'Resuscitatio,' either among the letters taken from Bacon's own register-book or in the supplementary collection nor is it to be found in the manuscript volume now in the British Museum,

---

[1] Birch, Mem of Eliz i pp 162, 178, 496, etc , ii p 41
[2] Ib i p 175, ii p 509   [3] Add MSS 5503, fo 20 b   'Resuscitatio,' p 21

which I take to be a contemporary copy of the register-book itself,
It was certainly delayed (as appears by a postscript which has been
added and then crossed out) in order that it might be accompanied
by a letter to the King; and it may be that it was stopped altogether by news that Bruce was already on his way to London, for the
despatch from the Lords of the Council was anticipated by Sir Robert Cary, who saw James on the night of the 26th, and informed
him that the Queen was dead upon which both Bruce and Foulis
were immediately despatched to London, and appear to have set out
before the official messenger arrived.

The letter, however, whether sent or not, is undoubtedly genuine,
for there is a copy (or draft to dictation) among the Lambeth papers,
written in the hand of one of Bacon's men, with additions in his own
And from this copy I take it

To Edward Bruce, Abbot of Kinloss [1]

My Lord,

The present occasion awaketh in me a remembrance of the
constant amity and mutual good offices, which passed between my
good brother deceased and your Lordship, whereunto I was less
strange than in respect of the time I had reason to pretend; and
withal I call to mind the great opinion which my brother (who
seldom failed in judgment of persons) would often express to me
of your Lordship's great wisdom and soundness both in head and
heart towards the service and affairs of the King our sovereign
lord. The one of these hath bred in me an election, and the
other a confidence to address my goodwill and sincere affection
to your Lordship, not doubting, in regard that my course of life
hath wrought me not to be altogether unseen in the matters of
this kingdom, that I may be of some use both in points of service to the King and in your Lordship's particular And on the
other side I will not omit humbly to desire your Lordship's favour,
in furdering a good conceit and impression of my most humble
duty and true zeal towards the King; to whose majesty words
cannot make me known, neither mine own nor others. but time
will, to no disadvantage of any that shall forerun his Majesty's
experience, by their humanity and commendation. And so I
commend your good Lordship to God's preservation From
Gray's-Inn, this xxv[th] of March, 1603. To do your L humble
service

---

[1] Lambeth MSS 976, fo 3 Addressed in Bacon's own ' nd "To his hon[ble]
good L Mr Breuze, L of Kynlosse be these delivered"

So the letter stood originally, but at the end the following post-script is added, I think in Bacon's own hand

Since my writing of this letter I have taken courage to make oblation of my most humble service by letter unto his Majesty, whereof I send your Lordship a copy, and shall esteem it an exceeding courtesy if you will take some speedy and good opportunity to present it to his royal hands: which if your L shall vouchsafe to undertake, I have desired this gentleman, Mr. Matthew, eldest son to my L. B. of Durham, to deliver the same unto your L desiring your L furder for my sake to show him what courtesies his occasions shall require which I assure your L. shall be towards a very worthy and rare young gentleman.

The letter to Foulis had gone by Mr. Lake, who was despatched from the Council on the 27th This, at the time when the postscript was written, was evidently intended to be carried and presented by Toby Matthew,[1] a private friend of Bacon's own—the same who acted the Squire in Essex's 'Device' on the Queen's day in 1595,[2] and a man for whom Bacon retained a great personal affection, through much variety of fortune on both sides, to the end of his life. Upon further thoughts however, or further news, he appears to have changed his mind again, for he struck out the postscript, and transferred it, along with the commission which it carried, to another letter addressed to another man, as we shall presently see.

Matthew set out on the 28th or 29th of March, charged with a letter from Bacon to the King, and another to Sir Thomas Challoner (enclosing a copy or duplicate of it) to serve by way of introduction his commission being to get it delivered in the handsomest way that offered Sir Thomas Challoner, an accomplished scholar, and a student in natural history and chemistry,[3] had been employed in Italy as an intelligencer in the service of the Earl of Essex upon Anthony Bacon's recommendation, who kept up a continual correspondence with him,[4] and whom he "acknowledged to be the first author of manifesting his firm zeal to his Lordship's service" When his acquaintance with Francis began, I do not know but on the 27th of October, 1596, when he was on the point of departure to Italy, I find him begging Anthony "most heartily to salute his brother" for him [5] How the business prospered, I cannot say but the letters

---

[1] In Sir Toby Matthew's collection of letters, edited by Dr Donne, the name is printed *Matthews* But as Bacon always writes it *Matthew*, I shall keep that form
[2] Vol I p 375
[3] Birch, ii pp 150, 182, 226, 270, 304
[4] Lodge, iii p 59, note
[5] Lambeth MSS 959, fo 222.

themselves are preserved in Bacon's own collection, and with the headings, which I suppose to have been inserted by himself or copied from his dockets, may be left to tell their own story

Of the letter to the King we have three copies, independent of each other and slightly differing   one in the Register-book, one in Sir Toby Matthew's collection, and one in the 'Remains'   Sir Toby Matthew's copies I do not hold very high as authorities for the exact text   for I suspect that he used the privilege of an editor rather freely in omitting or disguising personal allusions, and occasionally in mending the style by the alteration of a word or two   The copies in the 'Remains' are full of mere blunders   but in some cases, as in this, they appear to have been taken from the original letter, while those in the Register were taken from the rough draft   I have therefore in this instance formed my text from the 'Remains,' correcting obvious misprints from the Register, and giving the other differences in foot-notes

An offer of service to his Majesty K. James upon his first coming in [1]

It may please your most excellent Majesty,

It is observed upon a place in the Canticles by some, *Ego sum flos campi et lilium convallium*, that, *à dispari*, it is not said, *Ego sum flos horti, et lilium montium*, because the majesty of that person is not inclosed for a few, nor appropriate to the great And yet notwithstanding, this royal virtue of access, which nature and judgment have planted in your Majesty's mind as the portal of all the rest, could not of itself (my imperfections considered) have animated me to make oblation of myself immediately to your Majesty, had it not been joined with an habit of like liberty, which I enjoyed with my late dear Sovereign Mistress, a Prince happy in all things, but most happy in such a successor   And yet further and more nearly, I was not a little encouraged, not only upon a supposal that unto your Majesty's sacred ears (open to the air of all virtues) there might perhaps have come some small breath[2] of the good memory of my father, so long a principal counsellor in this your kingdom , but also by the particular knowledge of the infinite devotion and incessant endeavours (beyond the strength of his body, and the nature of the times) which appeared in my good brother towards your

---

[1] Remains, p 55   Add MSS 5503, fo 19, b   [2] *some knowledge*   A

Majesty's service; and were on your Majesty's part, through your singular benignity, by many most gracious and lively significations and favours accepted and acknowledged,[1] beyond the merit of anything he could effect   All which endeavours and duties for the most part were common to myself with him, though by design (as between brethren) dissembled   And therefore, most high and mighty King, my most dear and dread sovereign lord, since now the corner-stone is laid of the mightiest monarchy in Europe, and that God above, who is noted to have[2] a mighty hand in bridling the floods and fluctuations[3] of the seas and of people's hearts, hath by the miraculous and universal consent (the more strange because it proceedeth from such diversity of causes[4]) in your coming in, given a sign and token what he intendeth in the continuance,[5] I think there is no subject of your Majesty's, who loveth this island, and is not hollow and unworthy, whose heart is not set on fire, not only to bring you peace-offerings to make you propitious, but to sacrifice himself a burnt-offering[6] to your Majesty's service   amongst which number no man's fire shall be more pure and fervent than mine   But how far forth it shall blaze out, that resteth in your Majesty's employment.   For since your fortune in the greatness thereof hath for time debarred your Majesty of the princely[7] virtue which one calleth the principal—" Principis est virtus maxima nosse suos "—because your Majesty hath many of yours which are unknown to you, I must leave all to the trial of further time, and so thirsting after the happiness of kissing your royal hand, continue ever, etc.

A LETTER COMMENDING HIS LOVE AND SERVICES TO SIR THOMAS CHALLONER, THEN IN SCOTLAND, UPON HIS MAJESTY'S ENTRANCE [8]

Sir,

For our money matters, I am assured you conceived no insatisfaction, for you know my mind, and you know my means; which now the openness of the time, caused by this blessed con-

---

[1] Birch, Mem of Eliz 1 181.   [2] *who hath ever hand* A   [3] *motions* A
[4] For an exposition of these various causes, see the *Beginning of a History of Great Britain*, Works, VI 277
[5] *of great happiness in the continuance of your reign* A   [6] *or holocaust* A
[7] *finally* in the 'Remains' This whole sentence—from *for since* to *time*—is omitted in A, which has only, *so, thirsting*, etc
[8] Add MSS 5503, fo 21

sent and peace, will increase; and so our agreement according to our time be observed.

For the present, according to the Roman adage (that one cluster of grapes ripeneth best besides another,) I know you hold me not unworthy whose mutual friendship you should cherish, and I for my part conceive and hope that you are likely to become an acceptable servant to the King our Master, not so much for any way made heretofore (which in my judgment will make no great difference[1]) as for the stuff and sufficiency which I know to be in you, and whereof I know his Majesty may reap great service   And therefore my general request is, that according to that industrious vivacity which you use towards your friends, you will further his Majesty's good conceit and inclination towards me; to whom words cannot make me known, neither my own nor others, but time will; to no disadvantage of any that shall fore-run his Majesty's experience by their testimony and commendation   And though occasion give you the precedence of doing me this special good office, yet I hope no long time will intercede before I shall have some means to requite your favour and acquit your report   More particularly, having thought good to make oblation of my most humble service to his Majesty by a few lines, I do desire your loving care and help, by yourself or such means as I refer to your discretion, to deliver and present the same to his Majesty's hands, of which letter I send you a copy, that you may know what you carry, and may take of Mr. Matthew the letter itself, if you be pleased to undertake the delivery   Lastly, I do commend to yourself, and such your courtesies as occasion may require, this gentleman Mr. Matthew, eldest son to my Lord Bishop of Duresme, and my very good friend, assuring you that any courtesy you shall use towards him, you shall use to a very worthy young gentleman and one, I know, whose acquaintance you will much esteem.   And so I ever continue.

A LETTER TO MR FOULES, 28th OF MARCH 1603[2]
Mr Foules,

I did write unto you yesterday by Mr. Lake (who was dispatched hence from their Lordships) a letter of reviver of those

---

[1] Meaning, I suppose, that his having been engaged in Essex's service would not give him any special advantage over others
[2] Add MSS 5503, fo 22, b

sparks of former acquaintance between us in my brother's time,
and now upon the same confidence, finding so fit a messenger, I
would not fail to salute you; hoping it will fall out so happily
as that you shall be one of the King's servants which his Majesty
will first employ here with us, where I hope to have some means
not to be barren in friendship towards you We all thirst after
the King's coming, accounting all this but as the dawning of
the day before the rising of the sun, till we have his presence.
And though now his Majesty must be *Janus bifrons*, to have a
face to Scotland as well as to England, yet *quod nunc instat
agendum.* The expectation is here that he will come in state,
and not in strength So for this time I commend you to God's
goodness.

A Letter to Mr Davys, then gone to the King, at his
first entrance, March 28, 1603.[1]

Mr. Davis,

Though you went on the sudden, yet you could not go before you had spoken with yourself to the purpose which I will
now write. And therefore I know it shall be altogether needless, save that I meant to show you that I am not asleep. Briefly,
I commend myself to your love and to the well using of my name,
as well in repressing and answering for me, if there be any biting
or nibbling at it in that place, as in impressing a good conceit
and opinion of me, chiefly in the King (of whose favour I make myself comfortable assurance), as otherwise in that court. And not
only so, but generally to perform to me all the good offices which
the vivacity of your wit can suggest to your mind to be performed to one, in whose affection you have so great sympathy,
and in whose fortune you have so great interest So desiring
you to be good to concealed poets, I continue

Your very assured,

FR. BACON.

Gray's Inn, this
28th of March, 1603

[1] Lambeth MSS 976, fo 4 The original letter apparently for the seal remains The signature is Bacon's own, and the docket is in his hand the body
of the letter in the hand of one of his men There is a copy of it in the Register
book, with two or three slight verbal differences, and without the date Mr
Davis was no doubt John Davies, the poet,—author of 'Nosce Teipsum' and
afterwards Attorney-General for Ireland The allusion to "concealed poets" I
cannot explain But as Bacon occasionally wrote letters and devices, which were
to be fathered by Essex, he may have written verses for a similar purpose, and
Davis may have been in the secret

Another acquaintance of Bacon's in the Scotch Court was Dr Morison, who had been in confidential correspondence with the Earl of Essex in his loyal days, and supplied him with a great deal of valuable intelligence   He wrote in French under a cipher, and all the correspondence passed through Anthony Bacon's hands, who generally sent it to his brother on its way to the Earl   To him Bacon now sent a letter to refresh the old acquaintance. But I find no better copy of it than one in the 'Remains,' where it was first printed It is a genuine letter I have no doubt, though not a correct copy

A Letter to Doctor Morrison, a Scottish Physician, upon his Majesty's coming in.[1]

Mr. Doctor Morrison,

I have thought good by this my letter to renew the[2] ancient acquaintance which hath passed between us, signifying my good mind to you, to perform to you any good office for your particular, and my expectation and firm[3] assurance of[4] the like on your part towards me. wherein I confess you may have the start of me, because occasion hath given you the precedency in investing you with opportunity to use my name well, and by your loving testimony to further a good opinion of me in his Majesty, and the court

But I hope my experience of matters here will, with the light of his Majesty's favour, enable me speedily both to requite your kindness, and to acquit and make good your testimony and report.   So not doubting to see you here with his Majesty, considering that it belongeth to your art to feel pulses, and I assure you Galen doth not set down greater variety of pulses than do vent here in men's hearts, I wish you all prosperity, and remain

Yours, etc.

From my chamber at Gray's Inn, etc

Having despatched these personal matters, his next care was to consider what help he could give in smoothing the King's path to the hearts of the people   To touch the right vein at first was a matter by no means easy for a stranger, and a rub the wrong way might do much mischief   Addressing himself therefore to the Earl of Northumberland, by whom his recent offer of service seems to have been favourably entertained, he sent him a draft of a Proclamation, such as he thought fit for the time, and which, being an entirely volun-

---

[1] Remains, p 63   [2] this my, in orig   [3] and a fi, in orig   [4] on, in orig

tary performance of his own suggestion, may be taken as embodying
the advice which he would have given to the King at this conjuncture, if he had been in a position to advise   It is taken from a copy
preserved and corrected by himself, and shows, among other things,
that if depreciation of Elizabeth was really the fashion at Court
during the first few months of James's reign—a fact which I find it
hard to believe, though resting on the respectable evidence of Sully—
it was a mistake for which Bacon, at any rate, was not responsible ,
and its drift and purpose are sufficiently explained in the letter
which accompanied it

A LETTER TO MY LORD OF NORTHUMBERLAND MENTIONING A
   PROCLAMATION DRAWN FOR THE KING AT HIS ENTRANCE [1]

It may please your Lordship,

I do hold it a thing formal and necessary for the King to
forerun his coming (be it never so speedy) with some gracious
declaration, for the cherishing, entertaining, and preparing of
men's affections.   For which purpose I have conceived a draught,
it being a thing familiar in my Mistress' times to have my pen
used in public writings of satisfaction   The use of this may
be in two sorts: first properly, if your Lordship think convenient
to shew the King any such draught ; because the veins and pulses
of this state cannot be but best known here, which if your
Lordship should do, then I would desire you to withdraw my
name, and only signify that you gave some heads of direction of
such a matter to one of whose style and pen you had some opinion   The other collateral , that though your Lordship make
no other use of it, yet it is a kind of portraiture of that which I
think worthy to be advised by your Lordship to the King,[2] and
perhaps more compendious and significant than if I had set them
down in articles.   I would have attended your Lordship but for
some little physic I took.   To-morrow morning I will wait on
you   So I ever, etc

A PROCLAMATION DRAWN FOR HIS MAJESTY'S FIRST COMING IN,
              PREPARED BUT NOT USED.[3]

Having great cause at this time to be moved with diversity of
affections, we do in first place condole with all our loving subjects

[1] Add MSS 5503, p 23   'Remains,' p 62
[2] The copy in the 'Remains ' adds, "to express himself according to those
points which are therein conceived "
[3] Harl MSS 6797, fo 13   Copy, with some corrections in Bacon's hand
First printed in Stephens's second collection, A D 1734, p 301

of England for the loss of their so virtuous and excellent Queen; being a prince that we always found a dear sister, yea a mother to ourself, in many her actions and advices; a prince whom we hold and behold as an excellent pattern and example to imitate in many her royal virtues and parts of government, and a prince whose days we could have wished to have been prolonged, we reporting ourselves not only to the testimony of our royal heart, but to the judgment of all the world, whether there ever appeared in us any ambitious or impatient desire to prevent God's appointed time Neither are we so partial to our own honour, but that we do in great part ascribe this our most peaceable and quiet entrance and coming to these our crowns, next under the blessing of Almighty God and our undoubted right, to the fruit of her Majesty's peaceable and quiet government, accustoming the people to all loyalty and obedience As for that which concerneth ourselves, we would have all our loving subjects know that we do not take so much gladness and contentment in the devolving of these kingdoms unto our royal person, for any addition or increase of glory, power, or riches, as in this that it is so manifest an evidence unto us (especially the manner of it considered) that we stand (though unworthy) in God's favour, who hath put more means into our hands to reward our friends and servants, and to pardon and obliterate injuries, and to comfort and relieve the hearts and estates of our people and loving subjects, and chiefly to advance the holy religion and church of Almighty God, and to deserve well of the Christian commonwealth.

And more especially we cannot but gratulate and rejoice in this one point, that it hath pleased God to make us the instrument and as it were the corner-stone, to unite these two mighty and warlike nations of England and Scotland into one kingdom. For although these two nations are situate upon the continent of one island, and are undivided either by seas or mountains, or by diversity of language, and although our neighbour kingdoms of Spain and France have already had the happiness to be re-united in the several members of those kingdoms formerly disjoined, yet in this island it appeareth not in the records of any true history, no nor scarcely in the conceit of any fabulous narration or tradition, that this whole island of Great Brittany was ever united under one sovereign prince before

this day which as we cannot but take as a singular honour
and favour of God unto ourselves, so we may conceive good
hope that the kingdoms of Christendom standing distributed
and counterpoised as by this last union they now are, it will
be a foundation of the universal peace of all Christian princes,
and that now the strife that shall remain between them shall
be but an emulation who shall govern best and most to the weal
and good of his people.

Another great cause of our just rejoicing is the assured hope
that we conceive, that whereas our kingdom of Ireland hath
been so long time torn and afflicted with the miseries of wars,
the making and prosecuting of which wars hath cost such an
infinite deal of blood and treasure of our realm of England to
be spilt and consumed thereupon, we shall be able through
God's favour and assistance to put a speedy and an honourable
end to those wars   And it is our princely design and full purpose and resolution not only to reduce that nation from their
rebellion and revolt, but also to reclaim them from their barbarous manners to justice and the fear of God; and to popu-
late, plant, and make civil all the provinces in that kingdom
which also being an action that not any of our noble progenitors
kings of England hath ever had the happiness throughly to pro-
secute and accomplish we take so much to heart, as we are persuaded it is one of the chief causes for the which God hath
brought us to the imperial crown of these kingdoms

Further, we cannot but take great comfort in the state and
correspondence which we now stand in of peace and unity with
all Christian princes, and otherwise of quietness and obedience
of our own people at home whereby we shall not need to espouse
that our kingdom of England to any quarrel or war, but rather
have occasion to preserve them in peace and tranquillity, and
openness of trade with all foreign nations.

Lastly and principally, we cannot but take unspeakable comfort in the great and wonderful consent and unity, joy and alacrity, wherewith our loving subjects of our kingdom of England
have received and acknowledged us their natural and lawful king
and governor, according to our most clear and undoubted right,
in so quiet and settled manner, as if we had been long ago
declared and established successor, and had taken all men's
oaths and homages, greater and more perfect unity and readiness

could not have been. For considering with ourselves that notwithstanding difference of religion, or any other faction, and notwithstanding our absence so far off, and notwithstanding the sparing and reserved communicating of one another's minds, yet all our loving subjects met in one thought and voice, without any the least disturbance or interruption, yea hesitation or doubtfulness, or any shew thereof, we cannot but acknowledge it is a great work of God, who hath an immediate and extraordinary direction in the disposing of kingdoms and flows of people's hearts

Wherefore after our most humble and devout thanks to Almighty God, by whom kings reign, who hath established us king and governor of these kingdoms, we return our hearty and affectionate thanks unto the Lords spiritual and temporal, the knights and gentlemen, the cities and towns, and generally unto our Commons, and all estates and degrees of that our kingdom of England, for their so acceptable first-fruits of their obedience and loyalties offered and performed in our absence ; much commending the great wisdom, courage, and watchfulness used by the Peers of that our kingdom (according to the nobility of their bloods and lineages, many of them mingled with the blood royal, and therefore in nature affectionate to their rightful king), and likewise of the counsellors of the late Queen, according to their gravity and oath, and the spirit of their good Mistress (now a glorious Saint in heaven), in carrying and ordering our affairs with that fidelity, moderation, and consent, which in them hath well appeared · and also the great readiness, concord, and cheerfulness in the principal knights and gentlemen of several counties, with the head officers of great cities, corporations, and towns and do take knowledge by name of the readiness and good zeal of that our chiefest and most famous city, the city of London, the chamber of that our kingdom assuring them that we will be unto that city, by all means of confirming and increasing their happy and wealthy estate, not only a just and gracious sovereign lord and king, but a special and bountiful patron and benefactor

And we on our part, as well in remuneration of all their loyal and loving affections as in discharge of our princely office, do promise and assure them that as all manner of estates have concurred and consented in their duty and zeal towards us, so it shall be our continual care and resolution to preserve and maintain every several estate in a happy and flourishing condition, without confusion or over-growing of any one to the prejudice, discontentment, or discouragement of the rest and generally in all estates we hope God will strengthen and assist us not only to extirpate all gross and notorious abuses and corruptions, of simonies, briberies, extortions, exactions, oppressions, vexations, burdensome payments and overcharges, and the like, but further to extend our princely care to the supply of the very neglects and omissions of anything that may tend to the good of our people, so that every place and service that is fit for the honour or good of the commonwealth shall be filled, and no man's virtue left idle, unemployed, or unrewarded, and every good ordinance and constitution for the amendment of the estate and times be revived and put in execution

In the mean time, minding by God's leave (all delay set apart) to comfort and secure our loving subjects in our kingdom of England by our personal presence there, we require all our loving subjects joyfully to expect the same · and yet so, as we signify our will and pleasure to be, that all such ceremonies and preparations as shall be made and used to do us honour, or to express gratulation, be rather comely and orderly than sumptuous and glorious, and for the expressing of magnificence, that it be rather employed and bestowed upon the funeral of the late Queen, to whose memory we are of opinion too much honour cannot be done or performed.

The chief inconvenience which actually resulted from the want of an acknowledged successor to the Crown was, that authority derived from the Queen dying with her, and James being 400 miles away, there must be an interval of at least a week during which none of the officers of State could be formally authorized to execute his functions The only disorder, however, which arose from this cause, appears to have been confined within the walls of the council-chamber itself, and to have been kept so well within bounds that our only knowledge of it comes from the report of a French ambassador at the time, and a collector of gossip in the next generation On the authority of the French ambassador, we are told that the right of the Council to act was formally disputed by the Earl of Northumberland, and that the Lord Keeper offered, on behalf of himself and such of the Councillors as were not members of the Upper House, to resign to the Lords

their seats at the head of the table[1]   On the authority of Aubrey,
we learn that "at a consultation at Whitehall, after Queen Eliza
beth's death, how matters were to be ordered and what ought to be
done, Sir Walter Ralegh declared his opinion that 'twas the wisest
way for them to keep the government in their own hands, and set
up a commonwealth, and not be subject to a needy and beggarly
nation"[2]   The authority is not worth much in either case, but if
anything of this kind really occurred—and it does not appear that
any Englishman of the time had heard of it—Ralegh's proposal could
only be meant and taken as a jest, and the Lord Keeper's offer was
of course declined   The Council continued not only to act during
the interregnum, but to act with vigour   and the King made the
interval as short as possible by immediately directing that all persons
in office at the Queen's death should so continue till his further plea
sure were known   a direction which appears to have included everybody concerned, except Bacon

Bacon had for some years been employed and described as one of
the Learned Counsel, but it was by the verbal order of the Queen
he had never been sworn in, and had no written warrant   Not being
now mentioned by name in the King's letters, and not coming properly under the description of a person "in office at the Queen's
death," he was in effect left out   The omission however was altogether accidental, and as soon as the King was informed of it was
supplied at once[3]   What, in the meantime, had become of his letter
to the King, and whether either it or the personal influence of any
of his correspondents had done him any good, we do not know   It
appears, however, from the two private and familiar letters which
come next, and though not dated must belong to the first week in
April, that he was very well satisfied with the King's proceedings so
far

The first is addressed to Toby Matthew, from whose own collection it comes; and who no doubt inserted the heading, and probably suppressed the names of the persons alluded to   For his
object in making his collection was not to illustrate history or bio-
graphy, but to exhibit specimens of epistolary composition; and he

---

[1] Gardiner, i 51   An English narrative, apparently official, represents the Lord
Keeper as offering, on behalf of himself and the Councillors who were not peers,
to take the lower place at the table, but says nothing of any dispute about their
authority   "But as they began to sit in council in the Privy Chamber at White
hall, the Lord Keeper, Sir Thomas Egerton, and the rest of the Council that were
no Barons, offered to sit at the lower end of the Council table, and not above any
of the meanest nobility   but the noblemen in respect of their former authority,
called them to the higher end of the table, and wished them to keep their places"
—Add MSS 1786, 5, b   The ambassador's story would easily grow out of this
    Aubrey, ii p 515   [3] Egerton Papers (Camd Soc), p 268

has evidently taken pains to remove names and dates, and such particulars as might serve to identify persons In this case, however, there is little doubt that the persons alluded to are Foulis and Bruce, both of whom had certainly arrived in London before the 12th of April [1]

SIR FRANCIS BACON SIGNIFYING TO A FRIEND AND SERVANT OF HIS THE WISE PROCEEDING OF KING JAMES AT HIS FIRST ENTRANCE TO THIS KINGDOM [2]

Sir,

I was heartily glad to hear that you had passed so great a part of your journey in so good health My aim was right in my address of letters to those persons in the court of Scotland who are likeliest to be used for the affairs of England; but the pace they held was too swift; for the men were come away before my letters could reach them. With the first I have renewed acquaintance, and it was like a bill of reviver by way of cross-suits, for he was as ready to have begun with me The second did this day arrive, and took acquaintance of me instantly in the council-chamber, and was willing to entertain me with further demonstrations of confidence than I was willing at that time to admit But I have had no serious speech with him; nor do I yet know whether any of the doubles of my letter have been delivered to the King It may perhaps have proved your luck to be the first

Things are here in good quiet. The King acts excellently well, for he puts in clauses of reservation to every proviso [3] He saith, he would be sorry to have just cause to remove any He saith, he will displace none who hath served the Queen and state sincerely, etc The truth is, here be two extremes. Some few would have no change, no not reformation. Some many would have much change, even with perturbation. God, I hope, will direct this wise king to hold a mean between reputation enough and no terrors. In my particular I have many comforts and assurances; but in mine own opinion the chief is, that the canvassing world is gone, and the deserving world is come. And withal I find myself as one awaked out of sleep;

---

[1] Chamberlain to Carleton, 12 April, 1603
[2] A collection of letters made by Sir Tobie Matthews, Kt , etc (published, with a Dedicatory Letter by Dr Donne, in 1660), p 18
[3] So printed Qu promise?

which I have not been this long time, nor could, I think, have been now, without such a great noise as this, which yet is in *aura lene* I have written this to you in haste; my end being no more than to write, and thereby to make you know that I will ever continue the same, and still be sure to wish you as heartily well as to myself

The next is from Bacon's own collection, and is addressed to his cousin Robert Kempe—the "good Robin," I presume, with whom we are already acquainted.[1]

To Mr Robert Kempe, upon the Death of Queen Elizabeth.[2]

Mr Kempe,

This alteration is so great, as you mought justly conceive some coldness of my affection towards you if you should hear nothing from me, I living in this place. It is in vain to tell you with what wonderful still and calm this wheel is turned round, which whether it be a remnant of her felicity that is gone, or a fruit of his reputation that is coming, I will not determine· but[3] I cannot but divide myself between her memory and his name Yet we account it but a fair morn before sunrising, before his Majesty's presence though for my part I see not whence any weather should arise The Papists are contained with fear enough, and hope too much The French is thought to turn his practice upon procuring some disturbance in Scotland, where crowns may do wonders But this day is so welcome to the nation, and the time so short, as I do not fear the effect My lord of Southampton expecteth release by the next dispatch, and is already much visited and much well-wished There is continual posting by men of good quality towards the King, the rather, I think, because this spring time is but a kind of sport It is hoped that as the State here hath performed the part of good attorneys to deliver the King quiet possession of his kingdom, so the King will redeliver them quiet possession of their places, rather filling places void, than removing men placed So, etc

Of Bacon's personal relations with the Earl of Southampton we know little or nothing. The intimate connexion of both with the

Earl of Essex must, no doubt, have brought them together, but no
letters had passed between them that I know of, nor has any record
been preserved of any other communication In drawing up the
" Declaration of Treasons," Bacon had mentioned his name as slightly
as it was possible to do without misrepresenting the case in one of
its most material features; and there is some reason to believe that
he had used his private influence with the Queen after the trial, as
Cecil and Nottingham had certainly done,[1] to mitigate her displeasure
Yet considering the circumstances under which they had last seen
each other, it was too much to expect that Southampton (who did
not know what had passed since) was prepared to regard him as a
friend, and there were two ways in which Bacon might easily commit an error Others were visiting him with congratulations upon
his approaching liberation It was natural that he should do the
same, for there can be no doubt that he was really glad of it; and
if Southampton was disposed to take a true view of the case and to
be friends, it would seem churlish and unfriendly to stand aloof
But if, on the contrary, he saw the case with the eyes of his former
associates, and regarded Bacon as the ungrateful and ungenerous
enemy of his friend and himself, then it would seem indelicate and
unfeeling to intrude on him He thought it best therefore to begin
with a letter, excusing his *non*-attendance and explaining the reasons
of it The letter which he wrote is preserved in his own collection
and runs thus —

A LETTER TO THE EARL OF SOUTHAMPTON, UPON THE KING'S
COMING IN [2]

It may please your Lordship,

I would have been very glad to have presented my humble
service to your Lordship by my attendance, if I could have foreseen that it should not have been unpleasing unto you And
therefore, because I would commit no error, I choose to write;
assuring your Lordship (how credible soever it may seem to
you at first) yet it is as true as a thing that God knoweth,
that this great change hath wrought in me no other change

[1] " Was it anybody else," wrote the Earl of Northumberland to James, in the
secret correspondence, speaking of Cecil, " that saved Southampton ?" Correspondence, etc, Camd Soc p 68 " Those that would deal for him," writes
Cecil to Sir G Carew, " (of which number I protest to God I am one as far as I
dare) are much disadvantaged of arguments to save him "
" For the Earl of Southampton," writes Nottingham to Montjoy, " though he
be condemned, yet I hope well for his life for Mr Secretary and myself use all
our wits and power for it "
[2] Add MSS 5503, fo 23, b

towards your Lordship than this, that I may safely be now that which I was truly before   And so craving no other pardon than for troubling you with this letter, I do not now begin, but continue to be

Your Lordship's humble and much devoted

Southampton was released from the Tower on the 10th of April which determines within a few days the date of the last letter   Of the reception which it met with, I find no account anywhere

Meanwhile the news which Bacon received from his friends in the Scotch Court appears to have been favourable   sufficiently so, at least, to encourage him to seek a personal interview with the King   I cannot find the exact date, but it will be seen from the next letter that, before the King arrived in London, he had gone to meet him, carrying a despatch from the Earl of Northumberland, and that he had been admitted to his presence   The copy of this letter in the British Museum MS is in the same hand as the rest of the volume, but is distinguished from the others by having a few corrections and interlineations in another hand, which I believe to be Bacon's own, though I cannot speak with perfect confidence   His handwriting varied very much—according, I suppose, to pens, attitudes, moods, and times—and a few words inserted here and there are often difficult to identify   But it is certainly not the hand of the transcriber, the alterations are of a kind which it is not likely that anybody else would have made (no alteration being apparently required by the sense or grammar), and it is likely enough, considering his subsequent relations with James, that he may have looked back some time in his later life with great curiosity and interest to this fresh record of his first impressions of him, and made the corrections either from memory or taste, or from a better copy of the original which may have accidentally turned up   They are not at all material in substance, but are just such changes as he would naturally have made in writing a fair copy from a first draught   The text represents the letter as corrected   the notes as it stood in the original transcript

A LETTER TO THE EARL OF NORTHUMBERLAND AFTER HE HAD BEEN WITH THE KING [1]

It may please your good Lordship,

I would not have lost this journey, and yet I have not that for which I went.[2]   For I have had no private conference to

---

[1] Add MSS 5503, fo 24   [2] that I went for

any purpose[1] with the King; and[2] no more hath almost any
other English.   For the speech his Majesty admitteth with
some noblemen is rather matter of grace than of[3] business.
With the Attorney he spake, being[4] urged by the Treasurer of
Scotland, but yet no more[5] than needs must.   After I had received his Majesty's first welcome, I[6] was promised private
access, but[7] yet, not knowing what matter of service your Lordship's letter might carry[8] (for I saw it not) and well knowing
that primeness in advertisement is much, I chose rather to deliver it to Sir Thomas Erskins, than to cool it in my hands,
upon expectation of access   Your Lordship shall find a prince
the farthest from the appearance of vain-glory[9] that may be, and
rather like a prince of the ancient form than of the latter time
His speech is swift and cursory, and in the full dialect of his
country, and in point[10] of business, short; in point[11] of discourse
large.   He affecteth popularity by gracing such as he hath heard
to be popular, and not by any fashions of his own.   He is
thought somewhat general in his favours, and his virtue of access
is rather because he is much abroad and in press, than that he
giveth easy audience about serious things.[12]   He hasteneth to a
mixture of both kingdoms and nations, faster perhaps than policy
will conveniently[13] bear   I told your Lordship once before, that
(methought) his Majesty rather asked counsel of the time past
than of the time to come   But it is early yet to ground any
settled opinion   For the particularities I refer to conference,
having in these generals gone further in so tender an argument
than I would have done, were not both the reader and the bearer
assured[14]

[1] to purpose   [2] and, om   [3] matter of   [4] being, om
[5] but no more   [6] and   [7] but, om   [8] carried   [9] from vain glory
[10] speech   [11] speech   [12] about serious things, om
[13] well   [14] were not the bearer hereof so assured   So I continue.

CHAPTER III.

A D 1603. ÆTAT 43

1

JAMES's arrival in England brought no immediate prospect of improvement in Bacon's fortunes Nor was it likely that it should "Every new King," James thought, "ought at least to let a year and a day pass before he made any innovation,"[1] and he naturally left the administration of affairs in the hands in which he found it He made two or three new councillors, gave the Mastership of the Rolls, which was still vacant, to Edward Bruce, Abbot of Kinloss, removed Sir Walter Ralegh (probably not without what seemed the best advice) from the Captaincy of the Guard, putting in his place Sir Thomas Erskine (his own Captain of the Guard), but giving him at the same time a considerable pecuniary compensation,[2] placed two or three of his Scotch friends immediately about his person, but made no more changes of importance

Bacon was for the present to "continue to be of the Learned Counsel in such manner as before he was to the Queen"[3] But though this seemed like leaving his position unchanged, the practical effect was to give him a prospect of more leisure For his place among the Learned Counsel being an irregular one without any ordinary duties belonging to it as of course, his employment depended upon the pleasure of those who had the laying out of the business In this the Queen herself had been used to take a part, and by her direction he had in this irregular way been continually employed for many years. It would not be so now James, to whom the business and the persons were alike new, would naturally leave such arrangements, at least for a while, to Coke, who was not at all likely to want Bacon's help, nor is there any reason to think that Cecil, who kept the lead in council, and soon left the Earl of

[1] Sully   [2] Gardiner, i 61
[3] Warrant to the Lord Keeper, 21 April, 1603 —Egerton Papers (Camd Soc), p 368

Northumberland in the shadow, would go much out of his way to
put him forward.   What he had to do therefore was merely to hold
himself in readiness in case he were wanted, to recommend himself
to the King by such services or advices as he could offer without
impropriety, to make the most of the interval of leisure for the
great purpose to which all his leisure had long been dedicated, and
before all, if not above all, to clear off all remains of debt and bring
his living within his income

2.

The last-mentioned object was first in importance, and was (not
perhaps unfortunately) first forced upon him by an accident of which
the general character may be gathered from the next letter, though
none of the particulars are otherwise known

We have seen that he had been occupied since his brother's death
in endeavouring to settle some of his principal debts   It seems
however that he had not proceeded fast enough   For in the summer
of 1603 he had to apply to Cecil for help in some scrape, similar
apparently to that of 1598, when he was arrested on his way from
the Tower by Sympson, the goldsmith [1]   Something had been done
to him which he conceived to be an invasion of the privilege of
his office, and therefore an affront to the King's service, and it
had relation to some money transaction   And this is all we know
about it   The letter itself, however, which reveals the fact (and
which comes from the Hatfield collection, where it was found by
Murdin, who sent a copy to Birch) is unusually interesting, as
showing how his private affairs stood at the time, and what he was
now doing to set them straight and also as throwing further light
on his relations with Cecil, who, on this occasion at least, was giving
something more substantial than words,—preferring possibly a way
of obliging him which deserved his gratitude without risking his
rivalry

To Robert, Lord Cecil [2]

It may please your good Lordship,

They say late thanks are ever best.   But the reason was,
I thought to have seen your Lordship ere this.   Howsoever I
shall never forget this your last favour amongst others; and it
grieveth me not a little, that I find myself of no use to such an
honourable and kind friend.

For that matter, I think I shall desire your assistance for the

---

[1] Vol II p 106   [2] Letters, Speeches, etc, p 23

punishment of the contempt, not that I would use the privilege
in future time, but because I would not have the dignity of the
King's service prejudiced in my instance   But herein I will be
ruled by your Lordship.

It is fit likewise, though much against my mind, that I let
your Lordship know that I shall not be able to pay the money
within the time by your Lordship undertaken, which was a fortnight   Nay money I find so hard to come by at this time, as
I thought to have become an humble suitor to your Honour to
have sustained me with your credit for the present from urgent
debts, with taking up 300*l* till I can put away some land.   But
I am so forward with some sales, as this request I hope I may
forbear

For my estate (because your Honour hath care of it), it is
thus   I shall be able with selling the skirts of my living in
Hertfordshire to preserve the body; and to leave myself, being
clearly out of debt, and having some money in my pocket, 300*l*
land *per annum*, with a fair house, and the ground well timbered.
This is now my labour

For my purpose or course, I desire to meddle as little as I can
in the King's causes, his Majesty now abounding in counsel,
and to follow my private thrift and practice, and to marry with
some convenient advancement   For as for any ambition, I do
assure your Honour mine is quenched   In the Queen's, my
excellent Mistress's, time the *quorum* was small   her service was
a kind of freehold, and it was a more solemn time.   All those
points agreed with my nature and judgment.   My ambition
now I shall only put upon my pen, whereby I shall be able to
maintain memory and merit of the times succeeding.

Lastly, for this divulged and almost prostituted title of knighthood, I could without charge, by your Honour's mean, be content to have it, both because of this late disgrace, and because
I have three new knights in my mess in Gray's-Inn commons,
and because I have found out an alderman's daughter, an handsome maiden, to my liking   So as if your Honour will find the
time, I will come to the court from Gorhambury upon any
warning

How my sales go forward, your Lordship shall in a few days
hear.   Mean while, if you will not be pleased to take further
day with this lewd fellow, I hope your Lordship will not suffer

him to take any part of the penalty, but principal, interest, and costs.

So I remain your Lordship's most bounden,

Fr. Bacon.

3 July, 1603

Cecil's answer to this letter has not been preserved But it may be inferred from Bacon's reply (which comes from the same collection) that it was not only friendly as regarded the particular case, but contained also some general intimation that his professional services would be wanted

To the Same [1]

It may please your good Lordship,

In answer of your last letter, your money shall be ready before your day, principal, interest, and costs of suit So the sheriff promised, when I released errors, and a Jew takes no more The rest cannot be forgotten; for I cannot forget your Lordship's *dum memor ipse mei*. and if there have been *aliquid nimis*, it shall be amended. And, to be plain with your Lordship, that will quicken me now, which slackened me before. Then I thought you might have had more use of me, than now I suppose you are like to have. Not but I think the impediment will be rather in my mind than in the matter or times. But to do you service, I will come out of my religion at any time

For my knighthood, I wish the manner might be such as might grace me, since the matter will not, I mean, that I might not be merely gregarious in a troop. The coronation is at hand. It may please your Lordship to let me hear from you speedily. So I continue

Your Lordship's ever much bounden,

Fr. Bacon.

From Gorhambury, this 16th of July, 1603

It is probably to this time that a memorandum belongs, which I found in the State Paper Office, entitled ' a Note of my debts " It has no signature, or address, or date; but is written and docketed in Bacon's hand and may very well have been addressed to Cecil on the occasion which led to this correspondence Before the 16th of May, when he was created Baron Cecil of Essenden, ' Your Ho-

Letters, Speeches, etc, p 25

nour' is the title which Bacon would naturally have given him, and which indeed (as we see by the last letters) he still continued to use occasionally, and it is clear from the foregoing letters that he had been beholden to him for procuring a loan of money

A Note of my Debts [1]

My own proper debts.

That my L. Treasurer hath undertaken	2000*l*
That I was beholden to your Honour for procuring . .	500*l*
That Twicknam is mortgaged for	1200*l*
Sum tot . .	3700*l*

For my brother.

To Allen Mercer	500*l*
To Woolmer	500*l*
Other debts to the value of	300*l*.
Sum. tot .	1300

For the rest, Bacon obtained his title, but not in a manner to distinguish him   He was knighted at Whitehall, on the 23rd of July,' two days before the Coronation, but had to share the honour with 300 others

3

After this I find no more letters for a good while, nor indeed (until the meeting of Parliament on the 29th of March, 1603-4) any further news of his proceedings   I imagine, however that the intervening months were among the busiest and most exciting that he ever passed   For this is the time when I suppose him to have conceived the design of throwing his thoughts on philosophy and intellectual progress into a popular form, and inviting the co-operation of mankind

His old idea of finding a better method of studying the laws of Nature, having no doubt undergone in the endeavour to realise it many modifications, had at last taken the shape of a treatise in two parts   The first part was to be called *Experientia Literata*, and was to contain an exposition of the art of experimenting, that is. of proceeding in scientific order from one experiment to another, making the answer to one question suggest the question to be asked next The second part was to be called *Interpretatio Naturæ*, and was to explain the method of arriving by degrees at *axioms*, or general prin-

ciples in nature, thence by the light of those axioms proceeding to
new experiments, and so finally to the discovery of all the secrets of
nature's operation,—which would include the command over her
forces   This great speculation he had now digested in his head into
these two parts, and " proposed hereafter to propound "[1]   And being
a man whose mind found relief in utterance, though it were only to
a piece of paper in his cabinet, he drew up (either at, or about, or
at any rate with reference to this time) a short prefatory address,
which, had the work itself been then completed according to the design, would I suppose have stood as the introduction

As an exposition of the design it was superseded by completer
prefaces of later date, and was therefore not included among the
philosophical works selected for translation   But as bearing upon
the history of his own career it has a peculiar value, revealing as it
does an authentic glimpse of that large portion of his life, which
though to him as real as the rest and far more profoundly interesting, scarcely shows itself among these records of his career as a man of
business, and is in danger of being forgotten   And I do not know
how I can better help my readers to conceive the thing and to give
it its due prominence among his purposes and performances, than by
inserting a translation of it in this place   Of the practicability of
the enterprise and the reasonableness of the expectation, I say nothing   that question has been discussed in its proper place, and need
not concern us here   What we have to understand and remember is
the *nature* of the enterprise, and the fact that he *believed* it practicable   He believed that he had by accident stumbled upon a Thought,
which duly followed out would in the course of generations make
man the master of all natural forces.   The ' Interpretation of Nature" was, according to his speculation, the " Kingdom of *Man* "[2]
To plant this thought in men's minds under such conditions that it
should have the best chance of growing and bearing its proper fruit
in due season, was the great aspiration of his life, and though
diverted, interrupted, and baffled by a hundred impediments, internal and external,—by infirmities of body and of mind, by his own
business and other people's, by clients, creditors, and sheriff's officers, by the impracticability (say the wise) of the problem itself,
owing to a fundamental misconception of the case, by an imperfec-
tion (as I think) in his own intellectual organisation, which placed
him at a disadvantage in dealing with many parts of it,—he never

[1] Adv of Learn   Works, Vol III p 389   De Augmentis Scientiarum   lib v
c 2   Vol I pp 622-633
[2] Indicia vera *de Interpretatione Naturæ, sive de Regno Hominis*   Title of the
Novum Organum

doubted that the thing might be done if men would but think so, and
that it was his mission to make them think so and point out the way
And though many and many a day must have closed without shewing
any sensible progress in the work, I suppose not a single day went
down in which he did not remember with a sigh, or a resolution, or
a prayer, that the work was still undone   On one of these days, his
imagination, wandering far into the future, showed him in vision the
first instalment ready for publication, and set him upon thinking
how he should announce it to the world   The result of this meditation he fortunately confided to a sheet of paper, which being found
long after in his cabinet, revealed the secret which it had kept   The
original, written in stately Latin, may be seen in the third volume
of the Philosophical Works, p 518, accompanied with a long preface
of my own, to which I refer those who care to know what else I had
to say about it   For our present purpose, the following translation,
though in spirit and effect a poor copy, may serve sufficiently well

OF THE INTERPRETATION OF NATURE

Proem

Believing that I was born for the service of mankind, and regarding the care of the commonwealth as a kind of common
property which like the air and the water belongs to everybody,
I set myself to consider in what way mankind might be best
served, and what service I was myself best fitted by nature to
perform

Now among all the benefits that could be conferred upon
mankind, I found none so great as the discovery of new arts, endowments, and commodities for the bettering of man's life.   For
I saw that among the rude people in the primitive times the authors of rude inventions and discoveries were consecrated and
numbered among the Gods   And it was plain that the good
effects wrought by founders of cities, law-givers, fathers of the
people, extirpers of tyrants, and heroes of that class, extend but
over narrow spaces and last but for short times, whereas the
work of the Inventor, though a thing of less pomp and shew, is
felt everywhere and lasts for ever.   But above all, if a man could
succeed, not in striking out some particular invention, however
useful, but in kindling a light in nature—a light which should
in its very rising touch and illuminate all the border-regions that
confine upon the circle of our present knowledge, and so spread-
ing further and further should presently disclose and bring into

sight all that is most hidden and secret in the world,—that man
(I thought) would be the benefactor indeed of the human race,—
the propagator of man's empire over the universe, the champion
of liberty, the conqueror and subduer of necessities.

For myself, I found that I was fitted for nothing so well as
for the study of Truth, as having a mind nimble and versatile
enough to catch the resemblances of things (which is the chief
point), and at the same time steady enough to fix and distinguish
their subtler differences; as being gifted by nature with desire
to seek, patience to doubt, fondness to meditate, slowness to
assert, readiness to reconsider, carefulness to dispose and set in
order, and as being a man that neither affects what is new nor
admires what is old, and that hates every kind of imposture. So
I thought my nature had a kind of familiarity and relationship
with Truth

Nevertheless, because my birth and education had seasoned
me in business of state; and because opinions (so young as I
was) would sometimes stagger me, and because I thought that a
man's own country has some special claims upon him more than
the rest of the world; and because I hoped that, if I rose to any
place of honour in the state, I should have a larger command of
industry and ability to help me in my work;—for these reasons
I both applied myself to acquire the arts of civil life, and commended my service, so far as in modesty and honesty I might,
to the favour of such friends as had any influence In which
also I had another motive for I felt that those things I have
spoken of—be they great or small—reach no further than the
condition and culture of this mortal life, and I was not without
hope (the condition of Religion being at that time not very prosperous) that if I came to hold office in the state, I might get
something done too for the good of men's souls

When I found however that my zeal was mistaken for ambition, and my life had already reached the turning-point, and my
breaking health reminded me how ill I could afford to be so slow,
and I reflected moreover that in leaving undone the good that I
could do by myself alone, and applying myself to that which
could not be done without the help and consent of others, I was
by no means discharging the duty that lay upon me,—I put all
those thoughts aside, and (in pursuance of my old determination)
betook myself wholly to this work. Nor am I discouraged from

it because I see signs in the times of the decline and overthrow
of that knowledge and erudition which is now in use.   Not that
I apprehend any more barbarian invasions (unless possibly the
Spanish empire should recover its strength, and having crushed
other nations by arms should itself sink under its own weight)
but the civil wars which may be expected, I think, (judging
from certain fashions which have come in of late) to spread
through many countries,—together with the malignity of sects,
and those compendious artifices and devices which have crept
into the place of solid erudition—seem to portend for literature
and the sciences a tempest not less fatal, and one against which
the Printing-office will be no effectual security   And no doubt
but that fair-weather learning which is nursed by leisure, blos
soms under reward and praise, which cannot withstand the shock
of opinion, and is liable to be abused by tricks and quackery, will
sink under such impediments as these   Far otherwise is it with
that knowledge, whose dignity is maintained by works of utility
and power   For the injuries therefore which should proceed from
the times, I am not afraid of them, and for the injuries which
proceed from men I am not concerned.   For if any one charge
me with seeking to be wise overmuch, I answer simply that mo
desty and civil respect are fit for civil matters; in contempla
tions nothing is to be respected but Truth   If any one call on
me for *works*, and that presently, I tell him frankly, without
any imposture at all, that for me—a man not old, of weak
health, my hands full of civil business, entering without guide or
light upon an argument of all others the most obscure,—I hold
it enough to have constructed the machine, though I may not
succeed in setting it on work   Nay with the same candour I
profess and declare, that the Interpretation of Nature, rightly
conducted, ought in the first steps of the ascent, until a certain
stage of Generals be reached, to be kept clear of all application
to Works   And this has in fact been the error of all those who
have heretofore ventured themselves at all upon the waves of
experience—that being either too weak of purpose or too eager
for display, they have all at the outset sought prematurely for
works, as proofs and pledges of their progress and upon that
rock have been wrecked and cast away.   If again any one ask
me, not indeed for actual works, yet for definite promises and
forecasts of the works that are to be, I would have him know

that the knowledge which we now possess will not teach a man even what to *wish*. Lastly—though this is a matter of less moment—if any of our politicians, who use to make their calculations and conjectures according to persons and precedents, must needs interpose his judgment in a thing of this nature,—I would but remind him how (according to the ancient fable) the lame man keeping the course won the race of the swift man who left it and that there is no thought to be taken about precedents, for the thing is without precedent

Now for my plan of publication—those parts of the work which have it for their object to find out and bring into correspondence such minds as are prepared and disposed for the argument, and to purge the floors of men's understandings, I wish to be published to the world and circulate from mouth to mouth the rest I would have passed from hand to hand, with selection and judgment. Not but I know that it is an old trick of impostors to keep a few of their follies back from the public which are indeed no better than those they put forward but in this case it is no imposture at all, but a sober foresight, which tells me that the formula itself of interpretation, and the discoveries made by the same, will thrive better if committed to the charge of some fit and selected minds, and kept private   This however is other people's concern   For myself, my heart is not set upon any of those things which depend upon external accidents   I am not hunting for fame   I have no desire to found a sect, after the fashion of heresiarchs, and to look for any private gain from such an undertaking as this, I count both ridiculous and base   Enough for me the consciousness of well-deserving, and those real and effectual results with which Fortune itself cannot interfere

Such then was the project with which Bacon was all this time labouring in secret, such, and no less, the issues which he believed to be involved in it. But though his faith in the principle never failed, he knew that it could not be fairly tried without the cooperation of many men and of more than one generation, and when he came to sound men's opinions in the matter, he discovered that he had a preliminary difficulty to encounter in finding any who would listen to him [1]

---

[1] " Et quos socios habes ?   Ego certe (inquam) profecto nullos, quin nec quenquam habeo quocum familiariter de hujusmodi rebus colloqui possim, ut me saltem explicem et exacuam "—Philosophical Works, Vol III p 559

Now if he could get the King to take an interest in it, a great part of this difficulty would be removed; and to bring this about, the best chance would be to produce some practical and notable proof of proficiency in matters of which the King was already qualified to judge. For experimental philosophy James had not as yet shown any taste, and having been trained in the ancient learning, he was not likely to be attracted by a proposal to set aside all received doctrines and begin afresh from the beginning; but a general survey and criticism of the existing stock of knowledge was a work which few men then living were better qualified to appreciate, and in which he was almost sure to take a lively interest; and such a survey being the natural and legitimate foundation of any attempt at a large and general reform, it seems to have occurred to Bacon that this was the thing to begin with, and this the very time for it. Here was a King, still in the prime of life, devoted to peace, sympathizing largely with the interests of mankind, eminent even among learned men in a learned age for proficiency in all kinds of learning, coming out of straits and troubles into a great fortune, his imagination raised, his habits unfixed, his direction not yet taken: why should he not be excited to seek his greatness in a work like this? Accordingly, when Bacon told Cecil, on the 3rd of July, 1603, that he should put his ambition only upon his pen, it seems to me probable that he had newly conceived the design of writing his work on the 'Proficience and Advancement of Learning.' I say newly, for it was certainly not the same work on which he had been engaged before, nor any part of it: nor was it till some years after that he determined to include it in the general design.[1] If so, the first book,—which may be described as a kind of inaugural lecture on the dignity and merit of learning as a work for the kings and potentates of the earth,—must apparently have been written during this year;[2] and we need seek no further for an account of the way in which his time during the remainder of it was chiefly spent.

4.

It was not, however, his only occupation. Though he had little or nothing to do this year as a member of the King's Learned Counsel, there were one or two subjects of such pressing importance in the political department, that he made bold to offer his opinion upon them.

[1] See my preface to the *De Augmentis Scientiarum.* Philos Works, Vol I p 416
[2] See my preface to the 'Advancement of Learning.' Philos Works, Vol III p 255

The first that had to be dealt with was the union of England and Scotland   We have seen that he had come away from his first inter-view with the King with an impression that he was "hastening to a mixture of both kingdoms and nations, faster perhaps than policy would conveniently bear"   Now as much haste as was compatible with good speed, no man could wish for more than Bacon himself for no man saw sooner or more clearly that England, well united with Scotland, had all natural requirements for becoming the greatest monarchy in the world   But he knew that things would not unite by being merely put together, and that perfect mixture required many conditions, of which *time* was one of the most indispensable And I suppose it was in the hope, not merely of drawing a little at-tention to his own pretensions as a scholar and a thinker (though that was something), but also of tempering the King's impatience and reconciling him to the cautious pace at which it would be neces-sary to go, that he took leave to present him with a short philo-sophical treatise concerning the conditions under which perfect union takes place in nature—an essay still interesting, both as a specimen of the *Philosophia Prima*, applied to a particular business in the details and practical management of which he was soon to be deeply engaged, and as showing that it was not as a member of the Learned Counsel, but as a scholar, a student, and a man of contemplation, that he chose to make his first approaches —a fact agreeing very well with my supposition that he regarded this as (for the present at least) his proper vocation and most promising career   And yet his aim is not the less practical, and bearing on the immediate business, for the conclusion is, that Nature and Time must be left to do the work, and that artificial forcing will only spoil the operation. the very warning which the King stood most in need of.

This little tract is said to have been printed in 1603, in 12mo,[1] but I never met with a copy   There is, however, a good manuscript of it in the Harleian Collection, in the hand (if I am not mistaken) of the transcriber of the 'Valerius Terminus,' and if so, contem-porary and authentic,[2] and it is printed in the Resuscitatio   The text here given is formed upon a collation of these two

Whence Bacon derived his idea of the nature of the Persian Magic, is a question with which we need not trouble ourselves here For the present occasion it is enough to know that it was formerly the subject of many speculations, inferences perhaps from a remark in Plato, that the princes of Persia were instructed in politics and in magic by the same persons,—and that the method of analogy in

---

[1] Birch's edition of Bacon's Works, vol iii p 257.
[2] See Philosophical Works, Vol III p. 206

which Bacon supposed it to consist was believed by him, not only at this time but ever after, to be a sound one [1]

A Brief Discourse touching the Happy Union of the Kingdoms of England and Scotland.

Dedicated in private to His Majesty [2]

I do not find it strange (excellent King) that when Heraclitus, he that was surnamed the obscure, had set forth a certain book which is not now extant, many men took it for a discourse of nature, and many others took it for a treatise of policy and matter of estate. For there is a great affinity and consent between the rules of nature, and the true rules of policy: the one being nothing else but an order in the government of the world, and the other an order in the government of an estate. And therefore the education and erudition of the kings of Persia was in a science which was termed by a name then of great reverence, but now degenerate and taken in ill part; for the Persian magic, which was the secret literature of their kings, was an observation of the contemplations of nature and an application thereof to [3] a sense politic; taking the fundamental laws of nature, with the branches and passages of them, as an original and first model, whence to take and describe a copy and imitation for government.

After this manner the aforesaid instructors set before their kings the examples of the celestial bodies, the sun, the moon, and the rest, which have great glory and veneration, but no rest or intermission, being in a perpetual office of motion, for the cherishing, in turn and in course, of inferior bodies: expressing likewise the true manner of the motions of government, which though they ought to be swift and rapid in respect of dispatch and the occasions, yet are they to be constant and regular, without wavering or confusion.

So did they represent unto them how the heavens do not enrich themselves by the earth and the seas, nor keep no dead stock or untouched treasures of that they draw to them from below, but whatsoever moisture they do levy and take from

---

[1] See 'Advancement of Learning,' Philos Works, Vol III p 348, and De Aug Scient Vol I p 512

[2] Harl MSS 532, fo 61

[3] *an application of the contemplations and observations of nature unto*   R

both elements in vapours, they do spend and turn back again in showers, only holding and storing them up for a time, to the end to issue and distribute them in season

But chiefly they did express and expound unto them the fundamental law of nature, whereby all things do subsist and are preserved, which is, That every thing in nature, although it have his private and particular affection and appetite, and doth follow and pursue the same in small moments, and when it is delivered and free from more general and common respects, yet nevertheless when there is question or case for sustaining of the more general, they forsake their own particularities and proprieties, and attend and conspire to uphold the public

So we see the iron in small quantity will ascend and approach to the loadstone upon a particular sympathy · but if it be any quantity of moment, it leaveth his appetite of amity with the loadstone, and like a good patriot falleth to the earth, which is the place and region of massy bodies

So again the water and other like bodies do fall towards the centre of the earth, which is (as was said) their region or country · and yet we see nothing more usual in all water-works and engines, than that the water (rather than to suffer any distraction or disunion in nature) will ascend, forsaking the love to his own region or country, and applying itself to the body next adjoining

But it were too long a digression to proceed to more examples of this kind   Your Majesty yourself did fall upon a passage of this nature in your gracious speech of thanks unto your counsel, when acknowledging princely their vigilancies[1] and well-deservings, it pleased you to note, that it was a success and event above the course of nature, to have so great change with so great a quiet   forasmuch as sudden and great mutations, as well in state as in nature, are rarely without violence and perturbation. So as still I conclude there is (as was said) a congruity between the principles of Nature and Policy. And lest that instance may seem to oppone to this assertion, I may even in that particular, with your Majesty's favour, offer unto you a type or pattern in nature, much resembling this event in your estate, namely earthquakes, which many of them bring ever much terror and wonder, but no actual hurt, the earth trembling for a moment, and suddenly stablishing in perfect quiet as it was before.

[1] *vigilancie* MS

This knowledge then, of making the government of the world a mirror for the government of a state, being a wisdom almost lost (whereof the reason I take to be because of the difficulty for one man to embrace both philosophies) I have thought good to make some proof (as far as my weakness and the straits of time will suffer) to revive in the handling of one particular, wherewith now I most humbly present your Majesty. For truly (as hath been said) it is a form of discourse anciently used towards kings; and to what king should it be more proper than to a king that is studious to conjoin contemplative virtue and active virtue together?

Your Majesty is the first king that had the honour to be *lapis angularis*, to unite these two mighty and warlike nations of England and Scotland under one sovereignty and monarchy. It doth not appear by the records and monuments[1] of any true history, nor scarcely by the fiction and pleasure of any fabulous narration or tradition of any antiquity, that ever[2] this island of Great Britain was united under one king before this day. And yet there be no mountains nor races of hills, there be no seas nor great rivers, there is no diversity of tongue or language, that hath invited or provoked this ancient separation or divorce. The lot of Spain was to have the several kingdoms of the continent (Portugal only except) to be united, in an age not long past, and now in our age that of Portugal also, which was the last that held out, to be incorporate with the rest. The lot of France hath been much about the same time likewise to have re-annexed to that crown the several duchies and portions which were in former times dismembered. The lot of this island is the last, reserved for your Majesty's happy times by the special providence and favour of God, who hath brought your Majesty to this happy conjunction with great consent of hearts, and in the strength of your years, and in the maturity of your experience. It resteth therefore but that (as I promised) I set before your Majesty's princely consideration the grounds of nature touching the union and commixture of bodies, and the correspondency which they have with the grounds of policy in the conjunction of states and kingdoms.

First, therefore, that position *Vis unita fortior*, being one of the common notions of the mind, needeth not much to be in-

[1] *memories* R   [2] *tradition, that ever, of any antiquity* R

duced or illustrated. We see the sun (when he entereth and while he continues under the sign of Leo) causeth more vehement heats than when he is in Cancer, what time his beams are nevertheless more perpendicular The reason whereof, in great part, hath been truly ascribed to the conjunction and corradiation in that place of heaven of the sun with the four stars of the first magnitude, Sirius, Canicula, Cor Leonis, and Cauda Leonis.

So the moon likewise, by ancient tradition, while she is in the same sign of Leo, is said to be at the heart, or to respect the heart which is not for any affinity which that place of heaven can have with that part of man's body, but only because the moon is then (by reason of the conjunction and nearness with the stars aforenamed) in greatest strength of influence, and so worketh upon that part in inferior bodies which is most vital and principal.

So we see waters and liquors in small quantity do easily putrefy and corrupt, but in large quantity subsist long, by reason of the strength they receive by union

So in earthquakes, the more general do little hurt, by reason of the united weight which they offer to subvert; but narrow and particular earthquakes have many times overturned whole towns and cities.

So then this point touching the force of union is evident. And therefore it is more fit to speak of the manner of union. Wherein again it will not be pertinent to handle one kind of union, which is union by victory; when one body doth merely subdue another, and converteth the same into his own nature, extinguishing and expulsing what part soever of it it cannot overcome. As when the fire converteth the wood into fire, purging away the smoke and the ashes as unapt matter to inflame· or when the body of a living creature doth convert and assimilate food and nourishment, purging and expelling whatsoever it cannot convert. For these representations do answer in matter of policy to union of countries by conquest, where the conquering state doth extinguish, extirpate, and expulse any part of the state conquered, which it findeth so contrary as it cannot alter and convert it And therefore, leaving violent unions, we will consider only of natural unions.

The difference is excellent which the best observers in nature do take between *compositio* and *mistio,* putting together and mingling: the one being but a conjunction of bodies in place, the other in quality and consent the one the mother of sedition and alteration, the other of peace and continuance· the one rather a confusion than an union, the other properly an union Therefore we see those bodies which they call *imperfecte mista* last not, but are speedily dissolved. For take for example snow or froth, which are compositions of air and water, and in them you may behold how easily they sever and dissolve, the water closing together and excluding the air

So those three bodies which the alchemists do so much celebrate as the three principles of things, that is to say, Earth, Water, and Oil, (which it pleaseth them to term Salt, Mercury, and Sulphur), we see if they be united only by composition or putting together, how weakly and rudely they do incorporate for water and earth maketh but an imperfect slime if[1] they be forced together by agitation, yet upon a little settling the earth resides in the bottom So water and oil, though by agitation it be brought into an ointment, yet after a little settling the oil will float on the top. So as such unperfect minglings continue no longer than they are forced, and still in the end the worthiest gets above.

But otherwise it is of *Perfect Mixture* For we see those three bodies, of Earth, Water, and Oil, when they are joined in a vegetable or a mineral, they are so united, as without great subtlety of art and force of extraction they cannot be separated and reduced into the same simple bodies again So as the difference between *compositio* and *mistio* clearly set down is this, that *compositio* is the joining or putting together of bodies without a new form and *mistio* is the joining or putting together of bodies under a new form For the new form is *commune vinculum,* and without that the old forms will be at strife and discord

Now to reflect this light of Nature upon Matter of Estate, there hath been put in practice in government these two several kinds of policy in uniting and conjoining states and kingdoms; the one to retain the ancient forms still severed, and only conjoined in sovereignty, the other to superinduce a new form agreeable and convenient to the entire estate The former of

[1] *and if* R

these hath been more usual, and is more easy ; but the latter is more happy   For if a man do attentively revolve histories of all nations, and judge truly thereupon, he will make this conclusion, that there were never any states that were good *commixtures* but the Roman [1]   Which because it was the best state of the world, and is the best example in this point, we will chiefly insist thereupon.

In the antiquities of Rome, Virgil brings in Jupiter by way of oracle in[2] prediction speaking of the mixture[3] of the Trojans and the Italians :—

> " Sermonem Ausonii patrium moresque tenebunt,
>   Utque est nomen erit   commisti corpore tantum
>   Subsident Teucri, morem ritusque sacrorum
>   Adjiciam, faciamque omnes uno ore Latinos
>   Hinc genus, Ausonio mistum quod sanguine surget,
>   Supra homines, supra ire Deos pietate videbis "

Wherein Jupiter maketh a kind of partition or distribution · that Italy should give the language and the laws, Troy should give a mixture of men, and some religious rites, and both people should meet in one name of Latins.

Soon after the foundation of the city of Rome, the people of the Romans and the Sabines mingled upon equal terms wherein the interchange went so even, that (as Livy noteth) the one nation gave the name to the place, the other to the people. For Rome continued the name, but the people were called Quirites, which was the Sabine word, derived of Cures the country of Tatius.

But that which is chiefly to be noted in the whole continuance of the Roman government, they were so liberal of their naturalizations, as in effect they made perpetual mixtures   For the manner was to grant the same not only to particular persons, but to families and lineages ; and not only so, but to whole cities and countries , so as in the end it came to that, that Rome was *communis patria*, as some of the civilians call it.

So we read that St Paul, after he had been beaten with rods, and thereupon charged the officer with the violation of the privilege of a citizen of Rome, the captain said to him, " Art thou then a Roman ? That privilege hath cost me dear " To whom St Paul replied, " But I was so born." And yet, in another place,

---

[1] *Romans*, in both copies   [2] *or* R   [3] *mixtures* MS

St Paul professeth of himself, that he was a Jew by tribe So as it is manifest that some of his ancestors were naturalized to him and to his descendents [1]

So we read that it was one of the first despites that was done to Julius Cæsar, that whereas he had obtained naturalization for a city in Gaul, one of the city was beaten with rods by the commandment of the consul Marcellus

So we read that in the emperor Claudius time, the nation of Gaul, that part which was called *Comata,* the wilder part, were suitors to be made capable of the honour of being senators and officers of Rome   His words are these, " Cum de supplendo

Tacitus, xi.
Annal

senatu agitaretur, primoresque Galliæ quæ Comata appellatur, fœdera et civitatem Romanam pridem assecuti, jus adipiscendorum in urbe honorum expeterent, multus ea super re variusque rumor, et studiis diversis apud principes[2] certabatur " And in the end after long debate it was ruled that they should be admitted.

So likewise the authority of Nicholas Machiavel seemeth not to be contemned , who enquiring the causes of the growth of the Roman empire, doth give judgment, there was not one greater than this, that the state did so easily compound and incorporate with strangers

It is true that most estates and kingdoms have taken the other course of which this effect hath followed, that the addition of further empire and territory hath been rather matter of burthen than matter of strength unto them   yea and further it hath kept alive the seeds and roots of revolts and rebellions for many ages, as we may see in a fresh and notable example of the kingdom of Arragon : which, though it were united to Castile by marriage, and not by conquest, and so descended in hereditary union by the space of more than an hundred years, yet because it was continued in a divided government, and not well incorporated and cemented with the other crown, entered into a rebellion upon point of their *fueros,* or liberties, now of very late years.

Now to speak briefly of the several parts of that form, whereby estates and kingdoms are perfectly united , they are (besides the sovereignty itself) four in number , Union in Name, Union in Language, Union in Laws, and Union in Employments

For Name, though it seem but a superficial and outward

---

naturalized , and so it was conveyed to him and their other descendants R
[2] *Principem* in both copies

matter, yet it carrieth much impression and enchantment   The
general and common name of Græcia made the Greeks always
apt to unite (though otherwise full of divisions amongst themselves) against other nations, whom they called barbarous.   The
Helvetian name is no small band to knit together their leagues
and confederacies the faster.   The common name of Spain (no
doubt) hath been a special mean of the better union and conglu-
tination of the several kingdoms of Castile, Arragon, Granada,
Navarra, Valentia, Catalonia, and the rest, comprehending also
now lately Portugal.

For Language, it is not necessary to insist upon it, because
both your Majesty's kingdoms are of one language, though of
several dialects, and the difference is so small between them, as
promiseth rather an enriching of one language than a continuance of two.

For Laws, which are the principal sinews of government, they
be of three natures; *Jura* (which I will term freedoms or abilities), *Leges*, and *Mores*

For Abilities and Freedoms, they were amongst the Romans
of four kinds, or rather degrees. *Jus Connubii, Jus Civitatis,
Jus Suffragii*, and *Jus Petitionis* or *Honorum   Jus Connubii* is a
thing in these times out of use   for marriage is open between
all diversities of nations   *Jus Civitatis* answereth to that we call
Denization or Naturalization   *Jus Suffragii* answereth to the
voice in Parliament, or voice of election of such as have voice in
Parliament. *Jus Petitionis* answereth to place in counsel and
office. And the Romans did many times sever these freedoms,
granting *Jus Connubii sine Civitate*, and *Civitatem sine Suffragio*,
and *Suffragium sine Jure Petitionis*, which was commonly with
them the last.

For Laws,[1] it is a matter of curiosity and inconvenience to
seek either to extirpate all particular customs, or to draw all
subjects to one place or resort of judicature or session. It suffi-
ceth that there be an uniformity in the principal and fundamental
laws both ecclesiastical and civil. For in this point the rule
holds which was pronounced by an ancient father, touching the
diversity of rites in the Church, for finding the vesture of the
Queen (in the psalm), which did prefigure the Church, was of
divers colours, and finding again that Christ's coat was without

[1] *For those we called Leges*   R

a seam, he concludeth well, *In veste varietas sit, scissura non sit*

For Manners, a consent in them is to be sought industriously, but not to be inforced   For nothing amongst people breeds so much pertinacy in holding their customs, as sudden and violent offer to remove them

And as for Employments, it is no more but an indifferent hand, and execution of that verse

Virg
Eneid 1°
"Tros Tyriusque mihi nullo discrimine agetur"

There remaineth only to remember out of the grounds of Nature the two conditions of perfect mixture, whereof the former is Time   for the natural philosophers say well, that *compositio* is *opus hominis*, and *mistio opus naturæ*   For it is the duty of man to make a fit application of bodies together, but the perfect fermentation and incorporation of them must be left to Time and Nature, and unnatural hasting thereof doth disturb the work, and not dispatch it   So we see, after the grift is put into the stock and bound, it must be left to Nature and Time to make that *continuum*, which was at first but *contiguum*.   And it is not any continual pressing or thrusting together that will prevent nature's season, but rather hinder it   And so in liquors, those mixtures which are at the first troubled, grow after clear and settled by the benefit of rest and time

The second condition is, that the greater draw the less.   So we see when two lights do meet, the greater doth darken and drown the less.   And when a smaller river runs into a greater, it leeseth both the name and stream

And hereof, to conclude, we have an example in the kingdoms of Judah and Israel.   The kingdom of Judah contained two tribes, the kingdom of Israel contained ten   King David reigned over Judah for certain years, and after the death of Ishbosheth, the son of Saul, obtained likewise the kingdom of Israel   This union continued in him, and likewise in his son Salomon, by the space of seventy years at least between them both.   But yet, because the seat of the kingdom was kept still in Judah, and so the less sought to draw the greater, upon the first occasion offered the kingdoms brake again, and so continued divided ever after

Thus having in all humbleness made oblation to your Majesty

of these simple fruits of my devotion and studies, I do wish,
(and I do wish it not in the nature of an impossibility, to my
thinking), that the happy union of your Majesty's two kingdoms
of England and Scotland may be in as good an hour and under
the like divine providence, as that was between the Romans and
the Sabines.

FRA BACON

5

With regard to the policy to be pursued in Ireland, which was
perhaps the next question in immediate urgency,—so impossible it
was to stand still and yet so much depended upon the step taken,—
Bacon had communicated his thoughts not long before to Cecil and
as Montjoy was now in England and a councillor, he had no pretence
for interposing further in the matter at this time

But there was another question, if not so immediately urgent, yet
of a far more vital character, which forced itself upon James's attention, and upon the answer to which hung consequences beyond all
estimate or prediction, a question turning indeed upon arguments
which lay within his own province and which he was well qualified
to handle, but involving issues which it was hardly possible for him
to appreciate   This was the dispute between the High Churchman
and the Puritans, which Elizabeth had bequeathed to him still unsettled, but yet (for a new King coming to it unembarrassed by
personal antecedents, able to understand the fact, and willing to
accept and make the best of it) in a condition apparently very favourable for settlement

Elizabeth had made up her mind at the beginning of her reign
how much innovation she would allow   Protestantism was to go so
far, and no further   Nor had she miscalculated her own position
To the last, when a wave threatened to encroach, she could rebuke
it and it would go back   But the tide was coming in nevertheless ;
and had she reigned a few years longer, and in security from foreign
enemies, she would have had to choose between making terms with
the non-conformists and suffering from the want of subsidies   How
she would have dealt with them, it is of course vain to conjecture
But I suppose her principal difficulty would have lain in her own
mind and declared resolution   She would have had to retract a
policy to which she stood publicly committed, and though I dare
say she would have known how to do it and would have got it done,
the difficulty would have been considerable. To James the thing
was comparatively easy   He was not as yet personally committed

H 2

to either side in the controversy He was not naturally disposed to
sectarianism, in matters of opinion and doctrine, on any side His
tolerance towards Popery had no superstition in it it arose not
from an inclination to agree, but from a liberal admission of the right
to differ His objection to the Puritans was rather political than
theological, and was in fact a legitimate counterpart of his objection
to Popery he took them for a party which aimed to make the
Church supreme over the King, and themselves supreme in the
Church But apart from the political tendency of their opinions,
I do not find that he had any horror of the particular opinions which
they held for he was naturally a Protestant, aware that Truth had
many aspects, and willing to have all questions referred to reason
and argument There was nothing therefore to prevent him from
taking the course which seemed most politic and prudent His
difficulty was to know what *was* the prudent course for that de
pended upon the tendencies of popular opinion and the relative
strength of parties , of which he had not yet the means of judging
personally, and his advisers would no doubt tell him very different
stories

This was a question upon which Bacon, having been an active
member of the House of Commons for nearly twenty years, had had
good opportunities of forming a judgment He had been (as we
saw) by no means satisfied with the course formerly taken by the
authorities in the matter and being well aware of the weight of it,
could not but be anxious that the chance should not be missed of
taking up the right position now, when everything lay so fair and
open for it, for as in differences between neighbours the question
whether two families shall be friends or enemies for years to come
will often depend upon the temper of the first answer, so in the
larger theatres of the world the manner of entertaining the first
motion for reform may decide whether there shall be peace or war
half a century after

The right position no doubt was to treat the reformed Church as
a living and therefore a growing body , subject to the condition of
all growth, which is change to dispose it to take in and digest into
its own system as much as possible of all that was good in all that
was new not to attempt to fix it in the shape which appeared to
the wisest men then living to be the most perfect, but to leave it
open to receive new impressions from the wisdom of other men and
other times , and therefore to admit as disputable within its pre
cincts all questions which were among well instructed and earnest
men really matter of dispute . allowing as much liberty to each as
was compatible with the liberty of all, and trusting to the natural

authority of reason in a fair field to make good the truth against all
assailants   In any subject except theology this would undoubtedly
be allowed as the only rational way of proceeding   If a commission
were appointed to frame rules for a school of natural science or profane history, no one would think of prohibiting the promulgation of
theories inconsistent with those at present accepted and approved
or if any such thing were done the result might easily be foretold
The new schools which would not the less inevitably arise would
come as enemies and antagonists of the old, and they would spend
their time in quarrelling instead of enquiring   Now when the Scriptures were once accepted (as by all varieties of Protestantism they
then were) for the supreme authority in matters of religion, the interpretation and application of them became a work of human science,
subject to like conditions   To be pursued successfully it must be
pursued freely   It is true that this was not a view which could then
be taken by any party, in the Church or out of it   They all believed
in orthodoxy, and each held it for a first duty to establish its own
creed and exclude every other—if possible for ever.   Not the less,
however, was it the wisdom of the Protestant Church to make room
for as many varieties of honest opinion as were not incompatible
with each other, and it seems probable that the manifestation even
of a *tendency* in that direction would have sufficed to draw towards
it all that was most learned, weighty, and influential in the religious
opinions of the time.   For though the change of masters, joined
with the general uncertainty as to the policy which would find favour
with the new King, had awakened all hopes and set all discontents
free to express themselves, and James was greeted at his entrance
with many petitions for reformation in the orders of the Church, it
is impossible to look through the list of particular alterations proposed without feeling that most of the points in question might
have been left open without either danger or disturbance to the
establishment.   Where authority does not interfere, general opinion
keeps order, and there can be little doubt that the great majority
of churchmen, if left to themselves, would have followed the fashion,
and so established as much uniformity in practice as was desirable

The danger was in giving it to be understood that *nothing* would
be conceded . for opposition to a government which threatens dissatisfaction to all alike is the one thing in which all varieties of
dissatisfaction can agree   On the other hand, the indication of a
willingness on the part of the Church to tolerate differences,—to
allow more liberty for clergymen to think freely and to say freely
what they thought,—would to a certain extent have satisfied them
all, and united them in a common support of the government   And

this course, which a wise statesmanship would surely have prescribed, appeared to Bacon to be prescribed by reason and religion as well "A man that is of judgment and understanding shall sometimes hear ignorant men differ, and know well within himself that those which so differ mean one thing, and yet themselves would never agree And if it come so to pass in that distance of judgment which is between man and man, shall we not think that God above, that knows the heart, doth not discern that frail men in some of their contradictions intend the same thing, and accepteth of both?"[1] To "accept of both," therefore, was the course which he would have recommended to the Church in cases where religious men, intending acceptable service, brought different gifts, and now was the time when such a course might be most happily inaugurated

It was under these circumstances that (having received some gracious acknowledgment of his discourse touching the Union of the Kingdoms) he made bold to present the King, in a paper entitled "Certain considerations touching the better pacification and edification of the Church of England," with his opinion as to the best method of reconciling the prevailing dissensions

This paper—a worthy sequel to the "Advertisement touching Church Controversies" written in 1589,—was presented to the King "at his first coming in"[2] and was not (I presume) meant to be published at that time   There exists however a printed copy with the date 1604 —the same probably which Dr Rawley mentions in his commonplace book as having been "called in"[3]   In 1641, when there was a great demand for all Bacon's political tracts it was reprinted   And it was afterwards included in the Resuscitatio But the copy which I have taken as the ground of my text is a manuscript in the Rolls House, which has the great merit of having been revised and corrected by Bacon himself   The printed copies (which are independent authorities and may possibly be later) I have collated, and the result of the collation is given in the footnotes in which A means the first printed copy,[4] B the second[5] (apparently a reprint of the first, but without any date) ; R the copy in the Resuscitatio, MS the manuscript at the Rolls

[1] Essay of Unity in Religion
[2] These words are inserted in the title of one of the manuscript copies
[3] Lambeth MSS 1031 in a list of "Lo St Alban's works printed"
[4] London printed for Henrie Tomes An 1604   I have not met with or heard of any perfect copy of this edition , and it seems probable that the printing was stopped before it was completed   for the most perfect copy I have seen (bought 17 Aug 1865, from Mr Wilson, of Great Russell Street) has sheet k printed only on pages 1, 4, 5, and 8 (as if only one side had been completed) the blank pages being supplied in MS
[5] Printed for Henry Tomes   (No place or date)

CERTAIN CONSIDERATIONS TOUCHING THE BETTER PACIFICATION AND EDIFICATION OF THE CHURCH OF ENGLAND.[1]

Dedicated to his Most Excellent Majesty

The unity of your Church, excellent Sovereign, is a thing no less precious than the union of your kingdoms; being both works wherein your happiness may contend with your worthiness. Having therefore presumed, not without your Majesty's gracious acceptation, to say somewhat of the one, I am the more encouraged not to be silent in the other, the rather because it is an argument that I have travelled in heretofore. But Salomon commendeth a word spoken in season; and as our Saviour, speaking of the discerning of seasons, saith. *when you see a cloud rising in the west, you say it will be a shower*, so your Majesty's rising to this monarchy in the west parts of the world doth promise a sweet and fruitful shower of many blessings upon this Church and commonwealth, a shower of that influence as the very first dews and drops thereof have already laid the storms and winds throughout Christendom, reducing the very face of Europe to a more peaceable and amiable countenance.

But to the purpose, it is very true that these ecclesiastical matters are things not properly appertaining to my profession, which I was not so inconsiderate but to object to myself. But finding that it is many times seen that a man that standeth off, and somewhat removed from a plot of ground, doth better survey it and discover it than those which are upon it, I thought it not impossible but that I, as a looker on, might cast mine eyes upon some things which the actors themselves (specially some being interessed, some led and addicted, some declared and engaged) did not or would not see, and that knowing in my own conscience,[2] whereto God beareth witness, that the things which I shall speak spring out of no vein of popularity, ostentation, desire of novelty, partiality to either side, disposition to intermeddle, or any the like leaven, I may conceive hope that what I want in depth of judgment may be countervailed in simplicity and sincerity of affection. But of all things this did most animate me, that I found in these opinions of mine, which I have long held and embraced (as may appear by that which I have many years since written of them) according to the proportion nevertheless of my weakness, a consent and conformity with that which your Majesty hath published of your own most Christian most wise and moderate sense in these causes; wherein you have well expressed to the world, that there is infused in your sacred breast from God that high principle and position of government, *That you ever hold the whole more dear than any part.*

For who seeth not that many are affected and give opinion in these matters, as if they had not so much a desire to purge the evil from the good, as to countenance and protect the evil by the good? Others speak as if their scope were only to set forth what is good, and not to seek forth[1] what is possible; which is to wish, and not to propound. Others proceed as if they had rather a mind of removing than of reforming. But howsoever either side as men, though excellent men, shall run into extremities, yet your Majesty, as a most wise equal and Christian moderator, is disposed to find out the golden mediocrity, in the establishment of that which is sound, and in the reparation of that which is corrupt and decayed. To your princely judgment then I do in all humbleness submit whatsoever I shall propound, offering the same but as a mite into the treasury of your wisdom. For as the astronomers do well observe, that when three of the superior lights do meet in conjunction it bringeth forth some admirable effects, so there being joined in your Majesty the light of nature, the light of learning, and above all the light of God's holy spirit, it cannot be but your government must be as a happy constellation over the states of your kingdoms. Neither is there wanting to your Majesty that fourth light, which though it be but a borrowed light, yet is of singular efficacy and moment added to the rest, which is the light of a most wise and well compounded counsel, to whose honourable and grave wisdoms I do likewise submit whatsoever I shall say[2], hoping that I shall not need to make protestation of my mind and opinion, that until your Majesty doth otherwise determine and order, all actual and full obedience is to be given to ecclesiastical jurisdiction as it now stands, and when your Majesty hath determined and ordered, that every good subject ought to rest satisfied, and apply his obedience to your Majesty's laws, ordinances, and royal commandments, nor of the dislike I have of all immodest bitterness, peremptory presumption, popular handling, and other courses

---

[1] *forth*, om R   [2] *speak* R

tending rather to rumour and impression in the vulgar sort, than to likelihood of effect joined with observation of duty.

But before I enter into the points controverted, I think good to remove (if it may be) two opinions, which do directly confront and oppone to reformation,—the one bringing it to a nullity, and the other to an impossibility The first is, *that it is against good policy to innovate anything in Church matters*; the other, *that all reformation must be after one platform*

For the first of these, it is excellently said by the prophet, *Stale super vias antiquas, et videte quænam sit via recta et vera, et ambulate in ea*, so as he doth not say, *Stale super vias antiquas, et ambulate in eis*, for it is true that with all wise and moderate persons custom and usage obtaineth that reverence, as it is sufficient matter to move them to make a stand and to discover and take a view ; but it is no warrant to guide or[1] conduct them ; a just ground I say it is of deliberation, but not of direction   But on the other side, who knoweth not that time is truly compared to a stream, that carrieth down fresh and pure waters into that salt sea of corruption which environeth all human actions? And therefore if man shall not by his industry, virtue, and policy, as it were with the oar row against the stream and inclination of time, all institutions and ordinances, be they never so pure, will corrupt and degenerate   But not to handle this matter common-place-like, I would only ask why the civil state should be purged and restored by good and wholesome laws made every third or fourth year in parliaments assembled, devising remedies as fast as time breedeth mischiefs, and contrariwise the ecclesiastical state should still continue upon the dregs of time, and receive no alteration now for these five and forty years and more ? If any man shall object that if the like intermission had been used in civil causes also, the error had not been great, surely the wisdom of the kingdom hath been otherwise in experience for three hundred years' space at the least. But if it be said to me that there is a difference between civil causes and ecclesiastical, they may as well tell me that churches and chapels need no reparations though houses and castles do whereas commonly, to speak truth, dilapidations of the inward and spiritual edification[2] of the Church of God are in all times as great as the outward and material. Sure I am that the very word and stile

---

[1] *and* R

[2] *edifications* A, B, R

of reformation used by our Saviour, *ab initio non fuit ita*,[1] was applied to Church matters, and those of the highest nature, concerning the law moral Nevertheless, he were both unthankful and unwise, that would deny but that the Church of England, during the time of Queen Elizabeth of famous memory, did flourish. If I should compare it with foreign churches, I would rather the comparison should be in the virtues, than (as some make it) in the defects; rather I say as between the vine and the olive, which should be most fruitful, and not as between the briar and the thistle, which should be most unprofitable, for that reverence should be used to the Church, which the good sons of Noah used to their father's nakedness, that is, as it were to go backwards, and to help the defects thereof, and yet to dissemble them And it is to be acknowledged that scarcely any Church, since the primitive Church, yielded in like number of years and latitude of country a greater number of excellent preachers, famous writers, and grave governors But for the discipline and orders of the Church, as many and the chiefest of them are very[2] holy and good, so yet if St John were to indite an epistle to the Church of England, as he did to them of Asia, it would sure have the clause, *habeo adversus*[3] *te pauca*. And no more for this point, saving that as an appendix thereunto, it is not amiss to touch that objection which is made to the time, and not to the matter, pretending that if reformation were necessary, yet it were not now seasonable at your Majesty's first entrance Yet Hippocrates saith, *Si quid mores, a principio move*. And the wisdom of all examples doth[4] shew that the wisest princes, as they have ever been the most sparing in removing or alteration of servants and officers upon their coming in, so for removing of abuses and enormities, and for reforming of laws and the policy of their states, they have chiefly sought to ennoble and commend their beginnings therewith; knowing that the first impression with people continueth long, and when men's minds are most in expectation and suspense then are they best wrought and managed And therefore it seemeth to me that as the spring of nature, I mean the spring of the year, is the best time for purging and medicining the natural body, so the spring of kingdoms is the most proper season for the purging and rectifying of politic bodies

[1] *sic* R   [2] *very*, om R   [3] *adversum* MS   [4] *do* R

There remaineth yet an objection, rather of suspicion than of reason, and yet such as I think maketh a great impression in the minds of very wise and well-affected persons, which is, *that if way be given to mutation, though it be in taking away abuses, yet it may so acquaint men with sweetness of change, as it will undermine the stability even of that which is sound and good.* This surely had been a good and true allegation in the ancient contentions and divisions between the people and the senate of Rome, where things were carried at the appetite of multitudes, which can never keep within the compass of any moderation. But these things being with us to have an orderly passage, under a king who hath a regal[1] power and approved judgment, and knoweth as well the measure of things as the nature of them, it is surely a needless fear. For they need not doubt but your Majesty, with the advice of your counsel, will discern what things are intermingled like the tares amongst the wheat, which have their roots so enwrapped and entangled, as the one cannot be pulled up without endangering the other; and what are mingled but as the chaff and the corn, which needs but a fan to sift and sever them. So much therefore for the first point, of no reformation to be admitted at all.

For the second point, that there should be but one form of discipline in all churches, and that imposed by a necessity of a commandment and prescript out of the word of God, it is a matter volumes have en compiled of, and therefore cannot receive a brief redar   I for my part do confess, that in revolving the scriptu   could never find any such thing, but that God had left the like liberty to the Church-government, as he hath done to the civil government, to be varied according to time and place and accidents, which nevertheless his   nd divine providence doth order and dispose   For all c   vernments are restrained from God unto the general grounds of justice and manners, but the policies and forms of them are left free   So that monarchies and kingdoms, senates and seignories, popular states or[2] communalities, are all[3] lawful, and where they are planted ought to be maintained inviolate   So likewise in Church matters, the substance of doctrine is immutable, and so are the general rules of government, but for rites and ceremonies, and for the particular hierarchies, policies, and disciplines of church,[4]

---

[1] *royal* A, B, R   [2] *and* A, B, R   [3] *all*, om R   [4] *churches* A, B, R

they be left at large   And therefore it is good we return unto the ancient bands of unity in the Church of God, which was, *one faith, one baptism,* and not, *one hierarchy, one discipline,* and that we observe the league of Christians, as it is penned by our Saviour Christ,[1] which is in substance of doctrine this, *He that is not with us, is against us,* but in things indifferent and but of circumstance this, *He that is not against us, is with us* In these things, so as the general rules be observed,—that Christ's flock be fed, that there be a succession in bishops and ministers, which are the prophets of the new Testament, that there be a due and reverent use of the power of the keys; that those which[2] preach the Gospel, live of the Gospel, that all things tend to edification, that all things be done in order and with decency, and the like, the rest is left to the holy wisdom and spiritual discretion of the masters builders[3] and inferior builders in Christ's Church, as it is excellently alluded by that father that noted that Christ's garment was without seam and yet the Church's garment was of divers colours, and thereupon set[4] down for a rule *in veste varietas sit, scissura non sit*

In which variety nevertheless it is a safe and a[5] wise course to follow good examples and precedents. But then the rule of imitation and examples is, to consider not only which are the best, but which are the likest, and to choose the best of the likest,[6] as namely the government of the Church in the purest times of the first good Emperors that embraced the faith; for the times of persecution, before temporal princes received the[7] faith, as they were excellent times for doctrine and manners, so they be unproper and unlike examples of outward government and policy; and so much for this point   Now to the particular points of controversy,[8] or rather of reformation.

Circumstances in the government of Bishops.

First therefore for the government of Bishops, I for my part, not prejudging the precedents of other reformed churches, do hold it warranted by the word of God and by the practice of the

---

[1] *Christ* om R   [2] *that* A, B, R   [3] *master builders* A, B, R
[4] *setteth* A, B, R   [5] *a,* om R
[6] The last clause omitted in all the printed copies R has *But then, by the rule of imitation and example, to consider not only which are best, but which are the likeliest*
[7] *om* R   [8] *controversies* A, B, R

ancient Church in the better times, and much more convenient for kingdoms, than parity of ministers and government by synods. But then further it is to be considered, that the Church is not now to plant or build, but only to be pruned from corruptions, and[1] repaired and restored in some decays for it is worth the noting, that the scripture saith, *Translato sacerdotio, necesse est ut et Legis fiat translatio* It is not possible, in respect of the great and near sympathy between the state civil and the state ecclesiastical, to make so main an alteration in the Church, but it would have a perilous operation upon the kingdom. And therefore it is fit that controversy be in peace and silence

But there be two circumstances in the administration of Bishops, wherein I confess I could never be satisfied, the one, *the sole exercise of their authority*, the other, *the deputation of their authority*

For the first, the Bishop giveth orders alone; excommunicateth alone; judgeth alone This seems to be a thing almost without example in government,[2] and therefore not unlikely to have crept in in the degenerate and corrupt times We see the greatest kings and monarchs of the earth[3] have their councils There is no temporal court in England of the higher sort where the authority doth absolutely[4] rest in one person. The King's bench, Common-pleas, and the Exchequer, are benches of a certain number of judges The Chancellor of England hath an assistance of twelve masters of the Chancery The master of the Wards hath a council of the court so hath the Chancellor of the Duchy In the Exchequer-chamber, the Lord Treasurer is joined with the Chancellor and the Barons. The masters of the Requests are ever more than one The justices of Assize are two. The Lords[5] Presidents in the Marches and in the North[6] have councils of divers. The Star-chamber is an assembly of the King's privy council, aspersed with lords[7] spiritual and temporal. So as in all[8] courts the principal person hath ever either colleagues or assessors The like is to be found in other well-governed kingdoms[9] abroad, where the jurisdiction is yet more distributed,[10] as in the Courts of Parliament of France, and in other places. No man will deny but the acts that pass the Bishop's

---

[1] *pruned from corruption, and to be* R [2] *in good government* R
[3] *of the earth,* om A, B, R [4] *absolutely,* om A, B, R
[5] *Lord* A, B, R [6] *in the North and in Wales* R
[7] *the Lords* R. [8] *all,* om R [9] *commonwealths* R [10] *dispersed* R

jurisdiction are of as great importance as those that pass the
civil courts, for men's souls are more precious than their bodies
or goods, and so are their good names.   Bishops have their infirmities, and have no exemption[1] from that general malediction
which is pronounced against all men living, *Væ soli, nam si ceci-
derit,* etc.   Nay we see that the first warrant in spiritual causes
is directed to a number, *Dic[2] Ecclesiæ,* which is not so in temporal matters.   And we see that in general causes of Church-
government, there are as well assemblies of all the clergy in
councils, as of all the states in Parliament   Whence should this
sole exercise of jurisdiction come?   Surely I do suppose, and I
think upon ground,[3] that *ab initio non fuit ita,* and that the
Deans and Chapters were councils about the sees and chairs of
Bishops at the first, and were unto them a presbytery or consistory, and intermeddled not only in the disposing of their revenues
and endowments, but much more in jurisdiction ecclesiastical
But it is probable that the Dean and Chapter[4] stuck close to the
Bishops in matters of profit and the world, and would not leese
their hold, but in matters of jurisdiction (which they counted
but a trouble[5] and attendance,) they suffered the Bishops to encroach and usurp, and so the one continueth and the other is
lost.   And we see that the Bishop of Rome (*fas est[6] et ab hoste
doceri,* and no question in that church the first institutions were
excellent,) performeth all ecclesiastical jurisdiction as in consistory.   And whereof consisteth this consistory, but of[7] parish-
priests of Rome, which term themselves cardinals, *a cardinibus
mundi,* because the Bishop pretendeth to be universal over the
whole world?   And hereof again we see divers[8] shadows yet re-
maining· as that the Dean and Chapter *pro forma* chooseth the
Bishop, which is the highest point of jurisdiction   and that the
Bishop when he giveth orders, if there be any ministers casually
present, calleth them to join with him in imposition of hands,
and some other particulars   And therefore it seems to me a
thing reasonable and religious, and according to the first institution, that Bishops, in the greatest causes, and those which require
a spiritual discerning, namely in ordaining, suspending, or depriving ministers, in excommunication (being restored to the
true and proper use, as shall be afterwards touched), in senten-

---

[1] *exception* A, B, R   [2] *Dei* A, B   [3] *good ground* R
[4] *Deans and Chapters* R   [5] *accounted but trouble* A, B, R
[6] *enim* R   [7] *of the parish priests* A, B, R   [8] *many* R

cing the validity of marriages and legitimations, in judging causes
criminous, as simony, incest, blasphemy, and the like, should
not proceed sole and unassisted which point (as I understand
it) is a reformation that may be planted *sine strepitu*, without
any perturbation at all and is a matter which will give strength
to the Bishops, countenance to the inferior degrees of prelates or
ministers, and the better issue and[1] proceeding to those causes
that shall pass

And as I wish this strength given to the Bishops by council,
so it is not unworthy your Majesty's royal[2] consideration, whether
you shall not think fit to give strength to the general council of
your clergy, the Convocation-house, which was then restrained
when the state of the clergy was thought a suspected part to
the kingdom, in regard of their late homage to the Bishop of
Rome, which state now will give place to none in their loyalty
and devotion to your Majesty.

For the second point, which is the deputation of their authority, I see no perfect and sure ground for that neither, being somewhat different from the examples and rules of government The
Bishop exerciseth his jurisdiction by his Chancellor, Commissary,[3] Official, etc We see in all laws in the world, offices of
confidence and skill cannot be put over nor exercised by deputy,
except it be specially contained in the original grant, and in that
case it is doubtful,[4] and for experience, there was never any
Chancellor of England made a deputy; there was never Judge[5]
in any court made a deputy. The Bishop is a judge, and of a
high nature, whence cometh it that he should depute, considering that all trust and confidence, as was said, is personal and
inherent, and cannot or ought not to[6] be transposed ? Surely in
this again *ab initio non fuit ita* [7] but it is probable that bishops
when they gave themselves too much to the glory of the world,
and became grandes[8] in kingdoms, and great counsellors to
princes, then did they deleague their proper jurisdiction[9] as
things of too inferior a nature for their greatness, and then,
after the similitude and imitation of kings and counts palatine,
they would have their chancellors and judges But that example of kings and potentates giveth no good defence For
the reasons why kings administer by their judges, although

[1] or   A, B, R   [2] *royal*, om R   [3] *and commissary* A, B, R
[4] *dutiful* A, B, R   [5] *any judge* A, B, R   [6] *nor ought not be* MS R
[7] *sic* R   [8] *grandees* R   [9] *jurisdictions* R

themselves be supreme judges, are two The one because the offices of kings are for the most part of inheritance, and it is a rule in all laws that offices of inheritance are rather matters that found[1] in interest than in confidence, for as much as they may fall upon women, upon infants, upon lunatics and idiots, persons incapable to execute judicature in person; and therefore such offices by all laws might ever be exercised and administered by delegation The second reason is, because of the amplitude of their jurisdiction,[2] which is as great as either their birth-right from their ancestors, or their sword-right from God maketh it. And therefore if Moses, that was governor over no great people, and those collected together in a camp, and not scattered in provinces and cities, himself likewise[3] of an extraordinary spirit, was nevertheless not able to suffice and hold out in person to judge the people, but did by the advice of Jethro approved from God, substitute elders and judges, how much more other kings and princes? There is a third reason likewise not[4] much to the present purpose, and that is, that kings, either in respect of the commonwealth, or of the greatness of their[5] patrimonies, are usually parties in suits, and then their judges stand indifferent between them and the subject But in the case of bishops, none of these reasons hold for first their office is elective and for life, and not patrimonial or hereditary, an office merely of confidence, science, and qualification. And for the second reason, it is true that their jurisdiction is ample and spacious, and that their time is to be divided between their[6] labours as well in the word and doctrine, as in government and jurisdiction But yet I do not see, (supposing the Bishop's courts to be used incorruptly, and without any indirect course held to multiply causes for gain of fees,) but that the Bishop mought very well, for causes of moment, supply his judicial function in his own person For we see before our eyes that one Chancellor of England dispatcheth the suits in equity of the whole kingdom which is not[7] by reason of the excellency of that rare honourable person which now holdeth that[8] place, but it was ever so, though more or less burdenous to the suitor, as the Chancellor was more or less able to give dispatch And if hold be taken of that which was said before, that the Bishop's

[1] *ground* R   [2] *jurisdictions* R   [3] *likewise,* om R
[4] *though not* R   [5] *their own* A, B, R   [6] *the* A, B, R
[7] *not so much* R   [8] *the* R

labour in the word must take up a principal part of his time, so
I may say again that matters of state have ever taken up most
of the Chancellor's time, having been for the most part persons
upon whom[1] the kings of this realm have most itched for matters
of counsel. And therefore there is no doubt but the Bishop,
whose circuit is less ample and the causes in nature not so multiplying, with the help of references and certificates to and from
fit persons, for the better ripening of causes in their mean proceedings, and such ordinary helps incident to jurisdiction, may
very well suffice his office   But yet there is another help   For
the causes that come before him are these   tithes; legacies and[2]
administrations and other testamentary causes, causes matrimo-
nial, accusations against ministers, tending to their suspension,
deprivation, or degrading, simony, incontinency, heresy, blasphemy, breach of Sabbath,[3] and other like causes of scandal.
The first two of these, in mine opinion, differ from the rest;
that is, tithes and testaments   for these[4] be matters of profit
and in their nature temporal, though by a favour and connivance of the temporal jurisdiction they have been allowed and
permitted to the courts ecclesiastical; the one to the end the
clergy might sue for that that was their sustentation before their
own judges, and the other in a kind of piety and religion which
was thought incident to the performance of dead men's wills.
And surely for these two, the Bishop in mine opinion may with
less danger discharge himself upon his ordinary judges   And I
think likewise it will fall out that those suits are in the greatest
number   But for the rest which require a spiritual science and
discretion in respect of their nature or of the scandal, it were
reason in my opinion there were no audience given but by the
Bishop himself, he being also assisted, as was touched before
but it were necessary also he were attended by his chancellor, or
some other his officers being learned in the civil law, for his
better instruction in points of formality, or the courses of the
court   which if it were done, then were there less use of the
official's court (whereof there is now so much complaint), and
causes of the nature aforesaid being only drawn to the audience
of the bishop, it would repress frivolous and powling[5] suits, and

[1] *upon*, om MS   [2] *and*, om R
[3] *of the Sabbath* R   *of Saboth* A, B   *of Sabaoth* MS
[4] *those* A, B, R.   [5] *poling* B   *prowling* R

VOL III   1

give a grave and incorrupt proceeding to such causes as shall be
fit for the court

There is a third point also, not of jurisdiction, but of form
of proceeding, which may deserve[1] reformation, the rather be
cause it is contrary to the laws and customs of this land and
state, which though they do not rule those proceedings, yet may
they be advised with for better direction,[2] and that is the oath
ex officio whereby men are enforced to accuse themselves, and
(that that is more) are sworn unto blanks, and not unto accusations and charges declared   By the laws[3] of England no man is
bound to accuse himself   In the highest cases of treasons,[4] torture is used for discovery, and not for evidence   In capital
matters, no delinquent's answer upon oath is required, no, not
permitted.   In criminal matters not capital, handled in the
Star-chamber, and in causes of conscience, handled in the Chan
cery, for the most part grounded upon trust and secrecy, the
oath of the party is required.   But how ?   Where there is an
accusation and an accuser, which we call bills of complaint, from
which the complainant cannot vary, and out of the compass of
the which the defendant may not be examined, exhibited unto
the court, and by process notified unto the defendant.   But to
examine a man upon oath, out of the insinuation of fame, or out
of accusations secret and undeclared, though it have some coun
tenance from the civil law, yet it is so opposite *ex diametro* to
the sense and course of the common law, as it may well receive
some limitation.

Concerning the Liturgy, the Ceremonies, and Subscription

For the Liturgy, great respect and heed would be taken, lest
by inveighing against a[5] dumb ministry, due reverence be not
withdrawn from the liturgy   For though the gift of preaching
be far above that of reading, yet the action of the liturgy is as
high and holy as that of the sermon   It is said *Domus mea
domus orationis vocabitur* the house of prayer, not the house of
preaching   And whereas the Apostle saith, *How shall men call
upon him, on whom they have not believed ?   And how shall they
believe except[6] they hear ?   And how shall they hear, without a
preacher ?* it appeareth that as preaching is the more original,

---

[1] *discerne* A, B   [2] *directions* R   [3] *law* R   [4] *treason* A, B, R
[5] *the* A, B, R, corrected in MS   [6] *unless* A, B, R

so prayer is the more final, as the difference is between the
seed and the fruit; for the keeping of God's law is the fruit of
the teaching of the law, and prayer or invocation or divine service or liturgy (for these be but varieties of terms) is the immediate[1] hallowing of the name of God, and the principal work of
the first table, and of the great commandment of the love of
God It is true that the preaching of the holy word of God is
the sowing of the seed, it is the lifting up of the brazen serpent,
the ministry of faith, and the ordinary means of salvation But
yet it is good to take example, how that the best actions of the
worship of God may be extolled excessively and superstitiously
As the extolling of the Sacrament bred the superstition of the
Mass. The extolling of the Liturgy and prayers bred the superstition of the monastical orders and oraisons And so no doubt
preaching likewise may be magnified and extolled superstitiously,
as if all the whole body of God's worship should be turned into
an ear So as none, as I suppose, of sound judgment will derogate from the liturgy, if the form thereof be in all parts agreeable to the word of God, the example of the primitive Church,
and that holy decency which St. Paul commendeth. And therefore, first, that there be a set form of prayer, and that it be not
left either to an extemporal form or to an arbitrary form Secondly, that it consist as well of lauds, hyms, and thanksgivings,
as of petitions, prayers, and supplications. Thirdly, that the
form thereof be quickened with some shortness and diversity[2] of
prayers and hymns, and with some interchanges of the voice of the
people as well as of the voice[3] of the minister. Fourthly, that it
admit some distinctions of times and commemorations of God's
principal benefits, as well general as particular. Fifthly, that
prayers likewise be appropriated to several necessities and occasions of the Church Sixthly, that there be a form likewise of
words and liturgy in the administration of the sacraments and in
the denouncing of the censures of the Church, and other holy
actions and solemnities These things I think will not be much
controverted

But for the particular exceptions to the liturgy in form as it
now stands, divers[4] of them, (allowing they were just,) yet seem
they not to be weighty otherwise than that nothing ought to

---

[1] *mediate* A, B   [2] *diversities* A, B, R   [3] *of the voice*, om R
[4] *I think, divers* A, B, R   *I think* is crossed out in the MS

be counted light in matter[1] of religion and piety, as the heathen himself could say, *etiam vultu sæpe læditur pietas* That the word *Priest* should not be continued, especially with offence (the word *minister* being already made familiar), this may be said, That it is a good rule in translation, never to confound that in one word in the translation, which is precisely distinguished in two words in the original, for doubt of equivocation and tra ducing And therefore seeing the word πρεσβύτερος and ἱερεύς be always distinguished in the original, and the one used for a sacrificer, the other for a minister the word Priest being made common to both, whatsoever the derivation be, yet in use it con foundeth the minister with the sacrificer And for an example of this kind, I did ever allow the discretion and tenderness of the Rhemish translation in this point, that finding in the original the word ἀγάπη and never ἔρως, do ever translate *Charity* and never love, because of the indifferency and equivocation of that[2] word with impure love

Touching the *Absolution*, it is not unworthy consideration whether it may not be thought unproper and unnecessary, for there are but two sorts of absolution, both supposing an obliga tion precedent, the one upon an excommunication, which is religious and primitive, the other upon confession and penance which is superstitious or at least positive, and both particular, neither general Therefore since the one is taken away, and the other hath his proper case, what doth a general absolution, wherein there is neither penance nor excommunication prece dent? for the Church never looseth, but where the Church hath bound And surely I may think this at the first was allowed in a kind of spiritual discretion, because the Church thought the people could not be suddenly weaned from their conceit of as soiling, to which they had been so long accustomed

For *Confirmation*, to my understanding the state of the ques tion is whether it be not a matter mistaken and altered by time, and whether that be not now made a subsequent to *Baptism*, which was indeed an inducement to the *Communion* For whereas in the primitive Church children were examined of their faith before they were admitted to the Communion, time may seem to have turned it to refer as if it had been to receive a con firmation of their Baptism

[1] *matters* A, B, R   [2] *the* A, B, R

For private baptism by women or lay persons, the best divines do utterly condemn it, and I hear it not generally defended, and I have often marvelled, that when[1] the book in the preface to public baptism doth acknowledge that baptism in the practice of the primitive Church was anniversary,[2] and but at set and[3] certain times, which sheweth that the primitive Church did not attribute so much to the ceremony as they would break an outward and general order for it, the book should afterwards allow of private Baptism, as if the ceremony were of that necessity, as the very Institution which committed Baptism only to the ministers should be broken in regard of the supposed necessity. And therefore this point of all others I think was but a *Concessum propter duritiem cordis*

For the form of celebrating matrimony, the ring seemeth to many even of vulgar sense and understanding a ceremony not grave, specially to be made (as the words make it) the essential part of the action, besides, some other of the words are noted in common speech[4] to be not so decent and fit

For music in churches, That there should be singing of psalms and spiritual songs is not denied So the question is *de modo*, wherein if a man will look attentively into the order and observance[5] of it, it is easy to discern between the wisdom of the institution and the excess of the later[6] times For first, there are no songs or verses sung by the quire, which are not supposed by continual use to be so familiar with the people, as they have them without book, whereby the sound hurteth not the understanding, and those which cannot read upon the book, are yet partakers of the sense and may follow it with their mind So again, after the reading of the word of God,[7] it was thought fit there should be pause[8] for holy meditation, before they proceeded to the rest of the service, which pause was thought fit to be filled rather with some grave sound, than with a still silence, which was the reason of the playing upon the organs after the scriptures read All which was decent and tending to edification But then the curiosity of division and reports and other figures of music, hath[9] no affinity with the reasonable service of God, but were added in the more pompous times

---

[1] *where* A, R   [2] *anniversarie* A   [3] *set and*, om R
[4] *in speech* A, B, R   *common* inserted in MS in Bacon's hand
[5] *observation* R   [6] *late* A B R   [7] *of God*, om R
[8] *some pause*, A, B, R   [9] *have* A, B R   Corrected in the MS

For the cap and surplice, since they be things in their nature indifferent and yet by some held superstitious, so[1] that the question is between science and conscience, it seems to fall within the compass of the Apostle's rule, which is, that the stronger do descend and yield to the weaker. Only the difference is, that it will be materially said, that that[2] rule holds between private man and private man, but not between the conscience of a private man and the order of a Church. But since the question at this time is of a toleration, not by connivance which may encourage disobedience, but by law which may give a liberty, it is good again to be advised whether it fall not within the equity of the former rule; the rather because the silencing of ministers by this occasion is (in this scarcity of good preachers) a punishment that lights upon the people as well as upon the party.

And for the subscription, it seemeth to be[4] in the nature of a confession, and therefore more proper to bind in the unity of faith, and to be urged rather for articles of doctrine than for rites and ceremonies and points of outward government. For howsoever politic considerations and reasons of state may require uniformity, yet Christian and divine grounds look chiefly upon unity

Touching a Preaching Ministry.

To speak of a learned ministry, it is true that the worthiness of the pastors and ministers is of all other points of religion the most summary, I do not say the greatest, but the most effectual towards all[5] the rest. But herein to my understanding while men go on in zeal to hasten this work, they are not aware of as great or greater inconvenience than that which they seek to remove. For while they inveigh against a dumb ministry, they make too easy and too promiscuous an allowance of such as they account preachers, having not respect enough to years, except[6] their gifts be extraordinary,[6] not respect enough to their learnings in other arts, which are handmaids to divinity, not respect enough to the gift itself, which many times is none at all. For

---

[1] *and* A, B, R   [2] *the* A, B, R   [3] *But yet* A, B, R
[4] *me* R   [5] *all*, om R
[6] This clause is omitted in A and B. R has *Having not respect enough to the learnings*, etc, *not respect enough to years except it be in case of extraordinary gift, not respect enough*, etc

God forbid, that every man that can take unto himself boldness to speak an hour together in a Church upon a text, should be admitted for a preacher, though he mean never so well   I know there is a great latitude in gifts and a great variety in auditories and congregations, but yet so as there is *aliquid infimum* below which you ought not to descend.   For you must rather leave the Ark to shake as it shall please God, than put unworthy hands to hold it up, and when we are in God's temple, we are warned rather to put our hands upon our mouth than to offer the sacrifice of fools.   And surely it may be justly thought, that amongst many causes of Atheism which are miserably met in our age, as schisms and controversies, profane scoffing in holy matters, and others, it is not the least that divers do adventure to handle the word of God which are unfit and unworthy.   And herein I would have no man mistake me, as if I did extol curious and affected preaching, which is as much on the other side to be disliked, and breeds atheism and scandal as well as the other (for who would not be offended at one that comes into the pulpit as if he came upon a[1] stage to play parts or prizes?) neither on the other side as if I would discourage any who hath any tolerable gift

But upon this point I ground three considerations. whether[2] it were not requisite to renew that good exercise which was practised in this Church some years and afterwards put down (by order indeed from the Church, in regard of some abuse thereof, inconvenient for those times) and yet against the advice and opinion of one of the greatest and gravest prelates of this land, and was commonly called prophesying, which was this. That the ministers within a precinct did meet upon a week-day in some principal town, where there was some ancient grave minister that was president, and an auditory admitted of gentlemen, or other persons of leisure, then every minister successively, beginning with the youngest, did handle one and the same piece[3] of Scripture, spending severally some quarter of an hour or better, and in the whole some two hours, and so the exercise being begun and concluded with prayer, and the president giving a text for the next meeting, the assembly was dissolved And this was as I take it a fortnight's exercise, which in mine opinion was the best way to frame and train up preachers

---

[1] *the* A, B, R   [2] So MS A, B   R inserts *First*   [3] *part* R

to handle the word of God as it ought to be handled, that hath been practised. For we see orators have their declamations, lawyers have their moots, logicians have[1] their sophems, and every practice of science hath an exercise of erudition and imitation[2] before men come to the life, only preaching, which is the worthiest, and wherein it is most danger to do amiss, wanteth an introduction, and is ventured[3] and rushed upon at the first But unto this exercise of prophecy,[4] I could[5] wish these two additions the one, that after this exercise, which is in some sort public, there were immediately a private meeting of the same ministers, where they mought brotherly admonish the one the other, and especially the elder sort the younger, of any thing that had passed in the exercise in matter or manner unsound or[6] uncomely, and in a word, mought mutually use such advice, instruction, comfort, or encouragement, as occasion might minister, (for public reprehension were to be debarred) The other addition that I mean is, that the same exercise were used in the universities for young divines before they presumed to preach, as well as in the country for ministers For they have in some colleges an exercise called a *common-place*, which can in no degree be so profitable, being but the speech of one man at one time

And if it be feared that it may be occasion to whet men's speeches for controversies, it is easily remedied by some strict prohibition, that matters of controversy tending any way to the violating or disquieting of[7] the peace of the Church be not handled or entered into, which prohibition, in regard there is ever to be a grave person president or moderator, cannot be frustrated

The second consideration is, whether it were not convenient there should be a more exact probation and examination of ministers, namely that the Bishops do not ordain alone, but by advice, and then that the[8] ancient holy orders of the Church might be revived, by the which the Bishop did ordain ministers but at four set times of the year, which were called *Quatuor tempora*, which are now called Ember-weeks it being thought fit to accompany so high an action with general fasting and prayer and sermons, and all holy exercises, and the names

---

¹ *have*, om A, B, R   ² *imitation* R   ³ Here A has two pages of MS
³ *the prophecy* B R   ⁵ *would* B, R   ⁶ *and* B, R
⁷ *of*, om R   ⁹ *the*, om R

likewise of those that were[1] ordained, were published some days before their ordination; to the end exceptions might be taken, if just cause were.

The third consideration is, that if the case of the Church of England be, that when[2] a computation is taken of all the parochian churches,[3] (allowing the union of such as are[4] too small and adjacent), and again a computation be[5] taken of the persons who are worthy to be pastors, and if upon the said account it fall out that there be many more churches than pastors, then of necessity recourse must be had to one of these remedies, either that pluralities be[6] allowed, specially if you can by permutations make the benefices to be[7] more compatible; or else[8] there be allowed preachers to have a[9] more general charge, to supply and serve by turn parishes unfurnished For that some churches should be provided of pastors able to teach, and other wholly destitute, seemeth to me to be against the communion of Saints and Christians, and against the practice of the primitive Church.

Touching the abuse of Excommunication.

Excommunication is the greatest judgment upon the[10] earth, being that which is ratified in heaven, and being a precursory or prelusory judgment to the judgment[11] of Christ in the end of the world, and therefore for this to be used unreverently, and to be made an ordinary process to lackey up and down for fees, how can it be without derogation to God's honour, and making the power of the keys contemptible? I know very well the defence thereof, which hath no great force. That it issues forth, not for the thing itself, but for the contumacy I do not deny but this judgment is, as I said before, of the nature of God's judgment, of the which it is a model. For as the judgment of God taketh hold upon the least sin of the impenitent, and taketh not hold of the greatest sin of the penitent,[12] so *Excommunication* may in case issue upon the smallest offence, and in case not issue upon

---

[1] *were to be* R　　　　　　　[2] *where* B, R　　　　　[3] *parishes* B
[4] *were* B, R　　　　　　　　[5] *to be* B, R　　　　　　[6] *must be* B, R
[7] *to be*, om B, R　　　　　　[8] *or that* R *as* B
[9] Here follow two printed pages in A　　　　[10] *the*, om R
[11] *to the judgment*, om A, B *of the great judgment* R
[12] *and taketh no hold of the greatest sin of the convert or penitent* R The clause omitted in A and B

the greatest. But is this contumacy such a contumacy as excommunication is now used for? For the contumacy must be such, as the party (as far as the eye and wisdom of the Church can discern) standeth in the state[1] of reprobation and damnation, as one that for that time seemeth given over to final impenitence[2] Upon this observation I ground two considerations the one, that this censure be restored to the true dignity and use thereof, which is, that it proceed not but in causes of great weight, and that it be decreed, not by any deputy or substitute of the Bishop, but by the Bishop in person, and not by him alone, but by the Bishop assisted. The other consideration is, that in lieu thereof there be given to the ecclesiastical courts some ordinary process, with such force and coercion as appertaineth, that so the dignity of so high a sentence being retained, and the necessity of a[3] mean process supplied, the Church may be indeed restored to the ancient vigour and splendour. To this purpose, joined with some other holy and good purposes, was there a bill drawn in parliament, in the three-and-twentieth year of the reign of the Queen deceased, which was the gravest parliament that I have known, and the bill recommended by the gravest counsellor of estate in parliament, though afterwards it was staid by the Queen's special commandment, the nature of those times considered

Touching[4] *the Non residents and Pluralities*

For *Non-residence*, except it be in case of necessary absence, it seemeth an abuse drawn out of covetousness and sloth, for that men should live of the flock that they do not feed, or of the altar at which they do not serve, is a thing can[5] hardly receive just defence, and to exercise the office of a pastor in matter of word[6] and doctrine by deputy,[7] is a thing not warranted, as hath been touched before The questions in this point do chiefly[8] rise upon the cases of exception and excusation,—which shall be thought sufficient and reasonable,[9] and which not. For the case of chaplains, let me speak it[10] with your Majesty's pardon,

---

[1] *in state* A, B   [2] *impenitency* A, B, R
[3] *a*, om A, B, R   Inturlined in the MS
[4] *the*, om R   Here follow two pages of MS in A
[5] *that can* B, R   [6] *the word* R   [7] *deputies* R
[8] *The questions upon this point do arise* R   *The question upon this point doth chiefly arise* B   [9] *reasonable and sufficient* B, R   [10] *that* B, R

and with due reverence towards other peers and great persons
which are by statute privileged,[1] I should think that the attendance used and given in[2] your Majesty's court, and in the houses
and families of their lords, were a juster reason why they should
have no benefice, than why they should be qualified to have
two For as it standeth with Christian policy that such attendance be in no wise neglected, because the[3] good which en-
sueth thereof to the Church of God may exceed or countervail
that which may follow of their labours in any though never so
large a congregation, so yet[4] it were reasonable that their maintenance should honourably and liberally proceed thence where
their labours be employed. Neither are there wanting in the
Church dignities and preferments, not joined with any exact
cure of souls, by which and by the hope of which such attendants
in ordinary (who ought to be, as for the most part they are, of
the best gifts and sort) may be further encouraged and rewarded
And as for extraordinary attendants, they may very well retain
the grace and countenance of their places and the[5] duties at times
incident thereunto, without discontinuance or non-residence in
their pastoral charges Next for the case of intending studies
in the universities, it will more easily receive an answer, for
studies do but serve and tend to the practice of those studies,
and therefore for that which is most principal and final to be
left undone, for the attending of that which is subservient and
subministrant, seemeth to be against proportion of reason
Neither do I see but that they proceed right well in all knowledge which do couple study with their practice, and do not first
study altogether, and then practise altogether, and therefore
they may very well study at their benefices. Thirdly, for the
case of the[6] extraordinary service of the Church, as if some pastor
be sent to a general council, or here to the[7] Convocation, and
likewise[8] for the case of necessity, as in the particular of infirmity of body and the like, no man will contradict but that there
may be some substitution for such a time

But the general case of necessity is the case of pluralities (the
want of pastors and insufficiency of livings considered), *posito*
that a man doth faithfully and incessantly divide his labours

[1] *and with reverence towards the other peers and great persons, whose chaplains by statutes are privileged* R [2] *which chaplains give to* R
[3] *that* B, R [4] *yet,* om B, R [5] *the,* om B, R
[6] *the* om B, R [7] *a* B, R [8] here follows another printed page in A

between two cures, which kind of necessity I come now to speak of in the handling of pluralities

For pluralities, in case the number of able ministers were sufficient, and the value of the[1] benefices were sufficient, then pluralities were in no sort tolerable   But we must take heed we desire not contraries, for to desire that every parish should be furnished with a sufficient preacher, and to desire that pluralities be forthwith taken away, is to desire things contrary, considering *de facto* there are not sufficient preachers for every parish, whereto add likewise, that there is not sufficient living and maintenance in many parishes to maintain a preacher, and it makes the impossibility yet much the greater   The remedies *in rerum natura* are but three, union, permutation, and supply, union of such benefices as have the living too small, and the parish not too great, and are adjacent, Permutation, to make benefices more compatible, though men be over-ruled to some loss in changing a better for a nearer, Supply, by stipendiary[2] preachers to be rewarded with some liberal stipends, to supply as they may such places which are unfurnished of sufficient pastors as Queen Elizabeth, amongst other her christian[3] acts, did erect certain of them in Lancashire, towards which pensions, I see no reason also[4] but leading ministers, if they have rich benefices, should be charged.

Touching the provision for sufficient maintenance in the Church

Touching Church-maintenance, it is well to be weighed what is *jure divino*, and what *jure positivo*   It is a constitution of the divine law, whereunto[5] human laws cannot derogate, *that those which feed the flock should live of the flock, that those that serve at the altar should live of*[6] *the altar, that those which dispense spiritual things should reap temporal things*   Of which it is also an appendix, that the proportion of this maintenance be not meagre[7] or necessitous, but plentiful and liberal   So then, that all the places and offices of the Church have[8] such a dotation that they may be maintained according to their several degrees, is a constitution permanent and perpetual. But for the[9] particu-

[1] *the,* om R   [2] The rest is supplied in MS in A   [3] *gracious* R
[4] *also,* om B, R.   [5] *from which* R   *where from* B   [6] *at* B
[7] *small* B, R   [8] *be provided of* R   [9] *the* om B, R.

larity of the endowment, whether it shall[1] consist of tithes or
lands or pensions or mixt, it may[2] make a question of convenience,
but no question of precise necessity   Again, that the case of
this[3] Church *de facto* is such, that there is a want in the Church
patrimony,[4] is confessed   For the principal places, namely the
Bishops' livings, are in some particulars not sufficient, and
therefore enforced to be supplied by toleration of Commendams,
things in[5] themselves unfit, and ever held of no good report
But[6] as for the benefices and pastors' places, it is too manifest
that many[7] of them are very weak and penurious. On the
other side, that there was a time when the Church was rather
burdened with superfluity than with lack, that is likewise apparent, but it is long since, so as the fault was in others, the
want redoundeth to us   Again, that it were to be wished that
impropriations were returned to the Church as the most proper
and natural endowment[8] thereof, is a thing likewise wherein
men's judgments will not much vary   Also[9] that it is an impossibility to proceed now either to their resumption or redemption,
is as plain on the other side, for men are stated in them by
the highest assurance of the kingdom, which is act of Parliament, and the value of them amounteth much above ten subsidies, and the restitution must of necessity pass their hands
in whose hands they are in interest and possession [10] But of
these things which are manifestly true, to infer and ground some
conclusion.[11] First, for[12] mine own opinion and sense, I must confess (let me speak it with reverence) that all the parliaments since
27 and 31 of K Henry VIII which[13] gave away impropriations
from the Church, seem to me to stand in some[14] sort obnoxious
and obliged to God in conscience to do somewhat for the Church,
and[15] to reduce the patrimony thereof to a competency   For
since they have debarred Christ's wife of a great part of her
dowry, it were reason they made her a competent jointure. Next,
to say that impropriations should be only charged, that carrieth
neither possibility nor reason, Not possibility, for the reasons

[1] *should* B, R   [2] *might,* R   [3] *the* B, R
[4] *that there is want in the Church of patrimony* B, R
[5] *of* R   [6] *and* B, R
[7] *it is manifest that very many*   R   *it is manifest that many*   B
[8] *endowments* R   [9] *Nevertheless* R
[10] *they now are in possession or interest ·* R   *in whose hands there is interest
and possession* B   [11] *conclusions* B, R   [12] *in* R
[13] *who* B, R   [14] *a* R   [15] *and,* om B, R

touched before, not reason, because if it be conceived that if any other person be charged it should be a re-charge or double charge, inasmuch as he payeth tithes already, that is a thing mistaken. For it must be remembered, that as the realm gave tithes to the Church, so the realm hath taken that away again from the Church and gave them unto the king, as they mought give their ninth sheaf or eighth sheaf;[1] and therefore the first gift being evacuated it cannot go in defeasance or discharge of that perpetual bond, whereby[2] men are bound to maintain God's ministers, as[3] we see in example, that divers godly and well-disposed persons do put in ure, who are content[4] to increase their preachers' livings, which, though in law it be but a bene-volence, yet before God it is a conscience. Furder, that im-propriations should not be somewhat more deeply charged than other revenues of like value, methinks cannot well be denied, both in regard of the ancient claim of the Church, and the in-tention of the first givers,[5] and again because they have passed in valuation between man and man somewhat at the less rate, in regard of the said pretences or claim[6] in conscience before God. But of this point, touching Church-maintenance, I do not think fit to enter into furder particularity or project,[7] but reserve the same to a fitter time.

Thus have I in all humbleness and sincerity of heart, to the best of mine understanding, given your Majesty tribute of my cares and cogitations in this holy business, so highly tending to God's glory, your Majesty's honour and the peace and welfare of your states, insomuch as I am partly[8] persuaded that the Papists themselves should not need so much the severity of penal laws if the sword of the spirit were better edged, by strength-ening the authority and repressing the abuses in the Church. To conclude, therefore,[9] renewing my most humble submission of all that I have said to your Majesty's high wisdom, and again most humbly craving pardon for any errors committed in this writing which the same weakness of judgment which suffered me to commit them would not suffer me to discover,[10] I end with my

---

[1] since again hath given tithes away from the Church unto the King, as they may give their 8th sheaf or ninth sheaf R   tenth sheaf or ninth sheaf B
[2] wherewith R   [3] and so R
[4] persons, not impropriators, are content R   [5] giver B, R
[6] pretence or claim of the Church R   [7] or project, om B, R
[8] partly, om B, R   [9] therefore, om R
[10] that suffered me to commit them would not suffer me to discover them R

devout and fervent prayer to God, that as he hath made your
Majesty the cornerstone in joining your two kingdoms, so you
may be also as a corner-stone to unite and knit together these
differences in the Church of God   To whose heavenly grace and
never erring direction I commend your Majesty's sacred person
and all your doings.

6.

What the King thought of these suggestions we are not directly
informed, but, judging from his subsequent proceedings, I gather
that he generally approved, and was for his own part disposed to act
in the spirit of them   He began by treating the questions at issue
as matters deserving grave consideration, showed himself ready to
allow any alterations which could be proved to be requisite and
fit, and with that view invited the leaders of the party which desired alteration to appear and state their case for themselves   If
he had stopped there, playing the part of listener only, and reserv-
ing the expression of his own opinion for after-consideration, I
suppose he could not have done better.   His error—a characteristic
error, and springing out of what was best in him, considered as a
man—was in allowing himself to be drawn personally into disputation.   Even if the case of his opponents had been one which admitted of a refutation conclusive and unanswerable in itself, it
would have been better not to urge it   The old proverb tells us to
"let losers have their words," and upon the same principle the
authority which can overrule in action should not be too solicitous
to defeat in argument   But in this case there was no hope of
convincing the opponents that they were wrong, and the attempt
was sure to invite opposition and aggravate disappointment   And yet
to let an answerable argument pass unanswered was a piece of forbearance to which the scholar-King was not equal, and in comparing the second day of the Hampton Court conference with the first,
the consequences are traceable very distinctly   On the first day,
when he was taking order with his councillors what changes should
be made, and had only his own Bishops to dispute with, he seems to
have gone altogether in the direction which Bacon advised, and to
have been disposed to go a good way   Before he had got through
the second, when he was engaged in argument with the dissentient
doctors, he had committed himself to a position which Bacon would
certainly not have approved   "This (said he, in answer to a question how far the Church had authority to prescribe ceremonies) is
like Mr. John Black, a beardless boy, who told me, the last conference in Scotland, that he should hold conformity with his Majesty

in matters of doctrine, but every man, for ceremonies, was to be left to his own liberty But I will have none of that, I will have one doctrine, one discipline one religion, in substance and ceremony Never speak more on that point—how far you are bound to obey "[1] Now Ceremonies, in themselves indifferent, were precisely what the dissentient party most strained at, and such declarations as this, though intended to procure quiet, did in fact warn them that they must either abandon what they took for points of conscience or seek for relief elsewhere, and thereby undid the tranquillizing effect of the concessions which the King was willing to make, and which were not inconsiderable What they were it may be convenient to set down here. For they have a manifest and direct relation to the preceding paper, and this was the last occasion on which Bacon went out of his way to interpose in the quarrel, being ever after (in conformity with the profession with which he sets out) against all attempts to unsettle these questions, when they had once been by the legitimate authority "determined and ordered"

The resolution to have a conference for the consideration and settlement of them was taken in the summer or early autumn of 1603, and was announced by proclamation on the 24th of October, on occasion of postponing the meeting (originally fixed for the 1st of November) till after Christmas It took place on Saturday, the 14th of January, 1603-4 On the 18th, Dr Montague, who had been present, wrote a short and apparently a very fair account of it in a letter to his mother [2]

"The King assembling only the Lords of his Council and the Bishops, myself had the favour to be present by the King his command The company met, and himself sate in his chair He made a very admirable speech, of an hour long at least,

"His M prepounded six points unto them Three in the Common Prayer Book, two for the Bishops' jurisdiction, and one for the Kingdom of Ireland

"In the Prayer-book he named the General Absolution, the Confirmation of Children, and the Private Baptism by Women These three were long disputed between the King and the Bishops In the conclusion, the King was well satisfied in the two former, so that the manner might be changed, and some things cleared For the Private Baptism, it held three hours at least, the King alone disputing with the Bishops, so wisely, wittily, and learnedly, with that pretty patience, as I think never man living heard the like In the end he wan this of them, That it should only be administered by ministers, yet in private houses, if occasion required, and that whosoever else should baptize should be under punishment

[1] Fuller   [2] Winw Mem ii 13

"For the Commissaries' Courts and the Censures of Excommunication and Suspension, they shall be mended, and the amendment is referred to the Lord Chancellor and the Lord Chief Justice But for their common and ordinary excommunication for trifles, it shall be utterly abolished The fifth point was about the sole jurisdiction of Bishops, so he gained that of them, that the Bishops, in ordination, suspension, and degradation, and such like, they shall ever have some grave men to be assistants with them in all censures

"For Ireland, the conclusion was (the King making a most lamentable description of the state thereof), that it should be reduced to civility, planted with schools and ministers, as many as could be gotten

"These things done, he propounded matters whereabout he hoped there would be no controversy, as to have a learned ministry, and maintenance for them as far as might be And for Pluralities and Non-residences, to be taken away, or at least made so few as possibly might be"

This was the result of the first day's conference, which was between the King and the Bishops; the other party not being yet admitted and from this it would appear that the King had either anticipated or adopted most of the suggestions contained in Bacon's memorial, and was prepared to urge upon the Bishops the adoption of the principal changes which he recommended

'On Monday the King called the other party by themselves made likewise an excellent oration unto them, and then went to the matter, nobody being present but the Lords of the Council, and Dr Reynolds, Dr Sparke, Dr Field, Dr. King Mr Chadderton, and Mr Knewstubbs, all the Deans that were appointed, and myself

"They propounded four points The first, for purity of doctrine Secondly, for means to maintain it, as good ministers etc Thirdly, the Courts of Bishops, Chancellors, and Commissaries Fourthly, the Common Prayer book

"For doctrine, it was easily agreed unto by all For ministers also for jurisdiction likewise

"For the book of Common-prayer, and subscriptions to it, there was much stir about all the ceremonies and every point in it The King pleaded hard to have good proof against the Ceremonies, and if they had either the word of God against them, or good authority, he would remove them but if they had no word of God against them, but all authority for them, being already in the Church, he would never take them away For he came not to disturb the State, nor to make innovations, but to confirm whatever he found lawfully established, and to amend and correct what was corrupted by time. They argued this point very long The Bishops of Winchester and London, who of all the Bishops were present, laboured this point hard, and divers of the Deans, but at length the king undertook them himself, and examined them by the Word and by the Fathers There was not any of them that they could prove to be against the Word, but all of them confirmed by the Fathers, and that long before Popery So that, for the Ceremonies, I suppose nothing will be altered And truly the Doctors argued but weakly against them so that all wondered they had no more to say against them So that all that day was spent in Ceremonies and I think, themselves being judges, they were answered fully in everything At last it was concluded that day that there should be an uniform translation set out by the King of all the Bible, and one catechizing over all the realm, and nothing of the Apocrypha to be read that is in any sort repugnant to the Scripture, but to be still read, yet as Apocrypha, and not as Scripture, and for any point of the articles of Religion that is doubtful, to be cleared This was the second day's work '

It was a day of great honour and triumph for the King at the time and in some respects of very good service for the point of purity of *doctrine* was not in fact so easily settled as Dr Montague's report seems to imply there being a strong attempt to get inserted into the book of articles " the nine orthodoxal assertions concluded on at Lambeth " an attempt which the King resisted with spirit and firmness, to the great benefit of liberty and promotion of peace in the Church And yet it was this day's work that did the mischief, not the less The Doctors no doubt found plenty of answers to the King's arguments as soon as they got home, and plenty of audiences to appreciate them But they now knew that there was no hope of prevailing in those points *with* the King, if they were to prevail at all it must be *against* him And though it be true, as Fuller remarks, that ' thenceforward many cripples in conformity were cured of their former halting therein, and such who knew not their own till they knew the King's mind in this matter, for the future quietly digested the Ceremonies of the Church,' it was far otherwise with those who had learned to regard these points of ceremony as emblems and flags of that faith, which except every one do keep whole and undefiled, without doubt he shall perish everlastingly

" The third day, which was Wednesday, the King assembled all the Bishops (the Lords of the Council only being present), and took order how to have these things executed which he had concluded, that it might not be (as the King said) as smoke out of a tunnel, but substantially done to remain for ever So they were debated to whom they might most fitly be referred, and by them made fit to be hereafter enacted by Parliament so all the Bishops and all the Council have their parts given them This being done, the Ministers were called in, Dr Reynolds and the rest, and acquainted with what the King had concluded on They were all exceedingly well satisfied but only moved one thing That those ministers who were grave men and obedient unto the laws, and long had been exempted from the use of ceremonies, might not upon the sudden be obliged unto them, but have some time given them to resolve themselves in using or not using them. The King answered, his end being peace, his meaning was not that any man should be cruel in imposing those matters, but by time and moderation win all men unto them. Those they found peaceable, to give some connivency to such, and to use them brethren, as he had used them, with meekness and gentleness, and do all things to the edification of God and his Church. So they ended these matters till the Parliament, and then these matters shall be enacted.

"A Note of such things as shall be reformed.

"1. The *Absolution* shall be called the Absolution or General Confession of Sins.

"2. The *Confirmation* shall be called the Confirmation or further examination of the children's faith.

"3. The *Private Baptism* (now by laymen or women used) shall be called the Private Baptism by the Ministers and Curates only, and all those questions in that Baptism, that institute it to be done by women, taken away.

"4. The *Apocrypha*, that hath any repugnancy to the canonical Scriptures, to be laid aside; and other places chosen, which either are explanations of Scripture, or serve best for good life and manners.

"5. The *Jurisdiction of Bishops* shall be somewhat limited, and to have either the Dean and Chapter, or some grave ministers assistant unto them, in ordination, suspension, degrading, etc.

"6. The *Excommunication*, as it is now used, shall be taken away both in name and nature, and a writ out of Chancery shall be framed to punish the contumacies.

"7. The Kingdom of *Ireland*, the borders of *Scotland*, and all *Wales*, to be planted with schools and preachers, as soon as may be.

"8. As many *learned Ministers*, and maintenance for them, to be provided in such places in England where there is want as can be.

"9. As few *double beneficed men* and *pluralities* as may be, and those that have double benefices to maintain Preachers, and to have their livings as near as may be the one to the other.

"10. One uniform *translation* to be made, and only used in all the Churches of England.

"11. One *Catechism* only to be made and used in all places.

"12. The *Articles of Religion* to be explained and enlarged, and no man to teach or read against any of them.

"13. A care to be had to observe who doth not receive the Communion once in a year. The Ministers to certify to the Bishops, the Bishops to the Archbishops, the Archbishops to the King.

"14. A care had to inhibit *Popish books* from coming over; and if they come over, to be delivered into those men's hands that may give them out only to persons fit to have them.

"15. The *High Commission* to be reformed, and to be reduced to

K 2

higher causes, and fewer persons, and those of more honour and of better quality "

Such were the immediate results of the conference, as then under stood and intended which if they had been simply announced as decisions taken by the King in Council upon consideration of the complaints and petitions,—without any personal disputation,—would in all probability have done a good deal towards the pacification of controversies and the union of action among the different parties in the Church And here the matter, as far as Bacon had anything to do with it may be considered as resting for the present

CHAPTER IV.

A.D 1603. ÆTAT 43.

1.

How little disposition there was to employ Bacon in the business of the Learned Counsel at this time, is well seen in the fact that his name does not anywhere appear in connexion with that singular conspiracy, or series of conspiracies, which ruffled the otherwise universal quiet of James's entrance into England —a conspiracy in which so many representatives of different parties—the Catholic priest at open war with the Jesuits, the ordinary Catholic country gentleman, the high-couraged Puritan nobleman, the ambitious disappointed courtier, and (strangest of all) the soldier-sailor statesman distinguished in peace and war for inveterate enmity to Spain—having no common object to aim at, no pretence to put forward, no injuries to resent, no adherents to rely upon, but drawn, it seems, only by a common hope of profiting in their several ways by the chances of confusion,—met together in an insane project for overpowering the government As Bacon took no part either in the investigation or the trials, as he has not left on record so much as an opinion upon any of the questions at issue, and as the current of affairs was not materially affected either by the attempt or the proceedings which followed, I am happily relieved from the duty of attempting to make the history of it intelligible It is enough to say here that the main plot—commonly called the 'Priests' plot,' but in which Lord Grey the Puritan was an accomplice—came to the knowledge of the government about midsummer, and fell to pieces at once that before Christmas the several persons implicated had been tried and found guilty that the Priests, against whom the case was strongest and clearest, were hanged, and the rest, with general consent and applause, respited and that if it had not been for the manner in which the trial of Ralegh was conducted,—for which I think Sir Edward Coke must be held singly responsible,—the whole thing would have ended there, and produced no further effect, direct or indirect. The trial of Ralegh, however, had one very extraordinary result at the time, and became by a strange accident the cause of a serious embarrassment long after, with which we shall be more particularly concerned; it may be well therefore to add a few words as to the position in which he was left.

Ralegh had passed his fiftieth year, had been a brilliant and conspicuous figure in various fields of enterprise from his youth, had never been conspicuously engaged in actions hostile or offensive to the people, had already performed all the deeds (his great literary work excepted) on which his fame rests, and yet he had never been popular, but the contrary. And since his popularity dates from the day on which he was put upon his trial and made his own defence, it is natural to suppose that the cause in which he spoke and suffered was not only good in law but gracious with the people. This however was by no means the case. He went to his trial a man so unpopular that he was hooted and pelted on the road; he came out an object of general pity and admiration, and has held his place ever since as one of England's favourite and representative heroes; and yet, if we except his gallant bearing and splendid abilities (which were no new revelations) there was nothing in his case which could have tended either to excite popular sympathy or command popular respect; nor has anything been discovered since that enables us to explain his connexion with the plot in a way at all favourable to his character. By his own showing he had been in intimate and confidential relations with a man whom nobody liked or respected, and who was secretly seeking help from the hated Spaniard in a plot to dispossess James in favour of the Lady Arabella. By his own admission he had at least listened to an offer of a large sum of money,—certainly Spanish, and therefore presumably in consideration of some service to be rendered to Spain. And though it is true that we do not know with what purposes he listened, how much he knew, how far he acquiesced, or what he intended to do, it is impossible to believe that his intentions (whether treasonable or not) were, or were then supposed to be either popular or patriotic. He did not himself attempt to put any such colour upon his proceedings, declaring only that he did not know of the plot in which his confidential friends were engaged. His blindest advocates have not succeeded in doing it for him. And those who, though partial, have taken pains to examine and felt bound to respect the evidence, have scarcely succeeded even in believing him innocent. Among the students of his life in recent times there has been none more truly desirous to find heroic virtue in all his aims and actions than Mr. Macvey Napier; yet in endeavouring to explain his connexion with Lord Cobham, as disclosed in the course of this trial, he is driven to suspect him of a design so far from heroic in itself that it is hard to understand how it could find place in a mind in which the heroic element predominated.

"Old Major Stansby of   Hants," says Aubrey, "a most intimate friend and neighbour and coetanean of the late Earl of Southampton (Ld Treas) told me from his friend the Earl, that as to the plot and business about the Ld Cobham, &c, he [Ralegh] being then governor of Jersey, would not fully or &c [*sic*] unless they would go to his island, and that really and indeed Sir Walter's purpose was, when he had gotten them there, to have betrayed them and the plot, and so have delivered them up to the King, and made his peace."[1]

To this report Mr Napier refers us,[2] after an elaborate discussion of the evidence, as containing the explanation of Ralegh's connexion with the plot which he seems inclined to accept as upon the whole most probable. And it must be admitted that of the difficulties which his case presents one at least would be removed by it. Had his case been clear, it is incredible to me that, with such a head, such a heart, and such a tongue, he would have left it so ambiguous that a worshipper of his memory is driven to a conjecture like this. But if the conjecture be true—if it be possible to suppose that he had been really inviting his friend's confidence with the intention of betraying it[3]—that difficulty vanishes. Upon that supposition we may say that he purposely left the case dark, because he knew it would not bear the light. and if so, his handling of it so as to produce such a wonderful revolution of popular opinion in his own favour must surely be regarded as one of the most surprising feats of audacity and genius that the wit of man ever achieved.

I quote this however not as an explanation satisfactory to myself, but only as evidence that the case was and is still thought to require explanation. for beyond this the report is of little or no value. It proves only that Ralegh's famous defence left people to wonder and guess how far and in what way he was really implicated; and that this was one of the guesses in circulation half a century after.

But though the question of his guilt or innocence remains doubtful, and the verdict of the Jury (who were better acquainted with the evidence than their outside critics, whose judgment was formed

[1] Aubrey's Lives, iii p 516   Edin Rev, April, 1810, p 63
[3] Napier's own version of Aubrey's story is, "that Ralegh's intention really was to inveigle Cobham to Jersey, and then, having got both him and his Spanish treasure in his power, to make terms with the King."

upon very imperfect reports—for no official statement was published)
may for anything we know have been substantially just, the conduct
of the trial cannot be defended   The unfair advantages insisted on
by the Attorney General on behalf of the Crown, and allowed by the
Judges, turned by a natural reaction to the great disadvantage of
the Crown in the court of popular opinion, and left a blot in the
tables which imperilled the whole game, and the effect of which was
felt long afterwards—as we shall see in due time   For the present,
Ralegh remained a prisoner in the Tower, respited, not pardoned,
still under attainder for High Treason, and therefore, as the Law
phrased it, "civilly dead"—a man who, being alive in fact was still
capable of committing new crimes and offences, but being dead in
law, was not capable of being "drawn in question judicially"[1] for
any crime or offence he might afterwards commit —a man, in short,
to whom Justice was thenceforward forbidden by Law

In all this, Bacon, though no doubt an earnest and anxious ob
server, had no part as actor, adviser, or reporter   He came in for a
share in the subsequent embarrassment, but was no way concerned
in preparing the materials out of which it grew

Neither do I find that he had anything to do with the negotia
tions which ended not long after in the treaty of peace with Spain
a treaty of which the policy was and is disputed, but the considera
tion does not concern my subject.

2.

To this period however belongs one other paper of great importance, to which I have already had frequently to refer,—a paper very
interesting to me, as being one of those by which I was first at
tracted long ago to the study of Bacon's personal character and
history, and which grows in interest as the case is better understood   The exact date of the composition I do not know, further
than that the earliest printed copy bears 1601 on its title-page   If
printed *early* in 1601, here is its proper place, and here at any
rate it will come in most conveniently

If the popular disapprobation excited at the time by Bacon's conduct towards the Earl of Essex was as great and as universal as it is
usually assumed to have been by modern writers, it seems strange
that proofs of the fact should not be more abundant   I believe
however that the only contemporary witness who can be cited to

---

[1] Draft, in Coke's hand, of a letter to the King concerning the form and manner
of proceeding against Sir Walter Ralegh   Oct 18 1618   Lambeth MSS   Gib
Pap viii 21

prove the existence of any disapprobation at all, is Bacon himself,
and though his evidence proves conclusively that disapprobation
had been expressed, the absence or silence of other witnesses proves
almost as conclusively that it had not been expressed very generally
or very loudly

Such as it was, it had grown out of misinformation as to the part
which he had really taken in the matter   For when Essex on his
return from Ireland was committed to custody, those of his friends
who, not knowing the circumstances, could not otherwise account
for his loss of favour, naturally imputed it to the influence of some
enemy at Court, and as the news ran that "all the Lords were in
this matter his friends, for all spoke for him "[1] while of Bacon it
was only known that he was at that time frequently admitted to
speech with the Queen, their suspicion not unnaturally fell upon
him, and a suspicion in such cases soon becomes a rumour   Now a
rumour of this kind could not be satisfactorily met without the dis-
closure of confidential conversations in which others were concerned.
It was allowed accordingly to prevail, and produced its natural effect.
"Pity in the common people, if it run in a strong stream, doth
ever cast up scandal and envy,'[2] and the pity which ran so strongly
in favour of Essex had cast up scandal and envy against Bacon
From the duty of bearing it in silence he was now by the death of
the Queen partly released   he could now judge for himself what
and how much he was at liberty to disclose of that which had passed
between them   Whether any particular occasion impelled him to
speak at this time—any revival of the calumny (such as James's
supposed partiality for Essex and his open favour towards the surviving members of the party would naturally encourage), or some
expression which may possibly have fallen from the Earl of Southampton upon his offer of congratulation—or whether it was merely
that he wished to take the earliest opportunity of clearing himself
from a painful and undeserved imputation—I cannot say   for no
record remains to show what was said of him, or when, or by whom,
except what may be collected from the terms of his answer   But
the time was in one respect very convenient   For Lord Montjoy,
who was cognisant of the whole case—those parts of it which could
not yet be made public as well as the rest—was now in England and
in high reputation, newly created Earl of Devonshire and Lord
Lieutenant of Ireland   He had been deeply involved in some of
Essex's most secret intrigues,[3] and had only escaped the consequences

---

[1] Sydney Papers, ii 156   [2] Hist of Hen VII   Works, VI p 203
[3] See Vol II pp 167, 170   The fact that Montjoy had been implicated to an
extent which he felt to be dangerous, is fully confirmed by Fynes Morison's

through a bold connivance on the Queen's part, who wanted his service and felt that she could trust him, and made him understand that she meant to be ignorant of what had passed   No man could be less suspected of an inclination to judge Bacon's conduct too favourably   No man was so little likely to be deceived by a false story, nor was any man, on the other hand so well qualified to understand the full meaning of the true story in those parts where the meaning could not yet be fully explained   To him, therefore, as to the best and fairest representative of the party by whom he was censured or suspected, Bacon now addressed a letter of explanation, which I leave to speak for itself, premising only that the object of it is, not to justify himself for neglecting the duties which in the common understanding of the world a man owes to his benefactor but to show that he had to the best of his judgment and ability discharged them, up to the time when it became impossible to take his part further without betraying duties still more sacred   And if he does not enter into a formal vindication of the part he took at and after the trial, his motive may be easily conjectured   He could not have done it without repeating the story of Essex's offence, at a time when it would have served no higher object than the clearing of his own reputation

account of his proceedings upon the news of Essex's insurrection and apprehension   "The same two and twentieth of February, his Lordship received a packet out of England, by which he understood that the Earl of Essex was committed to the Tower for treason, which much dismayed him and his nearest friends, and wrought strange alteration in him   For whereas before he stood upon terms of honour with the Secretary, now he fell flat to the ground, and insinuated himself into inward love, and to an absolute dependency with the Secretary, so as for a time he estranged himself from two of his nearest friends, for the open declaration they had made of dependency on the Earl of Essex, yet rather covering than extinguishing his good affection to them   It is not credible that the influence of the Earl's malignant star should work upon so poor a snake as myself, being almost a stranger to him, yet my nearness in blood to one of his Lordship's above named friends made it perhaps seem to his Lordship improper to use my service in such nearness as his Lordship had promised and begun to do   So as the next day he took his most secret papers out of my hand, yet giving them to no other, but keeping them in his own cabinet   In truth his Lordship had good cause to be wary in his words and actions, since by some confessions in England, himself was tainted with privity to the Earl's practices, so that however he continued still to importune leave to come over, yet no doubt he meant nothing less, but rather (if he had been sent for) was purposed with his said friends to sail into France, they having privately fitted themselves with money and necessaries thereunto   For howsoever his Lordship were not dangerously engaged therein, yet he was (as he privately professed) fully resolved not to put his neck under the file of the Queen's Attorney's tongue "—Itinerary, part II book I c 2, p 89

SIR FRANCIS BACON HIS APOLOGIE,

IN

CERTAINE IMPUTATIONS

CONCERNING

THE LATE EARLE OF ESSEX

WRITTEN TO

THE RIGHT HONORABLE HIS VERY GOOD LORD, THE EARLE OF DEVONSHIRE,

LORD LIEUTENANT OF IRELAND.

LONDON

PRINTED FOR FELIX NORTON, AND ARE TO BE SOLD IN PAUL'S CHURCHYARD
AT THE SIGNE OF THE PAROT

1604

TO THE RIGHT HONOURABLE HIS
VERY GOOD LORD THE EARL OF DEVONSHIRE,
LORD LIEUTENANT OF IRELAND

It may please your good Lordship I cannot be ignorant, and ought to be sensible, of the wrong which I sustain in common speech, as if I had been false or unthankful to that noble but unfortunate Earl, the Earl of Essex and for satisfying the vulgar sort, I do no so much regard it, though I love good name, but yet as an handmaid and attendant of honesty and virtue For I am of his opinion that said pleasantly, *That it was a shame to him that was a suitor to the mistress, to make love to the waiting-woman*, and therefore to woo or court common fame otherwise than it followeth upon honest courses, I, for my part, find not myself fit nor disposed But on the other side, there is no worldly thing that concerneth myself which I hold more dear than the good opinion of certain persons, amongst which there is none I would more willingly give satisfaction unto than to your Lordship. First, because you loved my Lord of Essex, and therefore will not be partial towards me, which is part of that I desire next, because it hath ever pleased you to show yourself to me an honourable friend, and so no baseness in me to seek to satisfy you and lastly, because I know your Lordship is excellently grounded in the true rules and habits of duties and moralities, which must be they which shall decide this matter wherein (my Lord) my defence needeth to be but simple and brief namely, that whatsoever I did concerning that action and proceeding, was done in my duty and service to the Queen and the State, in which I would not show myself false-hearted nor faint-hearted for any man's sake living For every honest man, that hath his heart well planted, will forsake his King

rather than forsake God, and forsake his friend rather than forsake his King, and yet will forsake any earthly commodity, yea
and his own life in some cases, rather than forsake his friend
I hope the world hath not forgotten these degrees, else the
heathen saying, *Amicus usque ad aras*, shall judge them. And
if any man shall say that I did officiously intrude myself into
that business, because I had no ordinary place, the like may be
said of all the business in effect that passed the hands of the
learned counsel, either of State or Revenues, these many years,
wherein I was continually used For, as your Lordship may
remember, the Queen knew her strength so well, as she looked
her word should be a warrant, and after the manner of the
choicest princes before her, did not always tie her trust to place,
but did sometime divide private favour from office And I for
my part, though I was not so unseen in the world but I knew
the condition was subject to envy and peril, yet because I
knew again she was constant in her favours, and made an end
where she began, and specially because she upheld me with
extraordinary access, and other demonstrations of confidence
and grace, I resolved to endure it in expectation of better But
my scope and desire is, that your Lordship would be pleased
to have the honourable patience to know the truth in some particularity of all that passed in this cause wherein I had any
part, that you may perceive how honest a heart I ever bare to
my Sovereign and to my Country, and to that Nobleman, who
had so well deserved of me, and so well accepted of my deservings, whose fortune I cannot remember without much grief
But for any action of mine towards him, there is nothing that
passed me in my life-time that cometh to my remembrance
with more clearness and less check of conscience, for it will
appear to your Lordship that I was not only not opposite to my
Lord of Essex, but that I did occupy the utmost of my wits,
and adventure my fortune with the Queen to have reintegrated
his, and so continued faithfully and industriously till his last
fatal impatience (for so I will call it), after which day there was
not time to work for him, though the same my affection, when
it could not work on the subject proper, went to the next, with
no ill effect towards some others, who I think do rather not
know it than not acknowledge it And this I will assure your
Lordship, I will leave nothing untold that is truth, for any

enemy that I have to add , and on the other side, I must reserve much which makes for me, upon many respects of duty, which I esteem above my credit and what I have here set down to your Lordship, I protest, as I hope to have any part in God's favour, is true

It is well known, how I did many years since dedicate my travels and studies to the use and (as I may term it) service of my Lord of Essex, which, I protest before God, I did not, making election of him as the likeliest mean of mine own advancement, but out of the humour of a man, that ever, from the time I had any use of reason (whether it were reading upon good books, or upon the example of a good father, or by nature) I loved my country more than was answerable to my fortune, and I held at that time my Lord to be the fittest instrument to do good to the State, and therefore I applied myself to him in a manner which I think happeneth rarely amongst men for I did not only labour carefully and industriously in that he set me about, whether it were matter of advice or otherwise, but neglecting the Queen's service, mine own fortune, and in a sort my vocation, I did nothing but devise and ruminate with myself to the best of my understanding, propositions and memorials of any thing that might concern his Lordship's honour, fortune, or service And when not long afte I entered into this course, my brother Master Anthony Bacon came from beyond the seas, being a gentleman whose ability the world taketh knowledge of for matters of State, specially foreign, I did likewise knit his service to be at my Lord's disposing. And on the other side, I must and will ever acknowledge my Lord's love, trust, and favour towards me, and last of all his liberality, having infeoffed me of land which I sold for eighteen hundred pounds to Master Reynold Nicholas, and I think was more worth, and that at such a time, and with so kind and noble circumstances, as the manner was as much as the matter, which though it be but an idle digression, yet because I am not willing to be short in commemoration of his benefits, I will presume to trouble your Lordship with relating to you the manner of it. After the Queen had denied me the Solicitor's place, for the which his Lordship had been a long and earnest suitor on my behalf, it pleased him to come to me from Richmond to Twicknam Park, and brake with me, and said : Master Bacon, the Queen hath denied me you place for you, and hath placed another, I know you are the least part of your own matter, but you fare ill because you have chosen me for your mean and dependance, you have spent your time and thoughts in my matters, I die (these were his very words) if I do not somewhat towards your fortune you shall not deny to accept a piece of land which I will bestow upon you My answer I remember was, that for my fortune it was no great matter, but that his Lordship's offer made me call to mind what was wont to be said when I was in France of the Duke of Guise, that he was the greatest usurer in France, because he had turned all his estate into obligations meaning that he had left himself nothing, but only had bound numbers of persons to him Now my Lord (said I) I would not have you imitate his course, nor turn your state thus by great gifts into obligations, for you will find many bad debtors He bade me take no care for that, and pressed it whereupon I said My Lord, I see I must be your homager, and hold land of your gift, but do you know the manner of doing homage in law ? always it is with a saving of his faith to the King and his other Lords, and therefore, my Lord (said I), I can be no more yours than I was, and it must be with the ancient savings and if I grow to be a rich man, you will give me leave to give it back to some of your unrewarded followers. But to return sure I am (though I can arrogate nothing to myself but that I was a faithful remembrancer to his Lordship) that while I had most credit with him his fortune went on best And yet in two main points we always directly and contradictorily differed, which I will mention to your Lordship, because it giveth light to all that followed. The one was, I ever set this down, that the only course to be held with the Queen, was by obsequiousness and observance, and I remember I would usually gage confidently, that if he would take that course constantly, and with choice of good particulars to express it, the Queen would be brought in time to Assuerus question, to ask, *What should be done to the man that the King would honour* meaning, that her goodness was without limit, where there was a true concurrence, which I knew in her nature to be true My Lord on the other side had a settled opinion, that the Queen could be brought to nothing but by a kind of necessity and authority, and I well remember, when by violent courses at any time he had got his will, he would

ask me Now Sir, *whose principles be true?* and I would again
say to him *My Lord, these courses be like to hot waters, they
will help at a pang, but if you use them, you shall spoil the
stomach, and you shall be fain still to make them stronger and
stronger, and yet in the end they will lesse their operation;* with
much other variety, wherewith I used to touch that string.
Another point was, that I always vehemently dissuaded him from
seeking greatness by a military dependance, or by a popular
dependance, as that which would breed in the Queen jealousy,
in himself presumption, and in the State perturbation and I
did usually compare them to Icarus' two wings which were joined
on with wax, and would make him venture to soar too high,
and then fail him at the height. And I would further say unto
him, My Lord, stand upon two feet, and fly not upon two wings.
The two feet are the two kinds of Justice, commutative and distributive use your greatness for advancing of merit and virtue,
and relieving wrongs and burdens, you shall need no other art
or fineness but he would tell me, that opinion came not from
my mind but from my robe But it is very true that I, that
never meant to enthral myself to my Lord of Essex, nor any
other man, more than stood with the public good, did (though I
could little prevail) divert him by all means possible from courses
of the wars and popularity · for I saw plainly the Queen must
either live or die, if she lived, then the times would be as in the
declination of an old prince, if she died, the times would be as
in the beginning of a new, and that if his Lordship did rise too
fast in these courses, the times might be dangerous for him, and
he for them Nay, I remember I was thus plain with him upon
his voyage to the Islands, when I saw every spring put forth
such actions of charge and provocation, that I said to him : My
Lord, when I came first unto you, I took you for a physician
that desired to cure the diseases of the State, but now I doubt
you will be like those physicians which can be content to keep
their patients low, because they would always be in request
which plainness he nevertheless took very well, as he had an excellent ear, and was *patientissimus veri*, and assured me the case
of the realm required it and I think this speech of mine, and
the like renewed afterwards, pricked him to write that Apology
which is in many men's hands.

But this difference in two points so main and material, bred

in process of time a discontinuance of privateness (as it is the
manner of men seldom to communicate where they think their
courses not approved) between his Lordship and myself, so as
I was not called nor advised with, for some year and a half before his Lordship's going into Ireland, as in former time : yet
nevertheless touching his going into Ireland, it pleased him expressly and in a set manner to desire mine opinion and counsel
At which time I did not only dissuade, but protest against his
going, telling him with as much vehemency and asseveration as
I could, that absence in that kind would exulcerate the Queen's
mind, whereby it would not be possible for him to carry himself
so as to give her sufficient contentment; nor for her to carry
herself so as to give him sufficient countenance which would be
ill for her, ill for him, and ill for the State.   And because I would
omit no argument, I remember I stood also upon the difficulty
of the action, setting before him out of histories, that the Irish
was such an enemy as the ancient Gauls, or Britons, or Germans
were, and that we saw how the Romans, who had such discipline
to govern their soldiers, and such donatives to encourage them
and the whole world in a manner to levy them; yet when they
came to deal with enemies which placed their felicity only in
liberty and the sharpness of their sword, and had the natural
and elemental advantages of woods, and bogs, and hardness of
bodies, they ever found they had their hands full of them, and
therefore concluded, that going over with such expectation as he
did, and through the churlishness[1] of the enterprize not like to
answer it, would mightily diminish his reputation and many
other reasons I used, so as I am sure I never in any thing in my
life-time dealt with him in like earnestness by speech, by writing,
and by all the means I could devise For I did as plainly see
his overthrow chained as it were by destiny to that journey, as
it is possible for any man to ground a judgment upon future
contingents But my Lord, howsoever his ear was open, yet
his heart and resolution was shut against that advice, whereby
his ruin might have been prevented. After my Lord's going, I
saw how true a prophet I was, in regard of the evident alteration which naturally succeeded in the Queen's mind; and thereupon I was still in watch to find the best occasion that in the
weakness of my power I could either take or minister, to pull

[1] curlishness, in orig

him out of the fire if it had been possible: and not long after, methought I saw some overture thereof, which I apprehended readily, a particularity I think be[1] known to very few, and the which I do the rather relate unto your Lordship, because I hear it should be talked, that while my Lord was in Ireland I revealed some matter against him, or I cannot tell what; which if it were not a mere slander as the rest is, but had any though never so little colour, was surely upon this occasion The Queen one day at Nonesuch, a little (as I remember) before Cuffe's coming over, I attending her, shewed a passionate distaste of my Lord's proceedings in Ireland, as if they were unfortunate, without judgment, contemptuous, and not without some private end of his own, and all that might be, and was pleased, as she spake of it to many that she trusted least, so to fall into the like speech with me; whereupon I, who was still awake and true to my grounds which I thought surest for my Lord's good, said to this effect Madam, I know not the particulars of estate, and I know this, that Princes' actions must have no abrupt periods or conclusions, but otherwise I would think, that if you had my Lord of Essex here with a white staff in his hand, as my Lord of Leicester had, and continued him still about you for society to yourself, and for an honour and ornament to your attendance and Court in the eyes of your people, and in the eyes of foreign Embassadors, then were he in his right element for to discontent him as you do, and yet to put arms and power into his hands, may be a kind of temptation to make him prove cumbersome and unruly.   And therefore if you would *imponere bonam clausulam*, and send for him and satisfy him with honour here near you, if your affairs which (as I have said) I am not acquainted with, will permit it, I think were the best way. Which course, your Lordship knoweth, if it had been taken, then all had been well, and no contempt in my Lord's coming over, nor continuance of these jealousies, which that employment of Ireland bred, and my Lord here in his former greatness. Well, the next news that I heard was, that my Lord was come over, and that he was committed to his chamber for leaving Ireland without the Queen's licence this was at Nonesuch, where (as my duty was) I came to his Lordship, and talked with him privately about a quarter of an hour, and he asked mine

[1] So in orig

L 2

opinion of the course was taken with him, I told him, My Lord, *Nubecula est, cito transibit*, it is but a mist: but shall I tell your Lordship, it is as mists are, if it go upwards, it may haps cause a shower, if downwards, it will clear up. And therefore good my Lord carry it so, as you take away by all means all umbrages and distastes from the Queen, and specially, if I were worthy to advise you (as I have been by yourself thought, and now your question imports the continuance of that opinion) observe three points. First, make not this cessation or peace which is concluded with Tyrone, as a service wherein you glory, but as a shuffling up of a prosecution which was not very fortunate. Next, represent not to the Queen any necessity of estate, whereby, as by a coercion or wrench, she should think herself inforced to send you back into Ireland, but leave it to her. Thirdly, seek access *importunè, opportunè*, seriously, sportingly, every way. I remember my Lord was willing to hear me, but spake very few words, and shaked his head sometimes, as if he thought I was in the wrong; but sure I am, he did just contrary in every one of these three points. After this, during the while since my Lord was committed to my Lord Keeper's, I came divers times to the Queen, as I had used to do, about causes of her revenue and law business, as is well known, by reason of which accesses, according to the ordinary charities of Court, it was given out that I was one of them that incensed the Queen against my Lord of Essex. These speeches, I cannot tell, nor I will not think, that they grew any way from her Majesty's own speeches, whose memory I will ever honour; if they did, she is with God, and *miserum est ab illis lædi, de quibus non possis queri*. But I must give this testimony to my Lord Cecil, that one time in his house at the Savoy he dealt with me directly, and said to me, Cousin, I hear it, but I believe it not, that you should do some ill office to my Lord of Essex; for my part I am merely passive and not active in this action, and I follow the Queen and that heavily, and I lead her not; my Lord of Essex is one that in nature I could consent with as well as with any one living, the Queen indeed is my Sovereign, and I am her creature, I may not leese her, and the same course I would wish you to take· whereupon I satisfied him how far I was from any such mind. And as sometimes it cometh to pass, that men's inclinations are opened more in a toy, than in a

serious matter: A little before that time, being about the middle
of Michaelmas term, her Majesty had a purpose to dine at my
lodge at Twicknam Park, at which time I had (though I profess
not to be a poet) prepared a sonnet directly tending and alluding
to draw on her Majesty's reconcilement to my Lord, which I
remember also I shewed to a great person, and one of my Lord's
nearest friends, who commended it. this, though it be (as I
said) but a toy, yet it shewed plainly in what spirit I proceeded,
and that I was ready not only to do my Lord good offices, but
to publish and declare myself for him : and never was so ambitious of any thing in my life-time, as I was to have carried some
token or favour from her Majesty to my Lord. using all the art
I had, both to procure her Majesty to send, and myself to be
the messenger. for as to the former, I feared not to allege to
her, that this proceeding toward my Lord was a thing towards the
people very implausible, and therefore wished her Majesty, howsoever she did, yet to discharge herself of it, and to lay it upon
others, and therefore that she should intermix her proceeding
with some immediate graces from herself, that the world might
take knowledge of her princely nature and goodness, lest it
should alienate the hearts of her people from her.   Which I did
stand upon, knowing very well that if she once relented to send
or visit, those demonstrations would prove matter of substance for
my Lord's good   And to draw that employment upon myself,
I advised her Majesty, that whensoever God should move her to
turn the light of her favour towards my Lord, to make signification to him thereof, that her Majesty, if she did it not in
person, would at the least use some such mean as might not
intitle themselves to any part of the thanks, as persons that
were thought mighty with her, to work her, or to bring her
about; but to use some such as could not be thought but a mere
conduct of her own goodness. but I could never prevail with
her, though I am persuaded she saw plainly whereat I levelled;
but she had me in jealousy, that I was not hers intirely, but
still had inward and deep respects towards my Lord, more
than stood at that time with her will and pleasure.   About the
same time I remember an answer of mine in a matter which
had some affinity with my Lord's cause, which though it grew
from me, went after about in others' names.   For her Majesty
being mightily incensed with that book which was dedicated to

my Lord of Essex, being a story of the first year of King Henry
the fourth, thinking it a seditious prelude to put into the
people's heads boldness and faction, said she had good opinion
that there was treason in it, and asked me if I could not find
any places in it that might be drawn within case of treason
whereto I answered for treason surely I found none, but for
felony very many. And when her Majesty hastily asked me
wherein, I told her the author had committed very apparent
theft, for he had taken most of the sentences of Cornelius
Tacitus, and translated them into English, and put them into his
text. And another time, when the Queen would not be persuaded that it was his writing whose name was to it, but that
it had some more mischievous author, and said with great indignation that she would have him racked to produce his author,
I replied, Nay Madam, he is a Doctor, never rack his person,
but rack his stile, let him have pen, ink, and paper, and help of
books, and be enjoined to continue the story where it breaketh
off, and I will undertake by collecting[1] the stiles to judge
whether he were the author or no   But for the main matter,
sure I am, when the Queen at any time asked mine opinion of
my Lord's case, I ever in one tenour said unto her ; That they
were faults which the law might term contempts, because they
were the transgression of her particular directions and instructions: but then what defence might be made of them, in regard
of the great interest the person had in her Majesty's favour,
in regard of the greatness of his place, and the ampleness of
his commission , in regard of the nature of the business, being
action of war, which in common cases cannot be tied to strict-
ness of instructions, in regard of the distance of place, having
also a sea between, that demands and commands must be sub
ject to wind and weather, in regard of a counsel of State in
Ireland which he had at his back to avow his actions upon,
and lastly, in regard of a good intention that he would allege
for himself, which I told her in some religions was held to be
a sufficient dispensation for God's commandments, much more
for Princes' in all these regards, I besought her Majesty to be
advised again and again, how she brought the cause into any
public question nay, I went further, for I told her, my Lord
was an eloquent and well-spoken man, and besides his eloquence

[1] So in orig

of nature or art, he had an eloquence of accident which passed
them both, which was the pity and benevolence of his hearers;
and therefore that when he should come to his answer for himself, I doubted his words would have so unequal passage above
theirs that should charge him, as would not be for her Majesty's honour, and therefore wished the conclusion might be,
that they might wrap it up privately between themselves, and
that she would restore my Lord to his former attendance, with
some addition of honour to take away discontent   But this I
will never deny, that I did show no approbation generally of
his being sent back again into Ireland, both because it would
have carried a repugnancy with my former discourse and because I was in mine own heart fully persuaded that it was not
good, neither for the Queen, nor for the State, nor for himself:
and yet I did not dissuade it neither, but left it ever as *locus
lubricus*.   For this particularity I do well remember, that after
your Lordship was named for the place in Ireland, and not long
before your going, it pleased her Majesty at Whitehall to speak
to me of that nomination at which time I said to her; Surely
Madam, if you mean not to employ my Lord of Essex thither
again, your Majesty cannot make a better choice; and was
going on to shew some reason, and her Majesty interrupted
me with great passion · Essex! (said she), whensoever I send
Essex back again into Ireland, I will marry you, claim it of
me whereunto I said; Well Madam, I will release that contract, if his going be for the good of your State.   Immediately
after the Queen had thought of a course (which was also executed) to have somewhat published in the Star-chamber, for
the satisfaction of the world touching my Lord of Essex his restraint, and my Lord of Essex not to be called to it, but occasion
to be taken by reason of some libels then dispersed which when
her Majesty propounded unto me, I was utterly against it, and
told her plainly, that the people would say that my Lord was
wounded upon his back, and that Justice had her balance taken
from her, which ever consisted of an accusation and defence,
with many other quick and significant terms to that purpose:
insomuch that I remember I said, that my Lord *in foro famæ*
was too hard for her; and therefore wished her, as I had done
before, to wrap it up privately.   And certainly I offended her
at that time, which was rare with me . for I call to mind, that

both the Christmas, Lent, and Easter term following, though I came divers times to her upon law business, yet methought her face and manner was not so clear and open to me as it was at the first And she did directly charge me, that I was absent that day at the Star-chamber, which was very true; but I alledged some indisposition of body to excuse it and during all the time aforesaid, there was *altum silentium* from her to me touching my Lord of Essex causes.

But towards the end of Easter term, her Majesty brake with me, and told me that she had found my words true : for that the proceeding in the Star-chamber had done no good, but rather kindled factious bruits (as she termed them) than quenched them, and therefore that she was determined now for the satisfaction of the world, to proceed against my Lord in the Star-chamber by an information *ore tenus*, and to have my Lord brought to his answer howbeit she said she would assure me that whatsoever she did should be towards my Lord *ad castigationem, et non ad destructionem*, as indeed she had often repeated the same phrase before whereunto I said (to the end utterly to divert her) Madam, if you will have me speak to you in this argument, I must speak to you as Friar Bacon's head spake, that said first, *Time is*, and then *Time was*, and *Time would never be* · for certainly (said I) it is now far too late, the matter is cold and hath taken too much wind, whereat she seemed again offended and rose from me, and that resolution for a while continued, and after, in the beginning of Midsummer term, I attending her, and finding her settled in that resolution (which I heard of also otherwise), she falling upon the like speech, it is true that, seeing no other remedy, I said to her slightly, Why, Madam, if you will needs have a proceeding, you were best have it in some such sort as Ovid spake of his mistress, *Est aliquid luce patente minus*, to make a counsel-table matter of it, and there an end , which speech again she seemed to take in ill part , but yet I think it did good at that time, and help to divert that course of proceeding by information in the Star-chamber Nevertheless afterwards it pleased her to make a more solemn matter of the proceeding ; and some few days after, when[1] order was given that the matter should be heard at York-house, before an assembly of Counsellors, Peers, and Judges, and some audience of men of quality to be admitted,

[1] So in orig

and then did some principal counsellors send for us of the learned counsel, and notify her Majesty's pleasure unto us, save that it was said to me openly by one of them, that her Majesty was not yet resolved whether she would have me forborne in the business or no. And hereupon might arise that other sinister and untrue speech that I hear is raised of me, how I was a suitor to be used against my Lord of Essex at that time; for it is very true that I, that knew well what had passed between the Queen and me, and what occasion I had given her both of distaste and distrust in crossing her disposition by standing stedfastly for my Lord of Essex, and suspecting it also to be a stratagem arising from some particular emulation, I writ to her two or three words of compliment, signifying to her Majesty, that if she would be pleased to spare me in my Lord of Essex cause, out of the consideration she took of my obligation towards him, I should reckon it for one of her highest favours; but otherwise desiring her Majesty to think that I knew the degrees of duties, and that no particular obligation whatsoever to any subject could supplant or weaken that entireness of duty that I did owe and bear to her and her service; and this was the goodly suit I made, being a respect that no man that had his wits could have omitted. but nevertheless I had a further reach in it, for I judged that day's work would be a full period of any bitterness or harshness between the Queen and my Lord, and therefore if I declared myself fully according to her mind at that time, which could not do my Lord any manner of prejudice, I should keep my credit with her ever after, whereby to do my Lord service. Hereupon the next news that I heard was, that we were all sent for again, and that her Majesty's pleasure was, we all should have parts in the business, and the Lords falling into distribution of our parts, it was allotted to me, that I should set forth some undutiful carriage of my Lord, in giving occasion and countenance to a seditious pamphlet, as it was termed, which was dedicated unto him, which was the book before-mentioned of king Henry the fourth. Whereupon I replied to that allotment, and said to their Lordships, that it was an old matter, and had no manner of coherence with the rest of the charge, being matter of coherence with the rest of the charge, being matters of Ireland, and therefore that I having been wronged by bruits before, this would expose me to them more, and it would be said I gave in evidence mine own tales. It was

answered again with good shew, that because it was considered
how I stood tied to my Lord of Essex, therefore that part was
thought fittest for me which did him least hurt, for that whereas
all the rest was matter of charge and accusation, this only was but
matter of caveat and admonition.   Wherewith though I was in
mine own mind little satisfied, because I knew well a man were
better to be charged with some faults, than admonished of some
others · yet the conclusion binding upon the Queen's pleasure
directly *volens nolens,* I could not avoid that part that was laid
upon me; which part if in the delivery I did handle not tenderly
(though no man before me did in so clear terms free my Lord
from all disloyalty as I did), that, your Lordship knoweth, must
be ascribed to the superior duty I did owe to the Queen's fame
and honour in a public proceeding, and partly to the intention I
had to uphold myself in credit and strength with the Queen, the
better to be able to do my Lord good offices afterwards for as
soon as this day was past, I lost no time, but the very next day
following (as I remember) I attended her Majesty, fully resolved
to try and put in ure my utmost endeavour, so far as I in my
weakness could give furtherance, to bring my Lord again speedily
into Court and into favour, and knowing (as I supposed at least)
how the Queen was to be used, I thought that to make her conceive that the matter went well then, was the way to make her
leave off there: and I remember well, I said to her, You have
now Madam obtained victory over two things, which the greatest princes in the world cannot at their wills subdue, the one is
over fame, the other is over a great mind for surely the world
be now, I hope, reasonably well satisfied, and for my Lord, he
did shew that humiliation towards your Majesty, as I am persuaded he was never in his life-time more fit for your favour
than he is now therefore if your Majesty will not mar it by
lingering, but give over at the best, and now you have made
so good a full point, receive him again with tenderness, I shall
then think that all that is past is for the best.   Whereat I remember she took exceeding great contentment, and did often
iterate and put me in mind, that she had ever said that her pro
ceedings should be *ad reparationem* and not *ad ruinam,* as who
saith, that now was the time I should well perceive that that saying of hers should prove true   And further she willed me to set
down in writing all that passed that day   I obeyed her com-

mandment, and within some few days brought her again the
narration, which I did read unto her at two several afternoons .
and when I came to that part that set forth my Lord's own
answer (which was my principal care), I do well bear in mind
that she was extraordinarily moved with it, in kindness and re-
lenting towards my Lord, and told me afterwards (speaking how
well I had expressed my Lord's part) that she perceived old love
would not easily be forgotten whereunto I answered suddenly,
that I hoped she meant that by herself.   But in conclusion I did
advise her, that now she had taken a representation of the matter
to herself, that she would let it go no further For Madam (said
I) the fire blazeth well already, what should you tumble it ?
And besides, it may please you keep a convenience with yourself
in this case , for since your express direction was, there should
be no register nor clerk to take this sentence, nor no record or
memorial made up of the proceeding, why should you now do
that popularly, which you would not admit to be done judicially ?
Whereupon she did agree that that writing should be suppressed ,
and I think there were not five persons that ever saw it.   But
from this time forth, during the whole latter end of that summer,
while the Court was at Nonesuch and Oatlands, I made it my
task and scope to take and give occasions for my Lord s reinte-
gration in his fortune which my intention I did also signify to
my Lord as soon as ever he was at his liberty, whereby I might
without peril of the Queen's indignation write to him ; and having
received from his Lordship a courteous and loving acceptation of
my good will and endeavours, I did apply it in all my accesses to
the Queen, which were very many at that time, and purposely
sought and wrought upon other variable pretences, but only and
chiefly for that purpose   And on the other side, I did not forbear to give my Lord from time to time faithful advertisement
what I found, and what I wished   And I drew for him by his
appointment some letters to her Majesty, which though I knew
well his Lordship's gift and stile was far better than mine own,
yet because he required it, alleging that by his long restraint he
was grown almost a stranger to the Queen's present conceits, I
was ready to perform it and sure I am that for the space of six
weeks or two months it prospered so well, as I expected continually his restoring to his attendance   And I was never better
welcome to the Queen, nor more made of, than when I spake

fullest and boldest for him: in which kind the particulars were
exceeding many, whereof, for an example, I will remember to
your Lordship one or two. as at one time, I call to mind, her
Majesty was speaking of a fellow that undertook to cure, or at
least to ease my brother of his gout, and asked me how it went
forwards and I told her Majesty that at the first he received
good by it, but after in the course of his cure he found himself
at a stay or rather worse. the Queen said again, I will tell you,
Bacon, the error of it: the manner of these physicians, and especially these empirics, is to continue one kind of medicine, which
at the first is proper, being to draw out the ill humour, but after
they have not the discretion to change their medicine, but apply
still drawing medicines, when they should rather intend to cure
and corroborate the part. Good Lord Madam (said I) how wisely
and aptly can you speak and discern of physic ministered to the
body, and consider not that there is the like occasion of physic
ministered to the mind. as now in the case of my Lord of
Essex, your princely word ever was that you intended ever to
reform his mind, and not ruin his fortune. I know well you cannot but think that you have drawn the humour sufficiently, and
therefore it were more than time, and it were but for doubt of
mortifying or exulcerating, that you did apply and minister
strength and comfort unto him: for these same gradations of
yours are fitter to corrupt than correct any mind of greatness.
And another time I remember she told me for news, that my
Lord had written unto her some very dutiful letters, and that she
had been moved by them, and when she took it to be the abundance of the heart, she found it to be but a preparative to a suit
for the renewing of his farm of sweet wines whereunto I replied,
O Madam, how doth your Majesty conster of these things, as if
these two could not stand well together, which indeed nature
hath planted in all creatures. For there but two sympathies,
the one towards *perfection*, other towards *preservation* That
to perfection, as the iron contendeth to the loadstone, that to
preservation, as the vine will creep towards a stake or prop that
stands by it, not for any love to the stake, but to uphold itself.
And therefore, Madam, you must distinguish my Lord's desire
to do you service is as to his perfection, that which he thinks
himself to be born for, whereas his desire to obtain this thing of
you, is but for a sustentation And not to trouble your Lordship

with many other particulars like unto these, it was at the self-
same time that I did draw, with my Lord's privity, and by his
appointment, two letters, the one written as from my brother,
the other as an answer returned from my Lord, both to be by me
in secret manner shewed to the Queen, which it pleased my
Lord very strangely to mention at the bar, the scope of which
were but to represent and picture forth unto her Majesty my
Lord's mind to be such as I knew her Majesty would fainest
have had it · which letters whosoever shall see (for they cannot
now be retracted or altered, being by reason of my brother's or
his Lordship's servants' delivery long since comen into divers
hands) let him judge, specially if he knew the Queen, and do remember those times, whether they were not the labours of one
that sought to bring the Queen about for my lord of Essex his
good The troth is, that the issue of all his dealing grew to this,
that the Queen, by some slackness of my Lord's, as I imagine,
liked him worse and worse, and grew more incensed towards him.
Then she, remembering belike the continual and incessant and
confident speeches and courses that I had held on my Lord's side,
became utterly alienated from me, and for the space of at least
three months, which was between Michaelmas and New-year's-
tide following, would not as much as look on me, but turned away
from me with express and purpose-like discountenance wheresoever she saw me ; and at such time as I desired to speak with her
about law-business, ever sent me forth very slight refusals, insomuch as it is most true, that immediately after New-year's-tide I
desired to speak with her; and being admitted to her, I dealt with
her plainly and said, Madam, I see you withdraw your favour from
me, and now that I have lost many friends for your sake, I shall
leese you too you have put me like one of those that the French-
men call *enfans perdus*, that serve on foot before horsemen, so
have you put me into matters of envy without place, or without
strength ; and I know at chess a pawn before the king is ever
much played upon, a great many love me not, because they think
I have been against my Lord of Essex , and you love me not,
because you know I have been for him : yet will I never repent
me, that I have dealt in simplicity of heart towards you both,
without respect of cautions to myself, and therefore *vivus vi-
densque pereo* If I do break my neck, I shall do it in manner
as Master Dorrington did it, which walked on the battlements

of the church many days, and took a view and survey where he
should fall   and so Madam (said I) I am not so simple but that
I take a prospect of mine overthrow, only I thought I would tell
you so much, that you may know that it was faith and not folly
that brought me into it, and so I will pray for you   Upon which
speeches of mine uttered with some passion, it is true her Majesty
was exceedingly moved, and accumulated a number of kind and
gracious words upon me, and willed me to rest upon this, *Gratia
mea sufficit*, and a number of other sensible and tender words
and demonstrations, such as more could not be, but as touching
my Lord of Essex, *ne verbum quidem*   Whereupon I departed,
resting then determined to meddle no more in the matter, as
that that I saw would overthrow me, and not be able to do him
any good.   And thus I made mine own peace with mine own
confidence at that time, and this was the last time I saw her
Majesty before the eighth of February, which was the day of my
Lord of Essex his misfortune.   After which time, for that I performed at the bar in my public service, your Lordship knoweth
by the rules of duty that I was to do it honestly, and without
prevarication ; but for any putting myself into it, I protest before
God, I never moved neither the Queen, nor any person living,
concerning my being used in the service, either of evidence or
examination; but it was merely laid upon me with the rest of
my fellows   And for the time which passed, I mean between the
arraignment and my Lord's suffering, I well remember I was but
once with the Queen; at what time, though I durst not deal
directly for my Lord as things then stood, yet generally I did
both commend her Majesty's mercy, terming it to her as an excellent balm that did continually distil from her sovereign hands,
and made an excellent odour in the senses of her people, and
not only so, but I took hardiness to extenuate, not the fact, for
that I durst not, but the danger, telling her that if some base or
cruel-minded persons had entered into such an action, it might
have caused much blood and combustion, but it appeared well
they were such as knew not how to play the malefactors, and
some other words which I now omit   And as for the rest of the
carriage of myself in that service, I have many honourable witnesses that can tell, that the next day after my Lord's arraignment, by my diligence and information touching the quality and
nature of the offenders, six of nine were stayed, which otherwise

had been attainted, I bringing their Lordships' letter for their
say, after the jury was sworn to pass upon them, so near it went
and how careful I was, and made it my part, that whosoever was
in trouble about that matter, as soon as ever his case was sufficiently known and defined of might not continue in restraint, but
be set at liberty, and many other parts, which I am well assured
of[1] stood with the duty of an honest man   But indeed I will
not deny for the case of Sir Thomas Smith of London, the Queen
demanding my opinion of it, I told her I thought it was as hard
as many of the rest   but what was the reason? because at that
time I had seen only his accusation, and had never been present
at any examination of his; and the matter so standing, I had
been very untrue to my service, if I had not delivered that opinion
But afterwards upon a re-examination of some that charged him,
who weakened their own testimony; and especially hearing himself *viva voce*, I went instantly to the Queen, out of the soundness
of my conscience, and not regarding what opinion I had formerly
delivered, told her Majesty, I was satisfied and resolved in my
conscience, that for the reputation of the action, the plot was to
countenance the action further by him in respect of his place,
than they had indeed any interest or intelligence with him   It
is very true also, about that time her Majesty taking a liking of
my pen, upon that which I had done before concerning the proceeding at York-house, and likewise upon some other declarations which in former times by her appointment I put in writing,
commanded me to pen that book, which was published for the
better satisfaction of the world; which I did, but so as never secretary had more particular and express directions and instructions in every point how to guide my hand in it; and not only
so, but after that I had made a first draught thereof, and propounded it to certain principal counsellors, by her Majesty's
appointment, it was perused, weighed, censured, altered, and
made almost a new writing,[2] according to their Lordships' better
consideration, wherein their Lordships and myself both were
as religious and curious of truth, as desirous of satisfaction ·
and myself indeed gave only words and form of style in pursuing
their direction   And after it had passed their allowance, it was
again exactly perused by the Queen herself, and some alterations
made again by her appointment: nay, and after it was set to

print, the Queen, who, as your Lordship knoweth, as she was excellent in great matters, so she was exquisite in small, and noted that I could not forget my ancient respect to my Lord of Essex, in terming him ever My Lord of Essex, My Lord of Essex, in almost every page of the book, which she thought not fit, but would have it made Essex, or the late Earl of Essex whereupon of force it was printed *de novo*, and the first copies suppressed by her peremptory commandment   And this, my good Lord, to my furthest remembrance, is all that passed wherein I had part which I have set down as near as I could in the very words and speeches that were used, not because they are worthy the repetition, I mean those of mine own, but to the end your Lordship may lively and plainly discern between the face of truth and a smooth tale   And the rather also because in things that passed a good while since, the very words and phrases did sometimes bring to my remembrance the matters   wherein I report me to your honourable judgment, whether you do not see the traces of an honest man   and had I been as well believed either by the Queen or by my Lord, as I was well heard by them both, both my Lord had been fortunate, and so had myself in his fortune

To conclude therefore, I humbly pray your Lordship to pardon me for troubling you with this long narration , and that you will vouchsafe to hold me in your good opion, till you know I have deserved, or find that I shall deserve the contrary; and even so I continue

At your Lordship's honourable commandments very humbly

FINIS

This letter was published in a small volume very convenient for circulation; and as another impression was issued in the following year, we may infer that it was circulated widely   It would have been very interesting to know what was thought and said of it then but I can find no news of its reception   I do not remember to have met with a single allusion to it by any one living and forming his impressions at the time, a fact which does not countenance the notion that it was at the time felt to be unsatisfactory   for an ineffectual attempt to defend himself against a popular outcry is pretty sure to make the man more unpopular and the outcry louder   In later times judgment has been pronounced loudly enough   but later times have heard only half the case, and formed a conception of Essex's proceedings, not only partial, but utterly erroneous—mistaking altogether the meaning and spirit of them, and refusing to perceive the question of state which they involved   Bacon's ' apology " is indeed as well known by name, and as familiarly referred to, as any of his occasional writings, and as evidence of the facts which it relates, has been treated with due respect   being indeed the only authority for more of the circumstances in the story as now commonly told than readers are perhaps aware   But regarded as a justification of his own part in the matter, the popular judgment of recent times has certainly pronounced it a failure of the most egregious kind—not only failing to justify, but sufficing to condemn

Now those who say that it fails *of what it aims at* must (if they have read it—which I doubt) mean to say that they do not believe the story which Bacon tells   for what he asserts is that, up to the day of Essex's insurrection, he not only wished for his restoration to favour, but used all the influence he had to bring it about   and the question being whether he acted as a friend or an enemy, the answer is surely conclusive, if true   To the means which he resorted to for this purpose exception may be taken in one or two particulars on other grounds, for he did undoubtedly both advise and practise some indirect dealing, and indirect dealing is never justified in principle, and only approved in practice when—what shall we say?—when employed for a purpose which we approve, and which we perceive to be unattainable by direct dealing   But indirect dealing employed to serve a friend, however culpable otherwise, is not " falsehood or unthankfulness " to that friend, and falsehood or unthankfulness to the Earl of Essex was the charge against which he was defending himself   The question therefore comes simply to this —Is his narrative to be believed?   It is a perfectly fair question, and must have been anticipated and considered by everybody who

desired to form a fair judgment, for a story told in a man's own defence about things long past, concerning many of which he is himself
the sole surviving witness, may always be justly suspected of errors
both intentional and unintentional   But then, before I disbelieve
the positive statement of a man whose character for veracity has not
been otherwise forfeited, I want for my own part to know why
What reason can anybody give me for refusing my belief to the positive statements in this letter?   The two passages which may seem
at first sight to be inconsistent with other existing evidence—and
so far as I know, the only two—have been quoted at full length in
my own narrative, side by side with the evidence with which they
have been thought inconsistent,[1] and as my narrative in both cases
accepts and includes both, I cannot admit the inconsistency   In
other respects it has all the outward appearances of fairness and sincerity   It is full and circumstantial   it is written with a great deal
of feeling   it makes no attempt to throw blame on others, or to de-
preciate his own obligations, or to exaggerate his own services   it
resorts to no special pleading, indulges in no rhetoric, merely states
the facts and leaves them to suggest the judgment   What the judgment was, of those to whom he appealed, I cannot (as I said) produce any positive evidence   But the negative evidence is significant
"It is not probable," says Lord Macaulay, "that Bacon's defence
had much effect upon his contemporaries   But the unfavourable
impression which his conduct had made appears to have been gradually effaced"   From this I infer that Lord Macaulay's reading
furnished no expression or anecdote which implied, or could be made
to seem to imply, that the unfavourable impression continued after
the explanation had been heard   And as this is exactly what would
have happened on the supposition that his defence *did* produce its
natural effect upon his contemporaries, and is very hard to explain
upon any other supposition, (seeing that Bacon's course of life, as a
rising man in Court favour, in the House of Commons, and in his
profession, exposed him to envy and free criticism in a world which
was in this matter prejudiced against him), I think we may fairly
leave it there.

[1] Vol II pp 127-133, 150, 151

CHAPTER V

A D 1601   ÆTAT 11

1.

THE resolution to call a Parliament, having been postponed from month to month in consequence of the sickness then prevailing in London, was at length announced by Proclamation on the 11th of January 1603-4   The session began on the 19th of March and was opened by the King in person with a gracious and judicious speech, explaining his views on peace, on the union of the kingdoms, on the limits of toleration in religion, and on the general duties of government   in all which there seems to be nothing to find fault with   and if he had not called the Devil "a busy bishop"—upon which one of the Bench is said to have remarked that "his Majesty might have chosen another name"[1]—I am not aware that any exception would have been taken to it

But a clause in the Proclamation, introduced it seems by the Lord Chancellor,[2] had sown the seed of a difficulty which threatened to spoil the concert, and of which the history is worth telling at large, not only for the part which Bacon took in it, but also for the light which might have been taken from it as to the true method of arranging those disputes between Privilege and Prerogative which were destined to be the trouble of the times

The Proclamation had notified that all returns and certificates of Knights, Citizens, and Burgesses were to be brought to the Chancery, and there filed of record   and if any were found to have been made contrary to the Proclamation "the same was to be rejected as unlawful and insufficient"   A previous clause had forbidden the election of bankrupts or outlaws   Sir Francis Goodwin, who was returned for Buckinghamshire, was objected to as having been outlawed [3] the

---

[1] Nugæ Antiquæ, i 182   [2] Egerton Papers, p 38   Gardiner, i p 180
[3] With whom the objection originated does not clearly appear   In a letter to Winwood (Mem n p 18), Cecil seems to imply that it was an electioneering manœuvre advisedly adopted by the government   "Sir Francis Goodwyn (he says) having laboured to be Knight of Buckinghamshire, to the exclusion of an

return was accordingly refused by the Clerk of the Crown, and a
new writ being issued from the Chancery, Sir John Fortescue, a
Privy Councillor, was elected instead   This was before the meeting
of Parliament   and the very first motion made in the Lower House
after the election of the Speaker was for an examination of the return
and the admission of Sir F Goodwin as a member   The motion
was approved   the Clerk of the Crown was summoned to appear the
next morning with the writs, returns, indentures, etc , and Sir
Francis Goodwin was ordered to attend in person and explain his
case   a select committee being at the same time appointed (as usual
at the beginning of a session) to examine all questions touching pri
vileges and returns   Upon a full consideration and discussion of the
case (in which Bacon appears to have taken a prominent part, for
though there is no report of what was said, his name heads the list
of members named as speakers), it was resolved that Goodwin was
not an outlaw, and had been duly elected   upon which the Clerk of
the Crown was ordered to file the first return, and Goodwin took the
oaths and his seat

This was on Friday, March 23rd, and thus the House was brought
into collision with the Court of Chancery upon the question of ju
risdiction— to which of them it belonged to judge of the validity of
the return —a point of privilege important in the highest degree,
for if the judgment of the Court of Chancery was conclusive, the
Chancery could control the composition of the House   On the
following Tuesday the dispute was further complicated by a message
brought by the Attorney General from the Lords desiring a con

ancient Counsellor, Sir John Fortescue, *it was advised by the King's Learned
Counsel and Judges whether there were not some means by the laws to avoid it*
Whereupon it being found that he was outlawed (and so certified by the Sheriff),
consequently a new writ was sent forth," etc   And though nothing was said about
this in the House, it appears incidentally from the journals that Sir Edward Coke
had a principal hand in the Sheriff's certificate   To the question, " Who laboured
him to make the return so long before the day of the Parliament ?" the Sheriff
replied that, " he being here in London, Mr Attorney General, the 2nd of March,
at his chambers in the Inner Temple, delivered him two *cap utlegat* against Sir
Francis Goodwyn , and before he made his return, he went and advised with Mr
Attorney about his return *who penned it*, and so it was done by his direction
And the return being written, upon Friday after the King's coming through
London, near about my Lord Chancellor's gate, in the presence of Sir John For
tescue, he delivered the writ to Sir George Coppin   and at this time (it being
about 4 of the clock in the afternoon) and before they parted, Sir John Fortescue
delivered him the second writ sealed   Sir John Fortescue, Sir George Coppin, and
himself, being not above an hour together at that time , and never had but this
new writ of Parliament to him delivered " (Com Journ p 161)
Coke's part in the matter may perhaps have been merely ministerial but the
rapidity of the proceeding was a fatal blot in the case on the Chancery side, and
involved an irregularity which made it legally invalid —" the later writ being
awarded and sealed, before the Chancery was repossessed of the former —which
the Clerk of the Crown and the Sheriff of the County did both testify, and well
held to be a clear fault in law " (Id p 163)

ference on the subject to which the Commons replied that "it did not stand with the honour and order of the House to give account of any of their proceedings" This brought them into collision with the Lords And worse was behind For thus far the King had not been implicated but when the Attorney General returned presently with another message signifying that the Lords had acquainted his Majesty with the matter, who "conceived himself engaged and touched in honour that there might be some conference of it between the two Houses, and to that end signified his pleasure unto them, and by them to this House"—they were fairly in collision with all three,—the Chancery whose judgment they had reversed,—the Lords with whom they had refused to confer,—and the King who had taken part with the Lords.

Upon this they moved for access to the King himself which was granted for the next morning A committee was immediately named (Bacon's name the first on the list) "to set down the effect of that which Mr Speaker was to deliver from the House to the King" And on Wednesday at 8 o'clock in the morning he went, accompanied by a select committee, explained their whole proceeding, and the grounds of it, heard the King's answer to the several points, and received his "charge"—which was that they should first resolve amongst themselves, then confer with the Judges and report to the Council All which he related to the House the next day

And now came a grave difficulty For the King had argued the case himself, and (as he could not easily refrain from giving an answer when he had it ready) had personally committed himself to the legal doctrine which had been laid down, I suppose, by the Lord Chancellor and the Judges "By the law (he said) this House ought not to meddle with returns, being all made into the Chancery, and are to be corrected and returned by that Court only into which they are returned In 35 Hen VI, it was the resolution of all the Judges that matter of utlawry was a sufficient cause of the dismission of any member out of the House The Judges have now resolved that Sir Francis Goodwin standeth outlawed according to the laws of the land."[1] Not merely therefore upon the question whether they should confer with the Lords, but upon the entire constitutional question involved in the case, and upon each several point of it, they were now engaged in a direct dispute with the King himself Prerogative and Privilege found themselves suddenly face to face in a narrow passage one must stand aside to let the other pass, or each must be content with half the pathway What was to be done?

Their immediate resolution was to postpone the further considera-

tion of the question till the next morning   In the debate which
then took place, it appeared that upon one point they were at once
and unanimously resolved,—to stand fast by the principle that they
were judges of their own returns, sole and unaccountable   On that
point no one talked of a compromise.   But upon the question how
they should proceed in asserting it, opinions were much divided
And here it was that Bacon became, as I take it, an important actor
in the matter   All that we know of his speech is contained in the
following note, as entered in the Commons' Journals, but it is
enough to show the tenour of his advice

"That we ought not to contest with the King   That it is fit
to have a conference   That by it we shall lose no privilege, but
rather gain, for the matters of the conference will be two,
satisfaction of the King, and putting in certainty our privilege
All is not said that may be said   We are not to dispute with
one that is governor of 30 legions   *confitendum est, ne frustra
interrogasset.*   Let us deal plainly and freely with the Lords,
and let them know all the reasons.   They are jealous of the
honour of a Privy Counsellor, we of the freedom of election.   It
is fit great men maintain their Prerogative, so is it fit that we
maintain our privileges   This is a Court of Record, therefore
ought we by all means to seek to preserve the honour and dignity
of it.   If a Burgess be chosen for two places, the Burgess makes
his choice for which he will serve, and a warrant shall be directed from Mr Speaker, in the name of the House, to the
Clerk of the Crown, to send forth a writ for a new election for
the other place left, which is a direct proof that it is a Court of
Power and of Record   We have a Clerk and a Register   all
matters that pass here are entered of Record and preserved   As
they stand for the honour of a Counsellor, so we for our Privi
leges   It is to be wished that we had a law to declare our Privileges   That we have a Court of Record and a Register.
Object   We (they say) are but half of the body, and the
Lords are the parts nearest the head.
Answer   Nothing ascends to the head but by the breasts, etc
Conclusion   That we may pray, it may be explained by a law,
what our privileges are, and that no man outlawed may be
hereafter admitted

There must be a judge of the return before we sit, and this is
now judged according to the positive laws of the realm by the

King; which infringeth not our liberty, since we judge after the Court is set according to discretion.

No precedent that any man was put out of the House for utlawry. Therefore it had been fit we should have desired to inform the King that he was misinformed.

Let us now leave this particular case to the King, and consider and resolve of the material questions that will fall out in the debate of it. 1. Whether this Court hath power to take notice of returns made before we sit here. 2. Whether men outlawed may be of the House. 3. Whether a man pardoned, having not sued forth a writ of *Scire facias*, may be called in question. 4. Whether the writ were returned upon the 17th of February or no, upon oath of the Sheriff."[1]

Bacon's advice therefore amounted to this: establish the privilege; settle, and offer (if necessary) to amend, the law; but avoid a dispute upon the particular case. The King has desired that we should argue the question before the Judges: let us consent to do so, and in the meantime prepare for the argument by considering and resolving upon the "material questions" which it will raise.

Others however were strongly against yielding to the conference —as upon a matter which they had already decided; and the debate ended in the appointment of a Committee to set down in writing the reasons of their proceeding, and in a resolution—directly against Bacon's recommendation—*not* to confer with the Judges. These reasons,—which were drawn up in the form of an address to the King, setting forth in order all the objections made " by his Majesty and his reverend Judges,"[2] and answering them point by point,— having been read and approved, a committee was appointed to take them up to the Lords, and the same afternoon (April 3) they were delivered by the hands of Bacon: whose report of what passed is thus recorded in the Journals:

"Sir Francis Bacon, having the day before delivered to the Lords, in the Council Chamber at Whitehall, according to the direction of the House, the reasons in writing, penned by the Committee, touching Sir Francis Goodwyn's case, maketh report of what passed at the time of the said delivery. First, that though the Committees employed were a number specially deputed and selected, yet that the Lords admitted all Burgesses without distinction. That they offered it with testimony of their

own speed and care in the business, so as, they said, no one thing
had precedency, but only the Bill of Recognition That they
had such respect for the weight of it, as they had not committed
it to any frailty of memory, or verbal relation, but put it into
writing for more permanent memory of their duty and respect
to his Majesty's grace and favour   That in conclusion they
prayed their Lordships, sithence they had nearer access, they
would cooperate with them for the King's satisfaction : and so
delivered the writing to the hands of the Lord Chancellor, who,
receiving it, demanded whether they should send it to the King
or first peruse it.   To which was answered, That since it was the
King's pleasure they should concur, they desired their Lordships
would first peruse it   The Lord Cicell demanded, Whether they
had warrant to amplify, explain, or debate, any doubt or question made upon the reading To which it was said, they had no
warrant   And so the writing was read, and no more done at
that time."[1]

The writing in question was drawn up in a style very well suited
to the purpose, being clear and conclusive, and yet temperate and
respectful, and including an intimation that they had already, in
deference to the King's remarks, prepared an act disabling all outlaws thenceforth to serve in Parliament   and it seems probable
that the difference would have been arranged without further difficulty, had it not been for that formal resolution against consenting
to a conference with the Judges which had been passed so shortly
before   The King had professed to have no personal interest in
the dispute, and treated it merely as a question of constitutional
law, upon which he had been guided by the opinion of the Judges
The argument of the Commons went directly in the teeth of that
opinion, and he would naturally wish to hear what the Judges had
to say in reply, and what the Commons might have to say in reply
to them again   And as they had voluntarily waived their right of
refusing to give an account of their proceedings to anybody, there
seemed to be no reason why they should insist upon doing it in
the absence of those with whom the dispute really was.

Their answer to the King's and Judges' objections had been delivered to the Lords on the afternoon of the 3rd of April, without
any intimation of their resolution (passed the evening before[1])
against a conference with the Judges   On the morning of the 5th
the King—perhaps not knowing, certainly not having been formally

apprized of that resolution—sent for the Speaker told him that "he had seen and considered of the manner and the matter he had heard his Judges and Council, and that he was now distracted in judgment Therefore for his further satisfaction he desired and commanded as an absolute King, that there might be a conference between the House and the Judges, and that for this purpose there might be a select Committee of grave and learned persons out of the House, and that his Council might be present, not as umpires to determine, but to report indifferently on both sides"[1]

If there was any doubt before as to the expediency of the former resolution, there could be none now for upon receiving this "unexpected message," they consented at once, and very judiciously, to abandon it They were indeed involved in a dilemma, out of which the only escape lay backwards and the same member who had before been most vehement not only against conference, but apparently against compromise of any kind, was now foremost to retreat "The Prince's command," said Yelverton (for it was he who first broke the silence), "is like a thunderbolt. his command upon our allegiance is like the roaring of a lion. To his command there is no contradiction But how or in what manner we should now proceed to perform obedience, that will be the question" Another suggested that the King should be present himself at the conference, to hear, judge, and moderate the cause in person And a select committee was thereupon appointed " to confer with the judges of the law touching the reasons of proceeding in Sir Francis Goodwin's case, .. in the presence of the Lords of his Majesty's Council, according to his Majesty's pleasure signified by Mr Speaker this day to the House " the Committee to "insist upon the fortification and explaining of the reasons and answers delivered unto his Majesty, and not proceed to any other argument or answer, what occasion soever moved in the time of that debate "

The next day being Good Friday, the House was adjourned for a week and did not meet again till the 11th of April In the course of that day,—upon the return (I suppose) of the Committees from the conference,—Bacon, who had been spokesman, was called on for a report of what had passed, and when he replied that "he was not warranted to make any report,—and *tantum permissum quantum commissum* " it was ordered that the Committees should have another meeting for conference amongst themselves, and that he should then make his report The note of which is in these words

"Sir Francis Bacon, after the meeting of the Committees in

[1] C J pp 166, 943

the Court of Wards, reporteth what had passed in conference in the presence of his Majesty and his Council.

The King said he would be President himself.—This attendance renewed the remembrance of the last, when we departed with such admiration. It was the voice of God in man the good spirit of God in the mouth of man I do not say the voice of God, and not of man· I am not one of Herod's flatterers· a curse fell upon him that said it, a curse on him that suffered it We might say, as was said to Solomon, We are glad O King that we give account to you, because you discern what is spoken. We let pass no moment of time until we had resolved and set down an answer in writing, which we now had ready· That sithence we received a message from his Majesty by Mr Speaker, of two parts. 1. The one paternal 2. The other royal. 1 That we were as dear unto him as the safety of his person or the preservation of his posterity 2. Royal, that we should confer with his Judges, and that in the presence of himself and his Council That we did more now to King James than ever was done since the Conquest, in giving account of our judgments That we had no intent in all our proceedings to encounter his Majesty, or to impeach his honour or Prerogative.

This was spoken by way of preamble, by him you employed

How to report his Majesty's speeches he knew [not] The eloquence of a King was inimitable.

The King addressed·himself to him, as deputed by the House; and said he would make three parts of what he had to say. The cause of the meeting was to draw to an end the difference in Sir Francis Goodwyn's case.

If they required his absence, he was ready, because he feared he might be thought interessed and so breed an inequality on their part

He said, That he would not hold his Prerogative, or honour, or receive any thing of any or all his subjects.— This was his magnanimity

That he would confirm and ratify all just Privileges —This his bounty and amity, as a King, royally; as King James, sweetly and kindly, out of his good nature.

One point was, Whether we were a Court of Record and had power to judge of returns As our Court had power, so had the Chancery, and that the Court that first had passed their judgment should not be controuled

Upon a surmise, and upon the Sheriff's return, there grew a difference.

That there [were] two Powers, one permanent, the other transitory. That the Chancery was a confidentiary Court, to the use of the Parliament, during the time

Whatsoever the Sheriff inserts beyond the authority of his mandate, a nugation.

The Parliaments of England not to be bound by a Sheriff's return.

That our privileges were not in question That it was private jealousies, without any kernel or substance.   He granted it was a Court of Record and a Judge of returns   He moved that neither Sir John Fortescue nor Sir Francis Goodwyn might have place   Sir John losing place, his Majesty did meet us half way   That when there did arise a schism between a Pope and an Anti-Pope, there could be no end of the difference until they were both put down."[1]

I have thought it better to give these notes exactly as I find them, because the words themselves are probably genuine and the context may sometimes be guessed   It will be seen however that they are not *abstracts* of what was spoken, but merely disjointed fragments, made to look continuous by the simple process of writing them out in sequence   The note-taker seems to have set down as much as he could follow · sometimes the beginning of a sentence, sometimes the end, leaving gaps of all sorts and sizes   so that it is often difficult to assign the several sentences to the several speakers, or to make out so much as the general course of the argument

In this case, however, we may gather that the King began by maintaining that the Court of Chancery and the House of Commons being *both* courts of record, with power to judge of returns, neither of them could be called in question by the other, and therefore that the first judgment must stand. to which Bacon answered on behalf the Commons, that the Chancery was a judge of the returns only for the purpose of making the House, which as soon as it was made became itself the judge for otherwise, if the Chancery were governed by the Sheriff's return, and the House might not call the return in question, the sheriff's return did in effect bind the Parliament   It may be gathered further that upon this point (which was the material one), though the Judges were still prepared to contest it, the King was prepared to yield, but in order to settle the difference more handsomely, proposed that the two Courts should meet each other half-way and therefore that *both* returns should be set aside, a new writ be issued, and a new election proceed —that to this proposal (which was in accordance with his own former advice,—namely to content themselves with establishing their privilege, and avoid a contest with the King about the particular case) Bacon made no objection, but reported it to the House and recommended them to accede to it.

If in thus entertaining the question of a compromise he a little exceeded his commission (and exception was taken to his report on that ground by some members, as "drawing upon the House a note of inconsistency and levity") it was a wise liberty and well accepted by the great majority for "the acclamation of the House was, that it was a testimony of their duty, and no levity," and it was forthwith resolved (Sir Francis Goodwin's formal consent having been first obtained) to issue a writ for a new election and to send a message of thanks to the King which was delivered accordingly on the 12th of April, and accepted very graciously [1] And so that business ended

It was a good example to show how such differences might be successfully and satisfactorily arranged For the privilege was never afterwards called in question and in the meantime the concession, which was in itself quite immaterial, satisfied the King who, though jealous of his Prerogative, does not appear to have had any intention of interfering with their liberties,[2] but would have been ready, I think, to settle all such questions almost as they would, so long as he was allowed to feel that in assenting to their petitions he was *using* his Prerogative and not abandoning it.

2

While this was going on, the House had another privilege-dispute on hand, which (though the occasion was not so critical—the difference being with meaner persons, and neither King nor Lords nor Chancery being concerned in it) gave them more trouble and threatened at one time to drive them into violent measures A full account of all the proceedings (fragmentary notices of which are thickly scattered through the Journals, from the 22nd of March to

[1] C J p 171

[2] From a MS in the Cotton Collection in the handwriting of Ralph Starkey,—copied perhaps from Sir R Cotton's own notes—it would seem that the *Judges* were still prepared to stand by their original opinion, and that the proposal of the compromise came from the King himself "The King propounded the reasons and precedents to the Judges, who agreed unto them, and my Lord Chief Justice was about to disprove by another reason that Sir F G was not duly chosen Hereupon the King, desirous to compromit the matter, made offer to the Lower House to be contented that Sir Francis should not be also, and that a new writ should be sent out," etc Cott MSS Tit F iv fo 4, b

the 15th of May) would make too long a story   but enough to explain Bacon's part in them may be easily told

On the day of the King's solemn entry into London (15 March)
Sir Thomas Shirley, attending by command and being a member of
Parliament, had been arrested for debt at the suit of a goldsmith
named Sympson (the same I presume who arrested Bacon in 1598[1]),
and sent to the Fleet   The detention of a member from the House
was a breach of Privilege, and being complained of as such, and the
parties being sent for and heard at the Bar (27 March), was referred
to a select committee   upon whose report (11 April) it was resolved
that the arrest was a wilful contempt and that both Sympson and
the serjeant whom he employed should be committed to the Tower
for it   But because the delivery of Sir Thomas out of prison involved some doubtful questions of law, they agreed that before proceeding further the counsel of the parties should be heard

The doubt in law was whether the Warden of the Fleet, if he let
his prisoner go, would not become answerable to his creditor for what
he owed , and (opinions differing) it was judged best, before demanding the delivery of Sir Thomas, to put the matter out of doubt by
passing a special act for securing to Sympson the interest in his debt
and saving the Warden harmless   A bill for this purpose was accordingly brought in on the 17th of April, and passed and sent up to
the Lords on the 21st [2] and they were on the point of petitioning
the King (4 May) for a written promise that he would give his
assent to it, when it was objected that such a proceeding would be
"some impeachment to the privilege of the House "   So no doubt it
would   By going so far out of their way to ensure the Warden before they demanded the release of their member, they would seem to
admit by implication that they could not legally demand him without
such assurance   The caution being approved, and their intention
having been made sufficiently clear, they proceeded at once to serve
the Warden with a writ of *Habeas Corpus* for bringing Sir Thomas's
body into the House the next morning   And here began the difficulty
The Warden, not considering himself safe till the bill had become
a law, refused to obey the writ until it had received the royal assent
The Commons could not allow such a condition without creating a
precedent dangerous to their privilege   And what was to be done?

In the first place the Warden was called to the Bar and questioned
Persisting in his refusal, he was detained for that day in the custody
of the Serjeant at-arms, and (not to lose the chance of any better
thoughts which the night might bring) a second demand for the body
of Sir Thomas was made in due form the next morning , but with the

[1] See Vol II p 106   [2] C J p 180

same result   Upon this he was brought to the Bar a second time
(8 May), and, still refusing to promise obedience except upon con
ditions, was committed to the Tower.

Perhaps they might be more successful with his second in com
mand   and next day the Serjeant was sent for the third time upon
the same errand   But the second in command was the Warden's
wife, who having in the meantime taken possession of all the keys
and all the authority, referred him to her husband for his answer
and though armed with *Habeas Corpus* and mace, he could make no
impression on her

The House, which had thus far shown unusual patience and con
sideration in the matter, began now to get a little hot   a motion that
six members should accompany the Serjeant and bring Sir Thomas
by force, if he were not given up, was proposed and carried by a con
siderable majority   and appears to have been only stayed from exe
cution upon a suggestion that any member who took part in such a
proceeding would be liable to an action.   But the next day (10 May)
a new and a better chance offered itself   The King, who had pru
dently declined all interference in the dispute hitherto, volunteered
the promise which the House had forborne to ask for,—he would
engage *in verbo principis* to assent to the Bill at the end of the Parliament   Upon this the Serjeant was sent again to the Fleet, armed
as before, and (having first privately and of his own motion in
formed the Warden's wife of the King's promise) again demanded
the body of Sir Thomas   But the faithful and valiant woman knew
no authority except her husband's, declared that, without word from
him, if he carried Sir Thomas's body, he must carry her own, dead,
along with it, and when he offered to take her by the hand, lay
down.   To go further was beyond his commission, and so all three
—Serjeant, *Habeas Corpus*, and mace,—came back empty as before.

Then the Warden himself was brought to the Bar again, for the
third time, was formally acquainted with the King's promise, was
reasoned with   being found inexorable, was ordered into closer con
finement in a dungeon well known by the significant name of ' Little
Ease " and when this produced no better effect, some members were
sent to see whether the order had really been complied with   They
found that he had not been made uneasy enough, and upon their
report to that effect, a most distracted debate followed.   One would
have the Lieutenant of the Tower fined 2000*l* for not executing the
order   Another would have the Warden himself fined 100*l* a day
till he relented   A third was for an Act of Parliament disabling him
for all offices, etc   A fourth would have the Lessee of the Fleet sent
for, and get at their member that way   A fifth was for acquainting

the Lords and petitioning for the King's help [1] A sixth revived the former motion, that six members of the House should go with the Serjeant, and deliver Sir Thomas by force A seventh would have the House rise and strike work until they had power to execute their privileges And so they seemed to be at a non-plus; every man giving an opinion, and no two opinions alike

It was at this point that Bacon came forward with a suggestion Hitherto he had taken no part in the business, beyond giving an opinion (27 March) that the delivery of Sir Thomas did *not* (as the law stood) deprive the creditor of his remedy [2] But now the House seemed to be in imminent danger of committing some rash action The problem was, to vindicate the privilege without offending the law To call upon the Crown to enforce the demand for them would be to acknowledge a want of power in themselves To enforce it by the hands of their own members would be to exceed their powers To refuse to proceed with the public business would be foolish But there was a middle way left The Serjeant-at-arms might be ordered to recover their lost member by force, and the King might appoint persons to assist him in executing the order This appears to have been Bacon's suggestion The note of his speech runs thus

"This is a great case of Privilege —*Remora*, a little fish that stayeth great ships —We have had two of them this Parliament.—

No suit to the King, because he cannot do it, and it is a disclaimer of our power.—

Not to rise, like sullen fellows That is to give over our privileges to wind and weather —We shall displease the King, and hurt the Commonwealth.—

No members of the House to assist the serjeant —Judges cannot be ministers

Conclus. To be petitioners to the King, that he would appoint some to aid our Serjeant for the delivery of the prisoner with force." [3]

To this proposition however, when upon Bacon's motion it was formally put to the House, objection was taken by the Speaker as contrary to precedent, and though Bacon was prepared and allowed to give some answer to the objection (it being "overruled upon question that he might speak again in the same matter to expound himself" [4]) the motion appears to have been ultimately withdrawn,

[1] C J p 971   [2] Cott MSS Tit. F iv fo 4, b
[3] C J p 209, and compare p 971
[4] His object appears to have been to draw a distinction between petitioning the

and the question put in another form, though the measure agreed upon was not substantially different The King was not to be asked for material assistance—only moral and the debate ended in a resolution that the Serjeant-at-arms should be sent once more with a new writ, that the Warden should be carried to the door of the Fleet, and that the writ should be then delivered to him with commandment from the House to obey it the Vice-Chamberlain being at the same time privately instructed to go to the King, and humbly desire that he would be pleased (as from himself) to command the Warden upon his allegiance to set Sir Thomas free This measure at last succeeded They recovered their member, and established their privilege The Warden and other prisoners were in due time, after making due submission, released —and Sympson had to pay all the costs

<h3 style="text-align:center">3.</h3>

These disputes, though not without their importance in the development of our Parliamentary constitution, were serious and vexatious interruptions to the great businesses of the time, upon which the House had shown every disposition to enter promptly and earnestly The greatest of these was no doubt that which the King had especially recommended to them, and to which his own aspirations were at this time almost exclusively directed,—the Union of England and Scotland a national work of which it was hardly possible to overrate the importance But it was full of difficulties and had to be approached with caution In the meantime there were other questions which stood much in need of settlement and might be proceeded with at once, and though the results attained were not destined to be considerable for the present, the subsequent history of the reign, and especially of Bacon's political career, cannot be properly understood without careful observation of the first movements

1 The law which gave to the Crown the wardship of minors, springing originally out of the obligations of the feudal system, had ceased to be fit for the existing condition of society, and began to be felt as a burden and a grievance to the subject Being nevertheless a source of considerable revenue to the Crown, the legality of which was not disputed, it was a fit subject for Parliament to deal with by way of bargain.

King to assist them in executing their own order, and petitioning him to execute it for them But all that remains of what he said is this
" *Plenitudo potestatis, plenitudo tempestatis*
" To be petitioners to the King to assist no derogation a difference between execution and assistance in execution " (C J p 972)

2 The officers whose duty it was to provide food, carriage, and other necessaries for the Court in its journeys, had of old been in the habit of abusing their authority, and many acts had been passed to keep them in order, but the abuses still continued, and formed another serious grievance

3 The popular clamour against monopolies had been allayed for the time by Queen Elizabeth, as we have seen and one of James's first acts was to carry out her intentions, by a Proclamation prohibiting the use of any monopoly-licence ("except such grants only as had been made to any corporation, or company of any art or mystery, or for the maintenance or enlargement of any trade or merchandise") till it had been examined and allowed of by the King, with the advice of his Council, "to be fit to be put in execution without any prejudice to his loving subjects"[1] But the true state of the law with regard to these patents, and to the power exercised by the Crown of granting dispensations from penalties imposed by statutes—which was part of the same question,—was still doubtful, and it was a fit time to settle it

4 Since the Hampton Court Conference, a new edition of the Book of Common Prayer had been put forth by authority, with some alterations and explanations, and a confirmation of it by Act of Parliament was thought expedient

All these questions, with one or two others of less importance, were brought under consideration of the House on the first day (23 March), and being immediately referred to a Committee (of which Bacon was a member, and I suppose an active one, since he was selected to make their first report to the House) were proceeded with at once

The three last came within the powers of the House in its ordinary course of legislation For the abuses of Purveyors and Cartakers, a sub-committee was appointed to peruse the former statutes concerning them, and to draw a Bill for their restraint With respect to dispensations from Penal Statutes, a Bill was reported ready drawn, which was to be offered for the consideration of the whole House For Monopolies, all persons aggrieved were invited to bring in their complaints in writing, that the Committee might consider them and frame a law according to the cause For the Book of Common Prayer a sub-committee (in the list of which Bacon's name stands first) was appointed to "capitulate the alterations" and lay them before the Committee in writing, "together with their own opinion of the said book"

But the question of Wardship was of a different character Be-

[1] 7 May, 1603 Book of Proclamations, p 12

ing a matter of arrangement, which would require the concurrence beforehand both of the King and the Lords, who had a personal and legal interest in it, they judged it necessary to begin with a confe rence and the result of their deliberations was reported to the House by Bacon on the 26th of March   Of whose report I find in the Journals the following note

Sir Francis Bacon, one of his Majesty's Counsel learned, maketh report of the meeting of the Committees touching the matters formerly propounded by Sir Robert Wroth, and of the first endeavours and travel on the point of Wardship of men's children, relating briefly what was said *pro et contra*, viz.,

1. That it was a thing never petitioned, never won of any King

Answ But having his ground from the tenure of *Scutagium, Voyage Royal in Escosse*, that now determines, by his Majesty's possession of the Crown.

2. Next, the King's honour was considered

Answ It was the greatest honour to govern subjects mode- rately free

3. The justice of the matter was propounded, in respect it concerned divers officers in their right of credit, of profit, &c, divers mean Lords in their right of possession, of interest, &c.

Answ This House may take away the office, the countenance, the credit of any man   but that power the House hath always used tenderly   This no new thing, for King Henry VIII, King Edward VI, and Queen Mary had a power granted them by Parliament to dissolve the Court of Wards   That the intention of the House was, that both the King and mean Lords should be comprehended

The first resolution was for the matter, that petition should be made to the King   Then for the manner it was debated 1 Whether first to agree upon the plot, and to offer to the King the matter plotted. 2, or first to ask leave to treat, and then, whether first to pray a conference with the Lords, touching a petition to be offered to his Majesty for liberty to treat. Which last was thought the best course, and so resolved by the House."[1]

The Lords were quite ready to confer, and only desired that some other things of the same kind,—as Respite of Homage, Licence of

Alienation, and the general abuse of Purveyors and Car-takers,— might be included in the consultation To this the Commons readily agreed, and the proper number of Committees being appointed, the Conference took place the same afternoon of which Bacon, though he had not taken any part in the discussion, was again employed to make the report, which is thus recorded in the Journals

"Sir Fr Bacon maketh report of the conference yesterday between the Lords and this House, where, he said, he was merely a relator, no actor and said further, that the Lords upon their first meeting desired the Committees of this House to make the proposition Whereupon it was thought fit by the said Committee not to mention any objections, but only to show, 1 their dutiful respect in the handling of the matter and secondly to open the grief, adding some cautions and considerations to prevent mistaking

The grief was, That every man's eldest son or heir (the dearest thing he hath in the world) was, by Prerogative warranted by the laws of the land, to be in ward to the King for his body and lands, than which they conceived (to a free nation) nothing to be more grievous.

But they esteemed it only a grief, no wrong sithence it hath been patiently endured by our ancestors, and by ourselves, and therefore they did press to offer it to the King's grace, and not to his justice They knew it concerned the King in two sorts

1 In his revenue

2. And in reward to his well-deserving servants, and officers of his wards.

That the discharge of the wardship of mean Lords was also to be thought on —

And concluded, that their desire and resolution was, not to proceed by way of Bill, but by way of petition to his Majesty, for licence to treat, etc.

Of the Lords, first, one answered that they had as much feeling as any of the burden, and that with a double respect, because their families were planted in honour. That there was one other great grievance much complained of, in the matter of Respite of Homage, wherein though the King were interested in honour and profit, yet their desire was that it might be coupled in the petition with the matter of wardship, as growing upon that root.

It was affirmed by another Lord, that in the matter of Respite of Homage present order was to be taken, by special direction from his Majesty, and that for the grievance of Purveyors, there was some order taken already, and all convenient means daily thought on for relief and ease of the subject. But they knew the House did not intend to decry or dismiss the King of his Prerogative, and that this grievance was to be reformed by law, and not by petition .

Sir Francis continued his report of another Lord's speech, which (he said) he did but only report, not deliver as a message. It contained three points.

1 His affection to the House of the Commons
2 His good wishes unto it
3 The great benefits the King bringeth with him, as the peace we have by him, and the latitude and prospect of that peace.

That the King was born for us —That a people may be without a King, a King cannot be without a people —A persuasion that the House would answer him in all good correspondence

1. In modesty, that our desires be limited
2 In plainness, that we lay ourselves open in the naked truth of our hearts
3 In order and comeliness of proceeding, which is the band and ornament of all societies

The same Lord touched the case of Sir Francis Goodwin, as a thing he had heard at large, but did not understand it; and therefore desired to know it more particularly from this House

Answer was made that they had no warrant from the House to speak of it." [1]

Bacon will reappear hereafter in a more prominent position in connexion with this question of Wardship but in the subsequent proceedings during the present session I do not find any notice of the part he took, or whether he took any part. The cause appears to have been under the special charge of Sir Edwyn Sandys—one of the ablest of the independent members but it made no further way Many accidents intervened to postpone the proposed conference, and by the time it took place (which was not before the end of May) tempers were altered, and the result was unsatisfactory But of this I shall have occasion to speak further on, in connexion with the circumstances which brought the session to a somewhat sullen and cloudy end

[1] C J p 155

4.

The movement against the Purveyors, in the mean time, had fared a little better   Though the Commons had readily assented to the proposal of the Lords that this subject among others should be discussed at the Conference, they would not allow it to be put into the same boat with Wardship and Tenures, but resolved to deal with it separately   Instead however of dealing with it directly by a Bill—which was their first intention—they concluded upon further consideration that it would be more prudent to feel and prepare their way by a petition to the King, to be delivered "with some speech of introduction and explanation," and that speech to be made by Bacon which was accordingly done (27th April)   and of the way in which it was done we have on this occasion better means than usual of judging, a full report of his speech having been fortunately preserved by Bacon himself

It was first printed in the Resuscitatio (p 5)   But I take my text from a manuscript in the Harleian collection, which has corrections in Bacon's own hand

A Speech made by Sir Francis Bacon, Knight, chosen by the Commons to present a Petition touching Purveyors, delivered to his Majesty in the Withdrawing Chamber at Whitehall in the Parliament held 1° et 2do Jac , the first Session [1]

It is well known to your Majesty (excellent King) that the Emperors of Rome for their better glory and ornament did use in their titles the additions of the countries and nations where they had obtained victories, as *Germanicus, Britannicus,* and the like, but after all those names, as in the higher place, followed the name of *Pater Patriæ,* as the greatest name of all human honour immediately preceding that name of *Augustus,* whereby they took themselves to express some affinity that they had (in respect of their office) with divine honour   Your Majesty mought with good reason assume unto yourself many of those other names, as *Germanicus, Saxonicus, Britannicus, Francicus, Danicus, Gothicus,* and others, as appertaining to you, not by bloodshed (as they bare them) but by blood, your Majesty's royal person being a noble confluence of streams and veins, wherein the royal

[1] Harl MSS 6797, f 170   The last leaf, which has been displaced, will be found at f 17 of the same volume   There is another copy f 178, but it represents the MS before Bacon corrected it

blood of many kingdoms of Europe are met and united   But no name is more worthy of you, nor may more truly be ascribed unto you, than that name of *father of your people,* which you bear and express, not in the formality of your stile, but in the real course of your government   We ought not to say unto you as was said to Cæsar Julius, *Quæ miremur habemus, quæ laude mus expectamus* that we have already wherefore to admire you, and that now we expect somewhat for which to commend you, for we may (without suspicion of flattery) acknowledge that we have found in your Majesty great cause both of admiration and commendation   For great is the admiration wherewith you have possessed us since this Parliament began, in those two causes wherein we have had access unto you, and heard your voice, that of the return of Sir Francis Goodwin , and that of the Union Whereby it seemeth unto us, the one of these being so subtile a question of law and the other so high a cause of estate, that as the Scripture saith of the wisest king *that his heart was as the sands of the sea,* which though it be one of the largest and vastest bodies, yet it consisteth of the smallest motes and portions, so (I say) it appeareth unto us in these two examples, that God hath given your Majesty a rare sufficiency, both to compass and fadom the greatest matters, and to discern the least   And for matter of praise and commendation, which chiefly belongeth to goodness, we cannot but with great thankfulness profess, that your Majesty, within the circle of one year of your reign, *infra orbem anni vertentis,* hath endeavoured to unite your Church which was divided, to supply your nobility which was diminished, and to ease your people in cases where they were burdened and oppressed

In the last of these your high merits, that is, the ease and comfort of your people, doth fall out to be comprehended the message which I now bring unto your Majesty, concerning the great grievance arising by the manifold abuses of Purveyors, differing in some degree from most of the things wherein we deal and consult; for it is true that the knights citizens and burgesses in parliament assembled are a representative body of your Commons and third estate, and in many matters, although we apply ourselves to perform the trust of those that chose us, yet it may be we do speak much out of our own senses and discourses.   But in this grievance, being of that

nature whereunto the poor people is most exposed, and men of
quality less, we shall most humbly desire your Majesty to conceive, that your Majesty doth not hear our opinions or senses,
but the very groans and complaints themselves of your Commons,
more truly and vively than by representation   For there is no
grievance in your kingdom so general, so continual, so sensible,
and so bitter unto the common subject, as this whereof we now
speak. Wherein it may please your Majesty to vouchsafe me
leave first to set forth unto you the dutiful and respective carriage of our proceeding; next the substance of our petition; and
thirdly some reasons and motives which in all humbleness we
do offer to your Majesty's royal consideration or commiseration,
we assuring ourselves that never king reigned that had better
notions of head and motions of heart for the good and comfort
of his loving subjects

For the first, in the course of remedy which we desire we pretend not nor intend not in any sort to derogate from your
Majesty's prerogative, nor to touch, diminish, or question any
your Majesty's regalities or rights   For we seek nothing but the
reformation of abuses, and the execution of former laws whereunto we are born.   And although it be no strange thing in parliament for new abuses to crave new remedies, yet nevertheless
in these abuses (which if not in nature yet in extremity and
height of them are most of them new) we content ourselves with
the old laws, only we desire a confirmation and quickening of
them in their execution; so far are we from any humour of innovation or encroachment

As to the court of the green-cloth, ordained for the provision
of your Majesty's most honourable household, we hold it ancient,
we hold it reverend   Other courts respect your politic person,
but that respects your natural person   But yet notwithstanding
(most excellent king) to use that freedom which to subjects that
pour out their griefs before so gracious a king is allowable, we
may very well allege unto your Majesty a comparison or similitude used by one of the fathers in another matter, and not unfitly
representing our case in this point, and it is of the leaves and
roots of nettles, The leaves are venomous and stinging where
they touch, The root is not so, but is without venom or malignity; and yet it is that root that bears and supports all the
leaves   This needs no further application

To come now to the substance of our petition, it is no other than by the benefit of your Majesty's laws to be relieved of the abuses of Purveyors, which abuses do naturally divide themselves into three sorts. The first, they take in kind that they ought not to take, The second, they take in quantity a far greater proportion than cometh to your Majesty's use, The third, they take in an unlawful manner, in a manner (I say) directly and expressly prohibited by divers laws

For the first of these, I am a little to alter their name, for instead of takers they become taxers, instead of taking provision for your Majesty's service they tax your people *ad redimendam vexationem* imposing upon them and extorting from them divers sums of money, sometimes in gross, sometimes in the nature of stipends annually paid, *ne noceant*, to be freed and eased of their oppression   Again they take trees which by law they cannot do, timber-trees, which are the beauty, countenance, and shelter of men's houses, that men have long spared from their own purse and profit; that men esteem (for their use and delight) above ten times the value, that are a loss which men cannot repair or recover.   These do they take, to the defacing and spoiling of your subjects' mansions and dwellings, except they may be compounded with according to their own appetites, and if a gentleman be too hard for them while he is at home, they will watch their time when there is but a bailiff or a servant remaining, and put the axe to the root of the tree ere ever the master can stop it   Again they use a strange and most unjust exaction in causing the subjects to pay poundage of their own debts, due from your Majesty unto them, so as a poor man, when he hath had his hay or his wood or his poultry (which percase he was full loth to part with, and had for the provision of his own family, and not to put to sale) taken from him, and that not at a just price but under the value, and cometh to receive his money, he shall have after the rate of twelve pence in the pound abated for poundage of his due payment, growing upon so hard conditions.   Nay further, they are grown to that extremity, as is affirmed, though it be scarce credible (save that in such persons all things are credible) that they will take double poundage, once when the debenture is made, and again the second time when the money is paid

For the second point (most gracious Sovereign) touching the

quantity which they take, far above that which is answered to
your Majesty's use ; they are the only multipliers in the world ;
they have the art of multiplication   For it is affirmed ui to me
by divers gentlemen of good regard and experience in these
causes as a matter which I may safely avouch before your Majesty (to whom we owe all truth, as well of information as subjection) that there is no pound profit which redoundeth to your
Majesty in this course, but induceth and begetteth three pound
damage upon your subjects, besides the discontentment   And
to the end they may make this spoil, what do they ?   Where is
divers statutes do strictly provide that whatsoever they take shall
be registered and attested, to the end that by making a collation
of that which is taken from the country and that which is answered above their deceits might appear, they, to the end to
obscure their deceits, utterly omit the observation of this which
the law prescribeth.

And therefore to descend, if it may please your Majesty, to
the third sort of abuse, which is of the unlawful manner of their
taking, whereof this omission is a branch ; it is so manifold as it
rather asketh an enumeration of some of the particulars than a
prosecution of all   For their price by law they ought to take
as they can agree with the subject, by abuse they take at an
imposed and enforced price ; by law they ought to make but one
apprisement by neighbours in the country ; by abuse they make
a second apprisement at the court-gate and when the subject's
cattle come up many miles lean and out of plight by reason
of their travel, then they prize them anew at an abated price ;
by law they ought to take between sun and sun , by abuse they
take by twilight, and in the night-time, a time well chosen for
malefactors , by law they ought not to take in the highways, a
place by your Majesty's high prerogative protected, and by
statute by special word excepted , by abuse they take in the
ways, in contempt of your Majesty's prerogative and laws ; by
law they ought to shew their commission, and the form of commission is by law set down ; the commissions they bring down
are against the law, and because they know so much they will
not shew them   A number of other particulars there are,
whereof (as I have given your Majesty a taste) so the chief of
them upon deliberate advice are set down in writing by the labour of certain committees, and approbation of the whole house,

more particularly and lively than I can express them, myself having them but at the second hand by reason of my abode above. But this writing is a collection of theirs who dwell amongst the abuses of these offenders, and the complaints of the people; and therefore must needs have a more perfect understanding of all the circumstances of them

It remaineth only that I use a few words, the rather to move your Majesty in this cause a few words (I say) a very few For neither need so great enormities any aggravating, neither needeth so great grace as useth of itself to flow from your Majesty's princely goodness any artificial persuading There be two things only which I think good to set before your Majesty, The one the example of your most noble progenitors kings of this realm, who from the first king that endowed this kingdom with the great charter of their liberties until the last, have ordained, most of them,[1] in their several reigns some laws or law against this kind of offenders, and specially the example of one of them, that king who for his greatness, wisdom, glory, and union of several kingdoms, resembleth your Majesty most both in virtue and fortune, King Edward the third, who in his time only made ten several laws against this mischief The second is the example of God himself, who hath said and pronounced, *That he will not hold them guiltless that take his name in vain* For all these great misdemeanors are committed in and under your Majesty's name And therefore we hope your Majesty will hold them twice guilty that commit these offences, once for the oppressing of the people, and once more for doing it under the colour and abuse of your Majesty's dreaded and beloved name So then I will conclude with the saying of Pindarus, *Optima res aqua*, not for the excellency, but for the common use of it, and so contrariwise this matter of abuse of purveyance (if it be not the most heinous abuse) yet certainly it is the most common and general abuse of all others in the kingdom

It resteth that, according to the commandment laid upon me, I do in all humbleness present this writing to your Majesty's royal hands, with most humble petition on the behalf of your Com

---

[1] So corrected in Bacon's hand The passage had been originally written thus " All save one (who as she was singular in many excellent things, so I would she had not been alone in this) have ordained, every one of them," etc

mons, that as your Majesty hath been pleased to vouchsafe your gracious audience to hear me speak, so you would be pleased to enlarge your patience to hear this writing read, which is more material

This speech was delivered on the 27th of April, while the King was eagerly urging on the settlement of the Union,—a measure which was proceeding slowly through a variety of obstructions, very trying to his patience though they had not yet prevailed over it   He was not at all in a humour to make any new difficulty, and in this case he had no temptation   He had no sympathy with extortionate Purveyors, whom he was always ready to hand over to the Lord Chief Justice in case of complaint,[1] and having committed himself to no opinion which the motion threatened to assail, he was quite ready with a gracious answer and allowance   What he said we only know from the note of Bacon's report, made to the House the next day   But there can be no doubt that the movement, thus gracefully and judiciously conducted, was so far quite successful.   The Commons had his full consent to proceed with their professed object, and were only desired to confer with the Privy Council about it

That part of Bacon's report which relates to his own introductory speech I need not quote   It appears to have contained a full account of what he said, without any material variation ; the notes forming a series of memoranda from which one who had heard it might, while it was fresh in his memory, have reproduced the substance with great accuracy   Of the part which relates to the King's answer the notes are hardly sufficient, in the absence of a fuller commentary, to convey more than the general purport   But I give them as I find them

    His Majesty's answer
    A declaration of his mind
    Of his care already.
    Of his pleasure.
    The name of Father of the People greater than Emperor: Spoken of those that in fact would give comfort.
    Opposite to Rehoboam's answer —
    He would not answer so, but he would ease the burden — Hoped his fortune would be otherwise ; to unite where Rehoboam hath rent and torn
    He had cause to be sorry, and glad ·

[1] C J pp 189, 193

Sorry, that the general expectation of relief and solace should be frustrate by these men ·

Glad, that there was occasion for him so well to understand them

He would not neglect the punishment of that which is past — Provision for that which is to come —Satisfaction in both

His care hath been expressed .—

In summer last a definite and settled price of his provisions — A certain number of carts.

He appealed to his Council, who, being present, testified it —

His desire and pleasure, that they would have some conference with his Privy Council

The petition was then read [1] upon which, as the note proceeds,

The great officers of the Household gave some interruption by way of

Disproof

Justifying —

When complaint was made, they did justice.—

Never complaint in the stable since my Lord of Worcester's time

The like said by the Lord Admiral, the great officer of the Navy —

That they had these things only by relation.

Answered They would be verified.

They did according to ancient usage

Answ Usage or prescription, contrary to a positive statute, void

Not possible the King should be otherwise served

Answ *Quia mu um,—magnum mysterium,* that the King could not be served, if his laws observed.

Said by a great Lord

That their offences were

　　Felony .

　　Misdemeanour

To be prosecuted in the country, in course of Justice .—At the Assizes or Sessions.

This was all done or said at that time [2]

The next step therefore was to be a conference with the Lords,

[1] C J p 961　　　　　[2] C J p 192

which was held on the 8th or 9th of May, and seemed to show that the difficulty would be only in the terms of the arrangement This however, as the matter stood, was a considerable difficulty For the complaint was not (as in the case of Wardship) that the practice, though a legitimate source of profit to the Crown, was inconvenient, and therefore a fit subject for composition , but that it was against the law and therefore relief due without purchase

Of this conference Bacon was again the reporter, what part he had taken in it does not appear.

For Purveyors, etc , he said the Lords scope was to extermi-nate all Purveyors, etc   That they were sensible of our griefs, capable of our reasons, and careful of remedies. Purveyors termed by the Lords *Harpyiæ*   Wheresoever victuals were, there they wou'd seize

Our reasons had two heads ,

1 The Law was on our side —

His Majesty's means were increased , therefore the subject doth expect he will not press upon the people

Answ 1 *Summum jus summa injuria* —A rule between party and party , *a fortiori* in the King's case

2 *Necessitas non habet legem* —a thing impossible, to main-tain the King's charge without some help in this kind.

3. *Lex Talionis* —Many penal laws which the King doth ot press He looketh for the like measure of us.

2. Touching the King's ability and bounty.

Adhuc messis in herba

The King's charge in Ireland is yet 120,000*l* per annum

The cautionary towns 30,000*l*

Impositions in Spain 30 in the hundred :—We should be better gainers by war than by peace, if not for other consideration of state.

For remedy, they propounded composition by the subject, 50,000*l* per annum.

The Shires 27,000*l*   Supplies in specie 10,000*l*.

This concerns not the household and stable

King, Queen, Prince, Duke, and all included, with House-hold, Stable, etc , 50,000*l*

The Lords and Clergy should be assessed

Conclus   Omnia probate   quod bonum est tenete

190   LETTERS AND LIFE OF FRANCIS BACON.   [Chap V

From which side the proposal of an ar...l payment of £50,000 by way of composition proceeded, the terms of the note do not distinctly explain, and Mr Gardiner assumes that it came from the Commons[1] I cannot myself doubt however that "they" means the Committees of the House of Lords It cannot be supposed that the Committees of the Commons would have made such an offer without authority from the House, and it appears evidently from the notes of the subsequent debates that it was a good deal higher than the House was prepared to go But difficulties were found both as to matter and manner, and their consultations amongst themselves (in which I find no further traces of Bacon except in a recommendation to be content with the substance, if they could get it, and not to stand upon the form—"That we be not in Tantalus' case,— *Spectat aquas in aquis et poma fugacia captat* —Since it is to be hoped that his Majesty will give us satisfaction in the matter, let us give him satisfaction in the manner"[2]) ended at last in a resolution (2 June) to postpone all further proceeding till the next session, and to send a message to the Lords to that effect[3]

The truth was that other misunderstandings had arisen, which made smooth proceeding at present more and more difficult And, to explain these, we must now follow the great Union question through its first stages

5

The proceedings in relation to the Union began on the 14th of April with a message from the Lords inviting the Commons to a conference Their proposition (announced by the L Chancellor as "the King's purpose"[4]) was, to agree first upon a union in *Name*, and proceed afterwards to the consideration of laws and government,—their reason, I suppose, being that the Name appeared to be a simple thing which might be settled at once, while the other would be a long business

It soon appeared however that an alteration by Act of Parliament of the name and style of the two kingdoms was not so simple a thing as it seemed to be The debate upon the answer to be given to the Lords' proposition turned entirely upon that point, and after lasting four days ended in a resolution that the Union in *government* ought to be agreed on first[5]

[1] Hist of England, i 191   [2] C J p 978   [3] Ib p 231
[4] See a paper in Dudley Carleton's hand, entitled, "The several conferences with the Lords and debates in the Lower House touching the Union."—Domestic James I vol vii A valuable paper, but unfortunately imperfect
[5] C J p 179

In this debate Bacon took a prominent part The notes in the Journals however not being connected enough to show the tenour of his argument, it is better to take Carleton's account of what he said, though it is apparently but a small portion of it

Of his first speech (which seems to have been made on the 16th of April, upon the report of the propositions moved by the L Chancellor on the 14th) Carleton gives the following abstract.

That there were three considerations

Some things out of question, as the four unions named by the Lord Chancellor.[1]

Some things not properly in question; as the particular considerations of the union in substance

Some things now only in question the name, and the appointing of Commissioners to treat of the matter

That the name was Great Britany, wherein he considered the king's justice, his honour, and policy.

His justice, in regard of foreign Princes, upon whom he would not usurp by any unproper style of greatness, as that of Emperor or Great King, though the like was assumed by others, as by the Emperor of Germany and the Great King of Persia and Assyria

His honour, because honour contracted was better than honour divided, and compared it to one fair stone in a jewel, which was more precious than a jewel compacted of many That the name was honourable for the antiquity, and none known of old but Albion and Britany, but one of these was only poetical, the other true and historical

His policy, because a Union in name will draw on a unity in affection betwixt the two kingdoms; by example of the Cantons, who under the general name of Helvetia were better united The like of the several kingdoms under the name of Spain, and divers seignories under the title of Toscana.

Two objections made ·

That we should change our ancient name of England.

That we should prejudge the matter, and enwrap that which should be left free to the Committee.

Two answers

Every a good change for the better.

[1] Viz in sovereignty, in allegiance, in nature, and in religion — Carleton's paper

No danger to give by way of advance that which may be a
step forward to good action

Though the debate naturally ran upon the policy of the measures recommended, which involved the whole subject of the Union, the
immediate business which the House had to settle was, what to do
about the conference   And when the debate, having continued
through the 18th without result, was opened on the 19th with a
strong anti-Union speech, and seemed in danger of running the wrong
way, Bacon interposed with an attempt to bring it back within its
proper bounds.   Of this second speech Carleton gives the following
note

Sir Francis Bacon, directing his speech how to order a con
ference that was expected by the Lords touching this matter,
divided his speech into 3 parts

1   Matter of the Conference.
2   Limitation of the Commission
3   Disposing and ordering of the Conference

He began with the last, and wished that the Lower House
should not be the objectors only, but to make the case indiffe
rent betwixt the two Houses.

Touching the second part he advised that the Commissioners
might treat generally with the Lords, without limitation, but
conclude nothing.

For the matter which was now seasonably to be prepared, he
made a collection of 8 objections; whereof some were made by
Sir Maurice Barkley, who first turned the stream backward,
and others by particular members of that House the day before
and that morning

" He would seem " (adds Carleton) " to make answers to the ob
jections, and did only shew his good will in it   but no matter came
from him worth the noting "   But whatever may have been thought
of the value of his answers, it is clear that his candour and fairness
as a reporter was felt and valued at its worth, and that his speeches
had made a favourable impression on the House , for in all the sub
sequent proceedings (which were very many) the leading part was
by common consent assigned to him

The debate continued one day more, and ended at last (20th
April) in the appointment of a Committee to meet the Lords, and
hear their proposition   with instructions to assent to a conference
concerning the appointment of Commissioners to treat of a union

in *Government*, but till that were settled, *not* to assent to any conference concerning the alteration of the *Name* a limitation which was against Bacon's advice—namely that they should have commission to *treat* of everything though not to *conclude* upon anything —and which (as we shall see) was not a fortunate amendment

The King in the mean time had not been prepared to meet with any difficulty at this stage, and hearing of so many speeches made in criticism of a proposition which was in fact his own, he became desirous—very naturally, though I think not very judiciously—to make a speech for himself

"The Lower House" (says Carleton) "being thus prepared for conference with the Lords,—before the time or place was appointed, or their message sent, the King sent to the House that as many as could should come before him that afternoon   They came accordingly, and were placed in the gallery next St James' Park, whither the King came about 3 of the clock, accompanied with most of the Lords of the Parliament"

This was on Friday, the 20th of April   The next day, Bacon, who had been selected as spokesman and reporter, gave a full account of what passed to the House; but as the notes of his report in the Journals (p 953) are scarcely intelligible, and it is important to understand the position which the King really took up in this matter, it may be convenient to give Carleton's account of it in his own words.

"His Majesty's speech was directed to the Committees of both the Houses, and was to this effect

That he desired to be heard before they did consult

That the long debating in the Lower House was against his expectation that the doubts which were cast were but curiosities of ignorant persons, such as sought to find knots in bulrushes

He desired his breast were made of crystal and though he was unhappily embarked in former matters, in this he liked not to have his deliberations questioned.

That it was the greatest and the least question that ever came in Parliament

He made then a proposition of 3 parts.

That the union which is already in substance should be acknowledged by an Act

That a name should be presently given according to this union

That a commission should be appointed to treat of such things as do further concern the union

He repeated certain objections, as one that the change was dishonourable Wherein he held himself wronged and dishonoured, because as the honour of the Kings of England his predecessors doth descend upon

1st objection

him, so should he bear the burden of the dishonour, if there were any in the change

The question of names so foolish that it should not trouble wise men

The comparison in this to be like titles and honours given to great men, as the Earls of Dorset and Northampton had lost nothing by accession of their new styles

2nd objection   That an enumeration of titles in a Prince were more honourable than one single name

Answer   If so, then might he as well call himself Lord of Cornwall, Devon, Cumberland, Northumberland, &c

A bunch of arrows always better than one

And one Barony which is of great value more to be esteemed than many petty Lordships

3rd objection   Why should this matter be first propounded here, and what if Scotland should not assent?

Answer   He would have this realm have the honour of the first proposition, as being next to him in honour and if Scotland should refuse, he would compel their assents, having a stronger party there than the opposite party of the mutiners

That he would so unite it that the Crown of Scotland should be ever adherent and follow the succession of the blood of England

That the island was Britany, and therefore being King of the whole island, he would be King of Britany —as Brutus and Arthur were, who had the style and were kings of the whole island

That this was the reason of his haste, being interessed in honour to be called that which he was

That we were all likewise interessed, because shadows beget substance and unity in name an unity in affection

That to suspect him to bring in innovation were to slander him, and were no less offence than *Scandalum Regis* is in comparison of *Scandalum Magnatum*

That he cannot alter laws of himself nor will not, but that the Commissioners should treat of a participation of such laws as were good in each and defective in the other, without prejudice of the fundamental laws of both realms

For conclusion he proposed a project of an Act touching the present change of the name and appointing of a commission, and advised that in our consultations we should not look to sophistry, but substance "

It is probable that Bacon, in his report of this speech, managed his lights and shadows so as to throw some of the points into the background But it is well to see the worst of it, and from the foregoing abstract, which lies under no suspicion of partiality, it will be seen that the King's explanation was frank, courteous, and good-tempered and with regard to his own intentions and purposes, satisfactory enough. Only the last paragraph was of a nature to alarm the jealousy of the House for the 'project' seems to have been a draft in due form of such an Act as he wished Parliament to pass Such a draft is still extant among the State papers,[1] and if it be the one in question (which, though not stated, appears probable) nothing could be more harmless in itself, nor indeed more to the purpose And yet, as officially propounded by the King, it might look like an attempt to dictate and though Bacon, knowing that such ground required wary walking, had taken care to have it set down in writing, that there might be no mistake, it bred no little trouble nevertheless The result I give again in Carleton's words

Sir Francis Bacon made the report of his M speech on the day following, and observed three things to be demanded by the King

1. The union in substance to be acknowledged

2 The name to be presently allowed.

3 The Commission to be appointed.

Three things disclaimed.

1 That the King meant not to extinguish the name of England, but to superinduce a new to the whole island

2 That he would not alter the fundamental laws of the realm

3 That the Scotch should not encroach upon us

He ended with delivering in the King's 'project' as dictated at his own request, observing that it was not meant to ' prejudice the liberty of their conference, not to tie them to this or any other form This but a piece of crystal, to deliver him from mistaking "[2]

At first the House seems to have been taken by surprise with this, and not known how to receive it But as soon as the members came to talk it over among themselves, the effect showed itself in the temper of the discussion It "was read to the House," says Carleton, "and for that time not debated on but the next day and four days after, both in the House and in the Committee for this purpose, it was throughly sifted, and both the particularities of the King's speech and the project for the Act directly oppugned
And now all men's opinions went this way, and nothing said by any which was not against the Union either in the name or substance Only Sir Francis Bacon would seem to give a stop to this current, by a speech he made of three sorts of objections to be avoided —

1 Light objections lest it should be said *rebus arduis levia immisceri*

[1] Domestic James I April, 1604   [2] C J p 180

2 Subtile and curious lest in like manner it might be said *Rerum ponder a verborum fi enqit argutus*

3 High, and that we must not *scrutari arcana imperii* "

This, it appears from the Journals (for Carleton gives no dates), was on the 26th of April   In the mean time, the first conference with the Lords had been held, and the result reported by Bacon on the 23rd, which was that the Committees of the Lower House had been unable, from the limitation of their commission, to go into the argument ¹ the fact being, I suppose, that the Lords began with the question of union in *name*, whereas the Commons had forbidden their Committees to enter upon that until the question of union in *government* had been considered   It was now plain that the question of the name must be dealt with first, and the Committee was instructed to consider it

The King at the same time endeavoured to allay the alarm which his 'project' had excited, by a message² in which he assured the House that he had merely meant to explain himself, and did not wish at all to interfere with the freedom of their deliberations   an assurance of which I see no reason to doubt the sincerity   for the thing was in itself natural and rational, there being no way of showing how a thing may be done half so good as doing it   And—in further proof that he meant nothing unconstitutional,—finding that besides the objections to his proposal which he regarded (not I think without reason) as trivial, it was charged by the lawyers with one consequence of very serious character, he immediately referred it to the consideration of the Judges, with an earnest adjuration that they would   ground all their judgments upon reason, policy, and example of other kingdoms," and "upon their consciences to God and allegiance to him declare the truth "³

The Committee of the Commons meanwhile, according to the instructions given on the 23rd, went on with their preparations for the coming Conference with Lords about the name, and new objections came fast in   On the 25th Bacon reported that they found themselves in the case of Simonides when Hiero asked him what he thought of God, who asked first for six days to consider, then for twelve, then for twenty-four   "The more we wade" (he said) "the more we doubt," and then produced a list of the objections which had been urged by various members of the Committee against the

---

¹ "More silence than was meant, for want of warrant   Advice   that there might be free mandate and commission to debate, but not to conclude of anything" C J p 182
² C J p 183
³ See a paper in his own hand , docketed by Salisbury "The addition to his Speech "—Domestic James I. April, 1604

change of name which were 13 in number The next day Sir
Edwin Sandys made a long speech on the subject, adding other objections not included in the previous report and upon his motion,
supported by Bacon, it was settled that the parts should be distributed and the several arguments assigned to several persons Which
was done, as appears by the following report made by Bacon on the
27th, and printed apparently from the original manuscript [1]

Sir Francis Bacon reporteth from the Committee touching
the Union, that they had digested their resolution into heads,
and assigned several parts to several persons, of several qualities,
as they conceived fit

Light of order (he said) casteth beams upon the matter ·
and produced a paper containing all the objections heretofore
made in the House against the Union in Name and was directed by the House to stand at the Board and to read it himself, as being best acquainted with the order of it.

This paper had in the front this title —

Objections against the change of the name or style of
England and Scotland into the name or style of Great
Brittany, to be moved and debated in the Conference between the Lords and the Commons, and to that end by
the Committees of the House of Commons collected, reviewed, and reduced to order, for their better instruction.

The objections are of four several natures or kinds .—
Matter of generality or common reason
Matter of estate inward, or matter of law.
Matter of estate foreign, or matter of intercourse
Matter of honour or reputation.

The matter of generality or common reason hath two parts —
That there is no cause of the change.
That there is no precedent of the like change
The first objection therefore is —
That in constituting or ordaining of any innovation or
change, there ought to be either urgent necessity or evident
utility; but that we find no grief of our present estate,
and foresee no advancement to a better condition by this
change, and therefore desire it may be showed unto us
The second objection is —

[1] C J p 188.

That we find no precedent, at home or abroad, of uniting or contracting of the names of two several kingdoms
or states into one name, where the union hath grown by
marriage or blood, and that those examples which may be
alleged, as far as we can find, are but in the case of conquest.

Matter of estate inward, or matter of law, hath three main
heads —

The first, That the alteration of the name of the King
doth inevitably and infallibly draw on an erection of a new
kingdom or estate, and a dissolution and extinguishment of
the old; and that no explanation, limitation, or reservation
can clear or avoid that inconvenience, but it will be full
of repugnancy and ambiguity, and subject to much variety
and danger of construction

The second is an enumeration or recital of the special
and several confusions, incongruities, and mischiefs which
will necessarily and incidently follow in the time present,
as,

In the summoning of Parliaments, and the recitals of
Acts of Parliament

In the seals of the kingdom

In the great officers of the kingdom ·

In the laws, customs, liberties, and privileges of the
kingdom.

In the residence and holding of such Courts as follow
the King's person, which by this generality of name may
be held in Scotland.

In the several and reciproque oaths: the one, of his Majesty at his Coronation, which is never iterated, the other,
in the oaths of Allegiance, Homage, and Obedience, made
and renewed from time to time by the subjects

All which acts, instruments, and forms of policy and
government, with a multitude of other forms of Records,
Writs, Pleadings, and Instruments, of a meaner nature,
run now in the name of England, and upon the change
would be drawn into incertainty and question.

The third is a possibility of alienation of the Crown
of England to the line of Scotland, in case his Majesty's
line should determine (which God of his goodness defend);

for if it be a new-erected Kingdom, it must go, in the nature of a purchase, to the next heir of his Majesty's father's side.

The matter of state foreign, or matter of intercourse, consisteth of three points —

The first is, That Leagues, Treaties, foreign Freedoms of Trade and Traffic, foreign Contracts, may be drawn in question, and made subject to quarrel and cavillation.

The second is, that the King's precedence before other Christian Kings, which is guided by antiquity of kingdoms, and not by greatness, may be endangered, and his place turned last, because it is the newest

The third is, that the glory and good acceptation of the English name and nation will be, in foreign parts, obscured

The matter of honour and reputation standeth upon four points —

The first is, that no worldly thing is more dear to men than their name, as we see in private families, that men disinherit their daughters to continue their names: much more in States, and where the name hath been famous and honourable

The second is, that the contracted name of Brittaine will bring in oblivion the names of England and Scotland

The third is, that whereas now England, in the style, is placed before Scotland, in the name of Brittaine that degree of priority or precedence will be lost

The fourth is, that the change of name will be harsh in the popular opinion, and unpleasing to the country.

The maintenance of these several parts at the conference intended was reported to be thus distributed, viz —

Matter of generality or common reason, two parts

1 That there is no cause of change —Sir Francis Bacon.

2 That there is no precedent of like change —Sir Edwyn Sandys.

Matter of estate inward and of law —Mr Serjeant Hobart, Serjeant Dodridge, Serjeant Tanfield, Mr. Attorney of the Wards.

Matter of estate foreign, or matter of intercourse —Sir Henry Nevill, Sir Rich Spencer, Sir John Hollis, Sir Arthur Atye,

Sir Chro. Perkins, Sir Lewys Lewknor, Sir Geo Carey,
Master of Chancery.

Matter of honour and reputation —Sir Francis Hastings,
Sir Maurice Berkley, Sir Geo. Moore, Sir Herbert Crofts,
Mr Martin, Mr. Yelverton, Sir John Savill, Sir Rob
Wingfield, Sir Oliver St John, Sir Rob. Wroth, Mr Crewe,
Sir Edward Hobby, Mr. Hyde [1]

These preparations in effect settled the question For the Judges
had in the meantime given the opinion for which the King had
asked, and had given it against him   "All the judges of the realm'
(says Cecil writing on the 28th April to the Earl of Mar) "have
joined with the opinion of three parts of the House, that the first
hour wherein the Parliament gives the King the name of Great
Britany, there followeth necessarily by our laws a distraction, or
rather an utter extinction of all the laws now in force For, say
they, if the King be acknowledged by Act of Parliament King of
Britany, all processes, all writs, all executions of justice, yea the very
recognition of the King in this Parliament to be lawful possessor
of the Crown of England *secundum leges et consuetudines legum
Angliæ*, are made nothing, and therefore must have a new creation
an interim of a dangerous consequence in the apprehension of multi
tudes So as, to tell you what I conceive, his M (who never had
intention by his proposition of the name to change anything of that
nature, but to leave all those things to the event of future consulta
tions by Commissioners and to the resolutions of both Parliaments)
will be pleased for this cause only to forbear the urging of the pre
sent appellation, and will refer it with the rest to the Commis
sioners " &c [2]

And so accordingly it came to pass For when the Committees
met in conference, the Lord Chancellor, after a recapitulation of the
King's wishes in the matter, added in conclusion that "his desire
likewise was to give and receive satisfaction, and that he was not so
resolved on the name of Britany, as if it be found any prejudice to
the laws of the realm by any tacit signification, not to depart from his
purpose " and he was followed by Cecil, who "brought out in writ
ing an explanation of the King's former project,[3] which was read by
himself " Whereupon "a question grew betwixt the Lower House
and the Lords, whether the conference should proceed, the case

[1] C J p 188 (27 April)
[2] Domestic Jour I 28 April, 1604 Draft, corrected in Salisbury's own hand
[3] This was no doubt the paper docketed, "His M explanation of his meaning
in the project which he sent in writing to the Commons House," etc (C J p
180), which the editor of the Journals mistook for the project itself

being thus altered, and overruled that they should proceed, because the King's words were but conditional—in case better reason could be showed him, then to alter the course of his proceeding " [1]

Carleton's account of what followed unluckily breaks off in the middle, and we must look for the result in the Journals But his note of Bacon's speech, of which we have no other report, may be given here

Sir Francis Bacon entered first into the matter; with this protestation, that they spake but by way of argument and not of conclusion That they took the opposite side because the Lords were for the Union, and if they were against it, he for argument's sake would have been for it.

His theme was, that there was now neither necessity of change nor evident utility.

That we were now in a good haven and loth to put to sea · that we would not adventure upon a new condition unless there might appear some matter of improvement

Multa utilitate juvant, quæ novitate perturbant [2]

Sir Edwin Sandys followed with a long and learned speech upon the division of the argument which had been assigned to him, which raised much discussion in the middle of which the manuscript ends abruptly The result was however in accordance with Cecil's prediction It was agreed that the name should be dropped, and that they should confine themselves to the appointment of Commissioners to consider the other questions incident to a complete union and incorporation of both laws and kingdoms [3]

Of Bacon's report of this conference (made to the House on the 30th of April) we have the following note in the Journals

Sir Francis Bacon doth also make report of the conference had with the Lords on Saturday, touching the Union

The instructions read in the house, containing all the objections, he had in his hand, and said, the matter was prosecuted on those grounds

But the proceeding there divided itself into an Introduction, Matter, and Conclusion.

1 The Lord Chancellor's admonition ·—

The partition wall taken away, no man to repair it

[1] Carleton   [2] Carleton   [3] Letter to Mar, quoted before

The Lord Cecyll produced a project[1] from the King —

That it was not his meaning to take the name upon him, if the state could not be secured —

Maluit non dimicare quam non vincere.

Great magnanimity and policy to have the name.

Great moderation and justice to leave it

At length, from confutation,[2] the Lords fell into a commendation of their loyalty, their liberty, their gravity, their carriage, &c

The matter of the name to be left

The matter of naming the Commissioners to be proceeded in notwithstanding.

They shall hear from the Lords before any further proceeding.[3]

This concession removed the difficulty   The choice of Commissioners and the terms of the commission entailed of course a good deal of deliberation and several conferences between the Houses, but no important disagreement.   And the nature of the proceedings which followed will be sufficiently indicated by the notes of Bacon's successive reports, which I give in order, with the date of each

1 May

Sir Francis Bacon reported the Conference with the L

The Lord Chancellor made the overture, which ha⟨   ⟩
parts

   1   Repetition of the proceedings of the King

   2   Report of the opinion of the Judges

   3   A brief proposition, what was to be done.

1   His Majesty had thrice propounded this motion in Parliament, twice in open Parliament; never propounding the name definitively, but conditionally

There had not been only a fail in reason, but in point of honour, if there had been contradiction either *tacitè* or *implicitè*

2   The Judges' opinions

---

[1] So in the Journals but Carleton is undoubtedly correct in calling it "an *explanation* of the King's *former* project" There is a copy of it among the State Papers written entirely in Cecil's own hand, which is probably the draft, but whether of Cecil's own composition or written from the King's dictation, seems doubtful

[2] In the Journals, from which this is transcribed, the word is *consultation* But in the notes (p 961) from which the Journals have been compiled the words are, "then *confutation* into a commendation," etc which I have little doubt is right

[3] C J p 193 (30 April)

The name, a thing left, and no more to be spoken on.

He propounded six articles touching the Commission and naming of Commissioners *viz*

1 The number and naming to be left to ourselves.

2 The return to be made, upon prorogation, to the same body.

3 The Commissioners to treat and consult only, not to determine

4. The tenor of the Commission to be plain and general.

5 To be digested, and made ripe to be framed into an Act, by a sub-committee of both Houses, to that purpose to be selected.

6 That there may be another Conference for these purposes.

Conclus *Principia actionum tantum sunt in nostra potestate.* —The Lords, stars of influence, stars of brightness

Mr Secretary Herbert sent to the Lords with message that they will be ready to confer according to their Lordships' motion at the late Conference [1]

2 May.

Report made by Sir Francis Bacon of the Conference yesterday

Some things agreed

Some only moved.

1 Whether a commission should go forth ·—Admitted.

2 Whether a compounded nomination of Commissioners, or a separate —agreed to be severally named

3 The number to be competent, neither over great nor over small

Touching the quality of the persons; to be a mixture of Common Lawyers, Civilians, Men of State, Merchants, &c

The Commission first to be agreed on, and then Commissioners.

The Commission to begin the first of October.

The place, London, Westminster, *Camera depicta.*

The return to be made to the next Session of this Parliament.

Four things to be inserted in the Act

1 Acknowledgment of God's providence, and great blessing, in the Union already made

2 The Cause, contrariety and disconcurrence of some particular laws in the several kingdoms.

3. Recital of his Majesty's faithful promise, not to alter the laws

4. Proviso, that Scotland shall make a cession.

Exception to words, &c

Expedition in framing of a bill   To that purpose six of this House, four of that House, with Judges assistants to be named[1]

9 May

For the Conference touching the Union, he said the time was wholly spent in considering of instructions for the Bill to enable Commissioners, &c

They considered of the preface ·

The body.

Agreed to name the Commisioners before the Bill be drawn for it cannot be perfect before the Commissioners be named.

Urged, that the instructions for the Bill were directed to be delivered in writing and not verbally

Excused by the reporter that he heard of no such direction, neither had he any commission from the House[2]

On the 12th of May Bacon delivered in "a draft of the act for the authorising of Commissioners," etc (which I suppose had been approved by the Committee of the Commons), "with excuse that he did not obtrude it the last day, without some speech beforehand"[3] etc

Of this draft nothing more is said in the Journals but as I find one in the State Paper Office answering the description, written in a hand employed by Bacon himself on other occasions, and differing very much from the act which was ultimately passed, I presume that it is the one in question, and probably of his own composition There are two or three drafts of Proclamations, etc, preserved by himself in his collection of *Orationes, Acta, Instrumenta*, and described as "prepared but not used ,' and though this is not among them, I take it to be one of the same kind[4]

An Act for the better grounding of a further Union to ensue between the Kingdoms of England and Scotland.

Most gracious Sovereign We your Lords Spiritual and temporal and Commons in this present Parliament assembled do most

---

[1] C J p 196   [2] Ib p 204   [3] Ib p 208
[4] It is docketed (but in another hand and apparently at a later time, and certainly by mistake), "The Speaker's speech to the King declaring consent of Com[n]"

thankfully acknowledge that it is the great and blessed work of
Almighty God that these two ancient famous and mighty kingdoms of England and Scotland which have been so many ages
united in continent and language, but separated in sovereignty
and allegiance, are now grown to an union in your Majesty's
royal person, most lawfully and most happily holding and enjoy-
ing both the same kingdoms by undoubted title in most quiet
and peaceable possession, and in a most flourishing estate, and it
seemeth unto us most manifest now after the event is come to
pass, that God, unto whom all his works are from the beginning
known, did by his divine providence long ago and from time to
time prepare a way unto this excellent work, first by the long-
continued peace and amity now for many years last past between
both the nations, secondly, by knitting them both in God's true
religion, which is the perfectest bond of all unity and union;
thirdly by a commixture of the most noble bloods of the line
royal of both the kingdoms so often redoubled and renewed in
your Majesty's excellent person, and fourthly by the equal and
indifferent terms and motives of affection which the same providence of God doth necessarily draw your Majesty to hold between
both the nations, having ordained that your Majesty's birth and
the passing of the first part of your age should be in the one
kingdom, and your Majesty's principal seat and mansion and the
passing of the latter part of your age should be in the other
We do acknowledge likewise in most humble manner that it is
in your Majesty a most royal and virtuous desire and full of
magnanimity wisdom and goodness, that as your Majesty is now
become *lapis angularis* of both kingdoms, and that the partition wall is now taken away and the vail rent, so your princely
desire is to second this blessed work of God, and to build
upon the foundation which he hath laid, and to conjoin and
consolidate these two kingdoms more and more, as far as may
stand with the weal and good estate of them both Wherefore
your Majesty having now in your singular wisdom moderation
and loving course held towards us clearly delivered us from all
shadows and fears by your most gracious declaration, often published iterated and explained unto us, that your Majesty hath
no intention to alter change or diminish our fundamental laws
liberties and grounds of government, but that your princely purpose is to remove and extirpate all seeds of discord between

both the nations, and to remedy and accommodate such points
of incongruity and disconvenience as the several laws and customs
of both kingdoms, which were fit and reasonable in the policy of the
kingdoms when they stood divided, but are now become utterly
unproper impossible and absurd, may bring forth, and[1] generally
to reduce your subjects in both realms to a perpetual conformity
and agreement, to the furtherance of your Majesty's obedience
and their own weal and good estate And your Majesty having also
given unto us a pledge of this your most gracious intention by your
princely suspension and forbearance to require of us any present
act for alteration of your Majesty's royal style and name, upon
the discovery of the perils that might ensue thereupon unto the
state of this kingdom, in the which your Majesty's most gracious
benignity we do yield unto you our most humble and affectionate
thanks It is therefore (most gracious Sovereign) all our hearts'
desire, not only for the giving satisfaction to your Majesty, which
we esteem more than our own lives, but also in discharge of our
duties unto the state of this kingdom which we represent, and accordingly it is our most humble petition unto your Majesty, that
it may be enacted by the authority of this present Parliament, and
be it enacted by the same authority, that there be chosen and no
minated in this present Parliament by both the houses of Parlia
ment respectively, a number of selected Commissioners who may
convene and join with selected Commissioners to be chosen and
appointed by the realm of Scotland, and thereupon consult and
treat of all questions propositions and considerations whatsoever,
which may tend or pertain to the more indissoluble and perfect
union conjunction agreement and mutual comfort and good of
both kingdoms; without any authority nevertheless to conclude
otherwise than as amongst themselves upon any point, but that
the report and return of the propositions articles treaties and
other the labours of the said Commissioners be made and exhibited
to the present Parliament, for that purpose to be prorogued and
not dissolved, that thereupon such resolutions and ordinances may
be taken and enacted as may stand with the joint and several
good of both kingdoms, and that to the purpose aforesaid Commission be awarded under the great seal of England unto the
persons hereafter specified, authorising them to proceed accord
ing to the tenour and true meaning of this act[2]

[1] The MS has "and may bring forth generally," etc
[2] S P Dom James I vol viii no 5

On the same day the House proceeded to the choice of the persons who were to be trusted with the Commission, and having first agreed that the list should include two Privy Councillors, two Ambassadors, four Common Lawyers, two Civilians, four Merchants, and sixteen Country Gentlemen, they had the names proposed one by one, and a several question put upon every name, and so the number was filled up. The names were marshalled afterwards according to rank, but it seems that they were proposed in order of importance, for the first vote was given for Bacon[1] It now remained only to agree with the Lords upon the frame of the Act, which led to two or three additional conferences, but to no material disagreement, and the Bill being sent down from the Upper House on the 30th of May, went as fast as possible through its regular stages, and was passed by the Commons on the 2nd of June[2] Which was as much as could be done in the matter, to any good purpose, for the present

6.

Thus far the King had in fact conceded all that was necessary easily enough and in time enough, insomuch that if he had only kept his thoughts and feelings to himself, his *acts* would have appeared wise, prudent, and temperate. But though good sense and good nature had prevailed with him in action, he was in his heart a good deal disappointed and mortified at finding so many difficulties made, in a work from which he had looked for nothing but applause and congratulation and everlasting honour and this mortification, unfortunately, he could not help betraying On the 21st of April he had told a Committee of the Commons that " he wished his heart were of crystal, that all might see his cogitations,"[3] and on the 1st of May he wrote a letter to the House, which showed that his wish had been granted —a letter of which the business and practical errand was merely to say that the point to which they demurred was withdrawn, and that they were free to deal with the question in their own way, but in which the personal sensibilities of a man who felt that his affection had been ill-requited, his words ill-weighed, his intentions misunderstood, his hopes disappointed, showed through in every line, and in its turn so hurt the feelings of his faithful Commons—for the House (strange to say) had feelings almost as jealous and sensitive as his own—that they were hardly dissuaded

---

[1] " And that myself was by the Commons graced with the first vote of all the Commons selected for that cause "—*Certain articles or considerations touching the Union of the Kingdoms, etc* Printed further on, p 218
[2] C J pp 228, 230   [3] Ib p 953

from making a formal grievance of the letter, and petitioning for
access, that they might give him what they called 'satisfaction"—
which always meant an argumentative demonstration that they were
right and he was wrong   This danger was happily avoided for the
present by another message,[2] intimating his gracious acceptance both
of the intention and the forbearance   But wounded hearts remain
tender, and there were several businesses in progress which could
hardly be handled without danger of fresh irritation   The Committee was still engaged in collecting evidence of the abuses of Purveyance   The composition for Wardship—a money-bargain for relief
from an oppressive prerogative—was still under discussion   The
struggle with the Warden of the Fleet over the body of Sir Thomas
Shirley was at its hottest   A series of conferences with the Lords
and Bishops was bringing them nearer and nearer to points of inevitable and irreconcileable disagreement   Not a word had been
said as yet about Supply   And in the middle of all this there sprung
up a new and unexpected cause of quarrel, in a book just published
by one of the Bishops   a book tending (according to the description
given by the member who brought it under notice) "to the derogation and scandal of the proceedings of the House in the matter of
the Union, answering the objections made against the union in
Name, and taking knowledge of many other passages of the House
touching that matter, unmeet to be questioned by any, much less
by any member of the Higher House "[3]

Here again their first impulse was "to go to his Majesty and express their grief, because it seemed to be done *cum privilegio*"—
meaning (I suppose) that as a published book it must be held as
authorized by the King   But being reminded that the Bishop was
a member of the Upper House, they determined to make their complaint first to them, and it turned out, fortunately for the peace of
the time, that he had no friends there   for after an exchange of one
or two preliminary messages, it was answered in conference by Lord
Cecil that he had been rebuked and made to own his fault and express his regret   as we learn from the following note

Sir Francis Bacon reporteth the Conference had, touching the
book published by the Bishop of Bristowe

A speech of a great Lord (E S.) in three parts

---

[1] C J p 197   In the debate on this question Bacon (2 May) spoke, apparently
in deprecation of the proceeding   But the note says only, "Sir Fr Bacon —*Sed*
motos præstat componere fluctus —Qui dolorem habent et non sensum, iis mens
ægrotat —Sed adversus veritatem, sed pro veritate"
[2] 4 May   Ib p 199   [3] C J p 226 (26 May)

1. Their good correspondence with this House.

2. A declaration of the proceedings against the Bishop

3 Reason why they went no further.

[1] That they were interested as well as we —

If not, yet the union of the two Houses gave them an interest

[2] A rebuke to the Bishop —

That which durst not shew his head in Parliament should go to the Press in mean hands.—

That any man should presume to let the King see more than a Parliament could —

The King the head, we the body. if any man will swell above the circumference, it must be a wert or a wenn.

[3] The Bishop made submission with them —*Peccavi, pœnitet, non putaram* —They remitted in respect of his coat — That he was a member —That he came under the shadow of the Cypress-tree, the Union

Conclus Less severely reported than performed.[1]

Here Bacon (who appears to have confined himself to a report of Cecil's speech) would probably have wished the matter to rest And though the House was not quite satisfied, but (in order that the Press might better know the limits of its liberty) proceeded to demand the suppression of the book and the public delivery of the Bishop's submission in writing, that it might be placed on record,[2] the compiler of the Journals seems to have been unable to discover

---

[1] C J p 236 (11 June)   The proceeding of the Lords is recorded in their own Journals (5 June) thus   "After that the Lords had entered into speech and consideration of some meet course to be taken for yielding satisfaction to the Lower House touching that matter, they did all agree in opinion, that the same might best be done if the said Bishop would voluntarily acknowledge himself to have committed an error in that behalf, and to be sorry for it, which acknowledgment the said Bishop in the end did accordingly make, and did express the same in these words following, *videlicet* —

"'1 I confess that I have erred in presuming to deliver a private sentence in a matter so dealt in by the High Court of Parliament

"'2 I am sorry for it

"'3 If it were to do again, I would not do it

"'4 But I protest it was done of ignorance and not of malice towards either of the Houses of Parliament, or any particular member of the same, but only to declare my affection to the intended Union, which I doubt not but all your Lordships do allow of'"

As we shall have to deal from time to time with questions bearing upon the just limits of liberty in speech and writing, I thought it as well to give this at full length, as a good illustration of what was thought by the guardians of liberty to be a transgression of those limits

[2] C J p 244 (21 June)

what came of that demand :[1] and therefore I suppose it was not insisted on.

At the same time a more legitimate cause of remonstrance was given by a protest from the Convocation House against the pretensions of the House of Commons to "deal in any matters of Religion,"[2] accompanied with a threat that if the Bishops would not desist from conferring with them, " they would appeal to the King, who had given them authority to deal only in such matters " This protest having been publicly read by a Bishop at a Conference, put them upon searching for "precedents"—a search which is sure to end favourably to the stronger party , and would undoubtedly have raised a storm, had either the King or the Lords taken part with Convocation As it was, a declaration from the Bishop of London that " they conceived the privilege of Parliament to stand upright"[3] was accepted as sufficient

All these incidental troubles must have been very annoying to the King, if only as delays and interruptions, though he had the prudence to keep personally clear of them   and there were other measures coming on, in which it was hardly possible to avoid a direct disagreement   He had settled the Church question to his own satisfaction at the Hampton Court Conference , and now the Commons were urging a large measure of reform, in the interest of the nonconforming clergy [4] He had taken order for the revocation of all monopolies which should appear to himself and Council prejudicial to the subject   and now they were preparing a large measure for the liberation of Trade, aimed at the monopolies of the great companies[5] The discussion of the terms of the proposed composition for Wardship and Tenures led inevitably to enquiries into the true state of the Crown revenew , which was then reckoned one of the *arcana imperii*,—no fit subject for popular criticism.

Under these various trials, the scanty measure of patience with which he was endowed by nature had begun to fail, and the distastes against which he had hitherto been struggling, to re-assert themselves—encouraged no doubt by the sympathy they were sure to meet with from the conservatism which prevails in all Upper Houses, whether temporal or spiritual , when this same Wardship and Tenure question, which had been opened under Bacon's management at the beginning of the session with fair words and prospects, came at last (30 May) to be discussed in a conference managed by Sir Edwin Sandys, and found the weather quite changed Not that the Commons

<hr>

[1] " For the submission, that being a fault committed, etc , *quære* "—C J p 251 (2 July)
[2] C J p 235 (8 June)   [3] Ib p 251 (2 July)   [4] Ib p 199   [5] Ib p 218

had changed their ground   What they desired was no more than
the Lords had already in a general way and with seeming alacrity
agreed to,—namely that they would join with them in a petition to the
King for leave to treat   the particulars being to be arranged in conference   But they now discountenanced the proposition altogether,
and besides answering the reasons urged by the Commons, went on
to expostulate with them on the manner in which they had spent
their time —all speaking in the same sense   *Sensi ex composto rem
geri*, said Sir E. Sandys in concluding his report   And to make
matters worse, no sooner had the conference broken off on these
unsatisfactory terms, than the King, by a coincidence which if un-
designed was unlucky, desired the attendance of the whole House,
that he might speak to them   And his speech, being (as we gather
from what followed—for I find no report of it) a review of all their
proceedings during the session in a tone of censure and dissatisfaction, had the usual effect of hurting their feelings and provoking
them to reply

But the state of feeling which it produced will be best understood
from the 'order' entered in the Journals the next day—the result
of the debate on Sir E Sandys' report   Which, though very clumsily
drawn up, I give as it stands

Veneris 1° Die Junii, 1604.

This day Sir Edwyn Sandys, making report of the late conference had
with the Lords, according to a former commission of this House, touching
the matter of Wardship and other the incidents thereunto, instead of acceptation and assent to join in petition to his Majesty, delivered from
their Lordships no other than matter of expostulation opposition of
reason to reason, admonition, or precise caution, in proceeding which
suiting with the grounds of his Majesty's speech subsequent, advisedly
and of purpose made upon that occasion to the whole House, assembled
by his Majesty's direction at Whitehall, on Monday last (wherein many particular actions and passages of the House were objected unto them, with
taxation and blame), summoned the duty and judgment of the House to
consider, what were fittest to be done, and amongst others the motion of
Sir Thomas Ridgway, one of the Knights for Devonshire, induced the
House to this consideration, that since it appeared his Majesty had made
such an impression of mislike of the proceedings of the House in general,
as also that the grounds conceived touching Wardship and matters of that
nature, seemed to be so weakened and impugned, it were necessary and
safe for the House, and dutiful and convenient in respect of his Majesty,
instantly to advise of such a form of satisfaction, either by writing or
otherwise, as might in all humility inform his Majesty in the truth and
clearness of the actions and intentions of the House from the beginning,
thereby to free it from the scandal of levity and precipitation, as also of

P 2

the proceedings in particular touching the said matter of Wardship, with this special care, that a matter so advisedly and gravely undertaken and proceeded in, might not die or be buried in the hands of those that first bred it [1]

A proceeding like this,—entailing as it must a personal contro ... with the King on points to which he had thus publicly com mi ed himself,—could not be expected to have a satisfactory result But it would take time Time would allow feelings to cool on both sides and meanwhile they could give satisfaction of a more promi sing kind by making haste with what remained to be done The Union Act, which had just been sent down from the Lords, had been read once It was now read a second time, committed, reported, passed, and sent back to the Lords, by whom it was received with great applause[2]—all in a day the day after the King's speech And it was agreed at the same time that all further proceedings in the matter of Purveyors should be allowed to sleep till the next session Measures which were not lost upon the King as may be seen by the message which he sent to the House only three days after

Mr Speaker delivereth from the King a message of three parts
The motives of his Majesty's unkindness
Matter of his relation to us
Of his princely satisfaction
When he looked into the gravity and judgment of this House, and of the long continuance of the Parliament, so few matters of weight passed and that matter of Privilege had taken much time (which, notwithstand ing, he was as careful to preserve as we ourselves), he was moved with jealousy that there was not such proceeding as, in love, he expected This the cause of unkindness

That we should not think this declaration to us was any condemnation of our ingratitude or forgetfulness of him, but by way of commemoration and admonition, as a father to his children, neither did he tax us, but only remember us of expedition, omitted and desired

Lastly, that he is resolved, we have not denied anything which is fit to be granted That he had divers arguments of our good affections

1 Our doubt of his displeasure

2 Our desire to give him satisfaction, which he accepteth as a thing done, because desired by us

3 He observeth the difference of our proceeding, sithence his speech unto us, with greater expedition in those things desired to be effected by him, than before He giveth us thanks, and wisheth we would not trouble ourselves with giving him satisfaction

And he giveth what time we desire for finishing the matters of import ance depending [3]

[1] C J p 230   [2] Ib p 231   [3] Ib p 232 (5 June)

In spite however of this message, which may be regarded as the
King's Apology to the Commons, the Committee appointed to prepare the threatened Apology of the Commons to the King went on
diligently with their work, and at the end of a fortnight laid the
result before the House —a grave and important document, in which
all their proceedings that had been found fault with were recapitu-
lated and justified, point by point, and which, though not formally
placed on record, remains to this day a notable landmark in the progress of constitutional liberty.   The question was, what to do with
it   I do not know that any exception was or could be taken either
to the substance of it or the style   But seeing that the positions
which it maintained were threatened only in words and by implication, that the Commons remained masters of the field in fact, that
there was no pretence for a serious declaration of hostilities, and
that the formal delivery of such an argument could have led to nothing but an angry altercation and a quarrel in the honeymoon—
which would have been bad for all parties—those who wished to preserve harmony could not wish that it should be pressed further
Bacon was certainly among those who spoke against presenting it,
though we have no account of what he said [1]   And as the Journals
contain no notice of the final resolution, we may conclude that it
was in favour of letting the dispute rest, and that the document was
not officially brought under the King's notice.

Nevertheless, as it had been twice read in the House, we may be
sure that he heard of it   and that unluckily at a time when he was
endeavouring to digest a fresh disappointment   At the beginning
of the session, hoping to please everybody and wishing to avoid
everything that might cast a shadow over the general satisfaction,
he had resolved that no demand should be made on his subjects for
money, and in this resolution he had persevered so constantly and so
long that I have no doubt it was a true intention of his own   For
full three months he had refrained both his tongue and his pen from
all allusion to the subject—had not said so much as that he meant
to say nothing—but maintained on all occasions a politic and digni-
fied reserve which was very unusual with him   Now however that
the prorogation was near at hand, it was represented to him by
some who thought they understood the Lower House, that a session
closing without any vote of supply would have a bad appearance,
and be subject to unfavourable construction   Upon which it seems
to have been arranged that, the Lords having or making occasion to
confer with the Commons upon a Tonnage and Poundage Bill, the

[1] C J pp. 243, 995

opportunity should be taken to give them some information about the financial condition of the kingdom.—with a hint that an offer of subsidy would not be unwelcome. Of the communication which was thereupon made, we have the following partially intelligible note.

Sir Francis Bacon maketh report of the Conference with the Lords, touching the Bill of Subsidy of Tonnage and Poundage.

Reported the reading and consideration of sundry amendments in the Bill.

Collateral speeches.

That we were well fenced with Privileges.—That it was good husbandry to fence.—

A good account of this Parliament, to maintain privileges and preserve the King's favour.—

An insinuation of a message from the King, touching subsidy or gratuity.—

Excuse of the Lords that they propounded matter of charge or contribution.—

An approbation of the forbearing to offer by this House.

No meaning that this insinuation should possess the House as with a motion.

Not to preoccupate our thanks.

Not to prejudicate our assent or dissent.—

The state of the King. } Not within the knowledge of this
The nature of the Peace. } House.

Four last years of Queen Eliz. the charge of this state 2.200.000*l.*

Debt of the City of London, 80,000*l.*

The exchange of Ireland, 120,000*l.*

Entry, Funeral, Coronation, a great accumulation of charge.—

Peace only between the persons of the King of England and Spain.—Nothing articulate.—A mere cessation, or abstinence, from hostility.—

The proportion of the charge of Ireland is yet 30,000*l.*—The rebel hath put up, not put off, his sword.—

Conclus. To think of the point of honour, in respect of advertisement to foreign states.[1]

Simultaneously with this (for though the report was not made till the 22nd of June, the Conference appears to have been held on the

[1] C. J. p. 244 (22 June).

19th) a motion was made in the House of Commons for a committee to consider of some sort of gratuity to be offered to the King But whoever advised it, it was an unlucky motion Though introduced by two of the most independent and popular members,—Sir Francis Hastings and Sir Edward Hoby[1]—in the interest of national honour, harmony, and reputation abroad, it was received so doubtfully that the King thought it best to avoid the risk of a refusal by making it his personal request—a request conveyed in a letter too transparent to allow a doubt of its sincerity[2]—that they would not meddle any further in the question

This of course was not the issue which had been intended or anticipated, and (coming upon him at the same time with rumours of the 'Apology') proved more than he could comfortably digest And though the Speaker, by a lavish profession of affection, admiration, and loyalty, made in the name of all the Commons,—together with a liberal offer of all they had whenever it was wanted,—did as much as words could do to make the parting pleasant, the King could not bring himself to repay the flattery in kind, but frankly told them exactly what he felt [3] And so Parliament was prorogued on the 7th of July, and they parted for the present, each with better means of knowing what was to be expected of the other.

7

In Sir Toby Matthew's Collection of Letters (p 20) there is one with this title—"Sir Francis Bacon desiring a friend to do him a service" It has no date, and like many others in that collection it appears to have been stripped of all particulars which might serve to fix the occasion But I think it belongs to this session of this Parliament The 'service' desired is assistance in preparing a 'report' of some debate or conference in which Bacon had himself taken an active part The friend has always been supposed to be Matthew himself Now it has been seen that Bacon was continually employed during this session both as spokesman for the House in conferences, and as reporter to the House of what had passed The attention requisite for taking part in the discussion would of course interfere with the attention requisite for remembering the passages

[1] C J p 994 It was of course supported (though I think not advised) by Bacon of whose speech we have only this note
"The Kingdom in the Queen's time but as a tenant for life if for a state for life a gratuity, then much more for a planted posterity—a state of inheritance
"Let not this Parliament end, like a Dutch feast, in salt meats, but like an English feast, in sweet meats"—C J p 242 and compare p 994
26 June C J p 246 [3] S P Dom viii 93

of it while engaged in thinking what he should say himself, he
would be in danger of not hearing what others were say ig   When
called upon for a report, therefore—especially when the call was un
expected, as happened sometimes—the help of another man's memory
would be of great value.   And as Toby Matthew was a member
of Parliament, and of more than one Conference-Committee in
which Bacon had a principal part, nothing is more natural than that
on some occasion of this kind he should have had recourse to him
What the particular occasion was it is probably impossible to guess
That it was a matter of some importance, which had given some
trouble, may be inferred from the terms in which it is alluded to
But many such businesses were on hand, and almost all of them
sooner or later "fell and seized upon" Bacon

SIR FRANCIS BACON DESIRING A FRIEND TO DO HIM A SERVICE

Sir,

The report of this act, which I hope will prove the last of
this business, will probably, by the weight it carries, fall and
seize on me.   And therefore, not now at will but upon necessity,
it will become me to call to mind what passed; and (my head
being then wholly employed about invention) I may the worse
put things upon the account of mine own memory   I shall take
physic to-day, upon this change of weather and vantage of
leisure, and I pray you not to allow yourself so much business
but that you may have time to bring me your friendly aid before
night, &c

CHAPTER VI.

A D 1601. July—December. Ætat 41

i.

The King having now had a taste of Bacon's disposition and abilities, was not long in marking his appreciation of them On the 18th of August, 1604,[1] he granted him by patent the office of Learned Counsel, which he had hitherto held only by verbal warrant and at the same time conferred on him a pension for life of £60 For a man of Bacon's abilities and long service, it was not much ; but it was a beginning , and it came at a time when he had a very good opportunity to show how well it was deserved For the Commissioners for the Union were to meet in October, and his vacation's work was to prepare for the conference by taking a survey of all the questions which would fall under consideration

In such matters one of the best-informed men of the time was Sir Robert Cotton, and the following letter has been preserved by accident, to show that consultation with such men was not neglected

To Sir Robert Cotton.[2]

Sir,

Finding during Parliament a willingness in you to confer with me in this great service concerning the Union, I do now take hold thereof to excuse my boldness to desire that now which you offered then, for both the time as to leisure is more liberal, and as to the service itself is more urgent. Whether it will like you to come to me to Gray's Inn or to appoint me where to meet with you, I am indifferent, and leave it to your choice, and accordingly desire to hear from you ; so I remain your very loving friend

Fr. Bacon

Gray's Inn, this 8th day of Sept 1604

[1] This was the date of the warrant, the patents were dated August 25 S P O.
[2] Cott MSS Jul C iii fo 30 Original own hand

The first fruit of these studies and conferences was a concise but complete analysis of the whole subject, drawn up for the King's information in which all the particular questions that would have to be dealt with—questions which it took a hundred years to adjust—were enumerated and explained   What use was made of it at the time, besides submitting it to the King, and to what extent it was circulated I do not know   The only manuscript of it which I have met with—and that appears to be only a collector's copy, without any special value as an authority for the text—is in the Library of Queen's College, Oxford [1]   The earliest printed copy I know or have heard of is in Rawley's Resuscitatio   and from this the text is here taken

CERTAIN ARTICLES OR CONSIDERATIONS TOUCHING THE UNION OF THE KINGDOMS OF ENGLAND AND SCOTLAND

Collected and dispersed for his Majesty's better Service.

Your Majesty, being (I do not doubt) directed and conducted by a better oracle than that which was given for light to Æneas in his peregrination (*Antiquam erquirite matrem*), hath a royal and indeed an heroical desire to reduce these two kingdoms of England and Scotland into the unity of their ancient mother kingdom of Britain   Wherein as I would gladly applaud unto your Majesty, or sing aloud that hymn or anthem, *Sic itur ad astra*, so in a more soft and submisse voice, I must necessarily remember unto your Majesty that warning or caveat, *Ardua quæ pulchra* it is an action that requireth, yea and needeth, much not only of your Majesty's wisdom, but of your felicity   In this argument I presumed at your Majesty's first entrance to write a few lines, indeed scholastically and speculatively, and not actively or politicly, as I held it fit for me at that time, when neither your Majesty was in that your desire declared, nor myself in that service used or trusted.   But now that both your Majesty hath opened your desire and purpose, with much admiration even of those who give it not so full an approbation., and that myself was by the Commons graced with the first vote of all the Commons selected for that cause, not in any estimation of my ability (for therein so wise an assembly could not be so much deceived), but in an acknowledgment of my extreme labours and integrity in that business; I thought myself every way bound, both in

[1] xxxii 27

duty to your Majesty, and in trust to that house of Parliament, and in consent to the matter itself, and in conformity to mine own travels and beginnings, not to neglect any pains that may tend to the furtherance of so excellent a work. Wherein I will endeavour that that which I shall set down be *nihil minus quam verba.* For length and ornament of speech are to be used for persuasion of multitudes, and not for information of kings, especially such a king as is the only instance that ever I knew to make a man of Plato's opinion, *that all knowledge is but remembrance,* and that the mind of man knoweth all things, and demandeth only to have her own notions excited and awaked. Which your Majesty's rare and indeed singular gift and faculty of swift apprehension, and infinite expansion or multiplication of another man's knowledge by your own, as I have often observed, so I did extremely admire in Goodwin's cause, being a matter full of secrets and mysteries of our laws, merely new unto you, and quite out of the path of your education, reading, and conference: wherein, nevertheless, upon a spark of light given, your Majesty took in so dexterously and profoundly, as if you had been indeed *anima legis,* not only in execution, but in understanding · the remembrance whereof, as it will never be out of my mind, so it will always be a warning to me to seek rather to excite your judgment briefly, than to inform it tediously; and if in a matter of that nature, how much more in this, wherein your princely cogitations have wrought themselves, and been conversant, and wherein the principal light proceeded from yourself.

And therefore my purpose is only to break this matter of the Union into certain short articles and questions; and to make a certain kind of anatomy or analysis of the parts and members thereof. Not that I am of opinion that all the questions which I now shall open were fit to be in the consultation of the Commissioners propounded. For I hold nothing so great an enemy to good resolution as the making of too many questions, specially in assemblies which consist of many. For Princes, for avoiding of distraction, must take many things by way of admittance; and if questions must be made of them, rather to suffer them to arise from others, than to grace them and authorise them as propounded from themselves. But unto your Majesty's private consideration, to whom it may better sort with me rather to speak as a remembrancer than as a counsellor, I have thought good to lay before you all the branches, lineaments, and degrees of this Union, that upon the view and consideration of them and their circumstances, your Majesty may the more clearly discern and more readily call to mind which of them is to be embraced, and which to be rejected, and of those[1] which are to be accepted, which of them is presently to be proceeded in, and which to be put over to further time, and again, which of them shall require authority of Parliament, and which are fitter to be effected by your Majesty's royal power and prerogative, or by other policies or means, and lastly, which of them is liker to pass with difficulty and contradiction, and which with more facility and smoothness

First, therefore, to begin with that question, that I suppose will be out of question

Statutes
concerning
Scotland
and the
Scottish
nation Whether it be not meet, that the statutes which were made touching Scotland or the Scottish nation while the kingdoms stood severed, be repealed?

It is true, there is a diversity in these, for some of these laws consider Scotland as an enemy country, other laws consider it as a foreign country only as for example, the law of Rich II. anno 7° which prohibiteth all armour or victual to be carried to Scotland, and the law of 7° of K Henry VII that enacteth all the Scottish men to depart the realm within a time prefixed, both these laws, and some others, respect Scotland as a country of hostility but the law of 22° of Edward IV that endueth Barwick with the liberty of a Staple, where all Scottish merchandises should resort that should be uttered for England, and likewise all English merchandises that should be uttered for Scotland; this law beholdeth Scotland only as a foreign nation, and not so much neither; for there have been erected Staples in towns of England for some commodities, with an exclusion and restriction of other parts of England.

But this is a matter of the least difficulty, your Majesty shall have a calendar made of the laws, and a brief of the effect, and so you may judge of them. and the like or reciproque is to be done by Scotland for such laws as they have concerning England and the English nation

Laws, cus
toms, com-
missions,
officers of The second question is, what laws, customs, commissions, officers, garrisons, and the like, are to be put down, discontinued, or taken away, upon the borders of both realms

[1] these Res

To[1] this point, because I am not acquainted with the ordens of the Marches, I can say the less *the borders or marches*

Herein falleth that question, whether that the tenants who hold then tenant rights in a greater freedom and exemption in consideration of their service upon the borders, and that the countries themselves which are in the same respect discharged of subsidies and taxes, should not now be brought to be in one degree with other tenants and countries ; *nam cessante causa, tollitur effectus* Wherein, in my opinion, some time would be given, *quia adhuc eorum messis in herba est* but some present ordinance would be made to take effect at a future time, considering it is one of the greatest points and marks of the division of the kingdoms And because reason doth dictate that where the principal solution of continuity was, there the healing and consolidating plaister should be chiefly applied, there would be some further device for the utter and perpetual confounding of those imaginary bounds, (as your Majesty termeth them) : and therefore it would be considered, whether it were not convenient to plant and erect at Carlisle or Barwick some counsel or court of justice, the jurisdiction whereof might extend part into England and part into Scotland, with a commission not to proceed precisely or merely according to the laws and customs either of England or Scotland, but mixtly, according to instructions by your Majesty to be set down, after the imitation and precedent of the Counsel of the Marches here in England erected, upon the union of Wales.

The third question is that which many will make a great question of, though perhaps your Majesty will make no question of it, and that is, whether your Majesty should not make a stop or stand here, and not to proceed to any further union, contenting yourself with the two former articles or points. *Further union besides the removing of inconvenient and dissenting laws and usages.*

For it will be said, that we are now well (thanks be to God and your Majesty), and the state of neither kingdom is to be repented of, and that it is true which Hippocrates saith, that *Sana corpora difficile medicationes ferunt*, it is better to make alterations in sick bodies than in sound. The consideration of which point will rest upon these two branches : what inconveniences will ensue with time, if the realms

[1] *To om in R*

stand, as they are, divided, which are yet not found nor
sprung up   For it may be the sweetness of your Majesty's
first entrance, and the great benefit that both nations have
felt thereby, hath covered many inconveniences, which never
theless, be your Majesty's government never so gracious and
politic, continuance of time and the accidents of time may
breed and discover, if the kingdoms stand divided

The second branch is, allow no manifest or important
peril or inconvenience should ensue of the continuing of
the kingdoms divided ; yet on the other side, whether that
upon the further uniting of them there be not like to follow
that addition and increase of wealth and reputation, as is
worthy your Majesty's virtues and fortune to be the author
and founder of, for the advancement and exaltation of your
Majesty's royal posterity in time to come

Points
wherein
the nations
stand al-
ready
united But admitting that your Majesty should proceed to this more
perfect and entire union , wherein your Majesty may say, *Majus
opus moveo* , to enter into the parts and degrees thereof, I think fit
first to set down, as in a brief table, in what points the nations
stand now at this present time already united, and in what points
yet still severed and divided , that your Majesty may the better
see what is done, and what is to be done , and how that which is
to be done is to be inferred upon that which is done

The points wherein the nations stand already united are

In sovereignty
In the relative thereof, which is subjection.
In religion
In continent
In language
And now lastly, by the peace by your Majesty concluded
with Spain, in leagues and confederacies   for now both
nations have the same friends and the same enemies

Yet notwithstanding there is none of the six points, wherein
the union is perfect and consummate , but every of them hath
some scruple or rather grain of separation inwrapped and included in them.

Sovereign-
ty, line
Royal For the Sovereignty, the union is absolute in your Majesty
and your generation . but if it should so be (which God of
his infinite mercy defend) that your issue should fail, then
the descent of both realms doth resort to the several lines
of the several bloods royal

For Subjection, I take the law of England to be clear, Subjection, obedience (what the law of Scotland is I know not), that all Scottish-men, from the very instant of your Majesty's reign begun, are become denizens, and the *post-nati* are naturalized sub-jects of England for the time forwards for by our laws Alien, naturalization none can be an Alien but he that is of another allegiance than our sovereign lord the King's for there be but two sorts of Aliens, whereof we find mention in our law, an *Alien Amı*, and an *Alien Enemy*, whereof the former is a subject of a state in amity with the King, and the latter a subject of a state in hostility , but whether he be one or other, it is an essential difference unto the definition of an Alien, if[1] he be not of the King's allegiance, as we see it evidently in the precedent of Ireland, who since they were subjects to the crown of England, have ever been inheritable and capable as natural subjects, and yet not by any statute or act of Parliament, but merely by the common law, and the reason thereof So as there is no doubt that every subject of Scotland was and is in like plight and degree, since your Majesty's coming in, as if your Majesty had granted parti-cularly your letters of denization or naturalization to every of them, and the *post-nati* wholly natural But then on the other side, for the time backwards, and for those that were *ante-nati*, the blood is not by law naturalized, so as they cannot take it by descent from their ancestors, without act of Parliament and therefore in this point there is a defect in the union of subjection.

For matter of Religion, the union is perfect in points of Religion, church government doctrine, but in matter of discipline and government it is imperfect

For the Continent, it is true there are no natural boun- Continent, borders daries of mountains, or seas, or navigable rivers, but yet there are badges and memorials of borders, of which point I have spoken before

For the Language, it is true the nations are *unus labii*, and Language, dialect and have not the first curse of disunion, which was confusion of tongues, whereby one understood not another. But yet the dialect is differing, and it remaineth a kind of mark of distinction. But for that, *tempori permittendum*, it is to be

[1] *that* MS

left to time   For considering that both languages do con
cur in the principal office and duty of a language, which is
to make a man's self understood , for the rest, it is rather to
be accounted (as was said) a diversity of dialect than of lan
guage : and, as I said in my first writing, it is like to bring
forth the enriching of one language, by compounding and
taking in the proper and significant words of either tongue,
rather than a continuance of two languages.

Leagues,
Confedera-
cies, Trea-
ties
For Leagues and Confederacies, it is true that neither na
tion is now in hostility with any state wherewith the other
nation is in amity · but yet so, as the leagues and treaties
have been concluded with either nation respectively, and not
with both jointly , which may contain some diversity of arti
cles of straitness of amity with one more than with the
other

But many of these matters may perhaps be of that kind, as
may fall within that rule, *In veste varietas sit, scissura non sit*

Now to descend to the particular points wherein the realms
stand severed and divided, over and besides the former six points
of separation, which I have noted and placed as defects or abatements of the six points of the union, and therefore shall not need
to be repeated   The points, I say, yet remaining, I will divide
into external and internal

External
points of
separation
and union
The external points therefore of the separation are four

1 The several crowns, I mean the ceremonial and material crowns.

2 The second is, the several names, stiles, or appella
tions

3 The third is, the several prints of the seals.

4 The fourth is, the several stamps or marks of the
coins or moneys

It is true, that the external are in some respect and parts much
mingled and interlaced with considerations internal , and that
they may be as effectual to the true union, which must be the
work of time, as the internal , because they are operative upon
the conceits and opinions of the people, the uniting of whose
hearts and affections is the life and true end of this work

The cere-
monial or
material
crowns.
For the Ceremonial Crowns, the question will be, whether
there shall be framed one new imperial crown of Britain to
be used for the times to come?

Also, admitting that to be thought convenient, whether in the frame thereof there shall not be some reference to the crowns of Ireland and France?

Also whether your Majesty should repeat or iterate your own coronation and your Queen's, or only ordain that such new crown shall be used by your posterity hereafter?

The difficulties will be in the conceit of some inequality, whereby the realm of Scotland may be thought to be made an accession unto the realm of England. But that resteth in some circumstances. For the compounding of the two crowns is equal. The calling of the new crown the crown of Britain is equal. Only the place of coronation, if it shall be at Westminster, which is the ancient, august, and sacred place for the kings of England, may seem to make an inequality. And again, if the crown of Scotland be discontinued, then that ceremony which I hear is used in the Parliament of Scotland, in the absence of the kings to have the crowns carried in solemnity, must likewise cease.

For the Name, the main question is, whether the con- *The styles and names.* tracted name of Britain shall be by your Majesty used, or the divided names of England and Scotland.

Admitting there shall be an alteration, then the case will require these inferior questions.

First, whether the name of Britain shall not only be used in your Majesty's stile, where the entire stile is recited, and in all other forms the divided names to remain, both of the realms and of the people, or otherwise, that the very divided names of realms and people shall likewise be changed or turned into special or subdivided names of the general name, that is to say, for example, whether your Majesty in your stile shall denominate yourself King of Britain, France, and Ireland, etc. and yet nevertheless, in any commission, writ, or otherwise, where your Majesty mentioneth England or Scotland, you shall retain the ancient names, as *secundum consuetudinem regni nostri Angliæ*, or whether those divided names shall be for ever lost and taken away, and turned into the subdivisions of South-Britain and North-Britain, and the people to be the South-Brittains and North-Brittains, And so, in the example aforesaid, the tenour of the like clause to run *secundum consuetudinem Britanniæ Australis.*

Also, if the former of these shall be thought convenient, whether it were not better for your Majesty to take that alteration of stile upon you by proclamation, as Edward the third did the stile of France, than to have it enacted by Parliament.

Also, in the alteration of the stile, whether it were not better to transpose the kingdom of Ireland, and put it immediately after Britain, and so place the islands together, and the kingdom of France, being upon the continent, last in regard that these islands of the western ocean seem by nature and providence an entire empire in themselves, and also that there was never king of England so entirely possest of Ireland as your Majesty is so a your stile to run King of Britain, Ireland, and the islands adjacent, and of France, etc

The difficulties in this have been already throughly beaten over, but they gather but to two heads.

The one, point of honour and love to the former names

The other, doubt lest the alteration of the name may induce and involve an alteration of the laws and policies of the kingdom   Both which, if your Majesty shall assume the stile by proclamation, and not by Parliament, are in themselves satisfied for then the usual names must needs remain in writs and records, the forms whereof cannot be altered but by act of Parliament, and so the point of honour satisfied   And again, your proclamation altereth no law; and so the scruple of a tacit or implied alteration of laws likewise satisfied   But then it may be considered, whether it were not a form of the greatest honour, if the Parliament, though they did not enact it, yet should become suitors and petitioners to your Majesty to assume it

he seals

For the Seals, that there should be one great seal of Britain, and one Chancellor, and that there should only be a seal in Scotland for processes and ordinary justice, and that all patents of grants of lands, or otherwise, as well in Scotland as in England, should pass under the great seal here, kept about your person, it is an alteration internal, whereof I do not now speak.

But the question in this place is, whether the great seals of England and Scotland should not be changed into one and the same form of image and superscription of Britain;

which nevertheless is requisite should be with some one plain or manifest alteration; lest there be a buz and suspect that grants of things in England may be passed by the seal of Scotland, or *e converso*.

Also, whether this alteration of form may not be done without Act of Parliament, as the great seals have used to be heretofore changed as to their impressions.

For the Moneys, as to the real and internal consideration thereof, the question will be, whether your Majesty should not continue two mints, which (the distance of territory considered) I suppose will be of necessity.

Secondly, how the standards (if it be not already done, as I hear some doubt made of it in popular rumour) may be re-duced into an exact proportion for the time to come, and likewise the computation, tale, or valuation to be made exact, for the moneys already beaten.

That done, the last question is (which is only proper to this place) whether the stamp or the image and superscrip-tion of Britain for the time forwards should not be made the self-same in both places, without any difference at all. A matter also which may be done, as our law is, by your Ma-jesty's prerogative, without Act of Parliament.

These points are points of demonstration, *ad faciendum popu-lum.* But so much the more they go to the root of your Majesty's intention, which is to imprint and inculcate into the hearts and heads of the people, that they are one people and one nation.

In this kind also I have heard it pass abroad in speech of the erection of some new order of knighthood, with a reference to the Union, and an oath appropriate thereunto, which is a point like-wise deserveth a consideration. So much for the external points.

The internal points of separation are as followeth.

1. Several parliaments.
2. Several counsels of estate.
3. Several officers of the crown.
4. Several nobilities.
5. Several laws.
6. Several courts of justice, trials, and processes.
7. Several receipts and finances.

[1] *Separation and* om. in Res.

8 Several admiralties and merchandisings
9 Several freedoms and liberties
10 Several taxes and imposts

As touching the several states ecclesiastical, and the several mints and standards, and the several articles and treaties of intercourse with foreign nations, I touched them before.

In these points of the strait and more inward union, there will intervene one principal difficulty and impediment, growing from that root which Aristotle in his Politics maketh to be the root of all division and dissension in commonwealths; and that is equality and inequality For the realm of Scotland is now an ancient and noble realm, substantive of itself. But when this island shall be made Britain, then Scotland is no more to be considered as Scotland, but as a part of Britain, no more than England is to be considered as England, but as a part likewise of Britain, and consequently neither of these are to be considered as things entire of themselves, but in the proportion that they bear to the whole And therefore let us imagine, (*nam id mente possumus, quod actu non possumus*) that Britain had never been divided, but had ever been one kingdom, then that part of soil or territory which is comprehended under the name of Scotland is in quantity (as I have heard it esteemed, how truly I know not) not past a third part of Britain, and that part of soil or territory which is comprehended under the name of England is two parts of Britain, leaving to speak of any difference of wealth or population, and speaking only of quantity So then if, for example, Scotland should bring to Parliament as much nobility as England, then a third part should countervail two parts, *nam si inæqualibus æqualia addas, omnia erunt inæqualia* And this, I protest before God and your Majesty, I do speak, not as a man born in England, but as a man born in Britain And therefore to descend to the particulars

1 Parlia-
ments

For the Parliaments, the consideration of that point will fall into four questions

1 The first, what proportion shall be kept between the votes of England and the votes of Scotland

2. The second, touching the manner of proposition, or possessing of the Parliament of causes there to be handled, which in England is used to be done immediately by any

member of the Parliament, or by the Prolocutor, and in Scotland is used to be done immediately by the Lords of the Articles, whereof the one form seemeth to have more liberty, and the other more gravity and maturity and therefore the question will be, whether of these shall yield to other, or whether there should not be a mixture of both, by some commissions precedent to every Parliament, in the nature of Lords of the Articles, and yet not excluding the liberty of propounding in full Parliament afterwards.

3 The third, touching the orders of Parliament, how they may be compounded, and the best of either taken

4 The fourth, how those, which by inheritance or otherwise have offices of honour and ceremony in both the Parliaments, as the Lord Steward with us, etc, may be satisfied, and duplicity accommodated

For the Counsels of Estate, while the kingdoms stand divided, it should seem necessary to continue several counsels, but if your Majesty should proceed to a strict union, then howsoever your Majesty may establish some provincial counsels in Scotland, as there is here of York, and in the Marches of Wales, yet the question will be, whether it will not be more convenient for your Majesty, to have but one Privy Counsel about your person, whereof the principal officers of the crown of Scotland to be, for dignity sake, howsoever then abiding and remaining may be as your Majesty shall employ their service   But this point belongeth merely and wholly to your Majesty's royal will and pleasure

2 Counsels of Estate

For the Officers of the Crown, the consideration thereof will fall into these questions

3 Officers of the Crown

First, in regard of the latitude of your kingdom and the distance of place, whether it will not be matter of necessity to continue the several officers, because of the impossibility for the service to be performed by one

The second, admitting the duplicity of officers should be continued, yet whether there should not be a difference, that one should be the principal officer, and the other to be but special and subaltern   As for example, one to be Chancellor of Britain, and the other to be Chancellor with some special addition, as here of the Duchy, etc

The third, if no such specialty or inferiority be thought fit, then whether both officers should not have the title and the name of the whole island and precincts, as the Lord Chancellor of England to be Lord Chancellor of Britain, and the Lord Chancellor of Scotland to be Lord Chancellor of Britain, but with several provisos that they shall not intromit themselves but within their several precincts

4 Nobili-
ties

For the Nobilities, the consideration thereof will fall into these questions.

The first, of their votes in Parliament (which was touched before), what proportion they shall bear to the nobility of England wherein if the proportion which shall be thought fit be not full, yet your Majesty may, out of your preroga tive, supply it; for although you cannot make fewer of Scotland, yet you may make more of England

The second is, touching the place and precedence. Wherein to marshal them according to the precedence of England in your Majesty's stile, and according to the no bility of Ireland[1], that is, all English Earls first, and then Scottish, will be thought unequal for Scotland To marshal them according to antiquity, will be thought unequal for England, because I hear their nobility is generally more ancient And therefore the question will be, whether the indifferentest way were not to take them interchangeably, as for example, first, the ancient Earl of England, and then the ancient Earl of Scotland, and so *alternis vicibus*

5 Laws

For the Laws, to make an entire and perfect union, it is a matter of great difficulty and length, both in the collecting of them, and in the passing of them. For first, as to the collecting of them, there must be made by the lawyers of either nation a digest, under titles, of their several laws and customs, as well common laws as statutes, that they may be collated and compared, and that the diversities may appear and be discerned of. And for the passing of them, we see by experience that *patrius mos* is dear to all men, and that men are bred and nourished up in the love of it, and therefore how harsh changes and innovations are And we see likewise what disputation and argument the alteration of some one law doth cause and bring forth, how much

[1] So in Rea

more the alteration of the whole corps of the law? Therefore the first question will be, whether it be not good to proceed by parts, and to take that that is most necessary, and leave the rest to time. The parts therefore or subject of laws, are for this purpose fitliest distributed according to that ordinary division of criminal and civil, and those of criminal causes into capital and penal.

The second question therefore is; allowing the general union of laws to be too great a work to embrace, whether it were not convenient that cases capital were the same in both nations, I say the cases, I do not speak of the proceedings or trials; that is to say, whether the same offences were not fit to be made treason or felony in both places.

The third question is, whether cases penal, though not capital, yet if they concern the public state, or otherwise the discipline of manners, were not fit likewise to be brought into one degree, as the case of Misprision of Treason, the case of *Præmunire*, the case of Fugitives, the case of Incest, the case of Simony, and the rest.

But the question that is more urgent than any of these is, whether these cases at the least, be they of an higher or inferior degree, wherein the fact committed or act done in Scotland may prejudice the state and subjects of England, or *e converso*, are not to be reduced into one uniformity of law and punishment As for example, a perjury committed in a court of justice in Scotland cannot be prejudicial in England, because depositions taken in Scotland cannot be produced and used here in England. But a forgery of a deed in Scotland, I mean with a false date of England, may be used and given in evidence in England. So likewise the depopulating of a town in Scotland doth not directly prejudice the state of England but if an English merchant shall carry silver and gold into Scotland (as he may), and thence transport it into foreign parts, this prejudiceth the state of England, and may be an evasion to all the laws of England ordained in that case; and therefore had need to be bridled with as severe a law in Scotland as it is here in England

Of this kind there are many laws.

The law of the 5° of Richard II of going over without licence, if there be not the like law in Scotland, will be frustrated and evaded for any subject of England may go first into Scotland, and thence into foreign parts

So the laws prohibiting transportation of sundry commodities, as gold and silver, ordnance, artillery, corn, etc, if there be not a correspondence of laws in Scotland, will in like manner be deluded and frustrate, for any English merchant or subject may carry such commodities first into Scotland, as well as he may carry them from port to port in England, and out of Scotland into foreign parts, without any peril of law

So libels may be devised and written in Scotland, and published and scattered in England

Treasons may be plotted in Scotland and executed in England.

And so in many other cases, if there be not the like severity of law in Scotland to restrain offences that there is in England, (whereof we are here ignorant whether there be or no), it will be a gap or stop even[1] for English subjects to escape and avoid the laws of England

But for treasons, the best is that by the statute of 26 K Henry VIII cap. 13, any treason committed in Scotland may be proceeded with in England, as well as treasons committed in France, Rome, or elsewhere

6 Courts of Justice and administration of laws

For Courts of Justice, trials, processes, and other administration of laws, to make any alteration in either nation, it will be a thing so new and unwonted to either people, that it may be doubted it will make the administration of justice (which of all other things ought to be known and certain as a beaten way), to become intricate and uncertain And besides, I do not see that the severalty of administration of justice, though it be by court sovereign of last resort (I mean without appeal or error), is any impediment at all to the union of a kingdom as we see by experience in the several courts of Parliament in the kingdom of France. And I have been always of opinion, that the subjects of England do already fetch justice somewhat far off, more than in any nation that I know, the largeness of the kingdom considered, though it be holpen in some part by the circuits of the Judges, and the two Councils at York and in the Marches of Wales established.

But it may be a good question, whether, as *commune vinculum* of the justice of both nations, your Majesty should not erect some court about your person, in the nature of the Grand Council of France to which court you might, by way of evocation, draw causes from the ordinary judges of both nations, for so doth the French king from all the courts of Parliament in France, many of which are more remote from Paris than any part of Scotland is from London.

For Receipts and Finances, I see no question will arise, in regard it will be matter of necessity to establish in Scotland a receipt of treasure for payments and erogations to be made in those parts and for the treasure of spare, in either receipts, the custodies thereof may well be several, considering by your Majesty's commandment they may be at all times removed or disposed according to your Majesty's occasions. ^{7 Receipts, finances, and patrimonies of the Crown}

For the Patrimonies of both crowns, I see no question will arise, except your Majesty would be pleased to make one compounded annexation, for an inseparable patrimony to the crown out of the lands of both nations and so the like for the Principality of Britain, and for other appennages of the rest of your children. erecting likewise such duchies and honours, compounded of the possessions of both nations, as shall be thought fit

For Admiralty or Navy, I see no great question will arise For I see no inconvenience for your Majesty to continue shipping in Scotland And for the jurisdictions of the admiralties, and the profits and casualties of them, they will be respective unto the coasts over-against which the seas lie and are situated, as it is here with the admiralties of England ^{8 Admiralty, Navy, and Merchandizing}

And for Merchandising, it may be a question, whether that the companies of the Merchant Adventurers, of the Turkey merchants, and the Muscovy merchants (if they shall be continued), should not be compounded of merchants of both nations, English and Scottish. For to leave trade free in the one nation, and to have it restrained in the other, may percase breed some inconvenience

9 Free-
dom and
liberties

For Freedoms and Liberties, the charters of both nations may be reviewed, and of such liberties as are agreeable and convenient for the subjects and people of both nations, one Great Charter may be made and confirmed to the subjects of Britain, and those liberties which are peculiar or proper to either nation, to stand in state as they do

But for Imposts and Customs, it will be a great question how to accommodate them and reconcile them · for if they be much easier in Scotland than they be here in England, (which is a thing I know not,) then this inconvenience will follow; that the merchants of England may unlade in the ports of Scotland, and this kingdom to be served from thence, and your Majesty's customs abated.

And for the question, whether the Scottish merchants should pay strangers custom in England, that resteth upon the point of Naturalization, which I touched before

10 Taxes
and im-
posts

Thus have I made your Majesty a brief and naked memorial of the articles and points of this great cause, which may serve only to excite and stir up your Majesty's royal judgment, and the judgment of wiser men whom you will be pleased to call to it Wherein I will not presume to persuade or dissuade any thing, nor to interpose mine own opinion, but do expect light from your Majesty's royal directions, unto the which I shall ever submit my judgment and apply my travails And I most humbly pray your Majesty in this which is done to pardon my errors, and to cover them with my good intention and meaning, and desire I have to do your Majesty service, and to acquit the trust which was reposed in me, and chiefly in[1] your Majesty's benign and gracious acceptation

2

It will be seen that the question of the style and name, which it had been thought too dangerous to alter by Act of Parliament, is here recommended to be dealt with by Proclamation and it is not impossible that a draft of a Proclamation for that purpose accompanied this paper Such a draft Bacon did at any rate prepare, and as it cannot be supposed to have been written after the appearance

¹ So in Res a mistake, I think, for with

of the Proclamation by which the title of King of Great Britain was actually assumed, its proper place is here

It was first printed among the State-pieces appended to Stephens's second collection (1734), I presume from the manuscript now in the British Museum, which is fully authenticated by corrections written in Bacon's own hand, and from this it is here taken

A DRAUGHT OF A PROCLAMATION TOUCHING HIS MAJESTY'S STILE, PREPARED, NOT USED

Jacobi 2do.[1]

As it is a manifest token, or rather a substantial effect, of the wrath and indignation of God, when kingdoms are rent and divided which have formerly been entire and united under one monarch and governor, so on the contrary part, when it shall please the Almighty (by whom kings reign as his deputies and lieutenants) to enlarge his commissions of empire and sovereignty, and to commit those nations to one king to govern which he had formerly committed to several kings, it is an evident argument of his great favour both upon king and upon people, upon the king, inasmuch as he may with comfort conceive that he is one of those servants to whom it was said, *Thou hast been faithful in the less, I will make thee Lord of more*, upon the people, because the greatness of kingdoms and dominions, especially not being scattered but adjacent and compact, doth ever bring with it greater security from outward enemies, and greater freedom from inward burdens, unto both which people under petty and weak estates are more exposed. Which so happy fruit of the union of kingdoms is chiefly to be understood, when such conjunction or augmentation is not wrought by conquest and violence, or by pact and submission, but by the law of nature and hereditary descent. For in conquests it is commonly seen, although the bulk and quantity of territory be increased, yet the strength of kingdoms is diminished, as well by the wasting of the forces of both parts in the conflict, as by the evil coherence of the nation conquering and conquered, the one being apt to be

---

[1] Harl MSS 6797 f 17 *b* The words " prepared but much altered in that which was published " have been written on the margin (the five last in Bacon's hand) with a direction to insert them after ' style ' Then they have been struck out, and the words ' prepared not used ' written below whether meant to come in at the end or in the same place, is doubtful

insolent and the other discontent, and so both full of jealousies
and discord, and where countries are annexed only by act of
estates and submissions, such submissions are commonly grounded
upon fear, which is no good author of continuance, besides the
quarrels and revolts which do ensue upon conditional and articu
late subjections   But when the lines of two kingdoms do meet
in the person of one monarch as in a true point or perfect angle,
and that from marriage (which is the first conjunction in human
society) there shall proceed one inheritor in blood to several
kingdoms, whereby they are actually united and incorporate
under one head, it is the work of God and nature, whereunto the
works of force and policy cannot attain, and it is that which
hath not in itself any manner of seeds of discord or disunion,
other than such as envy and malignity shall sow, and which
groundeth an union, not only indissoluble, but also most comfortable and happy amongst the people   We therefore in all
humbleness acknowledge,[1] that it is the great and blessed work
of Almighty God, that these two ancient and mighty realms of
England and Scotland, which by nature have no true but an
imaginary separation, being both situate and comprehended in
one most famous and renowned island of great Britany, com-
passed by the ocean, without any mountains, seas, or other
boundaries of nature, to make any partition-wall or trench between them, and being also exempted from the first curse of
disunion, which was the confusion of tongues, and being people
of a like constitution of mind and body, especially in warlike
prowess and disposition, and yet nevertheless have in so many
ages been disjoined under several kings and governors, are now
at the last, by right inherent in the commixture of our blood,
united in our person and generation, wherein it hath pleased
God[2] to anoint us with the oil of gladness and gratulation above
our progenitors kings of either nation.   Neither can we sufficiently contemplate and behold the passages, degrees, and in-
sinuations, whereby it hath pleased the eternal God (to whom all
his works are from the beginning known and present) to open
and prepare a way to this excellent work, having first ordained

[1] So corrected in the MS from "We therefore taking counsel of the Providence
of God (which is the only vision and revelation which now remaineth, when all
other visions and revelations are ceased), do manifestly discern and in all humbleness acknowledge"
[2] "even our God," crossed out in MS

that both nations should be knit in one true and reformed religion, which is the perfectest band of all unity and union, and
secondly that there should proceed so long a peace continued between the nations for so many years last passed, whereby all seeds
and sparks of ancient discord have been laid asleep, and grown
to an obliteration and oblivion, and lastly that ourselves, in the
true measure of our affections, should have so just cause to embrace both nations with equal and indifferent love and inclination, inasmuch as our birth and the passing of the first part of
our age hath been in the one nation, and our principal seat and
mansion and the passing of the latter part of our days is like to
be in the other Which our equal and upright holding of the
balance between both nations, being the highest point of all
others in our distributive justice, we give the world to know that
we are constantly resolved to preserve inviolate against all emu-
lations and partialities, not making any difference at all between
the subjects of either nation in affection, honours, favours, gifts,
employments, confidences, or the like, but only such as the true
distinctions of the persons, being capable or not capable, fit or
not fit, acquainted with affairs or not acquainted with affairs,
needing our princely bounty or not needing the same, approved
to us by our experience or not approved, meriting or not meriting, and the several degrees of these and the like conditions,
shall in right reason tie us unto, without any manner[1] regard
to the country in itself, to the end that they may well perceive, that in our mind and apprehension they are all one and
the same nation, and that our heart is truly placed in the centre
of government, from whence all lines to the circumference are
equal and of one space and distance But for the further advancing and perfecting of this work, we have taken into our
princely care and cogitations, what it is that may appertain to
our own imperial power, right, and authority, and what requireth votes and assents of our Parliaments or estates, and
again, what may presently be done, and what must be left to
further time, that our proceeding may be void of all inconvenience and informality Wherein by the example of Almighty
God, who is accustomed to begin all his great works and design-
ments by alterations or impositions of names, as the fittest means
to imprint in the hearts of people a character and expectation of

[1] So MS Stephens inserted 'of' But the form in the text was not unusual

that which is to follow, we have thought good to withdraw and discontinue the divided names of England and Scotland out of our legal stile and title, and to use in place of them the common and contracted name of *Great Britany* . not upon any vain-glory whereof we persuade ourselves our actions do sufficiently free , in the judgment of all the world , and if any such humour should reign in us, it were better satisfied by length of stile and enume ration of kingdoms , but only as a fit signification of that which is already done, and a significant prefiguration of that which we further intend.   For as in giving names to natural persons, it is used to impose them in infancy, and not to stay till fulness of growth , so it seemed to us not unseasonable to bring in further use this name at the first, and to proceed with the more sub stantial points of the union after, as fast and as far as the com mon good of both the realms should permit , especially consider ing the name of Britany was no coined or new-devised or affected name at our pleasure, but the true and ancient name which God and time hath imposed, extant and received in histories, in cards, and in ordinary speech and writing, where the whole island is meant to be denominate ; so as it is not accompanied with so much as any strangeness in common speech [1]   And al though we never doubted, neither ever heard that any other pre- sumed to doubt, but that the form and tenor of our legal stile and title, and the delineation of the same, did only and wholly of mere right appertain to our supreme and absolute prerogative, to express the same in such words or sort as seemed good to our royal pleasure; yet because we were to have the advice and assent of our Parliament concerning other points of the union, we were pleased our said Parliament should amongst the rest take also the same into their consideration.   But finding by the grave opinion of our Judges who are the interpreters of our laws, that, in case that alteration of stile, which seemed to us but verbal, should be established and enacted by Parliament, it might involve by implication and consequence, not only a more present alteration, but also a further innovation than we any ways in- tended, or at least might be subject to some colourable scruple of such a perilous construction, we rested well satisfied to respite the same, as to require it by act of parliament.   But being still resolved and fixed that it may conduce towards this happy end

---

[1] 'A strangeness or jar to the ear' had been written first

of the better uniting of the nations, we have thought good by the advice of our Counsel to take the same upon us by our proclamation, being a course safe and free from any of the perils or scruples aforesaid And therefore we do by these presents publish, proclaim, and assume to ourselves from henceforth, according to our undoubted right, the stile and title of King of Great Britany, France, and Ireland,[1] and otherwise as followeth in our stile formerly used And we do hereby straitly charge and command our Chancellor, and all such as have the custody of any of our seals, and all other our officers and subjects whatsoever to whom it may in any wise appertain, that from henceforth in all commissions, patents, writs, processes, grants, records, instruments, impressions, sermons, and all other writings and speeches whatsoever, wherein our stile is used to be set forth or recited, that our said stile, as is before by these presents declared and prescribed, be only used, and no other And because we do but now declare that which in truth was before, our will and pleasure is, that in the computation of our reign, as to all writings or instruments hereafter to be made, the same computation be taken and made, as if we had taken upon us the stile aforesaid immediately after the decease of our late dear sister And we do notify to all our subjects, that if any person, of what degree or condition soever he be, shall impugn our said stile, or derogate and detract from the same by any arguments, speeches, words, or otherwise, we shall proceed against him as against an offender against our crown and dignity, and a disturber of the quiet and peace of our kingdom, according to the utmost severity of our laws in that behalf. Nevertheless our meaning is not that where in any writ, pleading, or other record, writing, instrument or speech, it hath been used for mention to be made of England or the realm of England, or any other word or words derived from the same, and not of our whole and entire stile and title, that therein any alteration at all be used by pretext of this our proclamation, which we intend to take place only where our whole stile shall be recited, and not otherwise, and in the other cases the ancient form to be used and observed.

A proclamation to this effect,—and probably founded upon this

---

[1] So corrected in Bacon's hand from "Great Britany, Ireland, and the islands adjacent, and of France," which had been written first Upon which point see above, p 226

draft, though almost wholly re-written,—was published on the 20th of October, the day on which the Commissioners for the Union were to meet and the kingdoms were thenceforth united in the King's style and title, without any contestation, difficulty, or inconvenience and so remained.

3.

The rest of the work was not so easily accomplished, though it began with fairer auspices than could have been looked for A council of forty-eight Englishmen and thirty-one Scotchmen, meeting on terms of perfect equality to make a bargain—a bargain involving interests so vast and so various—might have seemed to have no easy task before them yet in less than six weeks they had come to an agreement all but unanimous, and the work, so far as it depended upon them, was prosperously concluded

The reputation which Bacon brought with him from the House of Commons as the man in whose hands any business of delicacy or difficulty was always found to prosper best, would naturally give him great influence and authority in the Commission, and the order of proceeding, to which the harmonious progress of their deliberations was probably in great part due, was probably in great part due to him. Twenty years after, in revising his Essay on Counsel, he referred to this Commission as an example of good order. 'The counsels at this day in most places" (he says) "are but familiar meetings, where matters are rather talked on than debated And they run too swift to the order or act of counsel It were better that in causes of weight the matter were propounded one day, and not spoken to till the next day *In nocte consilium* So was it done in the Commission for Union between England and Scotland, which was a grave and orderly assembly "[1] This is confirmed by a Journal of the proceedings of the Commission, preserved among the manuscripts in the Library of Lincoln's Inn which contains however only a record of the business debated at each meeting without any account of the debates themselves, and though it appears to be an original and authentic record, and was very likely drawn up by Bacon himself, the following notes contain all that I thought worth extracting from it for the purpose of this work

Oct 20, 1604 The Commissioners meet but the Scottish Commissioners not having all arrived, adjourn till the 29th

Oct 29 Sub-committees of both nations for collection of hostile laws

Nov 2 Report made severally, first by Sir Francis Bacon, and

[1] Lit and Prof Works, vol 1 p 126

then by Sir T Hamilton, Lord Advocate of Scotland, of the services performed by the Sub-committees

"Agreed by a full consent that every time of assembly, after the matters concluded at that sitting, there shall be propositions made of such particular questions and matters as shall be debated at the next sitting and that after any matter debated, if the resolution be clear and without question, the votes may be given readily and publicly, but if the number of voices be doubtful, either part may retire and withdraw themselves to take knowledge of the voices in particular and afterwards make known publicly the resolution of the major part"

Nov 15 Matter of Naturalization debated from two till past nine P M and then the meeting adjourned[1]

Nov 21 Agreed to recommend the naturalization both of the Post nati and the Antenati

"This day all the articles that have been concluded since the first meeting of the Commissioners until this time were read accordingly as the same were set down and placed in the Journal book, and according to the times when they were concluded And thereupon direction was given to Sir Francis Bacon and the Lord Advocate of Scotland to review the said articles, and to reduce and join them together in such form and method as was meet and agreeable in coherence of matter, and would be fit to be set down in the instruments themselves to be propounded to the Parliaments And this to be done against Tuesday the 27th of this instant

"Moved also and assented, that the Lord of Cranbourne and the Lord Fivye[2] would confer against that day of some preface meet to be set before the articles of the said instrument"

Nov 27

' This day the articles were presented in writing, in such sort as they had been reduced into form and method according to the direction at the last sitting to Sir Francis Bacon and the Lord Advocate of Scotland, and likewise a preface to be set before the said articles in the instrument was presented by the Lord Cranbourne, as the same had been agreed by himself and the Lord Fivye, which preface and the said articles being presently read were allowed by the Commissioners, and thereupon order given for the engrossing of the in-

---

[1] At this point it seems that the opinion of the Law Officers of the Crown was taken on some questions relative to the naturalization of the Post nati who declared that all persons born in Scotland after the accession of James were already naturalized See S P Domestic, x 15

[2] Lord Fivye [File, I suppose] was President of the Council in Scotland Sir Robert Cecil had been created Baron Essendon on the 13th of May, and Viscount Cranbourn on the 20th of August

struments against Saturday the 1st of December, being the day appointed for the signing and sealing of the instruments."

The final meeting was afterwards deferred till Thursday, December 6, when the instruments were signed and sealed.[1]

1.

It will be observed that the charge of digesting the articles of the resolutions into their ultimate form was entrusted (on the English side) to Bacon; but that the composition of the preamble or prefatory introduction was undertaken by Cecil in conjunction with Lord Frye. It appears, however, that Bacon had made provision for this part of the work also, had it been wanted. For among the papers left by him, and by himself thought worth preserving, is a draft of precisely such a preface as was wanted for the occasion; and whatever reasons there may have been (personal or other) for preferring the production of the two great officers of state, there can be no doubt that for the modern purpose of throwing light upon the meaning and history of the business, Bacon's is much to be preferred. It is indeed a page of history ready written, and makes it unnecessary to offer in this place any further explanation of the results of the Commissioners' deliberations; the disputed points in which will not fail to force themselves upon our notice at a later time.

This was first printed in Stephens's second collection (1734), from a copy with a few interlineations in Bacon's own hand, now in the British Museum; from which copy it is here taken.[2]

THE MOST HUMBLE CERTIFICATE OR RETURN OF THE COMMISSIONERS OF ENGLAND AND SCOTLAND, AUTHORISED TO TREAT OF AN UNION FOR THE WEAL OF BOTH REALMS. 2 JAC. I. PREPARED, BUT ALTERED.[3]

We the commissioners for England and Scotland respectively named and appointed, in all humbleness do signify to his most excellent Majesty, and to the most honourable high Courts of Parliament of both realms, that we have assembled ourselves, consulted and treated according to the nature and limits of our commission; and forasmuch as we do find that hardly within the

[1] See Lincoln's Inn MSS. 83.
[2] Harl. MSS. 6797, fo. 16.
[3] These words are inserted in Bacon's hand. In the left-hand corner, at the top, is written in the same hand, 'prepared not used.'

memory of all times, or within the compass of the universal
world, there can be shewed forth a fit example or precedent of
the work we have in hand, concurring in all points material, we
thought ourselves so much the more bound to resort to the infallible and original grounds of nature and common reason, and
freeing ourselves from the leading or misleading of examples, to
insist and fix our considerations upon the individual business in
hand, without wandering or discourses. It seemed therefore
unto us a matter demonstrative by the light of reason, that we
were in first place to begin with the remotion and abolition of
all manner hostile, envious, or malign laws on either side, being
in themselves mere temporary, and now by time become directly
contrary to our present most happy estate, which laws, as they
are already dead in force and vigour, so we thought fit now to
wish them buried in oblivion, that by the utter extinguishment
of the memory of discords past, we may avoid all seeds of relapse
into discords to come Secondly, as matter of nature not unlike
the former, we entered into consideration of such limitary constitutions as served but for to obtain a form of justice between
subjects under several monarchs, and did in the very grounds
and motives of them presuppose incursions and intermixture of
hostility all which occasions, as they are in themselves now
vanished and done away, so we wish the abolition and cessation
thereof to be declared [1] Thirdly, for so much as the principal
degree to union is communion and participation of mutual commodities and benefits, it appeared to us to follow next in order,
that the commerce between both nations be set open and free,
so as the commodities and provisions of either may pass and
flow to and fro without any stops or obstructions into the veins
of the whole body, for the better sustentation and comfort of all
the parts, with caution nevertheless, that the vital nourishment
be not so drawn into one part, as it may endanger a consumption
and withering of the other Fourthly, after the communion and
participation by commerce, which can extend but to the trans-
mission of such commodities as are moveable, personal, and transitory, there succeeded naturally that other degree, that there be
made a mutual endowment and donation of either realm towards
other of the abilities and capacities to take and enjoy things
which are permanent, real, and fixed, as namely freehold and

[1] The words 'as they' and the last clause are inserted in Bacon's hand

inheritance, and the like and that as well the internal and
vital veins of blood be opened from interruption and obstruction
in making pedigree and claiming by descent, as the external and
elemental veins of passage and commerce , with reservation
nevertheless unto the due time of such abilities and capacities
only, as no power on earth can confer without time and educa
tion.   And lastly, because the perfection of this blessed work
consisteth in the union, not only of the solid parts of the estate,
but also in the spirit and sinews of the same, which are the laws
and governments, which nevertheless are already perfectly united
in the head, but require a furder time to be united in the bulk
and frame of the whole body, in contemplation hereof we did
conceive that the first step thereunto was to provide that the
justice of either realm should aid and assist, and not frustrate
and interrupt, the justice of the other, specially in sundry cases
criminal , so that either realm may not be abused by malefactors
as a sanctuary or place of refuge to avoid the condign punish
ment of their crimes and offences.   All which several points,—as
we account them, summed up and put together, but as a degree
or middle term to the perfection of this blessed work,—so yet we
conceived them to make a just and fit period for our present con
sultation and proceeding.   And for so much as concerneth the
manner of our proceedings, we may truly make this attestation
unto ourselves, that as the mark we shot at was union and unity,
so it pleased God in the handling thereof to bless us with the
spirit of unity, insomuch as from our first sitting unto the breaking up of our assembly (a thing most rare, the circumstances of
the cause and persons considered) there did not happen or inter
vene, neither in our debates or arguments, any manner alter
cation or strife of words, nor in our resolutions any variety or
division of votes, but the whole passed with an unanimity and
uniformity of consent · and yet so as we suppose there was never
in any consultation greater plainness and liberty of speech, argu
ment and debate, replying, contradicting, recalling any thing
spoken where cause was, expounding any matter ambiguous or
mistaken, and all other points of free and friendly interlocution
and conference, without cavillations, advantages, or overtakings [1]

---

[1] The words "used, permitted, or allowed, and not only so, but in all loving
manner called for, provoked, wished, and required," which followed in the MS , are
struck out

a matter that we cannot ascribe to the skill or temper of our own carriage, but to the guiding and conducting of God's holy providence and will, the true author of all unity and agreement, neither did we, where the business required, rest so upon our own senses and opinions, but we did also aid and assist ourselves as well with the reverend opinion of Judges and persons of great science and authority in the laws, and also with the wisdom and experience of merchants, and men expert in commerce   In all which our proceedings notwithstanding, we are so far from pretending or aiming at any prejudication, either of his royal Majesty's sovereign and high wisdom, which we do most dutifully acknowledge to be able to pierce and penetrate far beyond the reach of our capacities, or of the solid and profound judgment of the high Courts of Parliament of both realms, as we do in all humbleness submit our judgments and doings to his sacred Majesty and to the Parliaments, protesting our sincerity, and craving gracious and benign construction and acceptation of our travails.

We therefore with one mind and consent have agreed and concluded that there be propounded and presented to his Majesty and the Parliament of both realms, these articles and propositions following

If this introduction had been adopted it would have required in one place and I suppose in one place only, a slight correction

The "unanimity and uniformity of consent" with which all the resolutions are said to have passed, must of course be understood as referring to the conclusion of the whole business not that there were no differences of opinion among the Commissioners, but that they all agreed in what was ultimately recommended to be done And such was no doubt the result which Bacon anticipated from the tenour of the deliberations   The anticipation was not however destined to be strictly fulfilled   One of the English Commissioners, Sir Edward Hoby,—for some reason which he declined publicly to explain,—refused at the last to subscribe his name to the Instrument[1] The solitary exception however rather illustrates than throws doubt upon the substantial accuracy of the report which, after all due correction has been made, remains a notable record of a piece of business very effectually and prosperously despatched.

[1] C J 27 Nov 1606, p 1005

The history of its progress through Parliament will be a very different one, but belongs to a later time   Parliament was to have met in February, and the consideration of the measures recommended by the Commissioners was expected to be its principal business Apprehensions of a return of the Plague, of which some premonitory symptoms showed themselves in many parts of the country before Christmas, induced a further prorogation till the autumn [1] at which time the Gunpowder Plot came in the way and supplied business enough for the succeeding session   so that it was not till the winter of 1606 that the Instrument of the Union came under consideration The prorogation till autumn left Bacon with the best part of a year comparatively free from business, and available for the prosecution of the great literary work which I suppose him to have been so anxious at this time not only to go on with but to bring before the world as soon as possible   and of which the progress must have been much interrupted, if not completely suspended, by the heavy business which the last Parliament threw upon him   For the next ten months we have very little news of him   What there is shall begin a new chapter

[1] Proclamation for the proroguing of Parliament, 24 Dec 1601

CHAPTER VII.

A D 1605-6.   ÆTAT. 45.

1.

Tur importance of the part which had fallen to Bacon in the business of the last session—and that not through official patronage or private favour, but merely from experience of his ability and the necessities of the time calling for help—followed as it was by such happy success in his latest service—might have seemed to promise a speedy rise in his fortunes, had no opportunity occurred of making the promise good   But it so happened that on the 28th of October 1604 (the day after the first meeting of the Commissioners for the Union) the Solicitor General was made Chief Baron of the Exchequer, thereby vacating the very place to which a man in Bacon's position would naturally and reasonably aspire   It was given however on the same day to Serjeant Doderidge, a lawyer of good reputation, but no further conspicuous than as holding the office of Serjeant to the Prince of Wales   And the neglect of so fair an opportunity to raise Bacon looked almost like an intention to leave him below   I do not find traces however either of any application from him at the time for the place, or any complaint of having been passed over [1]   And the truth perhaps is that (as he had formerly said that "he could not expect that Coke and himself should ever serve as Attorney and Solicitor together"[2]) he really felt the relation which subsisted between them to be a valid objection to his appointment, and would not himself have asked for or recommended it

2

However that may be, the experience of the past year proved that, whether the King or Cecil or Coke wanted his help or not,

---

[1] Unless the following expression in a letter to the Lord Chancellor two years after, be taken to include an allusion to this appointment   "Otherwise for mine own private comfort it were better that   I should turn my course to endeavour to serve in some other kind, than for me to stand thus at a stop, and to have that little reputation which by my industry I gather to be scattered and taken away by continual disgraces, *every new man coming above me*"

[2] See above, p 1

his country had work for him to do, and that he must not reckon
upon having his time to himself, but if he meant to reform philosophy, must make the most of all intervals of leisure. The present
interval—the longest and least interrupted which he was destined to
enjoy for many years—came very seasonably to enable him to finish
the Advancement of Learning: which with due allowance made for
time consumed in the duties of courtship and the other business
which a treaty of marriage with an alderman's daughter would naturally involve, supplied work enough for nine or ten months.

The "two books of the Proficience and Advancement of Learning,
divine and human" were published in a single volume. But an
examination of the signatures of the sheets shows that the first book
must have been printed off before the second was sent to the press;
from which I infer that some considerable interval occurred in the
composition of them. And it seems very probable, as I have already
intimated, that the first book, which, though less important in its
argument than the other, is very full and elaborate in composition,
was written in 1603, when he expected an abundance of leisure for
such work, and that the second, which has many marks of haste
both in the writing and the printing and is in several parts pro-
fessedly unfinished, was hurried through in 1605, when he foresaw
that his times of leisure were not likely to come often or last long.
I speak of course only of the composition,—the arrangement of the
matter, the wording, and the putting into shape —for the matter
itself was the accumulation of his life, and many portions of it had
been already digested no doubt, in notes and essays.

This great work excepted, I find only one piece among the extant
writings of Bacon which appears to have been composed between
January and October, 1605, and that was probably suggested in the
progress of the work itself—being in fact a leaf taken out of it for
immediate use.

Near the beginning of the second book of the Advancement of
Learning, in speaking of the deficiencies of literature in the matter
of Civil History, he had pointed out the want of a better history of
England. And this being a thing which might, by the help of men
in authority, be put in course at once, and which through the perish-
ing of records and corruption of traditions would become more difficult with every year's delay, it occurred to him to bring the subject
immediately under the consideration of the government. With this
view he wrote, in April 1605, a letter to the Lord Chancellor Ellesmere, the original of which—a beautiful specimen of his fairest
handwriting—is still to be seen among the manuscripts at Bridgwater House.

It was first printed by Rawley in the Resuscitatio (p 28),—I presume from a copy preserved by Bacon himself in his Register-Book of letters, and shortly afterwards in Sir Toby Matthew's collection,—probably from an independent copy of his own   But both these are evidently taken from the first draft, in which Bacon made, as he wrote it fair, many alterations—as his manner was, without taking the trouble to have them copied into the draft which he kept. The letter which was actually sent was first printed by Mr. Payne Collier in his bibliographical catalogue of the Bridgwater library and a comparison of the two, which may be made here by the help of the foot-notes, will illustrate and confirm my conjecture (vol ii p 91) as to the true history of the differences between the letters as given in the Cabala and in the Resuscitatio, in certain cases

A Letter to the Lord Chancellor, touching the History of Britain.[1]

It may please your good Lordship,

Some late act of his Majesty, referred to some former speech which I have heard from your Lordship, bred in me a great desire, and by[2] strength of desire a boldness to make an humble proposition to your Lordship, such as in me can be no better than a wish   but if your Lordship should apprehend it, may[3] take some good and worthy effect.   The act I speak of, is the order given by his Majesty, as I understand,[4] for the erection of a tomb or monument for our late sovereign Lady[5] Queen Elizabeth [6] wherein I may note much, but this[7] at this time, That as her Majesty did always right to his Highness'[8] hopes, so his Majesty doth in all things right to her memory, a very just and princely retribution   But from this occasion, by a very easy ascent, I passed further, being put in mind, by this Representative of her person, of the more true and more firm[9] Representative[10], which is of her life and government.   For as Statues and Pictures are dumb histories, so histories are speaking Pic-

---

[1] The text is taken from the original   The collations are with the copy in the British Museum (Additional MSS 5503 25 b, which I call A), and that in the Resuscitatio, which I call R

[2] the R   [3] it may A, R
[4] as I understand om A, R   [5] Lady om A, R
[6] " His M hath commanded two stately tombs to be begun at Westminster, one for the Queen Elizabeth, and the other for his Majesty's mother."—Edmund Lascelles to the E of Shrewsbury April 11, 1605   Lodge, iii 115
[7] only this R   [8] Majesty's, A, R   [9] perfect, A, rue, R
[10] representation R

tures   Wherein if my affection be not too great, or my reading
too small, I am of this opinion, that if Plutarch were alive to
write lives by parallels, it would trouble him for virtue and fortune both to find for her a parallel amongst women   And
though she was of the passive sex, yet her government was so
active, as, in my simple opinion, it made more impression upon
the several states of Europe, than it received from thence.   But
I confess unto your Lordship I could not stay here, but went a
little further into the consideration of the times which have
passed since king Henry the 8th, wherein I find the strangest
variety that in like[1] number of successions of any hereditary
monarchy hath ever been known.   The reign of a child, the
offer of an usurpation, (though it were but as a Diary Ague); the
reign of a lady married to a foreign Prince,[2] and the reign of
a lady solitary and unmarried   So that as it cometh to pass in
massive bodies, that they have certain trepidations and waver-
ings before they fix and settle, so it seemeth that by the providence of God this monarchy, before it was to settle in his
Majesty and his generations (in which I hope it is now established for ever), it[3] had these prelusive changes in these
barren princes.   Neither could I contain myself here (as it is
easier to produce[4] than to stay a wish), but calling to remembrance the unworthiness of the history of England (in the main
continuance thereof), and the partiality and obliquity of that of
Scotland, in the latest and largest author[5] that I have seen   I
conceived it would be honour for his Majesty, and a work very
memorable, if this island of Great Britain, as it is now joined in
Monarchy for the ages to come, so were[6] joined in History for
the times past, and that one just and complete History were
compiled of both nations   And if any man think it may refresh
the memory of former discords, he may satisfy himself with the
verse, *olim hæc meminisse juvabit*   for the case being now altered,
it is matter of comfort and gratulation to remember former
troubles

Thus much, if it may please your Lordship, was[7] in the opta-
tive mood   It is true[8] that I did look a little in the potential,
wherein the hope which I conceived was grounded upon three

[1] so little A, R   [2] foreigner A, R   [3] hath A, R
[4] easier to multiply R, easier for a man to multiply A   [5] offer R
[6] so it were A, R   [7] is R   [8] and it was time A, R

observations The first, of the times,[1] which do[2] flourish in learning, both of art and language; which giveth hope not only that it may be done, but that it may be well done For when good things are undertaken in ill times, it turneth but to loss; as in this very particular we have a fresh example of Polydore Vergile, who being designed to write the English History by K. Henry the 8th (a strange choice to chuse a stranger), and for his better instruction having obtained into his hands many registers and memorials out of the monaster·s, did indeed deface and suppress better things than those he did collect and reduce [3] Secondly, I do see that which all the world seeth[4] in his Majesty, both a wonderful judgment in learning, and a singular affection towards learning, and the works of true honour which[5] are of the mind and not of the hand. For there cannot be the like honour sought in the building[6] of galleries, or the[7] planting of elms along highways, and the like manufactures,[8] things rather of magnificence than of magnanimity, as there is in the uniting of states, pacifying of controversies, nourishing and augmenting of learning and arts, and the particular actions appertaining unto these, of which kind Cicero judged truly, when he said to Cæsar, *Quantum operibus tuis detrahet vetustas, tantum addet laudibus* And lastly, I called[9] to mind, that your Lordship at sometimes hath[10] been pleased to express unto me a great desire, that something of this nature should be performed,[11] answerably[12] indeed to your other noble and worthy courses and actions, wherein your Lordship sheweth yourself not only an excellent Chancellor and Counsellor, but also an exceeding favourer and fosterer of all good learning and virtue, both in men and matters, persons and actions [13] joining and adding unto the great services towards his Majesty, which have, in small compass of time, been accumulated[14] upon your Lordship, many other[15] deservings both of the Church and Commonwealth and particulars; so as the opinion of so great and wise a man doth seem unto[16] me a good

---

[1] *the nature of these times* R   [2] *do, om* A, R
[3] This whole sentence, from "For when," etc , is omitted in A and R
[4] *sees* A, R   [5] *and works which* A, R
[6] *in building* R   [7] *and* A, R
[8] *and the outward ornaments wherein France now is busy* A, R   [9] *call* R
[10] *had* R   [11] *done* A   [12] *answerable* A, R
[13] This whole clause, from "wherein," is omitted in A and R
[14] *performed by* A *put upon* R   [15] *other great (many om)* A, R
[16] *to* A, R

warrant both of the possibility and worth of this matter   But all this while I assure myself, I cannot be mistaken by your Lordship, as if I sought an office or employment for myself For no man knoweth[1] better than your Lordship, that (if there were in me any faculty thereunto, as I am most unable),[2] yet neither my fortune[3] nor profession would permit it.   But because there be so many good painters both for hand and colours, it needeth but encouragement and instructions to give life and light[4] unto it

So in all humbleness I conclude my presenting to your good Lordship this wish,[5] which if it perish it is but a loss of that which is not   And thus[6] craving pardon that I have taken so much time from your Lordship, I always remain[7]

Your Lps very humbly and much bounden

Fr Bacon

Gray's Inn this 2d of April 1605

3

The great work now proceeded rapidly and in silence, and was ready for delivery about the end of October—just before Parliament was to meet again   The first news we have of it is in the following letters, accompanying presentation-copies —all from the Register book, and all without date; but needing no further introduction

To the Earl of Northampton, with request to present his Book to his Majesty [8]

It may please your good Lordship,

Having finished a work touching the Advancement of Learning, and dedicated the same to his sacred Majesty, whom I dare avouch (if the records of time err not) to be the learnedst king that hath reigned , I was desirous, in a kind of congruity, to present it by the learnedst counsellor in this kingdom , to the end that so good an argument, lighting upon so bad an author, might receive some reparation[9] by the hands into which, and by which, it should be delivered.   And therefore I make it my humble suit to your Lordship, to present this mean but well meant writing to his Majesty, and with it my humble and zealous duty , and also, my like humble request of pardon if I have too

---

[1] knows A, R   [2] This clause is omitted in A and R
[3] course of life A, R   [4] and light, om. A, R
   my presenting unto your Lordship of this wish R   [6] so A R
[7] I remain, etc A, R   [8] Add MSS 5507 f 29   [9] reputation Rs

often taken his name in vain, not only in the dedication, but in the voucher of the authority of his speeches and writings. And so I remain, etc

To Sir Thomas Bodley, upon sending him his Book of the Advancement of Learning.[1]

Sir,

I think no man may more truly say with the Psalm *Multum incola fuit anima mea*, than myself. For I do confess, since I was of any understanding, my mind hath in effect been absent from that I have done, and in absence are many errors[2] which I do willingly acknowledge; and amongst the rest this great one that led the rest, that knowing myself by inward calling to be fitter to hold a book than to play a part, I have led my life in civil causes, for which I was not very fit by nature, and more unfit by the preoccupation of my mind. Therefore calling myself home, I have now for a time enjoyed myself; whereof likewise I desire to make the world partaker. My labours (if I may so term that which was the comfort of my other labours) I have dedicated to the King, desirous, if there be any good in them, it may be as the fat of a sacrifice, incensed to his honour and the second copy I have sent unto you, not only in good affection, but in a kind of congruity, in regard of your great and rare desert of learning. For books are the shrines where the Saint is, or is believed to be and you having built an Ark to save learning from deluge, deserve propriety in any new instrument or engine, whereby learning should be improved or advanced

To the Earl of Salisbury, upon sending him one of his Books of Advancement of Learning[3]

It may please your good Lordship,

I present your Lordship with a work of my vacant time, which if it had been more, the work had been better It appertaineth to your Lordship (besides my particular respects) in some propriety, in regard you are a great governor in a province of learning,[4] and (that which is more) you have added to your place affection towards learning, and to your affection judgment, of which the last I could be content were (for the time) less, that

[1] Resuscitatio, p 31   The copy of this letter in the MS seems to be less correct
[2] *Errors are committed*, MS   [3] Add MSS 5503 f 28
[4] The Earl of Salisbury was Chancellor of the University of Cambridge

you might the less exquisitely censure that which I offer to you. But sure I am the argument is good, if it had lighted upon a good author. But I shall content myself to awake better spirits, like a bell-ringer, which is first up to call others to church. So with my humble desire of your Lordship's good acceptation, I remain

To the Lord Treasurer Buckhurst, upon the same occasion of sending his Book of Advancement of Learning [1]

May it please your good Lordship,

I have finished a work touching the Advancement or setting forward of Learning, which I have dedicated to his Majesty, the most learned of a sovereign or temporal prince that time hath known   And upon reason not unlike, I humbly present one of the books to your Lordship, not only as a Chancellor of an University, but as one that was excellently bred in all learning which I have ever noted to shine in all your speeches and behaviours   And therefore your Lordship will yield a gracious aspect to your first love, and take pleasure in the adorning of that wherewith yourself are so much adorned   And so humbly desiring your favourable acceptation thereof, with signification of humble duty, I remain.

A Letter of the like Argument to the Lord Chancellor [2]

May it please your good Lordship,

I humbly present your Lordship with a work, wherein as you have much commandment over the author, so your Lordship hath also great interest in the argument   For, to speak without flattery, few have like use of learning, or like judgment in learning, as I have observed in your Lordship.   And again, your Lordship hath been a great planter of learning, not only in those places in the Church which have been in your own gift, but also in your commendatory vote, no man hath more constantly held, *detur digniori*   and therefore both your Lordship is beholding to learning, and learning beholding to you   Which maketh me presume with good assurance that your Lordship will accept well of these my labours, the rather because your Lordship in private speech hath often begun to me in expressing your admiration of his Majesty's learning, to whom I have dedicated this work, and whose virtue and perfection in that kind did chiefly move me to a work of this nature. And so with signification of my most humble duty and affection towards your Lordship I remain

4.

The appearance of such a book by such a man was not likely in those days to make so much talk in the world as it would now, though the publication of "Sir F. Bacon's new book on Learning" was not forgotten by Chamberlain in reporting to Carleton the news of London on the 7th of November, 1605[1] But its appearance happened to coincide with an event which at any time would have drawn public attention away from everything else

In sending a copy to Toby Matthew, who had left England about the end of April, and was now in Italy Bacon enclosed a 'relation,' which was apparently a short account drawn up by himself of the discovery of the Gunpowder Plot But as I have not been able to find any paper answering the description, and Bacon does not appear to have had any part either in the investigation of the conspiracy or the trials of the conspirators, and as the general history of it is sufficiently notorious, it will not be necessary for me to go further into the particulars

The letter which enclosed the lost 'relation' comes from Matthew's collection, and has the following heading "Mr Bacon to a friend and servant of his, by way of advertisement concerning some books and writings of his own" It has no date, and the title "Mr" would suggest a wrong one But the matters alluded to prove that to be in error, and point clearly enough to the early part of November 1605 as the time when it must have been written And I suppose there is no reason to doubt that the 'friend and servant' was Matthew himself

To Mr Matthew[2]

Sir,

I perceive you have some time when you can be content to think of your friends, from whom since your have borrowed yourself, you do well, not paying the principal, to send the in-

---

[1] Domestic Papers, James I vol xvi
[2] Collection of Letters made by Sir Toby Mathews, Knt, London, 1660, p 11

terest at six months day. The relation which here I send you
inclosed, carries the truth of that which is public, and though
my little leisure might have required a briefer, yet the matter
would have endured and asked a larger

I have now at last taught that child to go, at the swadling
whereof you were. My work touching the *Proficiency* and
Advancement of *Learning*, I have put into two books, whereof the
former, which you saw, I count but as a Page to the latter   I
have now published them both , whereof I thought it a small
adventure to send you a copy, who have more right to it than
any man, except Bishop Andrews, who was my inquisitor

The death of the late great Judge concerned not me, because
the other was not removed.   I write this in answer to your good
wishes, which I return not as flowers of Florence, but as you
mean them; whom I conceive place cannot alter, no more than
time shall me, except it be to the better

Dr Launcelot Andrews, who had been Dean of Westminster since
1 July 1601,[1] was made Bishop of Chichester on the 3d of November
1605 [2] He was a friend of Bacon's student-days, being then preacher
at St Giles's,[3] and a man whom throughout his life he held in
special reverence   The nature of the inquisitorial office which he
performed for the *Advancement of Learning* may be partly inferred
from a letter of later date asking him to perform a similar office for
the *Cogitata et Visa*   "Now let me tell you" (Bacon writes) "what
my desire is If your Lordship be so good now as when you were
the good Dean of Westminster, my request to you is that not by
pricks, but by notes, you would mark unto me whatsoever shall
seem unto you either not current in the stile, or harsh to credit or
opinion, or inconvenient for the person of the writer, for no man
can be judge and party , and when our minds judge by reflexion on
ourselves they are more subject to error   And though for the
matter itself, my judgment be in some things fixed, and not accessible by any man's judgment that goeth not my way, yet even in
those things the admonition of a friend may make me express myself
diversely " He had consulted him, no doubt, upon the Advancement
of Learning in the same way, when he was "the good Dean of
Westminster," and sent him a presentation-copy shortly after he
became Bishop of Chichester

[1] Chamberlain to Carleton, 8 July, 1601, p 112
[2] Do 7 Nov 1605   Domestic Papers James I vol xvi
  See Vol I p 117

The light allusion to the "death of the late great Judge" as not concerning him because "the other" was not removed (in which I strongly suspect that the names have been suppressed by the editor) covers a fact which did really concern Bacon a good deal. In August 1605 Sir Edmund Anderson, Chief Justice of the Common Pleas, died. It was another opportunity for advancing Bacon, had the authorities wished to do it. If Coke had been promoted to the Common Pleas, and Doderidge succeeded him as Attorney, Bacon might have been made Solicitor. But Coke kept his place, Sir Francis Gawdy, one of the puisne Judges of King's Bench, succeeded Anderson, and Bacon remained where he was. In this case, as in the last, we hear of no application and no complaint, but unless there was some better reason against the arrangement than we know of, he could not but feel it as a discouragement.

5

I have said that Bacon had no part, so far as we know, in the investigations or trials which followed the discovery of the Gunpowder Plot. And indeed the only extant writing of his which connects him with it at all is a short note to Cecil (now Earl of Salisbury) enclosing an examination of a shoemaker's servant, who had heard a man say that "the plot would have been brave sport, if it had gone forwards." It was taken at the request of the Principal and Ancients of Staples Inn; and (to judge by the tone of his letter) was not thought by himself to be a matter of much importance.

The letter was printed (but without the enclosure) by Mr. Dixon in his "Personal History of Lord Bacon."

TO THE EARL OF SALISBURY.[1]

It may please your Lordship,

I send an examination of one was brought to me by the Principal and Ancients of Staple Inn, touching the words of one Braid, suspected for a Papist and practiser, being general words, but bad, and I thought not good to neglect anything at such a time. So with signification of humble duty I remain

At your Lordship's honourable commandments,
most humbly
FR. BACON

[1] Domestic Papers James I. vol. xv. to 29. Original; own hand. Docketed (but in another hand, and apparently at a later time) 8 Nov. 1605; which seems unlikely.

THE EXAMINATION OF JH DRAKE, SERVANT TO TH REYNOLLS, SHOEMAKER, DWELLING IN HOLBORN NEAR GRAY'S INN GATE, TAKEN THE 6TH NOVEMBER 1605.[1]

He sayeth that the morning of this present day he repaired to the lodging of one Mr Beard in the house of one Gibson in Fetter Lane over against the new Church yard, to take measure for new boots, and it was in the morning about seven of the clock, and finding him abed, Mr Beard asked him whether there were watching and warding abroad, to which this examinate said that the night before there was much watching and searching for Papists and Recusants, and named one Percye

And this Examinate said furder, that it was the most heinous treason that ever was which was intended, to which the said Beard said *It had been brave sport if it had gone forwards*, and this speech he spake as muttering to himself, so as the last words were scant heard, and not in any laughing or jesting manner, yet afterwards the said Beard spake against the fact very much

The said Reynolls being present at this examination sayeth that he hath served the said Beard of boots these two years' space, and that he used to lodge at Mrs Mayne's house at the upper end of St John's street, who is reported to be a Recusant and to bring up Recusants' children which are there to learn, but removed to Gibson's house about half a year ago.

JOHN DRAKE

V the mark of

TH REYNOLLS.

Ex per
  FR BACON.

After this we hear no more of Bacon till the meeting of Parlia ment in January 1605-6, except in a letter to his friend Hickes, now Sir Michael, which is interesting only as showing that their friend ship had not been disturbed by their money transactions It was written, if the docket be correct, on the 17th of January, 1605-6 But the allusion to "the Indictments at Westminster," as coming on the same day, makes me suspect that it is a mistake for the 27th for that was the day on which the first of the trials of the Gun powder Conspirators took place It appears to have been written

---

[1] Domestic Papers James I vol xvi fo 29 Original own hand Docketed, in Bacon's hand, " The Ex of Jh Drake "

at full finger-speed; but as a proof of the *temper* of the intercourse between the two men is the better evidence on that account

To Sir M. Hickes.[1]

Sir,

For your travel with all disadvantages, I will put it upon my account to travel twice so far upon any occasion of yours. But your wits seemed not travelled, but fresh, by your letter, which is to me an infallible argument of hearts-ease, which doeth so well with you, as I must entreat you to help me to some of the same. And therefore I will adjourn our conference to your return to the Strand on Monday, where I will find you, if it chance right. And this day would I have come to your Friery, but that I am commanded to attend the indictments at Westminster. And so, glad to perceive your good disposition, I remain

Your's assured
Fr Bacon.

6.

Parliament met on the 5th of November, according to the summons The Commons, having read a few bills, and talked a little about the great deliverance, adjourned till the 9th, when they heard the King's account of the discovery of the plot, and were again adjourned to the 21st of January Meditation upon the danger which the kingdom had so narrowly escaped had put them into a humour of great severity against the Papists, and warm personal affection for the King, and though the grievances which had been left unsettled in the last session were still to be dealt with, and not even allowed to sleep through this, they felt the danger of urging them so as to risk a rupture Measures for security and for demonstration of internal harmony took precedence, leaving the questions upon which the two Houses could not agree in such a position that they could be postponed without obstructing the general business of government An Act for public thanksgiving every year on the 5th of November passed at once and unanimously A very unconstitutional motion for making a special retrospective law for the trial and punishment of the "miners," was opposed by the new Solicitor-General, now the principal representative of the Government in the Lower

[1] Lansd MSS lxxxix 76 Original own hand Docketed "17 Jan 1605 Sir Fra Bacon" But the last figure is not clearly written, and might be meant either for a 1 or a 9 The allusion to the "Indictments at Westminster," makes me think that 27 Jan 1605, is the true date

House, and negatived by the good sense of the majority   Measures
' for the timely and severe proceeding against Jesuits, Seminaries, and
other Popish Agents and Practisers, and for the preventing and sup
pressing of their plots and practices''—which was their first care
—took more time, and led to many conferences, but met with no
opposition   The appointment of a Committee "to consider of the
fittest course to provide for the general planting of a Learned
Ministry, and for the meeting with non-residence in ministers already
placed," passed without remonstrance   Upon the question of Pur
veyance, in which a smooth passage could hardly be hoped for, they
resolved to proceed not by conference or petition, but by bill [1]—a
course which had the effect of postponing the critical period of the
discussion, while, at the same time, they showed no disposition to
keep back the question of supply, and make it wait upon the question
of Grievances (though they intended, as will appear presently, that
the two should go on together), but as early as the 10th of February
agreed to grant a double Subsidy—with the full assent of all the independent members who spoke, and without any dispute, except
upon the question (if I understand it correctly) whether the pro
posal should be referred to a Committee in the regular way, or passed
at once   "The Commons of the Lower House," writes the Earl of
Shrewsbury, on the 12th, "are much more temperate than they were
at the first Session, and now spend all their spirits and endeavours
in devising laws tending to his Majesty's safety, and suppressing of
the dangerous members of the state   I heard not any one trans
cendant speech uttered there as yet "[2]   It seemed, therefore, that the
attempt to overthrow Protestantism had only issued in a suspension
of those disputes and jealousies between the Commons and the Crown,
in which its chief weakness and danger lay

Bacon, though his name appears as usual in all the principal com
mittees, and though he was occasionally employed to bring up a re
port or assist in managing a conference, does not appear to have
taken a prominent part in the proceedings during this session   The
Solicitor, the Recorder, the Attorney of the Wards, and the second
Secretary of State, were all of the House   and in ordinary circum
stances the leading part would naturally fall to one or other of them

Nor did any difficulties arise, important enough to induce a de
parture from the ordinary course   In the matter of Papists and Re
cusants, the zeal of all parties on the side of severity needed no
enforcing, and a voice in favour of gentler measures would not easily

[1] C J Jan 21, p 259
[2] Shrewsbury to Edmunds, 12 Feb 1605-6—Court and Times of K Jas I
i 52

have obtained a hearing In granting liberal supplies without standing upon terms of bargain, the principal popular members concurred
with the majority, and the few murmurs of dissent which were heard
during the heat of the later debates might be safely left to be
answered by the general vote on the question, and would be disposed of in that way more effectually than by argument The question of the Union of the Kingdoms was postponed by common consent to the next session With regard to grievances in general,
Bacon approved of the course which the House was pursuing, which
was, first to hear the counsel of parties interested, and then to proceed by way of petition to the King And if in the particular
grievance of Purveyance,—which was to be dealt with by a Bill and
was in hot hands,—there was danger of their going faster and further
than seemed prudent —a sufficient remedy would be found in the
obstructive power of the Upper House, which encountered the shock,
and could count on the help of Sir Edward Coke in criticizing the
legal bearings of the law they proposed to pass

Of the part which he did take, I shall not be able to give a very
intelligible account, as it must be drawn almost entirely from the
notes in the Commons Journals, which are rather more fragmentary
than usual But the real records (broken and obscure as they are)
will at least help to exclude fanciful descriptions and as it is my
wish to collect all evidence that is authentic, I shall give them as I
find them, and make them as intelligible as I can

7.

The most convenient course will be to take the principal questions
in the order of the dates at which Bacon became prominent in connexion with them

The first appearance of his name in the Journals (otherwise than
in mere Committee-lists) was on the 7th of February when, after
the Solicitor-general had reported to the House the first conference
with the Lords on the Articles against Recusants, he followed with
a supplementary report

The appointment of a Committee to consider and report upon the
course to be taken in this matter had been the first business of the
House at its meeting on the 21st of January Of this Committee
Bacon was a member, and took some part in the debate, though we
do not know what [1] Their first measure appears to have been the
appointment of a sub committee, to draw up articles against Recu-

[1] Sir E Hoby to Sir T Edmunds, 10 Feb 1605-6 —Court and Times of
James I 16

sants,[1] the names of which Sub-committee have not been recorded
On the 3rd of February, while the proposed articles were still under
discussion in the House, the Lords, who had a measure of their own
for the same purpose under consideration, sent to desire a conference,
which was agreed to, and appointed for the 6th   The report of this
conference was made by Doderidge on the 7th   Each House had
drawn up articles, which being read on both sides showed "a great
agreement"   Each was to send a copy of its own articles to the
other, and a sub-committee of both houses was appointed, or recom
mended, "to draw things into form"[2]   When he had finished his
report, Bacon, either feeling that he had left unsaid something im
portant, or desiring to draw attention away from an injudicious hint
about supply[3] with which it seems that Salisbury (whose statesmanship was always rather near-sighted) had concluded his speech at the
Conference, rose, and referring to the King's "meditation" upon
the articles offered by the Lords, explained more fully the course
which it was proposed to hold with the different classes of Papists

But for what he said we must be content with the following notes
being all we have from which to conjecture it

Sir Francis Bacon, with a repetition of that which Mr. Solicitor reported —A glance in my Lord Salisbury's speech that
the Church must needs receive some storm if the Commonwealth
be not relieved —

The articles read —

The Lords propounded more strict articles than did arise from
this house —

The King's meditation touching these articles —

The ground —In repressing of Heresies in spiritual causes,
the sting of the law to the Heresy

Three sorts

1 Papists, old, rooted, and rotten

2. Novelists, the greatest danger

3 The youth, the future tense of the Papists

1. Like Queen Mary's Priests, small hope to reclaim them —
Rather superstitious than seditious.—

To be disarmed —No place of magistracy.—Left to the old
laws

---

[1] C J 25 Jan p 260   [2] Ib p 265
[3] ' It were not fit they should long stay, but think opportunely of that which
subjects use to do A gratification from the subject to the Sovereign " This, I
suppose, was the " other matter of importance " of which Salisbury had been
commissioned to make overture   See Lords' Journals Feb 3 and 6

2 Apostates, most malignant.—To be sifted by oaths before and after —Law of Reconcilement to extend in other countries, as well as in England.—Not use the words "beyond seas"

3 Take care of marriages and christenings —Nip them in bud —The beginning of procreation the acting

Priests in hold to be banished within a time —

After that, the law to be executed with all severity

The articles to be delivered [1]

After this, several other conferences were held between the two Houses, but all we hear further of Bacon in the matter is that on the 17th of February he and Doderidge were appointed to consult upon it "and to prepare themselves for conference," and that on the 5th of March he was put upon a Committee to draw the Bill In the end, the articles agreed upon were digested into two separate Acts,—an Act "for the better discovering and repressing of Popish Recusants," (of which the main object was to provide means of obliging all suspected persons to take the oaths of supremacy and allegiance)—and an Act "to prevent and avoid dangers which may grow by Popish Recusants," which aimed at limiting their means of action, and did undoubtedly impose many uncomfortable and vexatious restraints and taxes upon persons whose religious opinions and sympathies exposed them to suspicion of disloyalty, even where they were ready to give the required pledges of political obedience. It is not strange that at such a time public safety seemed to require such measures, and the indulgence which has been claimed for the act of indiscriminate murder attempted by the weaker party, on the ground that the grievance from which they hoped thereby to deliver themselves was "one which nobler hearts alone can feel,"—namely, that ' they were prohibited from worshipping God in the only way in which, as they believed, it was possible for Christian men to worship him at all,"[2]—cannot justly be refused to the intolerant legislation of the stronger party,—who were as fully convinced that they were thereby discouraging people from worshipping God in a way in which, as *they* believed, he could not be worshipped without danger of everlasting fire

8

A Committee "to consider of the fittest course to provide for the general planting of a Learned Ministry and for the meeting with non-residence in ministers already placed," was appointed on the 22nd of January, and bore its fruit in a "bill for the better establishing of true Religion,"—brought in by Sir Edwin Sandys, (a man whose relation to the Bishops may be inferred from the fact that on the 2nd of November preceding his " books were burned in Paul's Church Yard by order of the High Commission "[1]) on the 8th of February   With the preparation of this Bill Bacon does not appear to have had anything to do, and it was not till it had been committed, reported with amendments, and (upon some dispute arising on the report) sent back to the Committee again, that he was called on to help in it   At that time (Feb 24) it was thought advisable to strengthen the Committee by the addition of him and Sir Henry Hubbard [2] But this is all we know of his connexion with it, and it came to nothing   For though, after a delay of some weeks and a third commitment it had a smooth passage through the Lower House and was sent up to the Lords on the 26th of March, it came back on the 20th of May with amendments to which the Commons could not agree   " Upon the question of commitment, not any voice with it   Upon the question of rejection, a great cry to cast it out "[3]

Two or three other bills for the reform of the Church in this department were also passed and sent up by the Lower House but with no better success   while, on the other hand, a Bill for the restraint of Excommunication, which had been passed in the House of Lords upon the recommendation of the King himself, found no favour in the House of Commons, but was " upon the question rejected with much distaste "[4]   What the particular points in dispute were we have no means of knowing, but it is easy to understand that an Act of Parliament framed for such an object could hardly have satisfied the House of Commons, without infringing upon the authority of the Bishops, and it is not likely that Bacon, cordially as he approved of the object, thought this the best way of pursuing it   For I find that in another proceeding which aimed at the same end by a different way, he took a more prominent part

The silencing of ministers, when unjustly or injudiciously enforced, was an abuse of authority   and, as in the case of other abuses, the orderly course was to begin with a petition for redress   Immediately after the resolution to grant a double Subsidy had passed, a motion was made for a Committee to consider of the grievances of the Commonwealth [5]   When they were collected, the case of Deprived Ministers headed the list   Before putting it to the question, however, it was resolved, after a long debate, to desire a conference with the Lords upon this and other ecclesiastical grievances   And when asked by the Lords for a more particular statement of the points to

1 Chamberlain to Carleton, 7 Nov 1605 S P Dom   2 C J p 273
3 Ib p 311   4 Ib p 311 May 22   5 Ib p 267

be discussed, they resolved to distribute them under four heads namely, 1st, touching the deprivation, suspension and silencing of ministers 2nd, touching the multiplicity of ecclesiastical commissions 3rd, touching the form of citations 4th, touching Excommunication[1] Of these heads the charge of the first was assigned to .acon, the Archbishop of Canterbury being deputed to speak to it on the part of the lords And the following note contains what we know of the result[2]

Sir Francis Bacon reporteth the conference in ecclesiastical causes —

My Lord Archbishop's speech touching silenced ministers.—

Two parts of the Archbishop's speech

A narrative of the proceeding against ministers

Answer to propositions —

Eleven books A petition under hands[3]

That ministers might be restored —Precedent out of reformed Churches —Subscription in all —

A case forlorn, that Romish subtlety should underprop English formality

A protestation an exclusion of a conclusion —A negative

Kneeling, like All-hail to Christ —Cross, like broth at the Sacrament:—Surplice, like a coat with many patches —Coat with four elbows

Conclusion —*Immedicabile vulnus* —Leave off connivance. fall to further execution[4]

From this it would seem that the ground on which the Archbishop justified the proceedings complained of, was that the Ministers in question had not been content with the negative liberty of holding their opinions undisturbed, but had thought it their duty to turn upon aggressors, to vilify the ordinances of the Church, and teach

---

[1] C J p 291
[2] It seems that there were two conferences, one on the 16th of April, when the Committees of the Commons were heard the other when the Bishops gave their answer "For Church matters' (writes Dudley Carleton, 17 April 1606) "there were four points very curiously and learnedly handled by four apostles of the Lower House — deprivation, citation, excommunication, and the authority of the High Commission, by Sir Francis Bacon, the Attorney of the Wards, the Recorder and the Solicitor on which the Bishops took time till this day for answer, and is there was then a general fast and prayer among the brethren in the town for good success in their affairs, so do they now hasten Good Friday the sooner, and are all at their devotions" S P Dom The next day was Good Friday, and I suppose the answer was postponed till after the Easter recess
[3] So much Journals qu 'heads'?   [4] 29 April, 1606 C J p 302

their congregations to regard her appointed ceremonial with contempt In which it is likely enough that he had a good deal to say for himself

Other Conferences followed—in which however I do not find any report of anything said by Bacon and all ended in the verbal presentation by the Speaker to the King of two petitions—one concerning the execution of Jesuits, the other concerning deprived ministers With what effect we do not know , the King's answer, though reported to the House, being left blank in the Journals

9

The reason why the discussion and rejection of these ecclesiastical grievances passed so quietly I take to be, that the attention of the reformers was engrossed at the time by a grievance of another kind

It may be remembered that in the last session one of the grievances most complained of was Purveyance, and that the difficulty arose mainly from this The complaint of the Commons was that the proceedings of the Purveyors were against law , their demand, that the law should be made effectual to suppress them a concession for which the Crown could not justly claim any pecuniary compensation, because it was asked to give up nothing except what did not legally belong to it The Lords on the other hand (following the lead probably of Salisbury) thought that by carrying the concession a little further, a case for compensation might be made They proposed therefore (if I have put the fragments of information correctly together) that the Crown should give up altogether its claim to be supplied with provision for its progresses by the countries through which it passed, receiving in exchange on Parliamentary security an annual payment of 50,000*l* But the proposal being taken into consideration by the Commons, so many difficulties were found in it, that they agreed to let the whole question sleep till the next session

Taking the case up where they had left it, their first resolution (21 January) was to seek no further conference with the Upper House, but to bring in a bill A Bill was brought in accordingly, and (after a debate which seems to have turned chiefly upon the question whether they should compound or not) referred to a Committee , with instructions "to frame a form of a commission to be set down in the Act" But before it was brought back from the Committee, a message had been received which induced them to reconsider their resolution The King, in thanking the House

through the Speaker for the promised supply, had expressed himself
as "well pleased that consideration should be had how the people
might be eased of the grievances in Purveyance," and as wishing
that "a conference of Committees of both Houses might be appointed for the said causes,"[1] where matter would be communicated "nearly concerning the supply of his present estate"[2] This
pointed of course at the difficult question of composition; but a
request so conveyed from such a quarter could not either in courtesy or prudence be declined, and they agreed at once to forbear
further proceeding with their Bill until they had conferred with the
Lords Unfortunately, the member whom they selected for their
spokesman had a sharp tongue, and set forth the case in a style
which offended and irritated his hearers, thereby encumbering the
discussion with personal apologies and justifications, and nearly
bringing the two Houses into angry collision[3] But the substantial
question was, as before, the expediency of compounding by an annual
payment in money for "the removing and final taking away of these
grievances touching the Purveyors" This question it was agreed,
after much debating, to discuss in another Conference, in the presence of the Judges, and eight members were selected to conduct
the argument on behalf of the Commons,—with a special restriction,
however, not to make any offer of composition, but if any were made
on the other side, merely to hear and report

Bacon, who has not been mentioned hitherto as taking any part
whatever in this matter, was one of the members selected for this
duty, and to him also was assigned the task of reporting what
passed Of his report, which was made on the 1st of March, we have
this note

Sir Francis Bacon reporteth the Conference touching the
Purveyors.

A speech in the beginning by Mr Yelverton, in the end by a
Counsellor, not pertinent, but looking back

Silence of consent and approbation —The style of wisdom

[1] Lords' Journals, 12 Feb
[2] Sir E Hoby to Edmunds, 7 March (C and T of James I i 59)
[3] "The 11th, the great Committee met with the Lords, where Hare delivered
unto them a complaint out of sorrow and grief against the seed of the Devil,
namely, Purveyors and officers of the green cloth   The 15th relation was made
by the aforesaid committee by [to] the Commons, but so was it carried as the
House stood much ill affected towards the Lords' carriage, and Hyde yielded
many reasons why we should not yield more unto the king than we had, with
many invectives, and so far put the House in distaste, as that an expectation
grew of the sequel And if your Lordship had heard them, you would have said
that Hare and Hyde had represented the tribunes of the people"—Sir E Hoby
to Sir T Edmunds 7 March, 1605-6 (C and T of James I i 60)

Exceptions —Security, Conveniency, Proportion —

Two laws —A law of Right   a law of Love

The one will not bend, the other doth apply itself

Know first what shall be assured, before security be given

The King hath an inherent Prerogative —

The House to select some which should set forth the right of the subject —

The Lords to choose some, to maintain the Prerogative

To object to the security, as well as to the right

Apology touching the speech of Croesus' riches

Eighteen several articles in II. VII time for the unjust accumulating of treasure —

The day to be Monday.

The point, of the Right and Security —

The Judges to be present.—

The sub-committee to dispute it —The King's Prerogative and the Subject's liberty

Laws positive are never corrective of a King's right, but directive of a King's will

A necessity to admit a right if we lose the question.[1]

To this proposal for a fresh conference the Commons, again after long debate, assented   It took place according to appointment on the 4th of March, and appears to have been chiefly occupied with a speech from Coke, who had been called in to assist the Lords in maintaining "the Prerogative touching Purveyance." which was followed by a plain warning from Salisbury that "the King's necessity could not admit that their bill should pass," that the Lords would not allow the refusal of it to be put upon him, and that the arrangement must be by composition [2]

What line was taken by the managers of the conference on the part of the Commons, we are not informed, but upon their report to the House another long debate arose, lasting several days,—in the course of which Bacon made a speech which I judge by the notes to have been a considerable one

The question being whether they should agree to compound for the extinction of Purveyance, many difficulties were urged, not only as to the amount of revenue to be assured and the manner of raising it, but as to the security which could be taken for the performance of the other side of the bargain   For it was not easy to frame an act which should effectually secure the people against the claim of the

Crown for purveyance, without creating a precedent for "binding the Prerogative"—a thing which the Judges in those days would hardly have allowed that a statute could do [1] It will be seen that Bacon spoke in favour of Composition, and answered a series of objections   But I am afraid that nobody will be able to fill up the blanks completely enough to give a connected account of his argument

Composition disputed.

Sir Francis Bacon —A compact transaction .—Composition breeds mistaking —

Quest now, conveniency —

Neither against the Prerogative nor against public good.—

Fawning upon superiors ·—Pleasing a multitude —

In altero fœda species servitutis   In altero falsa species libertatis.

Humores moti et non remoti morbum aggravant.

Nec insidiis cœli capiere sereni.

First years of a King — Dancing — Triumphs — Afterthoughts of ambition —

Sinews of wars in coffers, as to have the sinews of peace in parchment —

Practice of Powder a *Supersedeas* to other practices —

Then despairs dangerous, but their hopes more dangerous —

Objections —

A perpetual tax

Ans A time of probation

Payments certain.—Royalties — Casualties —As fines for alienation, wards, fines of Alienations.

2 New precedent —

A new precedent of an offer.—Discharge him now or never

3 Precedent to redeem vexations.—

Prerogative buying.

1 Prerogative evicted, Dishonour —

Dismissed, Honour

5. King cannot part with his Prerogative —Quest. of Security. Whether he should live upon * * * *

Laws that trench to the Right bind the Prerogative   not simple Prohibitions

---

[1] " *Mr Fuller*—If the laws cannot bind the King in matter of Purveyance, *as the Judges delivered*, then the Composition to no purpose " C J. p. 278

6 Subsidy upon tonnage and poundage
The statute mistaken in the ground.

7 Instance of Prisage.—

Butlerage and Prisage ancient Rights of the Crown.—No affinity

8. Compositions already displeasant —

Compositions no squyre for this which we shall now make
The Green Cloth shall never deal with this.

9. Buying of Justice —

A buying of interest, possession, freedom, safety, ease.—The King hath more than a Preemption ·—Confessed *Terminum antiquum ne moveas* —

Compositions at Westminster for peace sake, buyings of Justice —

Prerogative as ancient as the Law —This as ancient as any —*Caput inter nubila conditur*

Children for the Chapel may be taken.—A preferment.— Small, for when their voices change, they shall be cast off —

The place not remedied by the old law.—The new doth

10 That we have ever proceeded by way of law.—*Penelope* — *Tantalus poma fugacia captat* —

Before the Lady Marie's Grace —Four funerals since one Christening.

E III. times many laws, because many mighty and noble issue —

Let not us bring ourselves into the like case.[1]

The debate had already lasted more than two days when this speech was made, and still there were no symptoms of a conclusion "The matter of conveniency was to be further proceeded in" the next day[2] Nevertheless, since ' the necessities of the King" had been openly alleged as the motive for standing upon terms of composition, and the policy of keeping him in straits by way of' bit and bridle (though Salisbury's huckstering system was fast teaching it) had not yet been adopted as the tactic of the reforming party, there was still an escape from the dilemma A perpetual tax was a serious matter to resolve on, but the present necessity might be met by a present supply What if they should offer a third Subsidy instead? Suggestions tending that way had already been thrown out in the course of the debate by some of the popular members And now

[1] C J p 279   [2] Ib p 280

the King, having understood probably that there was good hope of
a larger grant if that course were taken, intimated to the House
through the Speaker that though the proposal of composition came
originally from himself, if they did not like it he was content they
should leave it [1] This intimation of course settled that part of the
question, the discussion turned in effect into a debate on Supply
(which will be noticed presently) and the suspended bill having
passed quickly through its remaining stages (in spite of Salisbury's
attempts, through the help of the Speaker with whom he was in
constant communication, to keep it back) [2] was sent up to the Lords
by the hands of Bacon, with instructions to use some speech in commendation of it [3]

How he performed this office we have no means of knowing,—further than that his commendation did not secure its passage The
Archbishop of Canterbury reported from the Committee to which it
was referred, that "Mr Attorney-General having opened the parts
of the Bill at large unto the Committees, they found the same in
many things inconvenient, and not fit to be further proceeded in," [4]
and though the Commons were not satisfied without two more Conferences, (in which they had the advantage of hearing the defects of
their Bill explained by Coke in detail), [5] they did not succeed in

[1] 8 March C J pp 280, 281   "We had 2 whole subsidies given us" (writes
Salisbury to Mar, 9 March, 1605-6) "but there is such a heat because his M will
not put down Purveyors and Purveyance, by which he should lose 50,000*l* a year,
as we are now only seeking to temper that particular grievance by making a law
to punish the abuse, but in no wise to put down the use, and if it be possible, to
get somewhat more than 2 subsidies, whereof if we had made a good despatch,
than have on to our Union" (Dom James I vol xix)
    See the Speaker's letter to him 17 March, 1605-6   Dom James I vol xix
[3] 20 March C J p 287   [4] 10 April Lords' Journals, ii 412
[5] Dudley Carleton, in his letter of 17 April, gives the following account of the
matter as it then remained   "The Bill of Purveyors was the main matter which
bred trouble on all sides   For first it was arraigned by the Attorney at a Conference, and ten charges laid to it as impossibilities to have it pass, which was
reported to the Lower House, and Sir John Savile made a collection out of the
ten objections, reducing them to four—hanging the innocent, damning the ignorant, raising rebellion, and starving the King   For material points, they were
handled well and substantially   But the Judges overruled all on Prerogative side,
and gave it out for law that the King had both prising and preemption, and that
he was not bound to payment but upon these terms, *quand bonnement il peut* and
delivered one judgment in all mens opinions of dangerous consequence—that the
Prerogative was not subject to law, but that it was transcendent above the reach
of Parliament   In the end the Lords closed up the matter with the King's
favourable intentions, that in kindness he would do much, but upon constraint
nothing, and that of himself he would see that arrangement in this disorder which
Parliament could not provide for"   S P Dom
    Coke was not yet one of the Judges, and, as Attorney General, was no doubt
the retained advocate of the Crown   But is there any reason to doubt that this
decision in favour of Prerogative had his full personal concurrence? In Conferences
between the two Houses, he was called in as legal *adviser* of the Upper House,
"*ad tractandum et colloquium habendum cum Proceribus*"

making them think better of it So the Bill was lost, and the law had to remain for the present as it was

Inasmuch however as it was not the law, but the transgression of the law, which constituted the grievance, it was within the power of the executive to provide a remedy. And the King,—who had not meddled in this part of the business, and appears to have been really desirous to further the professed object of the Bill—which was to confine the Purveyors within the limits of their Commission, and the Commission within the limits of the law—was not slow to do what he could in the matter Within a week after the final rejection of the Bill by the Lords, "a Proclamation for the prevention of future abuses in Purveyance" was published: of which, as being the practical result of all these discussions, and as showing the state in which the question was allowed to rest for many years, it may be worth while to state the effect

The taking of timber-trees—which was one of the chief heads of complaint set forth by Bacon in his speech during the last session—it forbade altogether

It forbade the taking of carts, etc for the use of any but servants in necessary attendance, or from any place more than fourteen miles distant

It forbade the ordering of vehicles for carriage of coals and wood, without the concurrence of two Justices of Peace of the Counties next adjoining

It prescribed a several commission to be made out for each several shire, in which the kinds and quantities of provision to be taken were to be set down by the proper authorities, with blank schedules annexed, upon which every article taken was to be entered in the presence of the Constable or other local officer whose duty it was to see them delivered the same, when filled up, to be signed by the Constable and (if he chose) by the owner or seller, and a duplicate to be delivered to one of the next Justices of the Peace

It enjoined the Justices at Quarter Sessions to require from the Constables an account of what warrants they had received and what provisions had been taken and to certify the same every half year to the Board of Green Cloth

If it should appear upon a comparison of the accounts, or upon information otherwise received, that any Purveyor had infringed any of these regulations, it enjoined the principal officers of the Household to bring the person so offending before a Justice of Peace of the County where the offence had been committed who might then either bind him over to the Sessions to be proceeded against in the ordinary way, or recommend him to the Attorney General for prosecution in the Star Chamber

It said nothing however about the mode of settling the prices to be paid, and left the Board of Green Cloth in full possession of its authority; which was probably the reason why it was not accepted by the Commons as a satisfactory substitute for their rejected Bill For though it was read in the House on the 25th of April, and though, if their real object was only to enforce and not to alter the existing law, the securities taken seem to be sufficient they immediately proceeded to bring in another Bill, which, passing very rapidly through the usual stages, was sent up to the Lords on the 10th of May but could go no further the Lords declining to proceed with it, on the ground (then it seems for the first time distinctly laid down) that "when a Bill hath been brought into the House, proceeded withal, and rejected, another Bill of the same argument and matter may not be renewed and begun again in the same House and in the same Session where the former Bill was begun "¹

Here therefore for the present the matter ended.

10

The disputes and disappointments about this measure, upon which the Reformers spent their main force, though it troubled and retarded, did not materially interfere with the progress of the Subsidy Bill, the history of which is the rather worth telling, because Bacon referred to it at a later time as a proceeding in which "the manner was as worthy to be noted as the matter" "For (said he) the ancient majesty of the Kings of this realm was then preserved, in that those Subsidies were never demanded nor moved from the king, much less made the business or errand of the Parliament, but after the Parliament had sitten a good while, an honest gentleman (by name Sir Edward Montague) stood up, and in a plain familiar manner moved for two Subsidies and four fifteenths; concluding with these plain words, that so much he thought would content, and less would not be well accepted whereupon the two Subsidies passed upon question the same day and yet nevertheless upon conference with the Lords touching the occasions of the King, and by persuasion of some good servants of the King's which were gracious with the House, and chiefly out of their own good affections, came on afterwards to three "² And though in alleging this as evidence of "the affection of the subjects of England in their own nature to help their King," he did not perhaps take due account of the temporary fervour of loyalty produced by the Gunpowder Plot, it will

¹ 17 May, 1606 Lords' Journals, ii p 435
² Letter to the King in 1615 which will be printed in its place

be seen that this account of the spirit in which the question of Supply was carried in this Session is substantially true and just

The hint dropped by Salisbury at the Conference on the Recusants Bill on the 7th of February appears to have been received in silence   No notice was taken of it in the House, then or after   But on the 10th, when they had been engaged for three weeks in legislative business, Sir Thomas Ridgway, member for Devonshire, moved for a Committee of Supply   He was seconded by Sir Maurice Berkley   And then Sir Edward Montague proposed the amount—two Subsidies and four fifteenths   No trace is to be found in the Journals of any opposition   Only a motion "for a question presently" (meaning, I suppose, that the vote upon the proposed grant should be taken at once, without first referring it to a Committee) seems to have been made by way of amendment ; and the subsequent debate turned upon that   Such a grant involved of course many questions of form and manner, not suited for discussion in a general debate ; and the amendment being negatived or withdrawn, a Committee, of which Bacon was a member, was appointed to consider and report

They were to have met the next day in the afternoon   But on the morning of that day the King's message of thanks having been received, which included a request (see above, p 266) for a Conference between the two Houses on the Purveyance Bill, where some Lords would be deputed to deliver matters "nearly concerning his present estate,'—it was resolved to postpone their meeting till the Conference had taken place   Such at least I take to be the explanation of the note with which the Journal of 11th of February concludes—"Subsidy deferred to a time uncertain"

Upon this followed the discussions described in the last section which led to a full exposition of "the King's necessities," and ended in a resolution to give up the project of compounding for the extinction of Purveyance, and to consider rather of some increase to the grant of Subsidies already agreed on   This latter proposal met however with a good deal of opposition, and was warmly debated through the 13th and 14th of March ; without definite result ; but with much ripping up of *arcana imperii*, mixed with murmurs about grievance and proposals to give them precedence   of which, though grown naturally out of his own proposition, the King soon saw the inconvenience, and thereupon sent another message (18 March) requesting them not to betray to strangers abroad, by discourse upon the subject of his necessities, "those *arcana imperii* which he only wished to lay open to his loving subjects,' nor to impair the estimation of their gift by more   noise of doubts, debates, and contradiction but "to proceed to some such course as he might presently know their final determination."[1] The effect of which message (concluding as it did with a promise that all complaints of grievances should have a favourable hearing) was a resolution (carried the same day by a majority of 153 to 125) to add another Subsidy with its two fifteenths to the grant already resolved on, and an instruction to the Committee accordingly.

Whether Bacon took any part in the debate which ended in this resolution, it is impossible to say; for the Journals, though they mention several questions raised and "much disputed," give no particulars of what was said—not even the names of the speakers. It is most likely that he was himself one of those "good servants of the King which were gracious with the House," whose persuasion helped to carry the question. But however that may be, we need not doubt that he was an important person in the Committee, which had been appointed to meet on Thursday the 20th, and whose proceedings he was to report on Monday the 24th—as we learn from the following letter:—

To the Earl of Salisbury[2]

It may please your good Lordship,

I purpose, upon promise rather than business, to make a step to my house in the country this afternoon. Which because your Lordship may hear otherwise, and thereupon conceive any doubt of my return, to the prejudice of the King's business, I thought it concerned me to give your Lordship an account, that I purpose (if I live) to be here to-morrow evening; and so to report the Subsidy on Monday morning; which, though it be a day of triumph,[3] yet I hear of no adjournment, and therefore the house must sit. But if, in regard of the King's servants' attendance, your Lordship conceive doubt the house will not be well filled that day, I humbly pray your Lordship I may receive your direction for the forbearing to enter into the matter that day. I doubt not the success, if those attend that should. So I rest in all humbleness,

At your L. hon com⁰ˢ
                    Fr. Bacon

This Saturday the 22nd of March 1605.

The Report was not brought up (probably for the reason assigned; for though the House sate, no business was done besides receiving

[1] Message delivered to the House by the Speaker. S. P. Dom. vol. xix.
S. P. Dom. Original own hand.   [3] Anniversary of the King's accession.

a message of thanks from the King) till Tuesday the 25th   Mean
while an accident had happened, which helped to remind the mem
bers that worse things might befall the country than the continuance
of a grievance or the levy of an additional Subsidy   Early on
Saturday morning a rumour had gone abroad "that the King had
been slain in his bed at Oking "[1] and though a Proclamation was
immediately issued to contradict it, the alarm had lasted long enough
to make men consider what they would have had to expect if it had
been true   There can be little doubt that it told favourably upon
the disposition of the House, when, after an interchange of the com
pliments proper to such an occasion, the report was brought up by
Bacon, in a speech, of which we have the following note

Sir Francis Bacon reporteth from the Committee touching
Subsidy —

Excuseth memory —Distracted by one day of astonishment
two of gladness —Two contrary passions

Knights of all shires —Not distinct —Burgesses of all Port
Towns —Whether Cinque Ports —

The first Subsidy and two fifteens within the year being —
The first of May.

The first of November the first payment.—

500,000*l* a pressing and intractable debt —

The whole sum of the gift not above 400,000*l*

War, as preparation, so reparation.

Four Subsidies a Subsidy of State —When at the height
come fairly down —

First two roundly, therefore to be paid roundly   the rest more
slowly, because granted slowly —

Finis coronat opus —The evening commends the day precedent
The House to determine of the days of payment —

Assessing, Taxing, and Levying, [2] with Provisoes, to be also
committed

The debate which followed turned merely upon the periods at
which the several portions of the Subsidy should be made payable
nor was the difference large between the longest and the shorter
which were proposed —not above half a year altogether   The con
clusion was, that the first Subsidy with its two fifteenths should be
payable within the first year, the second within the second year, the

[1] C J 22 March, p 288   [2] 25 March, 1606   C J p 289

third ("more slowly because granted slowly") within the two years following, bringing the last payment to the 1st of May, 1610 which appears to have been according to the recommendation of the Committee

After this it only remained to draw the Bill, of which the Preamble was entrusted to Bacon, as we learn from another letter to Salisbury, written, I think, on the 27th of March

To the Earl of Salisbury.[1]

It may please your good Lordship,

I cannot as I would express how much I think myself bounden to your Lordship for your tenderness over my contentment But herein I will endeavour hereafter as I am able.

I send your Lordship a preamble for the Subsidy drawn, which was my morning's labour today This mould or frame if you like it not, I will be ready to cast it again *de novo*, if I may receive your hon. directions. For any particular corrections, it is in a good hand, and yet I will attend your Lordship (after tomorrow's business and tomorrow ended, which I know will be wearisome to you) to know your further pleasure. And so in all humbleness I rest

> At your Ls hon. Com^ts.
> more than ever bounden
> Fr. Bacon.

This letter, which bears no date either on face or back,[2] must have been written some time between the 25th of March (when the resolutions were passed upon which the Subsidy Bill was to be drawn) and the 10th of April, when the Bill itself was brought in And my reason for assigning it to the 27th of March is only that the trial of Father Garnett came on on the 28th, which would explain the allusion to "tomorrow's business"

Bacon's gratitude for Salisbury's "tenderness over his contentment" had reference, no doubt, to some promise of advancement which he had held out about this time—when (as we know other-

---

[1] S P Domestic, 1606 Original own hand.

[2] Mr Dixon, in his 'Personal History of Lord Bacon,' has printed it with the date, "Feb 10, 1606," at the top, as if forming part of the letter But this date must have been taken from a pencil note by the modern arranger of the State papers,—"probably 10th Feb 1605-6" which is obviously a conjecture, and surely a mistake Mr Gardiner (i p 289) has been misled by Mr Dixon, but will at once see how improbable it is that Bacon was occupied in drawing the Preamble on that particular morning

wise) there was some expectation of a shift of places among the Crown lawyers   But as I shall have to speak of this in connexion with some other letters in the next chapter, I will not interrupt the history of Bacon's parliamentary services with a discussion of it here

Of the Subsidy Bill all I need say further is, that having been presented on the 10th of April, read on the 12th, committed on the 16th, reported and ordered to be engrossed on the 18th, it was allowed to rest at that stage for three weeks: the fact being, I suppose, that the petition concerning Grievances, with which the House was busy in the interval, was meant to take precedence, as having a better chance of respectful consideration if it went up before the grant of supply was complete and irrevocable   For when the Subsidy Bill was at length brought up for its third reading on the 9th of May (the collection of grievances being then made out, the preamble actually engrossed, and the rest ready for engrossing), an attempt was made to stop it on that very ground, and so far successfully, that a special order " that the Subsidy should not *pass up* [meaning that the bill should not be sent to the Upper House] until the Grievances were ready and presented to the King," was entered on the journals —a measure which appears to have been accepted as a compromise to avoid a division upon the Bill itself   For the Journals tell us that on that day there was ' much dispute, whether a question should not be made for the third reading of the Subsidy   but that thought to be without precedent, and a very tender question, therefore forborne and in respect of the former order, the House satisfied and the Subsidy thirdly read "[1]   We find accordingly that the petition of Grievances having been presented to the King on the 13th, and the King's answer received on the 14th, the Subsidy Bill was sent up to the Lords the next morning,—and not before though the circumstances of the delivery appear to imply, and were probably meant to demonstrate, the reverse of dissatisfaction   " The Bill of Subsidy of the Temporalty," says the Journal of 15th May, 1606, " sent up by Mr Secretary Herbert, with the whole House attending him, not one man left but Speaker, Clerk, Serjeant —Never seen before "[2]

11

It might have been supposed from this that the House had obtained some very satisfactory concession in the matter of grievances But I do not find that anything passed beyond gracious words and assurances that their complaints should be favourably considered and attended to, which though as much as could have been reasonably

[1] C J p 307   [2] Ib p 309

expected, carried but a negative kind of satisfaction, that could never have turned a stream of popular discontent And therefore it is quite true that the predominant sentiment of the House was thus far one of affectionate loyalty

This collection of grievances became, however, afterwards so potent an engine in the hands of the popular party,—it was the motive or the instrument of such great alterations in its own time, and has left so dark a shadow in the popular judgment of later times upon the reputation not only of the King himself, but of every man who desired that such a King should reign in honour,—and it is a subject which will so often return upon us —that it may be worth while to explain at some length the spirit in which the King really regarded it, and the attitude which he took up when first appealed to And of this we have, in his own public declaration made to the Commons through the Speaker on the 18th of March, authentic evidence, for the message appears to have been delivered in writing, and a copy has been preserved The immediate occasion and object of this message I have already described (p 271), with the result But the concluding paragraph belongs more properly to this section, and as King James's characteristic vice of too much speaking and writing in his lifetime has left him since his death too much at the mercy of impatient abridgers, I will venture to ask my reader to study his meaning this once from his own words unabridged

"Secondly, his M hath given me in charge to open himself thus much further That where he hath understood, not only out of the house but by the common bruit of the vulgar abroad (whose minds are always apt to make the worst application of the best courses that can be held in things of that nature) that you are already entered into a course of reviewing and particular examining of all men's pretended grievances,—Although that be somewhat beyond his M expectation, yet because there may be something wherein the laws already standing may be defective (in which as there shall be cause found his M will readily add his authority for relief therein by Parliament), and because there may be some other things also wherein there need no other authority to be used than that which is invested in himself, and wherein his M may take some course of redress by advice of his Privy Council, according to the precedents of all those former princes (to whom, as he is no way inferior in power, so will he never be found less, but rather more in affection) — h is contented, when you have advisedly digested the same into such natures as shall be fit for you to prefer, and not unreasonable for him to grant, that you shall be favourably admitted into his presence with such convenient number as you shall choose, to present your petitions to the gracious eyes of his M royal person and understanding Not doubting but you will use so much discretion and expedition, as you will neither be any occasion to draw concourse of multitudes together for information nor yet so dwell upon the receiving of complaints so long, as if your house only were the place for the address of all sorts of grievances, or you disposed to entertain the unjust clamour or examination of those things by which (as one of the best branches of their revenues) all the Kings of this land (by the warrant of all laws) have used to support themselves, when they had not so large a posterity to care for. For that were to strike so deep at the root of his ordinary and lawful Prerogative, as such motions would ill sort with the voice of his necessities (which are commonly the laws of times), seeing they have already spoken so plainly and feelingly in that amongst you. All which may be just reasons to move you that every grant or constitution (by which his M. or his predecessors hath or may increase his ordinary revenues) may not be thought fit to make up the miss of just grievances, only because some few merchants may be abridged of some part of that gain which they would look for. in which kind his M. looketh to be preferred whensoever he and they shall be weighed in the balance of your discretions.

Besides, who knoweth not (as his M. saith) that there is no counsel nor assembly in any commonwealth (how well soever governed) to which complaints shall not flow with a strong current, if it be conceived once that men are apt to find faults. nay (which is more), those persons shall ever be in danger to have their ears filled with many untruths which shall but show the least facility in believing allegations without proof, or without hearing those that can show the fallacies and multiplication of vulgar reports and combinations, especially when gain is in question, which is never so justly raised but it must be displeasing to some in their own particular.

And of this true judgment and desire which his M. hath to remove all misadvertisements which may hinder your just satisfaction, his M. expect that you will be careful to contain yourselves within the limits of such informations as may concern matters of monopoly, hindrance of justice, general oppressions, and such corrupt devices as tend to general vexation or damage of his people. to all which (being laid before him) he will either by his own authority (with advice of his Council) give you just remedies, or else he will give them over without stay or interruption to be reformed by the ordinary course of his laws, and (which is more) will earnestly recommend the same to his ministers of justice to despatch the same with all possible expedition. "

Now if this was a true representation of the King's mind and intentions at the commencement of the controversy (which I see no reason to doubt), it is easy to understand that a proceeding on the other side so cautious and jealous as to imply distrust, even though it were no more than prudence and a just scepticism required, would be felt by a man of sensitive affections to be unkind and ungrateful. That such distrust was in fact implied in the proceedings of the Lower House during this session in the matter of the miscellaneou grievances, will not, I think, be disputed, and though it may have been right and unavoidable, we must not be surprised to find it hereafter bearing its natural fruit in misunderstandings and jealousies on both sides

For Bacon's part in these proceedings, it is not till a late stage that I find his name mentioned in connexion with them   but in order to understand the part he then took, the earlier stages must be shortly described

It appears to have been intended from the first that the Grievances and the Subsidies should proceed together   The first motion (which was made the day after the first motion for supply) was "for the great Committee for Subsidy to consider of such Grievances as should be offered by any member of the House"[1]   On the following day (certain special grievances having been set apart to be dealt with separately) a Committee was appointed (names not recorded) 'touching all other Grievances of the Commonwealth"   On the 15th of March—the day after the first debate on the *additional* Subsidy (and nothing further having been done in the meantime about the others),—the 'Collection of Grievances" was delivered in and read, and at the next sitting recommitted[2]   On the 27th,—only two days after the additional subsidy had been *voted*—motion was made 'that the Grievances, *so many as were ready*" (from which we see that the business was hurried on beyond its natural pace), "might be put into form, and thereupon a conference to be desired with the Lords, and to proceed with petition to his Majesty"[3]   On the same day on which the Subsidy Bill was brought in from the Committee and ordered to be engrossed (18th April), a Committee, including among its members the King's Learned Counsel, was appointed "to frame the Grievances" (which during the preceding fortnight had been severally read and discussed in the House,[4]

---

[1] 11 Feb 1605-6   C J p 267

[2] Through the management (it seems) of the Speaker   "May it please your Honour to know that the grievances pretended were that day so carried that the propounders themselves were driven to desire a recommitment , for that upon my opening of the several parts of them, they held them clean out of proportion in a fashion"—Sir R Phelipps to Salisbury, 17 March, 1605   Domestic James I vol xix

[3] C J p 290

[4] In the course of which, in the absence of counsel to speak against "the first grievance, touching the Imposition of Currants ' (meaning, I suppose, against the motion to vote it a grievance), "Sir Fr Bacon," says the Journal of April 11, "speaketh against it in the House

"Merchants the guides of Princes for raising customs —

"When they devise it, quiet , when it is reverted, they startle and stir —Unjust and cautelous"

This was the case upon which the whole question of the right of the Crown to levy impositions was afterwards argued in the Exchequer

counsel heard, and a vote taken upon each) "into a Petition"[1] On the 6th of May the preamble of this petition, having been read publicly, was ordered to be engrossed on parchment and made ready for the King On the 10th—after the Subsidy Bill had passed, but before it was sent up to the Lords—the collection of Grievances was read in the House On the 13th, "Sir Francis Bacon" was appointed "to read them to the King." And on the 15th, immediately after Secretary Herbert, accompanied by the whole House of Commons, had carried the Subsidy Bill up,[2]

Sir Francis Bacon maketh report of the King's speech yesterday —

Every man's spirit sinks towards the end of a Parliament —

His own speech first —

Answ by the King.

Grievances he had not yet heard —He would never deny —

Two parts —

One, a prudent challenge to some circumstance of proceeding —

A gracious answer —

Challenge four points —

Remember unto us —Matter of joy and gratulation, as well as grievance—

From a woman to a man —

From a prince in declination to a prince in full years

From a barren —

From a solitary .—

From Religion erected .—

From a State in faction —

From war in Ireland —

From delays in Justice.—

Asked whether these began not in the Queen's time, yet a just, a glorious Queen

An O-yes made for grievances —He arraigned these two months —

Remembered his proceeding in thanks for the Subsidy —Of leaving Purveyance for Composition[3]

Promise —That these grievances should be read and read again, and put every article to his proper forge

Matters of Law to Judges· other matters to men of that profession —

Admonishment —That we should carry an even mind —

If a little grievance to the subject and a little profit to the Crown —A little profit to the Crown —

Protestation —That he would hear the meanest subject in his grievance

Here for the present the matter rested

12

It will be seen from a letter which will be printed in the next chapter that there was another important measure passed by this Parliament with which Bacon had something to do—the Bill of Attainder of the offenders in the late Treason. But what he did was probably in the Committee, of which as one of the King's Learned Counsel he was of course a member; and no record remains of it. The only occasion in which his name appears in the Journals as taking a part at all conspicuous in that business was on the 10th of April. when upon the second reading of the Bill (which had been sent down from the Upper House, where it originated, a week before), a question was raised whether the King's Counsel that were of the House should be admitted to give evidence for the Crown. The objection taken (which is not without interest as bearing upon the history of the House of Commons) was that members of the House being Judges could not be counsellors, to which Bacon answered, in effect, that since all the King's Counsel except the Attorney General were members of one or other House, and the Attorney was bound to attend the Lords whenever they wanted him,—if it should happen that he could not come, the King could have no Counsel at all in the Lower House; also that the combination of the two functions was not without precedent in other cases

The note of his speech runs thus

"*Sr Fr. Bacon* All the King's Counsel be of the Upper or Lower House —·

If none here, if Mr Attorney be commanded by the Lords, we[1] cannot have it —

The oath of the King's Counsel, to serve the King and his people —

The Attorney in the Court of Wards and Duchy sign informations, which concern the King, and sit as Judges —

In the Star-chamber, reference to the King's Counsel as well as the Judges "[1]

The inconvenience however, whatever it might be worth, did not apply to the present case, for the Attorney was at liberty, and fully competent to do all that was necessary   And it was resolved that "Evidence touching the Bill of Attainder" should be given 'by Mr Attorney at the Bar, and not by Mr Solicitor and Sir Fr Bacon being members of the House "[2]   So Sir Edward Coke was heard on behalf of the Crown, and their own counsel on behalf of the parties, the Bill (with some amendments introduced by the Committee, to which the Lords had signified their assent) went through its stages, and whatever Bacon may have had to do with it in or out of the House—and we know that a proviso tendered by the Counsel of one of the parties was "much disputed "[3]—we hear no more of him in relation to it till it was passed   and then we only hear that he was deputed to carry it up to the Lords [4]

13.

There is a paper preserved among the Tanner MSS in the Bodleian Library, which is supposed by Mr Dixon (to whom we are indebted for the discovery of it) to be the notes of a speech made by Bacon during this session, against a bill for the regulation of fees payable for copies out of Courts of Record   Such a bill was brought in, it is true, on the 25th of January 1605-6, and after counsel had been heard (14 Feb) for the parties interested, was referred to a committee, by which it was reported (7 March) "as fit to sleep' Bacon's name however is not mentioned in the Journals either as one of the Counsel heard at the Bar, or as a member of the Committee, or as a speaker in the only debate upon it that is recorded   And on referring to the original manuscript, I find a note in the margin, which cannot be well reconciled with Mr Dixon's supposition   This note, if I have read it correctly, means that the original was a *certified copy* made on the 19th of January 1605-6   The words are "1605, Ext per Philipp et Rob 19 Janu "   Now if the date refer to the time when the copy was examined, the paper cannot refer to anything delivered in Parliament   and I rather think that it must have been a professional *opinion*,—of which certified copies might be wanted—given upon the Bill to the parties interested be

fore it was exhibited   If so,—and the fact that Bacon had given such
an opinion would account for his *not* being put on the Committee,—
the proper place for it would have been at the beginning of the
session instead of the end   The difference however is not material,
and the present arrangement, though accidental, will perhaps be found
more convenient   The paper has every appearance of being genuine

Sir Fran. Bacon's Arguments against the Bill of Shifts [1]

1 First, it hath sprung out of the ashes of a decayed monopoly by the spleen of one man, that because he could not continue his new exaction, therefore would now pull down ancient
fees.

2. Secondly, it knows the way out of the house, for in the
xxv Eliz the like bill was preferred,[2] and much called upon at
the first, and rejected at the engrossment, not having twenty
voices for it

3 Thirdly, it is without all precedent, for look into former
laws, and you shall find that when a statute erects a new office
or act to be done, it limits fees, as in case of enrolment, in case
of administration, &c, but it never limits ancient fees to take
away men's freeholds

4 Fourthly, it looks extremely back, which is against all justice of Parliament, for a number of subjects are already placed
in offices, some attaining them in the course of long service,
some in consideration of great sums of money, some in reward
of service from the Crown, when they might have had other
suits, and such officers again allied with a number of other subjects who valued them according to their offices.   Now if half
these men's livelihoods and fortunes should be taken from them,
it were an infinite injustice

5. Fifthly, it were more justice to raise the fees than to abate
them   For we see gentlemen have raised their rents and the
fines of their tenants, and merchants tradesmen and farmers
their commodities and wares, and this mightily within c years.
But the fees of officers continue at one rate.

6 Sixthly, if it be said the number of fees is much increased
because causes are increased, that is a benefit which time gives

[1] Lanner MSS 169, 42
[2] This I suppose was the "Bill for the better expedition of Justice in the Star
Chamber —concerning which see Vol I p 226

and time takes away It is no more than if there were an ancient toll at some bridge between Barwick and London, and now it should be brought down because that, Scotland being united, there were more passengers.

7. Seventhly, causes may again decrease, as they do already begin ; and therefore, as men must endure the prejudice of time, so they ought again to enjoy the benefit of time

8 Eighthly, men are not to consider the proportion between the fee and the pains taken, as if it were in a scrivener's shop because in the copies (being the principal gain of the officer) was considered *ab antiquo* his charge, his attendance, his former labours to make him fit for the place, his countenance and quality in the commonwealth, and the like

9 Ninthly, the officers do many things *sans fee*, as in causes *in formâ pauperis*, and for the King &c , which is considered in the fees of copies.

10 Tenthly, there is great labour of mind in many cases, as in the entering of orders, and in all examinations All which is only considered in the copies.

11 Eleventhly, these offices are either the gift of the King, or in the gift of great officers, who have their office from the King, so as the King is disinherited of his ancient right and means to prefer servants, and the great offices of the kingdom likewise disgraced and impaired

12 Twelfthly, there is a great confusion and inequality in the bill, for the copies in the inferior courts, as for example in the Court of the Marches, the Court of the North (being inferior courts) are left in as good case as they were, and high courts of the kingdom only abridged, whereas there was ever a diversity half in half in all fees, as Chancellor's, clerks', and all others [1]

13 Thirteenthly, if fees be abridged as too great, they ought to be abridged as well in other points as in copies, and as well in other offices as in offices towards the law For now prothonotaries shall have their old fees for engrossing upon the roll, and the like, and only the copies shall be abridged , whereas, if it be well examined, the copies are of all fees the most reasonable, and so of other offices, as customs, searchers, mayors, bailiffs, &c which have many ancient fees incident to their offices, which all may be called in question upon the like or better reason

[1] So in MS

11 Fourteenthly, the suggestion of the Bill is utterly false, which in all law is odious. For it suggesteth that these fees have of late years been exacted, which is utterly untrue, having been time out of mind, and being men's freehold, whereof they may have an assize, so as the Parliament may as well take any man's lands, common mynes, &c. as these fees.

15 Fifteenthly, it casts a slander upon all superior Judges, as if they had tolerated extortions, whereas there have been severe and strict courses taken, and that of late, for the distinguishing of lawful fees from new exactions, and fees reduced into tables, and they published and hanged up in courts, that the subjects be not poled nor aggrieved.

16 Sixteenthly, the law (if it were just) ought to enter into an examination and distinction what were rightful and ancient fees and what were upstart fees and encroacht, whereas now it sweeps them all away without difference

17 Seventeenthly, it requires an impossibility, setting men to spell again how many syllables be in a line, and puts the penalty of xx s. for every line faulty, which is xxm l. a sheet And the superior officers must answer it for clerks' fault or oversight

18. Eighteenthly, it doth disgrace superior Judges in Court, to whom it properly belongeth to correct those misdemeanours according to their oaths and according to discretion, because it is impossible to reduce it to a definite rule.

19. Lastly, this being a penal law, it seems there is but some commodity sought for, that some that could not continue their first monopoly mought make themselves whole out of some penalties.

And this I think is all that can be made intelligible concerning the part played by Bacon during this session which closed on the 27th of May without any sign of discontent on either side (and to the personal satisfaction of Sir Edward Coke[1]), and was prorogued to the 18th of November

[1] See his letter to Sir Thomas Lake, 22 May, 1606 (Dom James I. vol. xxi.) "Sir—I have made ready this general pardon (moulded in the former mould) for his M signature I perceive it not good that so many good men tarry so long together and therefore I wish an end of this Parliament.'

CHAPTER VIII

A D 1606-7, MARCH—JULY. ÆTAT 46

1.

We have seen that in March 1605-6 Salisbury had been showing some interest in Bacon's fortunes. And though we do not know precisely either what he had promised or how much his promises meant, there is reason to believe that he had favoured a proposed arrangement by which Bacon might have been advanced at last to the Solicitorship. Sir Henry Neville, writing to Winwood on the 11th of March in that year, says " We are in some expectation of a creation of four Barons viz the Lord Chief Justice, Mr Attorney *who is designed Chief Justice in Gaudie's room,* Sir John Fortescue and Sir Thomas Knevett,"[2] &c. The words which I have printed in italic are conclusive of the fact that a rumour to that effect was in circulation at that time, and as the same rumour is distinctly alluded to in the following letter, we need not hesitate to date it within a few days before or after the 11th of March, nor is there much room for doubt that Salisbury's demonstration of ' tenderness over Bacon's contentment" was subsequent to and consequent upon this letter. For if anything of the kind had passed between them before, it would have been impossible to avoid some reference to it on such an occasion.

This letter was first printed in the 'Remains' (1618) with this heading, " A Letter to the Earl of Salisbury touching the Solicitor's place, at what time he stood but in doubtful terms of favour with his Lordship " Although not to be found in the Resuscitatio, it appears to have been contained in Bacon's own collection, and is here taken from the copy in the British Museum, which differs from the other in one or two places, and is evidently more correct

To the Earl of Salisbury.[2]

It may please your Lordship,

I am not privy to myself of any such ill deserving towards

[1] Winwood's Memoi ii 198   [2] Add MSS 5503, fo 102

your Lordship, as that I should think it an impudent thing to
be suitor for your favour in a reasonable matter, your Lordship being to me as (with your good favour) you cannot cease
to be,—but rather it were a simple and arrogant part in me to
forbear it   It is thought Mr Attorney shall be Chief Justice
of the Common Pleas.   In case Mr Solicitor rise, I would be
glad now at last to be Solicitor, chiefly because I think it will
increase my practice, wherein God blessing me a few years, I
may amend my state, and so after fall to my studies and ease,
whereof one is requisite for my body, and the other sorteth with
my mind   Herein if I may find your Lordship's favour, I shall
be more happy than I have been, which may make me also
more wise   I have small store of means about the King, and
to sue myself is not so fit   And therefore I shall leave it to
God, his Majesty, and your Lordship   For if I must still be
next the door, I thank God in these transitory things I am well
resolved.   So beseeching your Lordship not to think this letter
the less humble, because it is plain, I remain

at your Lps. service very humbly,

FR. BACON.

The week before and the fortnight after the 11th of March was
a period of some anxiety for the Government,—the Lower House
having been engaged all the time in warm debates, first on the Purveyance Bill and afterwards on the question of a third Subsidy,—the
report of the Committee on the other two Subsidies not having yet
been brought in,—and the collection of general Grievances being
diligently proceeded with meanwhile   It was a time in which
Bacon's help in the House, where the representatives of the Government were not otherwise strong, could not be conveniently dis-
pensed with   And though I do not find that any of his former
disappointments and discouragements had on any occasion either
altered his course or slackened his industry, it was not a time
when Salisbury would have thought it prudent to neglect him, or
hesitated to hazard words of promise   Nor have I any reason to
doubt in this case the sincerity of his professions   The position in
which a man like Bacon was still left, at the age of forty-six, while
his cousin (though always friendly "*secundum exterius*") had been
in a position of such high influence for seven or eight years, makes it
hard to believe that he had been really anxious to advance him in the
service of the Crown.   But the fact that on this occasion nothing

followed the promises of favour, which (it seems) were his answer
to the foregoing letter,[1] may be sufficiently accounted for by the fact
that the arrangement talked of was not carried into effect and we
do not know where or with whom the obstruction lay   All we
know is that Gawdy, Coke, and Doderidge all kept their places, and
Bacon still remained ' next the door "

2

In his private affairs, however, Salisbury had not been wanting
(as we have already seen[2]) in giving Bacon substantial help, and
we know on Bacon's own authority that he had done something for
him,—though we are not told exactly what it was,—in furtherance
of an important domestic enterprise which was successfully accom
plished in the middle of this very session

Marriages in those days were treated more openly as matters of
business than they are now.   Fathers proposed to fathers, and
when the father was dead, great men were called in to countenance
and recommend the suitor   It is true that in the Order of the
Helmet instituted by the Prince of Purpoole in 1594, this practice
was strictly forbidden   "*Item* No Knight of this Order shall pro
cure any letters from his Highness to any widow or maid, for his
enablement or commendation to be advanced in marriage but a
prerogative wooing set apart, shall for ever cease as to any of
these Knights, and shall be left to the common laws of this land
declared by the Statute, *Quia electiones liberæ esse debent* "[3] But in
a satire on the fashions of the time, the prohibition of a practice is
proof of its prevalence   What obstructions Bacon met with on his
way to matrimony, we do not know   But they would probably be
such as a man who had the key of so many good places as Salis
bury had, might well help to smooth

The Lady was no doubt the same to whom he had alluded in 1603
—"an alderman's daughter," "an handsome maiden," and "to his
liking "   Alderman Barnham, her father, had been dead for 15 year
or more [4]   Her mother, by a second marriage, had been Lady Pack
ington since November 1598—a "little violent lady," according to
Chamberlain [5]   She herself was coheir to her father with three
sisters, and her name was Alice   which is nearly all we know
about her, unless a remark referring to a much later time, and re

[1] See the first paragraph of Bacon's letter about the preamble of the Sub-aid
Bill, p 277
[2] See p 79   [3] See Vol I p 329
[4] Note II II II to Montagu's Life of Bacon
[5] Chamberlain to Carleton, 20 Nov 1598   13 Feb. 1606-7.

corded more than twenty years after, be thought to imply that which
if true in 1620 must have been true also in 1606, namely that she
inherited some portion of her mother's weakness in the government
of the unruly member "One asked" (writes Dr Rawley in his
commonplace book) "how my La Darby came to make so good use
of her time whilst her husband[1] was Chancellor, and my La St.
Alban's made so little The other answered, because my La Darby's
wit lay backward, and my La St Alban's lay forward viz in her
tongue."[2]

The date of Bacon's marriage was not known, nor was there anything to be found in any printed book (so far as I am aware) by
which it could be fixed within less than a year, until the appearance
of Mrs Everett Green's Calendar of State Papers[3] from which it
appeared that there was a letter there from Dudley Carleton to
John Chamberlain, mentioning the marriage as fresh news on the
11th of May 1606 It had in fact taken place the day before, and in
a very busy time the Lower House having just passed the Subsidy
Bill, and being that very day engaged in passing the second Purveyance Act and in arranging a fresh conference with the Lords about the
Recusants As we know no particulars from any other source (for
I do not gather from Mr Dixon's story that he had any independent information) Carleton shall give the news in his own words

"Sir Francis Bacon was married yesterday to his young wench in
Marebone Chapel He was clad from top to toe in purple, and hath made
himself and his wife such store of fine raiments of cloth of silver and gold
that it draws deep into her portion The dinner was kept at his father-
in law Sir John Packington's lodging over against the Savoy, where his
chief guests were the three knights, Cope, Hicks,[4] and Beeston, and upon
this conceit (as he said himself) that since he could not have my L
of Salisbury in person, which he wished, he would have him at least in his
representative body."[5]

When the domestic relations of a man so conspicuous as Bacon
attract no notice, it may be inferred that they are peaceable and

[1] Lord Ellesmere.   [2] Lambeth MSS 1031
[3] Domestic Series James I (published under the direction of the Master of
the Rolls), p 307
[4] Sir Michael, no doubt, whom we know one of Salisbury's secretaries not
Sir Baptist, as Mr Dixon calls him. Sir Walter Cope and Sir Hugh Beeston had
also been long in the confidential employment of Salisbury (See Chamberlain's
letters (Camd Soc), p 151) All three were Members of Parliament It is
scarcely worth while to inquire on what ground Mr Dixon describes them is
' hard drinkers and men about town " It is probably a mere development of the
fact that he knew them to have been once the chief guests at a wedding dinner,
and knew no more
[5] Carleton to Chamberlain, 11 April, 1606 Domestic Papers, James I, 1606

quiet, and twenty years of married life in which the gossips and scandal-mongers of the time found nothing to talk about have a right to remain exempt from intrusion In outward circumstances it appears to have been a very suitable match the wife's fortune being a little less than the annual value of the husband's inherited estate, and her social rank a little lower, but not much Taking his position and prospects into account, it was certainly a good match for her, nor was it a bad one for him And I do not know why it should not be allowed to pass with as little remark now as it did then, or as any similar match would do in the present day.

3.

No change was made among the Law Officers during the session of Parliament But shortly after the prorogation, Sir Francis Gawdy died, and on the 29th of June Coke succeeded him as Chief Justice of the Common Pleas,—thenceforward to be no longer the champion of Prerogative in its encounters with Parliaments and Judges, but the champion of the Bench in its encounters with Prerogative and Privilege

A new Attorney General had now to be chosen The right of the Solicitor-General to the refusal of the office was not yet established by custom Since 1161, of 23 Solicitors only 9 had become Attorneys[1] And though it is true that three cases in succession had occurred in the last years of Elizabeth, and Fleming might possibly have made a fourth, had he not been removed by promotion before a vacancy occurred, yet the long delays and disputes in the appointment of Coke himself (who was the last of the three) are a sufficient proof that the custom was not then settled It did not follow therefore that 'Mr Solicitor would rise," and if he did not (since he still, I believe, held his office *quamdiu se bene gesserit*), he could not be compelled to vacate it And here it must be owned that the sincerity of Salisbury's professed desire to raise Bacon falls under just suspicion At any rate there was another man in whose behalf the same desire worked more effectually When the Attorney of the Court of Wards (of which Salisbury was Master) died, the King had left to him the choice of a successor,[2] and he chose Sir Henry Hobart Now that an Attorney General had to be chosen—whether it were that Doderidge had been found on trial to be inefficient, or that Hobart was more particularly suited to his own tastes and purposes—so it was that Doderidge remained Solicitor, and within

[1] Haydn's 'Book of Dignities'   [2] Chamberlain to Carleton, 24 Oct 1605

a week after Coke's promotion, Hobart became Attorney—Bacon being still left outside

It is true that another arrangement was in contemplation, by which this would have been avoided   It appears to have been the wish and the intention, certainly of the Lord Chancellor, probably of the king and possibly of Salisbury himself, to make way for Bacon's advancement by promoting Doderidge to the office of King's Serjeant,—an office of higher dignity,—and so vacating the Solicitorship Why this was not done, we do not know.   It may be (as Mr Gardiner has suggested) that it was thought necessary to wait for a vacancy among the King's serjeants, though it appears from the account of the office in Cowell's 'Interpreter,' a contemporary work, that the number of them was not limited [1]   But at any rate it was not done and Bacon thought it time at last to come to some distinct understanding as to his own prospects   He had had fair words enough, and upon them he had rested patiently until fair opportunities turned up of giving them effect   But a fairer opportunity than the present was not likely to come again, and it was fit he should know, with a view to the ordering of his own life and labours, whether he might reasonably expect to advance any further in his present career

It was certainly with reference to this occasion that the three letters which come next were written, though I cannot determine the exact date of them.   Hobart became Attorney General on the 4th of July, after which Bacon expected to hear news of the arrangement that had been intended for himself   Having waited long enough—how long I cannot say—and heard nothing, he wrote to ask about it.

These letters were first printed in the 'Remains,' and afterwards in the Resuscitatio   But as in other similar cases I take my text from the manuscript in the British Museum,—noting only such variations as appear to proceed from alterations introduced into the fair copy by Bacon himself   For I suppose the copies in the 'Remains' to have been taken from the letters sent,—though taken carelessly and full of blunders—and those in the Resuscitatio and in the manuscript from the drafts.

To the King, touching the Solicitor's place.[2]

How honestly ready I have been, most gracious Sovereign, to

---

[1] "And of these [Serjeants of the Coif] one is the King's serjeant,—being commonly chosen by the King out of the rest, in respect of his great learning, to plead for him in all his causes as, namely, in causes of treason.—And of these there may be more if it please the King '
Add MSS 5503, fo 38

do your Majesty humble service, to the best of my power, and and in a manner beyond my power, (as I now stand) I am not so unfortunate but your Majesty knoweth For both in the commission of Union, (the labour whereof, for men of my profession, rested most upon my hand,) and this last Parliament, in the bill of the Subsidy (both body and preamble), in the bill of Attainders both Tresham and the rest, in the matter of Purveyance, in the Ecclesiastical Petitions, in the Grievances, and the like, as I was ever careful (and not without good success sometimes to put forward that which was good, sometimes to keep back that which was not so good, so your Majesty was pleased to accept kindly of my services, and to say to me, such conflicts were the wars of peace, and such victories the victories of peace, and therefore such servants that obtained them were by kings, that reign in peace, no less to be esteemed than services of commanders in the wars In all which nevertheless I can challenge to myself no sufficiency, but that I was diligent and reasonable happy to execute those directions, which I received either immediately from your royal mouth, or from my Lord of Salisbury At which time it pleased your Majesty also to promise and assure me, that upon the remove of the then Attorney I should not be forgotten, but brought into ordinary place And this was after confirmed to me by many of my Lords, and towards the end of the last term,[1] the manner also in particular was spoken of, that is, that Mr Solicitor should be made your Majesty's Serjeant, and I Solicitor, for so it was thought best to sort with both our gifts and faculties for the good of your service And of this resolution both court and country took knowledge Neither was this any invention or project of my own, but moved from my Lords, and I think first from my Lord Chancellor Whereupon resting, your Majesty well knoweth I never opened my mouth for the greater place, although I am sure I had two circumstances, that Mr Attorney, that now is, could not alledge the one, nine years service of the crown, the other the being cousin german to the Lord of Salisbury, whom your Majesty esteemeth and trusteth so much [2] But for the less place, I conceived it was meant me But after that Mr Attorney Hubbard

---

[1] Trinity Term ended on the 10th of July The letter was probably written during the Long Vacation

[2] Instead of the last clause, the copy in the 'Remains' has, "for of my father service I will not speak

was placed, I heard no more of my preferment, but it seemed to be at a stop, to my great disgrace and discouragement   For (gracious Sovereign) if still, when the waters are stirred, another shall be put before me, your Majesty had need work a miracle, or else I shall be still a lame man to do your service.   And therefore my most humble suit to your Majesty is, that this, which seemed was to me intended, may speedily be performed and I hope my former services shall be but as beginnings to better, when I am better strengthened   For, sure I am, no man's heart is fuller (I say not but many may have greater hearts, but I say, not fuller) of love and duty towards your Majesty and your children, as I hope time will manifest against envy and detraction, if any be   To conclude, I most humbly crave pardon for my boldness, and rest

A LETTER OF LIKE ARGUMENT TO THE LORD CHANCELLOR [1]

It may please your good Lordship,

As I conceived it to be a resolution, both with his Majesty and amongst your Lordships of his Council, that I should be placed Solicitor, and the Solicitor to be removed to be the King's Serjeant, so I most thankfully acknowledge your Lordship's furtherance and forwardness therein, your Lordship being the man that first devised the mean   Wherefore my humble request to your Lordship is, that you would set in with some strength to finish this your work, which I assure your Lordship I desire the rather, because being placed I hope, for many favours, at last to be able to do you some better service.   For as I am, your Lordship cannot use me, nor scarcely indeed know me. Not that I vainly think I shall be able to do any great matters, but certainly it will frame me to use a nearer [2] observance and application to such as I honour so much as I do your Lordship, and not (I hope) without some good offices, which may now and then deserve your thanks   And herewithal, my good Lord, I humbly pray your Lordship to consider that time groweth precious with me, and that a married man is seven years elder in his thoughts the first day.   And therefore what a discomfortable thing is it for me to be unsettled still?   Certainly, were it not that I think myself born to do my Sovereign service (and there-

---

[1] Add MSS 5503, fo 37   [2] more industrious Rem

fore in that station I will live and die), otherwise, for my own private comfort, it were better for me that the King did blot me out of his book, or that I should turn my course to endeavour to serve him in some other kind, than for me to stand thus at a stop, and to have that little reputation which by my industry I gather to be scattered and taken away by continual disgraces, every new man coming above me.   Sure I am, I shall never have fairer promises and words from all your Lordships, for I know not what services[1] (saving that your Lordships[2] told me they were good) and I would believe you in a much greater matter.   Were it nothing else, I hope the modesty of my suit deserveth somewhat, for I know the Solicitor's place is not as your Lordship left it, time working alteration, somewhat in the profession, much more in that special place   And were it not to satisfy my wife's friends, and to get myself out of being a common gaze and a speech, I protest before God I would never speak word for it[3]   But to conclude, as my honourable Lady your wife was some mean to make me to change the name of another, so if it please you to help me[4] to change my own name, I can be but more and more bounden to you   and I am much deceived, if your Lordship find not the King well inclined, and my Lord of Salisbury forward and affectionate.

A LETTER TO MY LORD OF SALISBURY, TOUCHING THE SOLICITOR'S PLACE.[5]

It may please your good Lordship,

I am not ignorant how mean a thing I stand for, in desiring to come into the Solicitor's place   For I know well, it is not the thing it hath been, time having wrought alteration both in the profession, and in that special place   Yet because I think it will increase my practice, and that it may satisfy my friends, and because I have been noised to it, I would be glad it were done   Wherein I may say to your Lordship, in the confidence of your poor kinsman, and of a man by you advanced, *Tu idem fer opem, qui spem dedisti*   for I am sure it was not possible for

---

[1] So MS
[2] *your Lordships all* Rem   The 'Resuscitatio' has, "For I know not what my services are saving, etc
[3] This sentence, which is not in the MS or the 'Resuscitatio,' is inserted from the 'Remains'
[4] *as you said* Rem   Add MSS 5503, fo 36

any living man to have received from another more significant and comfortable words of hope, your Lordship being pleased to tell me, during the course of my last service, that you would raise me, and that when you had resolved to raise a man, you were more careful of him than himself; and that what you had done for me in my marriage, was a benefit to me, but of no use to your Lordship, and therefore I might assure myself, you would not leave me there, with many like speeches, which I know my duty too well to take hold of otherwise than by a thankful remembrance[1] And I know, and[2] all the world knoweth, that your Lordship is no dealer of holy water, but noble and real; and on my part I am of a sure ground that I have committed nothing that may deserve alteration[3] And therefore my hope is, your Lordship will finish a good work, and consider that time groweth precious with me, and that I am now *vergentibus annis*. And although I know your fortune is not to need an hundred such as I am, yet I shall be ever ready to give you my best and first fruits; and to supply (as much as in me lieth) worthiness by thankfulness

What answer Bacon received to these letters, or what was thought of them, we do not know. We know only that the proposed arrangement did not go forward at that time, and that he continued as he was for half a year longer, when he appears at last to have received a distinct *promise* of promotion to the Solicitorship whenever Doderidge should be removed.[4]

4.

About this time Bacon lost a private friend, for whom he appears to have had a great regard,—Jeremiah Bettenham, a Reader of Gray's Inn We hear of it by mere accident for having been appointed one of the executors, and had occasion to write a letter to Sir Thomas Hobby, upon whom it seems that the estate had some claim, the distinction of his own name has had virtue to preserve the letter, which being some years since carried by the chances of time into the possession of the late Mr Pickering (publisher of Mr Montagu's edition of Bacon's works), he very kindly, when he heard what I was

---

[1] *to take any other hold of than the hold of a thankful remembrance* 'Remains' and ' Resuscitatio '
[2] *and* om in MS
[3] *And if I cannot observe you as I would, your Lordship will impute it to my want of experience, which I shall gather better when I am once settled* Rem
[4] Foster to Matthew, Feb 22, 1606-7 (Dom James I)

about, showed it to me and allowed me to take a copy for insertion
in this collection   The original, which is all in Bacon's own hand
has been sold, I believe, since I saw it, and in whose possession it
now remains I do not know   It is printed here from my own copy
but as it was a copy taken by myself and collated with the original
by Mr Pickering and myself together, it may be depended upon for
accuracy as much as any other in the book

It is the more valuable as belonging to a class of letters which
would not in ordinary cases be kept and of which therefore we have
few specimens   And it is one of those which are of great use to
a biographer, as helping him to form a notion of the ordinary manners
and familiar behaviour of the man in his private relations   of which as
it is impossible to endeavour to follow a man closely through his
life without making *some* kind of picture to oneself, it is of no small
importance that the picture shall be something like the original

"Like men, like manners like breeds like, they say
Kind nature is the best   those manners next
That fit us like a nature, second hand
Which are indeed the manners of the great"

Judging from this and other letters of the same kind that have
come down to us I imagine Bacon's manners to have been "the
best '

To the Right Worshipfull his very loving cousin, Sir Thomas Posr Hobby [1]

Good Cousin   No man knoweth better than yourself what
part I bear in grief for Mr Bettenham's departure   For in
faith I never thought myself at better liberty than when he
I were by ourselves together.   His end was Christian and comfortable, in parfite memory and in parfite charity, and the dis
position of that he left wise, just and charitable

For your bonds or bills, I take it they be three, amounting to
about nine score pounds , I left them with Mr. Peccam, because
of your nearness to me   But I shall be able and will undertake
to satisfy your desire that you may take time till Allhallow tide
But then we shall need it, lest we subject ourselves to importu
nity and clamour   Your privy seal is forthcoming, but no
money was by Mr Bettenham by it received , and if the con
duit run, we will come with our pitcher, as you write

Your loving congratulation for my doubled life, as you call it

[1] Youngest son of Bacon's aunt Elizabeth (now Lady Russell) by her first
marriage

I thank you for   No man may better conceive the joys of a good wife than yourself, with whom I dare not compare   But I thank God I have not taken a thorn out of my foot to put it into my side   For as my state is somewhat amended, so I have no other circumstance of complaint   But herein we will dilate when we meet, which meeting will be much more joyful if my Lady bear a part to mend the music   to whom I pray let me in all kindness be commended   And so I rest

Yours assured,

Fr. Bacon

This 4th of Aug 1606

Sir Thomas, I suppose, had borrowed money of Mr Bettenham upon bond, and delivered to him as part of the security his privy seal, that is, his claim upon the Exchequer for money lent to the King   If " the conduit ran " that is, if repayment of such loans was obtainable, the executors would apply it towards the liquidation of the debt

Bacon afterwards erected a memorial to his friend, a seat under the elms, where they had been used to walk and talk together

"There was still standing in 1771" (says Pearce in his 'History of the Inns of Court') " an octagonal seat covered with a roof, within the circle of trees on the west side of Gray's Inn Gardens, with the following inscription

Franciscus Bacon,

Regis Solicitor generalis,

Executor testamenti Jeremiæ Bettenham,

nuper Lectoris hujus hospitii,

viri innocentis, abstinentis, et contemplativi,

hanc sedem   memoriam ejusdem Jeremiæ

extru   An Dom 1609 "

The inscription is given in Seward's "Anecdotes of Distinguished Persons," vol iv p 332, but not in the lapidary form, and I am not aware that the original shape has been preserved   It is a pity that somebody did not think of taking a sketch of the octagonal seat before it was removed

Bacon's temperate estimate of the result of his recent "experiment solitary" touching matrimony, I take rather as evidence that " his wisdom likewise remained with him," than that the experiment had been unsuccessful, so far

5.

I am not aware of any other writing of his that seems to belong to the summer vacation of 1606 (in which much time would probably be spent in preparations for the debates on the Union that were to be the special business of the coming Session, and his leisure would be sufficiently occupied with his *Experientia Literata* and *Interpretatio Naturæ*, a work which he had announced as in progress), unless it be a letter to Dr Playfere about the translation into Latin of the Advancement of Learning. The letter has no date; nor is the date of much consequence but it was certainly written "some while" after November 1605, when the book was published, and certainly *not* after July 1608, and August or September 1606 being as likely a date as any, I will place it here.

Dr Playfere was Margaret Professor of Divinity at Cambridge, and a distinguished preacher and latinist and if it be remembered that in those days all scholars could read Latin, and few except Englishmen could read English, the letter (which was preserved by Bacon himself in his Register-book, and first printed in the Resuscitatio) may be left to speak for itself without further introduction

A LETTER OF REQUEST TO DR. PLAYFER, TO TRANSLATE THE
ADVANCEMENT OF LEARNING INTO LATIN [1]

Mr. Doctor Playfer,

A great desire will take a small occasion to hope and put in trial that which is desired. It pleased you a good while since to express unto me the good liking which you conceived of my book of the Advancement of Learning, and that more significantly (as it seemed to me) than out of courtesy or civil respect Myself, as I then took contentment in your approbation thereof, so I should esteem and acknowledge not only my contentment increased, but my labours advanced, if I might obtain your help in that nature which I desire Wherein, before I set down in plain terms my request unto you, I will open myself what it was which I chiefly sought and propounded to myself in that work, that you may perceive that which I now desire to be pursuant thereupon. If I do not err, (for any judgment that a man maketh of his own doings, had need be spoken with a *Si nunquam fallit imago*,) I have this opinion, that if I had sought my own commendation, it had been a much fitter course for me to have done as gardeners use to do, by taking their seeds

[1] Add. MSS. 5503, f 29, b.

and ships, and rearing them first into plants, and so uttering them
in pots, when they are in flower, and in their best state. But for
as much as my end was merit of the state of learning to my
power, and not glory, and because my purpose was rather to
excite other men's wits than to magnify my own, I was desirous
to prevent the uncertainness of my own life and times, by uttering rather seeds than plants nay and further (as the proverb is)
by sowing with the basket, than with the hand. Wherefore,
since I have only taken upon me to ring a bell to call other
wits together, (which is the meanest office,) it cannot but be con-
sonant to my desire, to have that bell heard as far as can be.
And since that they are but sparks, which can work but upon
matter prepared, I have the more reason to wish that those sparks
may fly abroad, that they may the better find and light upon those
minds and spirits which are apt to be kindled. And therefore
the privateness of the language considered wherein it is written,
excluding so many readers, (as, on the other side, the obscurity
of the argument in many parts of it excludeth many others), I
must account it a second birth of that work, if it might be translated into Latin, without manifest loss of the sense and matter.
For this purpose I could not represent to myself any man into
whose hands I do more earnestly desire that work should fall
than yourself; for by[1] that I have heard and read, I know no
man a greater master in commanding words to serve matter.
Nevertheless, I am not ignorant of the worth of your labours,
whether such as your place and profession imposeth on you, or
such as your own virtue may, upon your voluntary election, take
in hand. But I can lay before you no other persuasions than
either the work itself may affect you with, or the honour of his
Majesty, to whom it is dedicated, or your particular inclination
to myself, who, as I never took so much comfort in any labours
of my own, so I shall never acknowledge myself more obliged
in any thing to the labour of another, than in that which
shall assist this. Which your labour if I can by my place,
profession, means, friends, travel, word, deed, requite unto you,
I shall esteem myself so straitly bound thereunto, as I shall be
ever be most ready both to take and seek occasions of thankfulness. So leaving it nevertheless *salva amicitia* (as reason is) to
your own good liking, I remain

[1] *by* om. in MS

Dr Playfere appears to have undertaken the task with alacrity But nothing came of it , whether because his way of doing it did not suit Bacon's taste, or because of his own failing health, is uncertain Tenison, who had means of knowing through Dr Rawley, gives the following account of the matter   " The Doctor was willing to serve so excellent a person and so worthy a design , and within a while sent him a specimen of a Latin translation   But men generally come short of themselves when they strive to outdo themselves   They put a force upon their natural genius, and in straining of it crack and disable it   And so it seems it happened to that worthy and elegant man   Upon this great occasion he would be over-accurate , and he sent a specimen of such superfine Latinity, that the Lord Bacon did not encourage him to labour further in that work, in the penning of which he desired not so much neat and polite, as clear, masculine, and apt expression "[1]

On the other hand there is a memorandum in ' the *Commentarius Solutus*, dated 25 July, 1608—' Proceeding with the translation of my book of Advancement of Learning hearkening to some other, *if Playfere should fail* "[2]—which proves that at that time Dr Playfere was still engaged upon the translation, though Bacon had begun to doubt whether he would get it done   And as he died only half a year after, at the age of 17[3]—and I gather from Fuller's short notice of him among the worthies of Kent, that during the last year or two he was not the man he had been[4]—it seems probable that the apprehension of failure was suggested by the state of his health or faculties, and the failure caused by his death

There is also a short note belonging to this autumn, which must come in here to make the collection complete , though I have no conjecture to offer as to the occasion of it

    To his assured friend Sir Mich Hickis[5]

Sir,

    I pray try the conclusion I spoke to you of, out of hand For it is a mind I shall not continue in if it pass this very tide So I rest

                    Yours,
                        Fr Bacon.

---

[1] Baconiana, p 25   [2] See the next Volume, p 64
[3] See his epitaph in Cooper's ' Athenæ Cantabrigienses ' He died on the 2nd of February 1608 9
[4] " It added to his distemper, that when his re election to his place (after his first two years' end) was put into the Regent-house, a great Doctor said, *Detur digniori* "
[5] Lansd MSS 89, f 203 Original own hand Docketed " No 1606 Sr Fr Bacon

G

Parliament met again, according to appointment, on the 18th of November, and the Commons having heard the King's speech and received a written answer to their petition of Grievances—an answer quite in accordance with the King's previous promise, and in which if there was anything unconstitutional, all the recognised constitutional authorities (Coke included) were as much implicated as the King[1]—addressed themselves at once to the business of the Union

The "Instrument of Union" (agreed upon by the Commissioners in December 1604) having been laid before the House and read on the 21st, and a Committee, of which Bacon was a member, having been appointed on the 24th to hear and report what the Lords had to propound, the question on receiving the report was, how to proceed Upon which question Bacon made a speech, of which there remains, in the hand I think of Sir Robert Cotton, the following sufficiently intelligible note

[SPEECH OF] SIR FRANCIS BACON, NOV. 25, 1606 [2]

Lest silence now in any particular should be noted, as it hath been already in general, I will in this cause give some brief though pertinent advice

That this should not be spoken of in the mass (as it hath been called before) I think we all hold necessary   For so perchance *Plebs amittet quod vult*,[3] the people shall want what they desire, and have put upon them what they would not. which was well provided for in Rome *lege Cecilia*, in ordaining that *Rogationes* should be *simplices* and it was a grave custom even in that Senate that any member might say *Postulo quod dividatur relatio*. A second reason of partition is expedition for if we speak in general, it will be temptation to lead men to ingratiate themselves, sometimes for favour, often for fame, both vices, and to speak as orators only, and not as lawmakers   A third reason, because it is good for caution, to escape traducing, for being an adversary to a part one may be taxed so of the whole.

[1] 'A memorial of such resolutions as his M hath taken with the advice of his Privy Council, assisted with the two Chief Justices, the Lord Chief Baron, and his Majesty's Counsel at Law, upon examination of those grievances which were presented to his M by the Lower House of Parliament, at the last session, wherein there hath not only been a just consideration how all those grants from whence these grievances are supposed to arise are warranted by the laws of the realm, but a due examination of all such inconveniences as do or may fall out in the execution of the same'—C J p 316

[2] Harl MSS 6842, fo 5, 6850, f 55

[3] *debet* in MS

The thing divides itself into three parts. 1 laws of Hostility, 2 Commerce, 3 Naturalizing These are of greatest conse quence Of the two first, the one included in streams of water, the other of blood, and the third of both *non in aqua tantum, sed in aqua et sanguine.* It was prettily and pithily said in my mind, if children, why tribute? if tribute, why are we called children?

Whether it be to be carried severally in the houses, or by con ference? I incline to the latter because it is a matter of state, a matter of future providence, and not of present feeling Our state is good now, and therefore to see what it may be, let us take help of those who sitting upon the higher ground by such advantage have the further prospect to see more Con ference is also suitable to our beginning So was the proposi tion of the Name, the act of Commission, and the meeting of the Commissioners, and by Conference the Continuance was re newed by act And besides, if the Lords proceed alone by a Bill, they will rest more inflexible from their first resolutions

If then Conference, the question is where to begin. *Dies diem docet* Imitate yourselves in the last great bill of Recusants (provided always it be not so long) That was to make one Church, this to make one Nation Then we made a selected Committee to prepare so did the Lords and our labours fell all out with that consent, that when the King's letter came from Royston, it made a unison, and therefore I wish this should have the like course

The immediate resolution of the House was not exactly in accord ance with this recommendation They resolved not only to distri bute the subject into branches, but to divide the branches between the two houses proposing to leave matters concerning Naturaliza tion and the Borders to the Lords, and reserve to themselves matters concerning Commerce and Hostility This proposal being however declined by the Lords, and on reconsideration immediately withdrawn, the ultimate conclusion was according to Bacon's suggestion The two Houses were to meet and confer upon the whole question, and for this conference the former Committee, with some new members added, was instructed (29 Nov.) to prepare

The Committee began with the hostile laws in which they met with no material difficulty, until they came across the point of *Escuage* which being "a kind of Knight's service, called service of the shield, whereby the tenant holding was bound to follow his Lord into the Scottish or Welch wars at his own charge,"[1]—a question was raised whether this should not now cease, no such wars being any longer possible   The difficulty, I suppose, lay in this,—that Escuage was one of "the flowers of the Crown," closely allied to Wardship,[2] and did actually perhaps give a right of wardship in the case of such tenants   and it was considerable enough to suggest the expediency of a special conference upon it with the Lords   What part Bacon had taken on it in the Committee the notes in the Jour nals are not full enough to explain [3] but the House had so much confidence in him as a representative, that he was selected, along with the Attorney, the Solicitor, and the Recorder, "to propound and maintain argument at the Conference," and though he asked to be excused, as being unprepared, he was nevertheless ordered to stand [4]   In the mean time however another division of the Com mittee had been discussing the article of Commerce, which presented more formidable difficulties, and had not been able to come to any conclusion   On this point their reporter declared (9 December) that he had "nothing to report but confusion and disorder"   At a sub sequent conference on the subject with the Lords (17 Dec) some sharp speeches passed, and the merchants of London having set down in writing their reasons against community of trade with the Scots, "were roundly shaken up by the Lord Chancellor"[5]   And as it was now close upon Christmas, the houses were adjourned on the 18th, and further proceeding postponed till after the recess [6]

Time, which is the best medicine for some kinds of discontent, aggravates others by giving the discontented more opportunities of talking them over and knowing one another's minds   And when the house met again on the 10th of February, these minor arrange ments, bearing upon the relations of two separate nations under the same crown, were set aside for awhile to make room for a protest against the project for making those two nations one, towards which the first step was a general naturalization

[1] Cowell's Interpreter
[2] "'The most and best part that spake' (writes Sir T Wilson in a note dated 4 Dec 1606) " was for the remaining of escuage   but the generalest applause was upon them that would have it taken away " (Dom James I)   It appears from the same note that Salisbury was suspected of secretly furthering the dispute, as a step towards the extinction of Wardship, which he wished to be the glory of his own administration
[3] In the House (according to Wilson's note above quoted) he put in a word for Wardship, on the authority of the Greek philosophers in their imaginary com monwealths
[4] 13 Dec 1606   C J p 330, 1010
[5] Carleton to Chamberlain, 18 Dec 1606   Dom James I
[6] C J p 331

The Commissioners of Union appointed in 1604 had agreed to recommend the passing of two acts, one for the *Post-nati*, the other for the *Ante-nati*. For the *Post-nati*, an act *declaring* "that all the subjects of both the realms born *since* the decease of Elizabeth and that shall be born hereafter   *are* by the common law of both realms, and shall be for ever, enabled to obtain, succeed, inherit, and possess all lands, goods, chattels, honours, dignities, offices, liberties privileges and benefices ecclesiastical or civil, in Parliament and all other places of the said Kingdoms, and in every one of the same, in all respects and without any exception whatever, is fully and amply as the subjects of either realm respectively might have done or may do in any sort within the Kingdom where they were born." For the *Ante-nati*, a new law, *enacting* "That all the subjects of both realms, born *before* the decease of the late Queen, may be enabled and made capable to acquire purchase inherit succeed use and dispose of all lands, inheritances, goods, offices, dignities, liberties, privileges, immunities, benefices, and preferments whatsoever, each subject in either kingdom with the same freedom and as lawfully and peaceably as the very native and natural born subjects of either realm, where the said rights states and profits are established; not withstanding whatsoever law statute or former constitution heretofore in force to the contrary   *other than to acquire possess succeed or inherit any office of the Crown, office of Judicature, or any voice place or office in Parliament* all which to remain still free from being claimed, held or engaged by the subjects of the one kingdom within the other, born before the decease aforesaid   until there be such a perfect and full accomplishment of the Union as is mutually desired by both realms;' it being nevertheless understood that the proposed act was not to interfere with the prerogative of the Crown "to denizate, enable, and prefer to such offices, etc, all English and Scottish subjects born before the decease of the late Queen as freely, as sovereignly and absolutely, as any his M. royal progenitors Kings of England and Scotland might have done at any time heretofore."[1]

The meditations of the recess had conjured up a host of terrors at the prospect of thus opening the gate and letting the lean kine into the fat pasture. And those who had been so little alarmed by the proposition during the first week after it was laid before them, that they desired to leave it entirely to the consideration of the other House, were now disposed to set all the rest aside and make their special stand upon this. The feeling broke out first on the 13th of February, in a vehement invective from the member for Bucks against Scotland and Scotchmen in general; which, though received "with

[1] C J p 323

a general amazement," was allowed at the time to pass without reply
or remark   Next day "the article of the Instrument concerning
Naturalization was read" in the House by the Speaker, and the
debate opened with a speech *against* it from Nicholas Fuller, who
seems to have been recognized as leader of the opposition, in so far
as that office can be said to have been recognized in those days, in
which the apprehensions that so readily suggest themselves to Englishmen when invited to alter anything found fluent and forcible
utterance   England, it seems, was already full to overflowing in all
her departments   there was no room for a Scotchman anywhere
The universities had more men who deserved preferment than could
find it   London was so pestered with new buildings, that they had
a bill then before the House to restrain them   The merchants had
made no profit for three years past. Trades were all overstocked
And so forth   His argument appears to have occupied the whole
day, and it was not till the 17th[1] that it received a reply, when
Bacon delivered a speech, of which he was afterwards at the pains to
set down a full report   and of which the text is here taken from two
independent manuscripts, both having corrections in his own hand

It was first printed in 1641, along with two other speeches relating
to the Union,[2] and afterwards in the Resuscitatio   But the manuscripts are the best authority[3]

A SPEECH[4] USED BY SIR FRANCIS BACON, IN THE LOWER HOUSE
OF PARLIAMENT, CONCERNING THE ARTICLE OF NATURALIZA-
TION.[5]

It may please you (Mr Speaker) preface I will use none, but
put myself upon your good opinions, to which I have been accustomed beyond my deservings, neither will I hold you in suspense what way I will choose, but now at the first declare myself,
that I mean to counsel the house to naturalize this nation
wherein nevertheless I have a request to make unto you, which

---

[1] The 15th was a Sunday, and the 16th was spent in discussing a motion for the
censure of the Member for Bucks for his speech on the 13th   which resulted in
his expulsion from the House
[2] " Three speeches of the Right Honourable Sir Francis Bacon, Knight,
concerning Post nati, Naturalization *of the Scotch in England, Union of the Laws
of England and Scotland*   Published by the author's copy, and licensed by authority   London 1641 "
[3] The King's MS (which I have called R) is a fair copy, revised and corrected
by Bacon himself, but the Harleian (which I have called H) has corrections
which must have been made subsequently
[4] King's MSS 17 A 56, fo 63 (K), Harl MSS 6797, fo 93 (H), Ib fo 182
(H 2) Rawley's ' Resuscitatio ' (R)
[5] Naturalization of the Scots, 5° Jacobi H 2, *the General Naturalization of
the Scottish Nation* R

x 2

is of more efficacy to the purpose I have in hand than all that I shall say afterwards, and it is the same request,[1] which Demosthenes did more than once in great causes of estate make to the people of Athens, *ut cum calculis suffragiorum sumant magnam mutatem reipublicæ*, that when they took into their hands the balls, whereby to give their voices (according as the manner of them was), they would raise their thoughts, and lay aside those considerations which their private vocations and degrees mought minister and present[2] unto them, and would take upon them cogitations and minds agreeable to the dignity and honour of the estate. For, Mr. Speaker, as it was aptly and sharply said by Alexander to Parmenio, when upon the recital of the great offers which Darius made, Parmenio said unto him, I would accept these offers, were I as Alexander: he turned it upon[4] him again, So would I, saith he, were I as Parmenio. So in this cause,[5] if an honest English merchant, (I do not single out that estate[6] in disgrace, for this island ever held it honourable, but only for an instance of a private profession,) if an English merchant should say, Surely I would proceed no further in the Union, were I as the King; it mought be reasonably answered, No more would the King, were he as an English merchant. And the like may be said of a gentleman in the country, be he never so worthy and sufficient, or of a lawyer, be he never so wise and learned, or of any other particular condition of persons[7] in this kingdom. For certainly, Mr. Speaker, if a man shall be only or chiefly sensible of those respects which his particular vocation and degree shall suggest and infuse into him, and not enter into true and worthy considerations of estate, he shall never be able aright[8] to give counsel or take counsel in this matter. So that if this request be granted, I account the cause obtained.

But to proceed to the matter itself. All consultations do rest upon questions comparative; for when a question is *de vero*, it is simple, for there is but one truth; but when a question is *de bono*, it is for the most part comparative, for there be differing degrees of good and evil, and the best of the good is to be preferred and chosen, and the worst of the evil is to be declined and avoided. And therefore in a question of this nature you may

---

[1] *request* om. R   [2] *represent* H 2   [3] *offer* H 2   [4] *it* om. H 2
[5] *case* H 2   [6] *state* H 2   [7] *of persons* om. R   [8] *aright* om. H 2

not look for answer[1] proper to every inconvenience alleged, for somewhat that cannot be specially answered may nevertheless be encountered and over-weighed by matter of greater moment And therefore the matter which I shall set forth unto you will naturally receive this distribution of three parts

First, an answer unto those inconveniences which have been alleged to ensue, if we should give way to this Naturalization, which I suppose you will find not to be so great as they have been made, but that much dross is put into the balance to help to make weight

Secondly, an encounter of the remain of those inconveniences which cannot properly be answered but[2] by much greater inconveniences which we shall incur if we do not proceed to this Naturalization

Thirdly, an encounter likewise, but of another nature, that is, of the good[3] and benefit which we shall draw and purchase to ourselves by proceeding to this Naturalization

And yet, to avoid confusion, which evermore followeth of [4] too much generality, it is necessary for me[5] (before I proceed to persuasion) to use some distribution of the points or parts of Naturalization, which certainly can be no better, nor none[6] other, than the ancient distinction[7] of *Jus Civitatis, jus Suffragii id Tribus,* and *Jus Petitionis sive Honorum* For all ability and capacity is either of private interest of *meum* and *tuum,* or of public service And the public consisteth chiefly either in Voice, or in Office Now it is the first of these (Mr. Speaker) that I will only handle at this time and in this place, and reserve the other two for[8] a committee, because they receive more distinction and restriction.

To come therefore to the inconveniences alleged on the other part The first of them is, that there may ensue of this Naturalization a surcharge of people upon this realm of England, which is supposed already to have the full charge and content and therefore there cannot be an admission of the adoptive without

---

[1] *answers* R   [2] *but* om R   [3] *by the gain* R   [4] *upon* H 2
[5] In K it had been written *a necessary for me* A mark of separation has been made between *for* and *me,* probably by Bacon himself, but *a* has not been struck out, no doubt by accident Up to this place K is probably the best authority for the text being a fair copy revised and corrected by Bacon himself For the rest I prefer H (which begins it "proceed"—the first leaf being lost—), and has corrections which must have been made afterwards
[6] *nor* K   [7] *distribution* R
[8] *to* K A correction in Bacon's hand for *of* which had been written first

a[1] diminution of the fortunes and conditions of those that are native subjects of this realm. A grave objection (Mr Speaker) and very dutiful; for it proceedeth not of any unkindness to the Scottish nation, but of a natural fastness to ourselves. For that answer of the Virgins, *Ne forte non sufficiat vobis et nobis*, proceeded not out of any envy or malign humour, but out of providence and the[2] original charity, which begins with ourselves. And I must confess (Mr Speaker) that as the gentleman said, when Abraham and Lot, in regard of the greatness of their families, grew pent and straitened, it is true that,[3] brethren though they were, they grew to difference, and to those words, *Vade tu ad dextram, et ego ad sinistram*, etc. But certainly, I should never have brought that example on that side. For we see what followed of it, how that this separation *ad dextram* and *ad sinistram* caused the miserable captivity of the one brother, and the dangerous though prosperous war of the other, for his rescue and recovery.

But to this objection (Mr Speaker) being so weighty and so principal, I mean to give three several answers; every one of them being, to mine[5] understanding, by itself sufficient.

The first is, that this opinion of the numbers of the Scottish nation, that should be likely to plant themselves here amongst us, will be found to be a thing rather in conceit than in event. For (Mr Speaker) you shall find those plausible similitudes, of a tree that will thrive the better if it be removed into the more fruitful soil, and of sheep or cattle, that if they find a gap or passage open, will leave the more barren pasture, and get into the more rich and plentiful, to be but arguments merely superficial, and to have no sound resemblance with the transplanting or transferring of families. For the tree, we know, by nature as soon as it is set in the better ground can fasten upon it, and take nutriment from it; and a sheep, as soon as he gets into the better pasture, what should let him to graze and feed? But there longeth more, I take it, to a family or particular person, that shall remove from one nation to another. For if (Mr Speaker) they have not stock, means, acquaintance and custom, habitation, trades, countenance, and the like, I hope you doubt not but they will starve in the midst of the rich pasture, and are far enough

---

[1] *the* K   [2] *that* R   [3] *it is true that*, omitted in K, interlined in H
[4] spelt *reasons* in all the copies   [5] *my* K

off from grazing at their pleasure And therefore in this point, which is conjectural, experience is the best guide, for the time past is a pattern of the time to come I think no man doubteth (Mr Speaker) but his Majesty's first coming in was as the greatest spring-tide for the confluence and entrance of that nation Now I would fain understand, in these four years' space, and in the fulness and strength of the current and tide, how many families of the Scottishmen[1] are planted in the cities, boroughs, and towns of this kingdom For I do assure myself, that, more than some persons of quality about his Majesty's person here at the Court, and in London, and some other inferior persons that have a dependancy upon them, the return and certificate, if such a survey should be made, would be of a number extremely small. I report me to all your private knowledges of the places where you inhabit

Now (Mr Speaker) as I said, *Si in ligno viridi ita fit, quid fiet in arido?* I am sure there will be no more such spring-tides. But you will tell me of a multitude of families of the Scottish nation in Polonia, and if they multiply in a country so far off,[2] how much more here at hand? For that (Mr Speaker) you must impute it of necessity to some special accident of time and place that draweth them thither For you see plainly before your eyes, that in Germany, which is much nearer, and in France, where they are invited with privileges, and with[3] this very privilege of Naturalization, yet[4] no such number can be found. So as it cannot be either nearness of place or privilege of person that is the cause But shall I tell you (Mr Speaker) what I think? Of all the[5] places in the world, near or far off, they will never take that course of life in this kingdom, which they content themselves with in Poland For we see it to be[6] the nature of all men that they will rather discover poverty abroad than at home There is never a gentleman that hath overreached himself in expense, and thereby must abate his countenance, but he will rather travel, and do it abroad, than at home and we know well they have good high stomachs, and have ever stood in some terms of[7] emulation with us and therefore they will never live here, except they can live in good fashion[8] So as I assure you (Mr Speaker) I am of opinion that the strife which we now have to admit them, will have like sequel as that contention had between the nobility and people of Rome for the admitting of a plebeian consul, which while it was in passage[1] was very vehement, and mightily stood upon, and when the people had obtained it, they never made any plebeian consul, not[2] in sixty years after   And even so[3] will this be for many years, as I am persuaded, rather a matter in opinion and reputation[4] than in use or effect   And this is the first answer that I give to this main inconvenience pretended, or surcharge of people

The second answer which I give to this objection, is this I must have leave to doubt (Mr Speaker) that this realm of England is not yet peopled to the full.   For certain it is, that the territories of France, Italy, Flanders, and some parts of Germany, do in equal space of ground bear and contain a far greater quantity of people, if they were mustered by the poll   Neither can I see that this kingdom is so much inferior unto those foreign parts in fruitfulness, as it is in population, which makes me conceive we have not our full charge   Besides, I do see manifestly amongst us the badges and tokens rather of scarceness, than of press of people, as drowned grounds, commons, wastes, and the like, which is a plain demonstration, that howsoever there may be an over-swelling throng and press of people here about London, which is most in our eye, yet the body of the kingdom is but thin sown with people   And whosoever shall compare the ruins and decays of ancient towns in this realm with the erections and augmentations of new, cannot but judge that this realm hath been far better peopled in former times, it may be in the Heptarchy or otherwise   For generally the rule holdeth, *the smaller state the greater population, pro rata*   And whether this be true or no, we need not seek further than to call to our remembrance how many of us serve here in this place for desolate and decayed boroughs   Again (Mr Speaker) whosoever looketh into the[5] principles of estate, must hold that it is the mediterrane countries, and not the maritime, which need to fear surcharge of people   For all sea provinces, and specially[6] islands, have another element besides the earth and soil, for their sustentation   For what an infinite number of people are, and may be, sustained by fishing, carriage by sea, and merchandising? Wherein I do again discover, that we are not at all pricked[1] by multitude of people. For if we were, it were not possible that we should relinquish and resign such an infinite benefit of fishing to the Flemings, as it is well known we do. And therefore I see that we have wastes by sea as well as by land, which still is an infallible argument that our industry is not awaked to seek maintenance by any over-great press or charge of people.

And lastly (Mr Speaker) there was never any kingdom in the ages of the world had, I think, so fair and happy a[2] means to issue and discharge the multitude of their people, if it were too great, as this kingdom hath, in regard of that desolate and wasted kingdom[3] of Ireland, which (being a country blessed with almost all the dowries of nature, as rivers, havens, woods, quarries, good soil, and temperate climate, and now at last under his Majesty blessed also with obedience) doth, as it were, continually call unto us for our colonies and plantations. And so I conclude my second answer to this pretended inconvenience of surcharge of people.

The third answer (Mr Speaker) which I give, is this. I demand what is the worst effect that can follow of surcharge of people? Look into all stories, and you shall find it none other than some honourable war for the enlargement of their borders, which find themselves pent, upon foreign parts, which inconvenience, in a valorous and warlike nation, I know not whether I should term an inconvenience or no, for the saying is most true, though in another sense, *Omne solum forti patria*. It was spoken indeed of the patience of an exiled man: but it is no less true of the valour of a warlike nation. And certainly (Mr Speaker) I hope I may speak it without offence, that if we did hold ourselves worthy, whensoever just cause should[4] be given, either to recover our ancient rights, or to revenge our late wrongs, or to attain the honour of our ancestors, or to enlarge the patrimony of our posterity, we would never in this manner forget the[5] considerations of amplitude and greatness, and fall at variance about profit and reckonings, fitter a great deal for private persons than for Parliaments and Kingdoms. And thus (Mr

---

[1] *punched* R   [2] *a* om. R   [3] *realm* K, H 2   [4] *shall* K
[5] *the* om. R

Speaker) I leave this first objection to such satisfaction as you have heard.

The second objection is, that the fundamental laws of both these kingdoms of England and Scotland are yet divers and several, nay more, that it is declared by the Instrument that they shall so continue, and that there is no intent in his Majesty to make innovation in them: and therefore that it should not be seasonable to proceed to this Naturalization, whereby to endow them with our rights and privileges, except they should likewise receive and submit themselves to our laws, and this objection likewise (Mr. Speaker) I allow to be a weighty objection, and worthy to be well answered and discussed.

The answer which I shall offer is this. It is true for mine own part (Mr Speaker) that I wish the Scottish nation governed by our laws, for I hold our laws, with some reducement, worthy to govern, and[1] it were the world   But that is that which I say, and I desire therein your attention.   That according to true reason of estate, Naturalization is in order first and precedent to union of laws, in degree, a less matter than union of laws, and in nature, separable, not inseparable, from union of laws   For Naturalization doth but take out the marks of a foreigner, but union of laws makes them entirely as ourselves   Naturalization taketh away separation; but union of laws doth take away distinction.   Do we not see (Mr Speaker) that in the administration of the world under the great monarch, God himself, that his laws are divers, one law in spirits, another in bodies, one law in regions celestial, another in elementary,[2] and yet the creatures are all one mass and lump, without any *vacuum* or separation   Do we not see likewise in the state of the Church that amongst people of all languages and lineages[3] there is one Communion of Saints, and that we are all fellow-citizens and naturalized of the heavenly Jerusalem,[4] and yet nevertheless divers and several ecclesiastical laws, policies, and hierarchies; according to the speech of that worthy father, *In veste varietas sit, scissura non sit?*   And therefore certainly (Mr Speaker) the bond of law is the more special and private bond, and the bond of naturalization the more common and general   For the laws are rather *figura reipublicæ* than *forma*, and rather bonds of perfection than bonds of entireness   And therefore we see

---

[1] *if* R   [2] *elementar* R   [3] *lineages* R   [4] *Hierusalem* R

in the experience of our own government, that in the kingdom
of Ireland all our statute laws since Poyning's law are not in
force, and yet we deny them not the benefit of Naturalization
In Gersey and Garnesey and the Isle of Man, our common laws
are not in force, and yet they have the benefit of Naturalization
Neither need any man doubt but that our laws and customs must
in small time gather and win upon theirs, for here's the seat of
the kingdom, whence come the supreme directions of estate
here is the King's person and example, of which the verse saith,

" Regis ad exemplum totus componitur orbis."

And therefore it is not possible, although not by solemn and
formal act of estates, yet by the secret operation of no long
time, but they will come under the yoke of our laws, and so
dulcis tractus pari jugo. And this is the answer I give to this
second objection

The third objection is some inequality in the fortunes of these
two nations England and Scotland, by the commixture whereof
there may ensue advantage to them and loss to us Wherein (Mr
Speaker) it is well that this difference or disparity consisteth but
in the external goods of fortune· for indeed it must be confessed, that for the goods of the mind and[1] body, they are *alteri
nos*, other ourselves. For to do them but right, we know in
their capacity and understanding they are a people ingenious,
in labour industrious, in courage valiant, in body hard, active,
and comely. More mought be said, but in commending them
we do but in effect commend ourselves. For they are of[2] one
piece and continent with us, and truth is, we are participant
both of their virtues and vices For if they have been noted to
be a people not so tractable in government, we cannot, without
flattering ourselves, free ourselves altogether from that fault,
being indeed a thing incident to all martial people; as we see it
evident by the example of the Romans and others, even like
unto fierce horses, that though they be of better service than
others, yet are they harder to guide and manage

But for this objection (Mr Speaker) I purpose to answer it,
not by authority of Scripture, which saith, *Beatius est dare quam
accipere*, but by an authority framed and derived from the judgment of ourselves and our ancestors in the same case, as to this

[1] *the body* R   [2] *as of* h

point.   For (Mr Speaker) in all the line of our kings none useth to carry greater commendation than his Majesty's noble progenitor king Edward the first of that name, and amongst his other[1] commendations, both of war and policy, none is more celebrated than his purpose and enterprise for the conquest of Scotland, as not bending his designs to glorious acquests abroad, but to solid strength at home, which nevertheless if it had succeeded,[2] could not but have brought in all those inconveniences of the commixture of a more opulent kingdom with a less, that are now alleged   For it is not the yoke either of our arms or of our laws that can alter the nature of the climate or the nature of the soil, neither is it the manner of the commixture that can alter the matter of the commixture   And therefore (Mr Speaker) if it were good for us then, it is good for us now, and not to be prized the less because we paid not so dear for it   But a more full answer to this objection I refer over to that which will come after to be spoken, touching Surety and Greatness

The fourth objection (Mr Speaker) is not properly an objection, but rather a pre-occupation of an objection of the other side   For it may be said, and very materially, whereabout do we contend?   The benefit of Naturalization is by the law, in as many as have been or shall be born since his Majesty's coming to the crown, already settled and invested   There is no more then desired[3] but to bring the *Ante-nati* into the degree of the[4] *Post-nati*, that men grown, that have well deserved, may be in no worse case than children which have not deserved, and elder brothers in no worse case than younger brothers   So as we stand upon *quiddam* not *quantum*, being but a little difference of time of one generation from another

To this (Mr Speaker) it is said by some, that the law is not so, but that the *Post-nati* are aliens as[5] the rest   A point that I mean not much to argue, both because it hath been well spoken to[6] by the gentleman that spake last before me, and because I do desire in this case and in this place to speak rather of convenience than of law.   Only this I will say, That that opinion seems to me contrary to reason of law, contrary to form of pleading in law, and contrary to authority and experience of law

For reason of law, when I meditate of it, methinks the wis-

---

[1] *other his*   K
[2] *succeeded well*   R
[3] *desired* om H, R
[4] *the* om   K
[5] *as well as*   R
[6] *to* om   H

dom of the common laws of England well observed, is admirable
in the distribution of the benefit and protection of the laws, according to the several conditions of persons, in an excellent proportion   The degrees are four, but bipartite, two of *Aliens* and
two of *Subjects*   The first degree is of[1] an Alien born under a
king or estate[2] that is an enemy   If such a one come into this
kingdom without safe-conduct, it is at his peril   the law giveth
him no protection, neither for body, lands, nor goods, so as if
he be slain, there is no remedy by any appeal at the party's suit,
although his wife were an English woman   marry at the king's
suit, the case may be otherwise, in regard of the offence to the
peace and crown[3]   The second degree is of an Alien that is born
under the faith and allegiance of a king or state that is a friend
Unto such a person the law doth impart a greater benefit and
protection, that is, concerning things personal, transitory, and
moveable, as goods and chattels, contracts, and the like, but
not concerning freehold and[4] inheritance   And the reason is,
because he may be an enemy, though he be not, for the state
under the obeisance of which he is may enter into quarrel and
hostility, and therefore as the law hath but a transitory assurance of him, so it rewards him but with transitory benefits
The third degree is of a subject, who having been an Alien, is
by charter made Denizen   To such a one the law doth impart
yet a more ample benefit, for it gives him power to purchase
freehold and inheritance to his own use, and likewise enables
the children born after his denization to inherit.   But yet nevertheless he cannot make title or convey pedigree from any an-
cestor paramount, for the law thinks not good to make him in
the same degree with a subject born, because he was once an
alien, and so mought once have been[5] an enemy   and *nemo
subito fingitur*, men's affections cannot be so settled by any benefit, as when from their nativity they are imbred and inherent
And the fourth degree, which is the perfect degree, is of such a
person that neither is enemy, nor can be enemy in time to come,
nor could have been enemy at any time past, and therefore
the law gives unto him the full benefit of Naturalization   Now
(Mr Speaker) if these be the true steps and paces of the law,

---

[1] *of* om K   [2] *state* K, R
[3] *peace and* om K, H 2, interlined in H, *and crown* om R   [4] *or* K
[5] So corrected in H by Bacon, from *may once be*

no man can deny but whosoever is born under the King's obedience, never could *in aliquo puncto temporis* be an enemy (a rebel he mought be, but no enemy), and therefore in reason of law is naturalized   Nay contrariwise, he is bound *jure naturaliæ* to defend this kingdom of England against all invaders or rebels, and therefore as he is obliged to the protection of arms, and that perpetually and universally, so he is to have the perpetual and universal benefit and protection of laws,[1] which is Naturalization

For form of pleading, it is true that hath been said, That if a man would plead another to be Alien,[2] he must not only set forth negatively and privatively, that he was born out of the obedience of our sovereign Lord the King, but affirmatively, under the obedience of a foreign king or state in particular, which can never be done in this case [3]

As for authority, I will not press it ; you know all what hath been published by the King's proclamation[4]

And for experience of law we see it in the subjects of Ireland, in the subjects of Gersey and Gernesey, parcels of the duchy of Normandy, in the subjects of Calais, when it was English, which was parcel of the crown of France   But, as I said, I am not willing to enter into an argument of law, but to hold myself to point of convenience   So as for my part I hold all *post-nati* naturalized *ipso jure*, but yet I am far from opinion that it should be a thing superfluous to have it done by Parliament, chiefly in respect of that true principle of estate,[5] *Principum actiones præcipue ad famam sunt componendæ*   It will lift up a sign to all the world of our love towards them, and good agreement with them [6]   And these are (Mr Speake) the material objections which have been made on the other side, whereunto you have heard mine answers   Weigh them in your wisdoms, and so I conclude that general part

Now (Mr Speaker) according as I promised, I must fill the other balance, in expressing unto you the inconveniences which we shall incur if we shall not proceed to this Naturalization

[1] *law* R   [2] *an Alien* K, R
[3] The last clause (which is not in K) is interlined in H
    by the K's procl interlined in H   [5] *of estate* om R
    This sentence (from " but yet ") is inserted in the margin of H, and is not found in K   R contains all the interlineations, and differs from H, as corrected, only in a few words which are probably errors of the transcriber or printer

Wherein that inconvenience which above all others, and alone by itself if there were none other, doth exceedingly move me, and may move you, is a position of estate, collected out of the records of time, which is this that wheresoever several kingdoms or estates have been united in sovereignty, if that union hath not been fortified and bound in with a further union, and namely that which[1] is now in question, of Naturalization, this hath followed, that at one time or other they have broken again, being upon all occasions apt to revolt and relapse to the former separation.

Of this assertion the first example which I will set before you, is of that memorable union which was between the Romans and the Latins, which continued from the battle at the lake of Regilla, for many years, unto the consulships of[2]

at what time there began, about this very point of Naturalization, that war which was called *Bellum Sociale*, being the most bloody and pernicious war that ever the Roman state endured. Wherein after numbers of battles, and infinite sieges and surprises of towns, the Romans in the end prevailed and mastered the Latins. But as soon as ever they had the honour of the war, looking back into what perdition and confusion they were near to have been brought, they presently naturalized them all. You speak of a Naturalization in blood, there was a Naturalization indeed in blood.

Let me set before you again the example of Sparta, and the rest of Peloponnesus then associates. The state of Sparta was a nice and jealous state in this point of imparting Naturalization to their confederates. But what was the issue of it? After they had held them in a kind of society and amity for divers years, upon the first occasion given, which was no more than the surprise of the castle of Thebes by certain desperate conspirators in the habit of maskers, there ensued immediately a general revolt and defection of their associates, which was the ruin of their state, never afterwards to be recovered.

---

[1] *that* K

[2] A blank is left in all the MSS after "consulships of" In H the words have been struck out by Bacon's own pen, and "tymes of Sylla" inserted which words have been again struck out, and the original words, with the blank space after them, carefully restored by the same pen. In the 'Resuscitatio' the blank is filled with the names of *T. Manlius and P. Decius.* In the copy printed in 1641 it is filled with the names of *C. Plautius and L. Æmilius Mamercus,* and there is the following note in the margin. "169 years after that battle. There are extant at this day coins or medals, in memory of a battle fought by this C. Plautius at Privernum." But Rawley is right. See Liv. viii 3, 5   [3] *that* K.

Of later[1] time let me lead your consideration to behold the like events in the kingdom of Aragon, which kingdom was united with Castile and the rest of Spain in the persons of Ferdinando and Isabella, and so continued many years, but yet so as it stood a kingdom severed and divided from the rest of the body of Spain in privileges, and directly in this point of Naturalization, or capacity of inheritance. What came of this? Thus much, that now of fresh memory, not past twelve years since, only upon the voice of a condemned man out of the grate of a prison towards the street, that cried *Fueros*, which is as much as liberties or privileges, there was raised a dangerous rebellion, which was suppressed with difficulty with[2] an army royal, and their privileges disannulled, and they incorporated with the rest of Spain.[3] Upon so small a spark, notwithstanding so long continuance, were they ready to break and sever again.

The like may be said of the states of Florence and Pisa; which city of Pisa[4] being united unto Florence, but not endued[5] with the benefit of Naturalization, upon the first light of foreign assistance by the expedition of Charles the eighth of France into Italy, did revolt, though it be since again re-united and incorporated.

The same effect we see in the most barbarous government, which shews it the rather to be an effect of nature. For it was thought a fit policy by the council of Constantinople, to retain the three provinces of Transylvania, Valachia, and Moldavia (which were as the very nurses of Constantinople, in respect of their provisions) to the end they mought be the less wasted, only under Vayvodds, as vassals and homagers, and not under Bassaes, as[6] provinces of the Turkish empire. Which policy we see by late experience proved unfortunate, as appeared by the revolt of the same three provinces under the arms and conduct of Sigismund Prince of Transylvania, a leader very famous for a time: which revolt is not yet fully recovered. Whereas we seldom or never hear of revolts of provinces[7] incorporate to the Turkish empire.

On the other part (Mr Speaker) because it is true which[8] the

---

¹ *latter* K   ² *by* K
³ So this passage stands in all the MSS., and in the edition of 1611 (except that it leaves a blank at the word *Fueros*), and in the 'Resuscitatio.' Blackbourn, I do not know on what authority, gives it thus: "After which victory nevertheless, to shun farther inconvenience these privileges were disannulled, and they were incorporated with Castile and the rest of Spain."
⁴ *city of Pisa* om. K   ⁵ *endowed* K   ⁶ *and* R   ⁷ *Princes* R.   ⁸ *that* K

logicians say, *Opposita juxta se posita magis elucescunt,* let us take a view, and we shall find that wheresoever kingdoms and states have been united, and that union corroborate by the bond of mutual Naturalization, you shall never observe them after-wards, upon any occasion of trouble or otherwise, to break and[1] sever again as we see most evidently before our eyes in divers provinces of France, that is to say,[2] Guienne, Provence, Normandy, Brytaine, which, notwithstanding the infinite infesting troubles of that kingdom, never offered to break again

We see the like effect in all the kingdoms of Spain which are mutually naturalized, as Leon, Castile, Valencia, Andaluzia, Granada and the rest,[3] except Aragon, which held the contrary course, and therefore had the contrary success, as was said, and Portugal, of which there is not yet sufficient trial

And lastly, we see the like effect in our own nation, which never rent asunder after it was once united, so as we now scarce know whether the Heptarchy were a story or a fable. And therefore (Mr Speaker) when I revolve with myself these examples and others, so lively expressing the necessity of a Naturalization to avoid a relapse into a separation, and do hear so many arguments and scruples made on the other side, it makes me think on the old Bishop, which upon a public disputation of certain divines Christians with some learned men of the Heathen, did extremely press to be heard, and they were loth to suffer him, because they knew he was unlearned, though otherwise an holy and well-meaning man but at last, with much ado, he gat to be heard And when he came to speak, instead of using argument, he did only say over his belief . but did it with such assurance and con-stancy, as it did strike the minds of those that heard him more than any argument had done And so (Mr Speaker) against all these witty and subtile arguments, I say that I do believe, and I would be sorry to be found a prophet in it, that except we proceed with this Naturalization (though perhaps not in his Majesty's time, who hath such interest in both nations) yet in the time of his descendents, these realms will be in continual danger to divide and break again Now if any man be of that careless mind, *maneat nostros ea cura nepotes,* or of that hard mind, to

---

[1] *or* K
[2] *in the provinces of France* K The alteration made by Bacon in H
[3] So in all the MSS , in the copy printed in 1641, and in the 'Resuscitatio' Blackbourn adds, *Murcia, Toledo, Catalonia*

leave things to be tried by the sharpest sword   sure I am he is not of St Paul's opinion, who affirmeth that whosoever useth not fore-sight and provision for his family is worse than an un believer. Much more, if we shall not use fore-sight for these two kingdoms, that comprehend so many families, but leave things open to the peril of future divisions.   And thus have I ex pressed unto you the inconvenience, which of all other sinketh deepest with me, as the most weighty

Neither do[1] there want other inconveniences (Mr. Speaker), the effect and influence whereof I fear[2] will not be adjourned to so long a day as this that I have spoken of   for I leave it to your wis doms[3] to consider whether you do not think, in case by the denial of this Naturalization any pique or[4] alienation or unkindness, I do not say should be, but[5] should be thought to be, or noised to be, between these two nations, whether it will not quicken and excite all the envious and malicious humours wheresoever (which are now covered) against us, either foreign or at home, and so open the way to practices and other engines and machinations, to the disturbance of this state   As for that other inconvenience of his Majesty's engagement into[6] this action, it is too binding and pressing to be spoken of, and may do better a great deal in your minds than in my mouth, or in the mouth of any man else, be cause, as I say, it doth press our liberty too far   And therefore (Mr Speaker) I come now to the third general part of my divi sion, concerning the benefits which we shall purchase by this knitting of the knot surer and straiter between these two king doms, by the communicating of Naturalization

The benefits may appear to be two ; the one surety, the other greatness.

Touching surety (Mr. Speaker), it was well said by Titus Quintius the Roman touching the state of Peloponnesus, that the tortoise is safe within her shell. *Testudo intra tegumen tuta est*   But if there be any parts that lie open, they endanger all the rest. We know well, that although the state at this time be in a happy peace, yet for the time past, the more ancient enemy to this kingdom hath been the French, and the more late the Spaniard, and both these had as it were then several

---

[1] *doth* K   [2] *fear me* K   [3] *wisdom* R   [4] *of* R
[5] *should be, but* om R   [6] *to* K , corrected in H
[7] *to come* K , corrected in H

postern gates, whereby they mought have approach and entrance to annoy us France had Scotland, and Spain had Ireland , for these were the two accesses which did comfort and encourage both these enemies to assail and trouble us We see that of Scotland is cut off by the union of both these kingdoms, if that it shall be now made constant and permanent That of Ireland is likewise cut off by the convenient situation of part[1] of Scotland towards the north of Ireland, where the sore was. which we see, being suddenly closed, hath continued closed by[2] means of this salve, so as now there are no parts of this state exposed to danger to be a temptation to the ambition of foreigners, but their approaches and avenues are taken away · for I do little doubt but those[3] foreigners which had so little success when they had these advantages, will have much less comfort now that they be taken from them.   And so much for surety

To greatness (Mr Speaker) I think a man may speak it soberly and without bravery, that this kingdom of England, having Scotland united, Ireland reduced, the sea provinces of the Low Countries contracted, and shipping maintained, is one of the greatest monarchies, in forces truly esteemed, that hath been in the world For certainly the kingdoms here on earth have a resemblance with the kingdom of heaven, which our Saviour compareth not to any great kernel or nut, but to a very small grain, yet such a one as is apt to grow and spread.   And such do I take to be the constitution of this kingdom, if indeed we shall refer our counsels to greatness and power, and not quench them too much with consideration of utility and wealth.   For Mr Speaker) was it not, think you, a true answer that Solon of Greece[4] made to the rich king Croesus of Lydia, when he shewed unto him a great quantity of gold that he had gathered together, in ostentation of his greatness and might But Solon said to him, contrary to his expectation, Why, sir, if another come that hath better iron than you, he will be lord of all your[5] gold Neither is the authority of Machiavel to be despised, who scorneth the proverb of estate taken first from a speech

[1] So K, where there seems to have been some erasure The two other MSS, the copy printed in 1641, and the ' Resuscitatio,' have all of them " the north of Scotland' Blackbourn substituted " the west of Scotland ," on what authority I do not know but probably (in this as in the other cases) on the authority of a marginal note made by somebody who had observed the inaccuracy
[2] partly by K , partly crossed out in H.   [3] these K   [4] Græcia K
[5] all we your K

of Mucianus, that *Moneys are the sinews of Wars*, and saith there are no true sinews of wars but the very sinews of the arms of valiant men   Nay more (Mr Speaker), whosoever shall look into the semmary[1] and beginnings of the monarchies of the world, he shall find them founded in poverty.   Persia, a country barren and poor, in respect of the Medes whom they subdued   Macedon, a kingdom ignoble and mercenary, until the time of Philip the son of Amyntas   Rome had poor and pastoral be ginnings   The Turks, a band of Sarmatian Scithes, that in a vagabond manner made impression upon that part of Asia, which is yet called Turcomania, out of which, after much variety of fortune, sprung the Othoman family, now the terror of the world   So we know the Goths, Vandals, Alans, Huns, Lom bards, Normans, and the rest of the northern people, in one age of the world made their descent or expedition upon the Roman empire, and came not as rovers to carry away prey and be gone again, but planted themselves in a number of fruitful and rich provinces, where not only their generations, but their names, remain till this day, witness *Lombardy, Catalonia*, a name com pounded of *Goth* and *Alane, Andaluzia*, a name corrupted from *Vandelicia, Hungarie, Normandy*, and others

Nay the fortune of the Swisses of late years, which are bred in a barren and mountainous country, is not to be forgotten, who first ruined the Duke of Burgundy, the same who had almost ruined the kingdom of France; what time, after the battle of Grançon, the rich jewel of Burgundy, prized at many thousands, was sold for a few pence by a common Swiss, that knew no more what a jewel meant than did Æsop's cock   And again the same nation, in revenge of a scorn, was the ruin of the French king's affairs in Italy, Lewis the 12th.   For that king, when he was pressed somewhat rudely by an agent of the Swisses to raise their pensions, brake into words of choler What, said he, will these villains of the mountains put a tax upon me?   Which words lost him his duchy of Milan, and chased him out of Italy   All which examples (Mr. Speaker) do well prove Solon's opinion of the authority and mastery that iron hath over gold.   And therefore if I shall speak unto you mine own heart, methinks we should a little disdain that the nation of Spain, which howsoever of late it hath grown to rule

yet of ancient time served many ages, first under Carthage,
then under Rome, after under Saracens, Goths, and others, should
of late years take unto themselves that spirit as to dream of a
Monarchy in the West, according to that device, *Video solem
orientem in occidente*, only because they have ravished from some
wild and unarmed people mines and store[1] of gold, and on the
other side, that this island of Brittany,[2] seated and manned as it
is, and that hath (I make no question) the best iron in the world,
that is the best soldiers of the world, should think of nothing
but reckonings and audits,[3] and *meum* and *tuum*, and I cannot
tell what

Mr. Speaker, I have, I take it, gone through the parts which
I propounded to myself. wherein if any man shall think that I
have sung *placebo*, for mine own particular, I would have him
know that I am not so unseen in the world but that I discern it
were much alike for my private fortune to rest[4] a *tacebo* as to sing
a *placebo* in this business. But I have spoken out of the foun-
tain of my heart. *Credidi propter quod locutus sum* I believed,
therefore I spake. So as my duty is performed. The judgment
is yours. God direct it for the best

7

What was the exact form of the question before the House when
this speech was made, the Journals do not distinctly explain. Bacon
evidently wished to turn it upon the consideration of general policy
—or ' conveniency " as it was called—which was indeed the proper
province of the Legislature, for upon the question what the existing
law *was*, they had no authority to decide. And if they were satisfied
that a general naturalization was expedient, though not prepared to
affirm that the Post-nati were naturalized already, there was no need
to meddle with the question. It would have been easy to frame the
Act so as either to include them under the new law or leave them to
the operation of the old. But the truth was that they were not prepared to admit any of the Scots to the benefits of naturalization, except upon conditions, and therefore it was necessary to put a veto,
if possible, upon the doctrine that the Post-nati were entitled to
admission as the law stood. Hence, as the debate went on, it
shifted more and more from the point of ' conveniency ' towards the

point of law, and ended at last on the 5th day in an instruction to the Committee to discuss it among themselves and "report their opinion on that point only"[1] Their opinion was that the Post-nati were *not* naturalized *de jure* and upon their report to that effect (23 Feb)—the House having in the meantime passed a resolution (21 Feb) that it was not fit to handle the point of conveniency before the point of law were determined—they were again instructed "to collect and set down in writing the heads of the arguments touching the point of law," and to consider who should be deputed to maintain each of the heads at the Conference with the Lords, which was to be the next step.[2]

The object of the conference being to establish a position which Bacon had just declared to be in his opinion "contrary to reason of law, contrary to form of pleading in law, and contrary to authority and experience of law," he could not be asked to take a part in maintaining it by argument. But he was not the less fit to set forth the state of the question at issue, and to explain the proposed method of discussion and accordingly the part assigned to him by the House was—"to make the entrance, by way of preamble and insinuation of the order of argument appointed to the Committee" to which was added the duty (which proved a very heavy one) of making report of the proceedings to the House the next morning.[4]

It seems that at these Conferences between the Lords and the Commons, the rule was that the Commons should stand all the time, bare headed which was found a great hurt and danger to the health of their bodies, and almost impossible for the strongest body to endure considering the length of conferences and the crowding and thronging there."[5] On this occasion, the conference having lasted very long and been continued through two successive days, the fatigue appears to have been too much for Bacon's constitution, and on the next morning he was ill and unable to appear in the House. But on Saturday, the 28th of February, he began his report which "being," says the Journal, "very long, consisting of many divisions and particulars and interlaced with much variety of argument and answer on both parts, the time would not allow him to finish, and so was deferred till Monday morning."[6]

Of this report there remains among the State papers an abstract in the hand of Dudley Carleton, drawn up apparently by himself and though several leaves are missing, it will help us to understand the position of the question as between the two Houses, and to interpret the proceedings which followed.

[1] 20 Feb C J p 339   [2] C J p 340   [3] 21 Feb   [4] 26 Feb
[5] Fuller's report, 14 March, 1606-7 C J p 352   [6] C J p 345

SIR FRANCIS BACON'S REPORT OF THE FIRST DAY'S CONFERENCE TOUCHING THE QUESTION WHETHER THE SCOTCHMEN BORN SINCE THE KING CAME TO THE CROWN BE NATURALIZED IN ENGLAND [1]

If want of health may not excuse attendance, nor want of hearing answer for not reporting, he knew not what to say for himself. For others they have stood as peremptories, but to him they cannot serve as dilatories. To bring out the whole and entire body he would not undertake, but to make an anatomy of it, and shew the lines and parts, which might serve to give a light, though not delight.

The speeches used by the Lower House divided into two parts, first into matter of introducement, secondly into matter of argument.

The introducement chiefly tended to prevent mistakings, and to persuade that this proceeding was no opposition to the main point of the Union, nor a wilful contradiction to his Majesty's proclamation, but a desire to make the Scottishmen more beholding to the State than to our laws, because our laws were firm and stable, and could neither impart favours nor expect thanks. This is not a matter *in deliberativo genere* but *in judiciali*, and the question not *de bono* but *de vero*, which might argue the insatisfaction of our judgments, not the indisposition of our wills. We might not be thought to oppose against the proclamation, because that had another main and principal intent, and these words only a passage set down by some skilful in the laws, which they term according to their usual form, *sages aux loyes.*

That we[2] acknowledge the power of proclamations to be great, yet not such as might explain laws. And that the explanation of a law was all one if not more than the enacting, because it was like *Janus bifrons*, and looked as well back how the law was ever to be taken, as forward how it should be taken hereafter, and was therefore left only to Parliament. Yet had this proclamation effected so much that in all this proceeding, which had suffered much debate, there was no flash of heat, or any unrespective word cast out.

In novo casu veritas tanquam germen quod spiritu humano

[1] Domestic, James I vol xxvi. no 65.   [2] *we not* in MS

aperitur et afflatur, and that therefore discourse and debate would serve to ripen it as well as bring it forth. The commendation of our law is that it is no jealous law but doth admit the society of other sciences, as of Grammar, Logic, Physic, &c., wherein the Judge doth aid himself in divers questions with the help of such as are skilful in those sciences   and therefore in a doubtful case in laws, inducement may many times help the judgment as well as proofs   We were therefore to lay open such induce-ments as did lead us to our opinion, and those were fetched out of the law of reason, out of the law of nations, and out of the civil law [1]

In the law of reason there is an axiom, *Deficiente lege recur-ritur ad consuetudinem, deficiente consuetudine recurritur ad ratio-nem*   and that therefore this case was so to be adjudged because there was neither example in this state to be suited with it, nor case in law expressly for it   But by the law of reason there were seven considerations made against it   First the difference of times   because states were in the beginning but heaps of people confusedly drawn together, without law or custom which might rule them,[2] and amongst them subjection might import naturali-zation, but after that by process of time there were forms of States and government, they then submitted themselves to the course of laws, and naturalization went according to laws.   Se-condly there would be much inequality in it, because by our law they should be naturalized here, and then law would admit no such privilege for us amongst them.   Thirdly the extent would be too large, because it should import naturalization of all which should at any time join with this Crown   and the altera-tion of States, by example of the often changes in the State of Rome, would breed much inconvenience   Fourthly there was another reason of inequality, because this naturalization would put them in better state than ourselves, and make them enjoy the whole benefit of our privileges, whereas they would be liable but to half of the burden   Fifthly our kind of naturalization was too large and bountiful, because there was no distinction, as is amongst others who could give Jus Civitatis, Jus Imperii or

---

[1] This appears to have been the conclusion of Bacon's own part in the con-ference   of which I gather from the entry in the Journals (p 1023) that the Lords signified their approval   The next paragraph contains an account of the argument maintained by Sir Edwin Sandys   (See Journals, p 315)

[2] Compare Case of *Post-nati,* Vol VII p 671

Provinciæ, as they saw cause, but if they had any part they had presently the benefit of all. Lastly there were no reasons for naturalization, which might not as well extend to the Ante-nati as the Post-nati. Yet must it be granted that they are somewhat in better state than aliens, though not in so good as naturalized subjects [1]

For the law of nations and precedent of foreign estates, there were three principal observations to be made

First that in the whole course of the Roman story there was never any naturalized *ipso jure*, but all by charters of constitutions. Secondly there is a good avoidance of any precedent of naturalization in Spain, because the State having been there in times past entire under one King, afterwards divided into many kingdoms, and since under one King again, it is now no union, but a reunion or a remitter

       *   *   †   *

Here the first sheet of the manuscript ends, and the rest is missing. What we have appears, from the notes in the Journals, to be about half the report of the first day's conference, which ended (after some answers made by the Lords) with an adjournment to the next day, when the Judges were to give their opinion [2] Of the proceedings on that day Bacon continued his report on Monday, March 2, and of this also we have an account drawn up by Carleton, though the last leaves are again missing

Sir Francis Bacon's Report, this 2 of March, [3] of the Conference had with the Lords the week before, wherein is first contained the reasons of the lower house in point of law, in the question *whether the Scots born since the King came to the Crown be naturalized in England,* which they held *negative,* and the opinion of the Judges for the affirmative

First he used some preamble to shew that this was a matter of substance and not of discourse, and therefore would breed more attention but less delight. His duty was to report truly and nakedly *rem gestam,* and not add nor diminish, nor express

---

[1] This is the conclusion of Sir E Sandys' part. The next point was argued by Sir Roger Owen

[2] C J p 312

[3] Dom James I vol xxvi no 66. The word "March" is now worn away, but it was distinctly legible when I made my copy

anything with unequal advantage, wherefore he would add nothing of his own, but the order only

In point of law, the question was held affirmatively by the Judges, and negatively by the House. Wherein there were first *concessa* on both sides, as the House did yield there was a union made in the King's person, and the Judges that there was a distinction betwixt the two kingdoms in regard of the separation in the laws. Now whether the one of these do draw on or involve the other, that is *oculus quæstionis*.

For the negative the arguments were 9 but might be contracted judicially into a less distinction of matter of allegiance and matter of jurisdiction like the ten commandments, which were all comprised under two heads, of love of God and love of our neighbour

1. Several laws do draw in consequence several allegiances, which argument is drawn *ex notatione nominis*, because *lex* and *ligantia* come both *a ligando*

2 The second argument was taken out of the statute of aliens of 15° Ed 3, *de natis ultra maria*, which was interpreted out of the allegiance of the kingdom and crown

3 The Scots are not subject to the jurisdiction of our laws, and therefore they were not to enjoy the benefit of them because it is not fit that law should impart favours and rewards which cannot enjoin obedience

4. Every law hath his precinct and limit within which it is bounded, and therefore this law cannot naturalize men born in Scotland, where it hath no force

5 Where our laws can effect anything they must have a potential act, as by virtue of the great seal or otherwise, which hath no power in Scotland yet hath it power in Ireland, Garnsey, and Jarsey, which it doth hold potentially though not execute it actually.

6. There is no subordination of the crown of Scotland to the crown of England, but they stand as distinct and entire sovereignties; whereas Aquitaine, Anjou, and other places in France were subordinate to this crown, as appears by good records that a *corpus capias* or any writ under the great seal was of force amongst them, and they had access here for their complaints in Parliament, as to this day it appears by the recital of the names of those places; yet were not those of these countries

naturalized . *ergo, a fortiori*, the Scots, who remain still distinct souveranities cannot be

7 *Rex et Regnum* are relatives, and the subjects of a king are naturalized in that kingdom whereof he is king, and when our King here in England was King of France, lest that greater kingdom should take to itself any greater predominance over this, it was expressly declared by an Act here in Parliament that our King, as King of France, could effect nothing here in England, nor the French enjoy any part of the privileges of this country

8 No man can be subject to two allegiances, therefore if they ought allegiance there in respect of the crown of Scotland, they could owe none here in respect of the crown of England.

9 An inconvenience of the commixture of jurisdictions, and a confusion that would grow by the Scots having honours and offices here amongst us.

THE ANSWER OF MY LORDS THE JUDGES

First they endeavoured to cut off our auxiliary forces and *nudare latera*, which they did by a distinction that in particular cases of judgment between person and person there might be help of other sciences, but not in this where the question only was what was law.

A discourse was then made of the worth of our law, and that set out in three points

1 In the continuance · the law having been ever as a rock, and stood firm against all storms and against the change of all nations here in England, as against the Danes, the Saxons, the Romans, and Normans, and had there not been found some excellency in it, it would surely have been altered by some of them, as by the Romans who gave laws to all the world

2 In the price · because they were written in blood, as at the time when the Magna Charta was obtained of the King to be confirmed by Act of Parliament.

3 In the security because the Judge as long as his judgment was contained within the compass of law was excused, the subject knew by what law he was to govern himself and his actions, nothing was left to the Judge's discretion; and where it was required long since by a bill in Parliament to have somewhat left to the Judge to allow or dislike in a particular case

which should be made arbitrary by the said bill, it was rejected, and upon this reason, that men were better be subject to a known inconvenience than to an unknown discretion.

The answers to the arguments which concerned allegiance, and were all to be comprised in one objection, as one branch divided into many buds or leaves, were three in gross and three in particular.

1. Allegiance is more spacious than laws, and that both in extent of time and extent of place. For time three reasons 1 Allegiance was before laws 2 Continued after. 3 Was in force and virtue when laws were asleep 1 At the first Kings did *dare jura*, and after came laws, and therefore allegiance begat laws, and not laws allegiance. 2 Allow a King were expulsed his kingdom and some—

Here again we come to the end of the only sheet that has been preserved, and the rest of Bacon's report of the Judges' answer (concerning which little more can be gathered from the Journals than that it was long and learned) must be left to imagination which however is the less to be regretted because the whole question was, not long afterwards, solemnly argued before them all in their own court For the present, Bacon having at last finished his long report, "in conclusion prayed the House that at other times they would use some other, and not oppress him with their favours"[1]

8

They had now had their conference upon the point of law, and received their answer which left them in a difficulty For upon the question what the law *was*, though they might dispute, the Judges must decide It was now plain that the Judges would decide against them, and what more could they do? To do nothing, would be to leave all the *Postnati* in unconditional possession of the privileges to which, except upon conditions, they thought it dangerous to admit them To alter the law by an Act of Parliament would be the constitutional remedy but it would require the consent of the Lords and the King, which was more than they could expect To proceed to a conference on the 'conveniency' of naturalization, would seem to imply acquiescence in the decision on the point of law Long debates followed both in the House and in the Committee, and some fine fencing with the Upper House as to the terms on which the next conference should be held the Lords pressing for a conference "concerning naturalization in general," the Commons trying to commit them to an interpretation of the words which should imply not only that the discussion was to be confined to the question of "convenience and limitations," but that the cases of the *Antenati* and the *Postnati* were not to be treated as distinct [1] failing in which, they proceeded to instruct their own Committee to decline the discussion if such distinction were insisted on [2] And on these terms a conference was held on the 11th of March, at which nothing could be concluded because of that restriction [3]

Of this proceeding it is easier to understand the motive than the justification for the distinction which they insisted upon ignoring was, upon any view of it, wide and important The question was, under what 'limitations' it was 'convenient' that the Scotch should be admitted to the privileges of naturalization Now the Postnati *had*, and the Antenati had *not*, a claim by the common law to be admitted to those privileges without any limitation, and though the claim might be disputable, it was not one which the House of Commons had any authority to decide Whatever privileges therefore they bestowed upon the one, with whatever limitations accompanied, were a benefit and free gift whatever limitations they imposed upon the other, with whatever privileges accompanied, were a disfranchisement

Had they consented to recognize the *distinction* of the cases, they might have had much to say upon the inconveniences involved in the interpretation of the law upon which the distinction rested One consequence it certainly had which might on some other occasion have proved very mischievous, and against which it might have been judicious to provide them by legislation for if true in this, it would

[1] C J pp 345-349
[2] "And it is resolved by the Committee that if their Lps still urge a disjunction, not by law, which they seem to have wished, but by reason, that there shall be no reply unless they admit them in equal state"—Cott MSS Tit f ii p 55
[3] "It is well known unto you that the last meeting brought forth little fruit, in regard of the unexpected course which was observed in the proceeding as your unexpected reservation *to hear without any speech* took away the use and life of that intended conference "—Message from Lords to Commons, 27 March, 1607 Lords' Journals, p 495 The conference alluded to was held on the 11th of March, and opened by Sir Edwin Sandys, whose "conclusion," according to a note of his speech in the hand of Dudley Carleton, was to this effect "Not fit to grant perfect privileges of naturalisation unlimited to an imperfect union therefore by order from the House no yielding to a difference between the ante nati and post nati , not upon any jealousy of the LL's meaning, *but to give no assent to the reason of this difference expressed in the instrument* and therefore unless we might treat of them both together, we would humbly give their Lps audience, but no further proceed in conference " (Domestic, James I xxvi 85)

be true in all cases of union under the same crown without distinction   And if that had been the point at which they aimed, it does not seem probable that they would have met with any obstruction   But that was a remote and contingent evil, which (though used to reinforce other objections) was not, I think, the real motive of their opposition.   It was the second objection touched in Bacon's speech,—namely, that the Scotch not being subject to the English laws, it was unfair that they should be endowed with English privileges and liberties—which really stood in the way, and this objection was even stronger as against the Postnati, who in another generation would be all, than against the Antenati, who had only a life interest in the matter   When they found therefore that the authorized interpreters of the law considered the Postnati to be in actual possession of all the privileges belonging to naturalization, and that the Upper House was too wary to engage in a proceeding by which they might seem to commit themselves to an opposite opinion, they tried to get at their end another way   Many were in favour of some action to be taken by the Lower House for the purpose of invalidating or counteracting the Judges' opinion on the point of law   and for a few days after the abortive conference of the 11th of March, Salisbury was so apprehensive of some such issue, that (the Speaker being luckily unwell at the time) he contrived to prevent the formation of a House by advising him to be too ill to attend[1]   The delay, or the difficulty, or reflexion upon the many mischiefs which such a course might bring, gave an advantage to more prudent counsels, and another solution of the problem, which appears to have been already suggested by Sir Edwin Sandys, began to find favour.

The objection was good only as against an *imperfect* union   "The cause of this imperfectness" (said Sandys to the Lords at the last conference) was "in the Scottish nation, by inserting this clause into the body of their Act, that their fundamental laws or privileges should not be altered, and that therein they have expressed their meaning to be, to stand   free monarchy"

The desire of the Commons of England (he added) was for ' a per-

[1] "His M rightly noteth that to which indeed the House is most inwardly affected, which is to get some such definitive sentence passed in the House of the invalidity of the Judges' resolution, as may make them daint hereafter to judge the question, or make the judgment less acceptable" (Salisbury to Lake, 15 March)   'I may not hide it from you that in this point of the difference between the post nati and ante nati, there is great heat of spirit kindled to decide it by a question in the Lower House   whereof as long as I am doubtful,   my Lords (I mean such of us as wrote the letter to his M) have all thought the safer way to prevent all causes," etc , namely, by advising the Speaker to be still too ill to go   (Same to same, 18 March)   Domestic, James I. vol xxvi no 91.

feet union, which with consent of the Scottish nation might be effected, and by the direction and aid of their Lordships such an one might be set down as would be both honourable and profitable to both nations " [1]

Let the two nations, in short, be united under the same law, and the objection to naturalization would disappear

The suggestion (though to any one who had fairly considered the number and the nature of the questions that would have to be encountered it could not but appear equivalent to an indefinite postponement of the whole thing) had a fair sound and show, and the debates drew gradually nearer and nearer to this solution of the present difficulty, till at last, on the 28th of March, upon occasion of a new and pressing message from the Lords, inviting them to a free discussion "on the point of conveniency only, without reference to anything that had been said before, or that might be said, in point of law," it took the shape of a distinct motion   Upon which Bacon, —who, I need hardly say, had no part assigned him in the last abortive conference, and does not indeed appear to have taken any share in the discussions since his long report on the 2nd of March,— came forward to oppose it, in the following speech   of which some notes may be seen in the Journals (p 1031), but this copy is taken from his own report, preserved, and in part corrected, by himself

A Speech used by Sir Francis Bacon, Knight, in the Lower House of Parliament, by occasion of a Motion concerning the Union of Laws [2]

And it please you, (Mr Speaker,) were it now a time to wish as it is to advise, no man should be more forward or more earnest than myself in this wish, that his Majesty's subjects of England and Scotland were governed by one law   and that for many reasons.

First, because it will be an infallible assurance that there will never be any relapse in succeeding ages to a separation

Secondly, *Dulcis tractus pari jugo*. If the draught be most upon us, and the yoke lightest [3] upon them, it is not equal

Thirdly the qualities and (as I may term it) the elements of their laws and ours are such as do promise an excellent temperature in the compounded body; for if the prerogative here be

---

[1] Dom James I vol xxvi 85
[2] King's MSS 17 A, bis to 96 (K)   Harl MSS 6797, fo 128 (only one leaf) (H)   Ib p 195 (H 2)
[3] *lye least* K   Corrected in H

too indefinite, it may be the liberty there is too unbounded, if our laws and proceedings be too prolix and formal, it may be theirs are too informal and summary.

Fourthly, I do discern to my understanding, there will be no great difficulty in this work. For their laws, by that I can learn, compared with ours, are like their language compared with ours For as their language hath the same roots that ours hath, but hath a little more mixture of Latin and French; so their laws and customs have the like grounds that ours have, with a little more mixture of the civil law and French customs.

Lastly, the mean to this work seemeth to me no less excellent than the work itself for if both laws shall be united, it is of necessity for preparation and inducement thereunto, that our own laws be reviewed and re-compiled, than the which I think there cannot be a work that his Majesty can undertake in these his times of peace, more politic, more honourable, nor more beneficial to his subjects for all ages.

> Pace data terris, animum ad civilia vertit
> Jura suum, legesque tulit justissimus auctor

For this continual heaping up of laws without digesting them, maketh but a chaos and confusion, and turneth the laws many times to become but snares for the people, as was well said *Pluet super eos laqueos, non sunt autem*[1] *pejores laquei, quam laquei legum* And therefore this work I esteem to be indeed a work (rightly to term it) heroical[2] So that for this good wish of Union of Laws I do consent to the full, and I think you may perceive by that which I have said, that I come not in this[3] to the opinion of others, but that I was long ago settled in it myself. Nevertheless, as this is moved out of zeal, so I take it to be moved out of time, as commonly zealous motions are, while men are so fast carried on to the end, as they give no attention to the mean For if it be time to talk of this now, it is either because the business now in hand cannot proceed without it, or because in time and order this matter should be precedent, or because we shall leese some advantage towards this effect so much

---

[1] *as is said in the Scripture, Pluet, etc   Non, Non sunt, etc*   R
[2] *and that which if I mought live to see, I would not desire to live after*   K, H 2   These words have been drawn through them in H Bacon having felt, no doubt, in reading them over, that they went beyond the truth
[3] *this om* K, H 2   interlined in H

desired, if we should go on in the course we are about. But
none of these three in my judgment are true, and therefore the
motion, as I said, unseasonable.

For first, that there may not be a naturalization without an
union in laws, cannot be maintained. Look into the example of
the Church[1] and the union thereof. You shall see several
Churches that join in one faith, one baptism, which are the points
of spiritual naturalization, do many times in policy, constitutions,
and customs differ. And therefore one of the fathers made an
excellent observation upon the two mysteries, the one, that in
the gospel[2] the garment of Christ is said to have been without
seam; the other, that in the psalm[3] the garment of the Queen
is said to have been of divers colours, and concludeth,[4] *In veste
varietas sit, scissura non sit*[5] So in this case (Mr Speaker) we
are now in hand to make this monarchy of one piece, and not of
one colour. Look again into the example of foreign countries,
and take that next us of France, and there you shall find that
they have this distribution, *pars du droit escrit*, and *pars du droit
custumier* For Gascoigne, Languedock, Provence, Dolphinie,
are countries governed by the letter or text of the civil law but
the Isle of France, Tourayne, Berry, Anjou, and the rest, and
most of all Brittain and Normandy, are governed by customs,
which amount unto a municipal law, and use the civil law but
only for grounds, and to decide new and rare cases, and yet
nevertheless naturalization passeth through all.

Secondly, That this union of laws should precede the naturalization, or that it[6] should go on *pari passu*, hand in hand, I
suppose likewise can hardly be maintained: but the contrary,
that naturalization ought to precede, and that not in the pre-

---

[1] In K, H 2, and H, as originally written, this sentence went on thus: "And
there you shall see the original bonds to be one faith, one Baptism, and not one
policy, one custom: and so it is in the civil estate, the main bonds are one allegiance, one birthright or naturality, and not one law, or one administration of
law." The correction is in Bacon's hand, in the margin of H.

that in the Gospel, where R, a conjectural correction apparently, and clearly
wrong.

[3] *that in the psalm, where* R

[4] *whereupon he draweth this conclusion* K, H 2, corrected in H

[5] *allowing divers forms of ecclesiastical laws and usages, so as there be no
schism or separation* K, H 2, crossed out in H

[6] The rest of the corrected MS (H) is wanting. It will be observed that the
copy in the 'Resuscitatio' has been taken so far from H, as corrected; but that
it has a few variations, which appear to be due to the editor, and are wrong.
Where it differs therefore from K and H 2 in what follows, we are not entitled to
assume that it represents Bacon's own corrections.

cedence of an instant, but in distance of time. Of which my
opinion, as I could yield many reasons, so because all this is but
a digression, and therefore ought to be short, I will hold myself
now only to one, which is briefly and plainly this, that the
union of laws will ask a great time to be perfected, both for the
compiling and for the passing, during all which time if this
mark of strangers[1] should be denied to be taken away, I fear it
may induce such a habit of strangeness, as will rather be an impediment than a preparation to further proceeding. For he was
a wise man that said, *Opportunium magnis conatibus transitus rerum*,
and in these cases, *non progredi est regredi.* And like as in a
pair of tables, you must put out the former writing before you
can put in new, and again, that which you write in[2] you write
letter by letter, but that which you put out, you put out at
once: so we have now to deal with the tables of men's hearts
wherein it is in vain to think you can enter the willing acceptance of our laws and customs, except you first put forth all notes
either of hostility or foreign condition. And these are to be put
out *simul et semel*, at once, without gradations, whereas the
other points are to be imprinted and engraven distinctly and by
degrees.

Thirdly, whereas it is conceived by some that the communication of our benefits and privileges is a good hold that we have
over them to draw them to submit themselves to our laws, it is
an argument of some probability, but yet to be answered many
ways. For first, the intent is mistaken, which is not, as I conceive it, to draw them wholly to a subjection to our laws, but to
draw both nations to one uniformity of law. Again, to think
that there should be a kind of articulate and indented contract
that they should receive our laws to obtain our privileges, is[3] a
matter in reason of estate not to be expected, being that which
scarcely a private man will acknowledge, if it come to that
whereof Seneca speaketh, *Beneficium accipere est libertatem ven-
dere.* No, but courses of estate do describe and delineate another way, which is to win them either by benefit or by custom.
For we see in all creatures that men do feed them first, and reclaim them after. And so in the first institution of kingdoms,
kings did first win people by many benefits and protections,
before they pressed any yoke. And for custom, which the poet

[1] *strangeness* H 2   *write in new* H 2   [3] *it is* R

calls[1] *imponere morem*—who doubts but that the seat of the kingdom and the example of the king resting here with us, our[2] manners will quickly be there,[3] to make all things ready for our laws?

And lastly, the naturalization which is now propounded is qualified with such restrictions, as there will be enough kept back to be used at all times for an adamant of drawing them further on towards[4] our desires. And therefore to conclude, I hold this motion of Union of Laws very worthy, and arising from very good minds, but yet not proper for this time.[5]

To come therefore to that which is now in question. It is no more but whether there should be a difference made, in this privilege of naturalization, between the *Ante-nati* and the *Post-nati*, not in point of law, (for that will otherwise be decided) but only in point of convenience, [as if a law were now to be made *de novo*][6] In which question I will at this time only answer two objections, and use two arguments, and so leave it to your judgment.

The first objection hath been, that if a difference should be, it ought to be in favour of the *Ante-nati*, because they are persons of merit, service, and proof, whereas the *Post-nati* are infants that (as the Scripture saith) know not the right hand from the left.

This were good reason (Mr Speaker) if the question were of naturalizing some particular persons by a private bill, but it hath no proportion with the general case. For now we are not to look to respects that are proper to some, but to those which are common to all. Now then how can it be imagined, but that those which[7] took their first breath since this happy union inherent in his Majesty's person, must be more assured and affec-

---

[1] *ports call* R　　　[2] *that our* K　　　[3] *theirs* H 2　　　[4] *to* R

[5] The copy of this speech which was printed in 1641 (along with the argument in the case of the *Post-nati* and the speech on General Naturalization), ends here: and so does the MS which I call K. It is a small 4to paper book, containing all the three speeches, very fairly transcribed. The two first have been carefully read over by Bacon himself, as appears by corrections here and there, very neatly inserted, certainly by his own hand. But there are none in the last, which seems to have been left incomplete.

[6] So R H 2 has, " whether there should be a difference made between the *ante-nati* and the *post-nati* in point of law, but only in point of convenience, as if a law were newly to be framed." If the rest of H should ever turn up, I should expect to find an interlineal correction here in Bacon's hand, agreeing with the text.

[7] *that* R

z 2

tionate to this kingdom, than those generally can be presumed to be which were sometimes strangers? for *Nemo subito fingitur* the conversions of minds are not so swift as the conversions of times. Nay in effects of grace, which exceed far the effects of nature, we see St Paul makes a difference between those he calls Neophytes, that is newly grafted into Christianity, and those that are brought up in the faith. And so we see by the laws of the Church that the children of Christians shall be baptized, in regard of the faith of their parents but the child of an ethnic may not receive[1] baptism till he be able to make an understanding profession of his faith.

Another objection hath been made, that we ought to be more provident and reserved to restrain the *Post-nati* than the *Ante-nati*, because during his Majesty's time, being a prince of so approved wisdom and judgment, we need no better caution than the confidence we may repose in him; but in the future reigns of succeeding ages, our caution must be in *re* and not in *persona*

But (Mr Speaker) to this I answer, that as we cannot expect a prince hereafter less like to err in respect of his judgment, so again, we cannot expect a prince so like to exceed (if I may so term it) in this point of beneficence to that nation, in respect of the occasion. For whereas all princes and all men are won either by merit or conversation, there is no appearance, that any of his Majesty's descendants can have either of these causes of bounty towards that nation in so ample degree as his Majesty hath. And these be the two objections which seemed[2] to me most material, why the *Post-nati* should be concluded in the same restrictions or greater with the *Ante-nati*,[3] whereunto you have heard the answers.

The two reasons which I will use on the other side, are briefly these the one being a reason of common sense, the other, a reason of estate

We see (Mr Speaker) the time of the nativity is in most cases principally regarded. In nature, the time of planting and setting is chiefly observed. And we see the astrologers pretend

[1] *have* H 2   [2] *seem* H 2
[3] So in H 2   R has "why the Post nati should be *left free and not* be concluded in the same restrictions with the *Ante-nati*" Which I take to be a conjectural correction made by some one who had mistaken the tenour of the argument The "objection" was *against* the naturalization of the *Post nati* therefore in favour of their being concluded in the same *restrictions* with the *Ante nati*, who were certainly *not* naturalized

to judge of the fortune of the party by the time of the nativity
In laws, we may not unfitly apply the case of legitimation to the
case of naturalization.   For it is true that the canon [1] law doth
put the *ante-natus* and the *post-natus* in one degree   But when
it was moved to the Parliament of England, *Barones una voce
responderunt, Nolumus leges Angliæ mutare*   And though it
must be confessed that the *ante-nati* and *post-nati* are in the
same degree in dignities, yet were they never so in abilities
For no man doubts, but the son of an Earl or Baron, born [2] before
his creation or call, shall inherit the dignity, as well as the son
born after.   But the son of an attainted person, born before the
attainder, shall not inherit, as the after-born shall, notwithstanding charter of pardon.

The reason of estate is, that any restriction of the *Ante-nati* is
temporary, and expireth with this generation, but if you make
it in the *Post-nati* also,[3] you do but in substance pen a perpe-
tuity of separation

Mr Speaker, in this point I have been short, because I little
expected this doubt as to point of convenience, and therefore
will not much labour, where I suppose there is no greater opposition.

This was spoken on Saturday the 28th of March, on which day
the House separated once more without coming to any conclusion,
and on Monday, while they were still in dispute upon the answer
they should send to the proposal of Conference, for which the Lords
were still waiting, they were informed that the King desired to
speak to the House the next day, upon which further proceeding
was of course suspended

The next Sunday was Easter Day, and the King being well informed as to the tenour of the debates both in the Houses and the
Committees, thought it expedient, before they separated for the
usual recess, to review the state of the question, to explain once
more his own views and wishes, and to answer the objections that
had been urged on the other side   His speech is given at full length
in the Commons' Journals, and though long is well worth reading, if
it were only that we may understand why the men of his own time
formed so different an estimate of his character and abilities from that

[1] *comon law* H 2, *common canon law* R   Bacon had probably made the
correction, and forgotten to strike out "common"   The canon law made no difference, but England had refused to adopt the canon law.
[2] *born* om H 2, R
[3] *if you make the Post-nati in all one degree* H 2

which is now popular   His audience, looking forward into an uncertain future peopled with the phantoms of danger which the English imagination is so quick in inventing, would be much less disposed to assent to his conclusions than we are who know by experience that those dangers were not substantial   But no man of judgment could have listened to that speech without great respect both for the ability and the temper of the speaker, and I think no man can read it now without feeling that wherever he was at variance with the popular judgment of his own time, it was by being in advance of it   It may be well doubted indeed whether it is ever prudent in a King to come forward as a disputant in a matter which must be decided by votes   but the very disposition to put it upon the issue of reason and fair argument was in evidence of simplicity and humanity and could not but give a favourable impression of the personal character of the man

His object, of course, was to persuade them to pass at once an Act of general naturalization by way of preparation for the more perfect union which he hoped would follow in due season   and the adjournment of Parliament for three weeks immediately after, gave time for the speech to make its impression   But though it was well received and though there was a general desire on all sides to avoid anything which would discontent the King, the dislike which was felt to the proposition itself could not be got over so   It was not the Crown they were jealous of, but their fellow-subjects   When they met again they took the business up where they had left it, and opinion still ran so strongly in favour of a union of laws as an indispensable preliminary to a general naturalization,[1] that it was found impracticable to proceed further with the measure   Once more the King tried the effect of a speech[2] to remove misunderstandings, but it was not so well considered as the last, and having too much of complaint and remonstrance in it, it touched the feelings of the House in the tender place, provoked remonstrance in return,[3] and led again to further explanations[4]   And upon these terms the project was allowed for the present to drop

9

But though naturalization, so far as the House of Commons could forbid it, was indefinitely postponed, laws made for a state of hostility between the two kingdoms might be repealed, and there being now no hope of good from further Conferences, a bill was next

[1] C J Ap 28, 29, 30, May 1   [2] Ib May 2   [3] Ib May 6, 7
[4] Ib June 2

brought in "for the continuance and preservation of the blessed
union of the Realms of England and Scotland, and for the abolishing
and taking away of all hostile laws, statutes, and customs that might
tend to disturb or hinder the same" the handling of which bill in
the Committee to which it was referred on the second reading, (as
described at the time by Sir Thomas Wilson for the information I
suppose of Salisbury),—will give the best idea of the difficulties
which any large measure would have had to encounter in the Lower
House, and sufficiently explain why no more could be attempted in
the present session

8 May

There hath been such ado this afternoon at the Committee, that it was
never more truly verified that which heretofore was alleged in the like
case—*Tua non volentis est in sept spina, um*

The first difficulty arose about taking the chair   Mr Solicitor and Sir
Fr Bacon being nominated were reclaimed by the populars, it being
secretly alleged amongst them that their hands were in penning the bill
and by those therefore Mr Fuller was named   yet in some doubtfulness
of the voices of the callers out of either side, Sir Fr B took the chair

The next question was whether they should begin with the title or the
bill itself   it being alleged that it were to make a monster of it to make
the body before the face and therefore the title to be first agreed upon
before the bill were framed, but that was wittily answered by Mr Martin,
that then the maker of the world and of all things therein made none
but monsters, who made things first and then brought them to Adam to
be named   It was further answered by Mr Attorney, that in ancient
times bills and laws were made without titles, whereof he alleged precedents, so it was fain to be decided by a question, with whether they
should begin, and by cunning mistaking of the question the title was first
dealt withal

Then fell they to mincing every word both in the title and the preamble

The first exception was to the words "continuance and preservation of
the Union," which they said seemed to presuppose an union already made,
to which they would not in any wise assent, no not to any naming of the
Union at all in the title   So, after much debating the title was propounded
to be thus,—' An Act for the abolishing of all hostile laws betwixt England and Scotland" Some would have the word 'all' taken out, and
'certain' or 'sundry' put in   But that was answered would imply that
there were some remaining yet untaken away   which would not do well
and so at last it was concluded that those words 'all,' certain,' 'sundry,'
etc should all be left out, and so much of the title pass as before, and so
it was set down

The next exception was to the word 'Customs,' it being alleged that the
custom was in the borders in regard of hostility between England and

Scotland, to the end they might be the better peopled, that every man's land and goods should be equally divided amongst his children, which custom if it should be taken away, it would alter the whole state of in heritance, and many other inconveniences. So it was agreed that the word 'Customs' should be left out or deferred till after the bill were formed, and then to be used or left as occasion should be found requisite. And it might be the better left out because it was not named in the Bill but only in the title, as was alleged by Sir R. Owen.

Then was there a bone cast in about *Escuage*, that hostile laws being taken away, whether that should not be thought of; but that was offered only by my L. Treasurer's man Mr. Bowyer for others to take hold of, but neither he nor any other apprehended it or prosecuted it.

Thus much and much more passed about the title, and so they went to the preamble.

The first that spoke to that was Sir Roger Owen, who said that the first line of the preamble was to follow the course of the title; for if there the words 'preservation of the Union' were to be left out, then the like was to be done here, and instead of 'preservation' he would have a word put in (near unto it in sound) that should be 'preparation.'

For the words 'establishment of the Union' they would have 'furtherance and advancement' put in.

And instead of that long preamble some would have only these words used—'that for the good and weal of both kingdoms be it enacted, etc.

It seemed they thought the word 'Union' a spirit, for they shunned the very shadow and the name of it until Mr. Attorney, seconded by Sir Francis Bacon, showed them that in two former acts the words 'of union made and kingdoms united' that were propounded now, had been used, and therefore if we should now refuse the name we should seem to go backward in our affection, which we cannot do without disreputation. So with much contestation pro and con, they made at last a contraction of the fair and well composed large preamble into these few words, viz.

The words of the preamble as now it is set down—

"For the honour, weal, and good of these two mighty famous and ancient kingdoms, and for the furtherance of the happy Union already begun in his Ma^{ts} royal person, be it enacted," etc.

And this Sir Francis Bacon had much ado to get assented unto, and it went so hard that it was fain to be decided by voices, and the question being first made, that all that liked it should pass thus should say, Yea, the Noes (being the fewer) carried the lesser sound; and so it is set down as before.

Then went they to the body of the Bill, the first being the passage out of England into Scotland, wherein there was such debate that it was fain to be left to the House till to-morrow. Sir Mau. Barklay upon this point offered a new bill for the taking away of all the laws of restraint in Rich. 2 his time, as was agreed at the Conference about that matter, but it was not accepted of to be read there until it had been first offered to the House.

Divers other matters passed which time serves not now to report, but it will be fitter and better to-morrow after the report in the House of this afternoon's work [1]

It was not till the 30th of June that this Bill was finally passed by both Houses several questions having been raised which led to much dispute,—especially concerning the provision to be made for the trial of offenders on either side of the border but though Bacon had a good deal to do with them both as reporter and actor in the subsequent proceedings,[2] I do not find any record of the part he took personally on the points disputed I shall only add therefore that the act was settled at last to the general satisfaction of both houses, and took its place in the Statute-book—the principal fruit of the long session

10

The esteem in which Bacon was held as a reporter of other men's speeches is so well established by the continual demands upon him for that service, and yet his perfection in the art is so poorly represented in the notes which remain, and of which for want of better I have been obliged to give so many specimens,—that a really good report of one of these performances at full length is worth studying and with one such this session supplies us

On the 17th of June, we read in the Commons' Journals, that

"Sir Francis Bacon maketh report of the Conference with the Lords on Monday last, as well touching the doubts and questions of the Bill for the abolition of all memory of hostility, etc as the petition of the merchants for redress of Spanish wrongs, etc

"Wherein, by the way, he said that divers precedents were produced, proving that upon the petition of the Commons such wrongs had been redressed

"That it was conceived and uttered by the Lords, that if the Commons were at any time made acquainted with such causes, it was with one of these two purposes that either they should make some declaration of their affections, or else minister aid of money, the sinews of war "[1]

This is all, and upon comparing it with the original notes (p 1053) nothing more can be extracted that is intelligible The occasion however was important enough to induce Bacon himself to set down and preserve among his own writings a full report of what he said and we are thus enabled to form some conjecture of the relation which the notes of such speeches bear to the speeches themselves

[1] Domestic, James I vol xxvi no 17   - May 28, June 1, 11 12, 15
[1] C J p 381

The importance of the matter, as a thing worth placing on record, lay in this It represented the attitude taken by the Government upon a motion proceeding from the House of Commons and relating to negotiations with foreign powers a motion symptomatic of a change in the constitution, which to a thoughtful observer, being at once a member of Parliament and a servant of the Crown, must have been very interesting That the Commons as they found their strength, should advance their pretensions, was inevitable , but the mode, the direction. the extent, and the spirit, in which those pretensions should be asserted, would depend upon the entertainment of the first approaches The particular case though likely to rouse popular passion to the height—for the offenders were Spaniards, and the offence complained of was injustice and cruelty of the most atrocious kind—was not one upon which the people were at all it variance with the Government Since the treaty with Spain was concluded Spanish officers had not only stopped and searched English merchant ships on suspicion of containing contraband goods , but had in some cases conducted the inquisition after the example of their own higher powers, by help of torture Remonstrances had been made by the Government, and civil answers had been received , but two years had passed, or thereabouts, without bringing any redress Now in the time of Henry V , on an occasion more or less analogous, a statute had been passed authorizing the issue of ' letters of Marque" to the parties aggrieved on the strength of which they might make reprisals and the merchants now resolved to petition Parliament that they might have ' letters of mart granted them, to the value of their loss," under the authority of that statute

Their petition was addressed "to the King s most excellent Majesty, the Lords Spiritual and Temporal, and the rest of this honourable Court," and being laid before the House of Commons, was referred to a Committee, (28 Feb 1606-7) upon whose report (13 May), a message was sent to the Lords ' for a conference touching joining in petition to his Majesty for redress of Spanish wrongs,' and ' expressing the desire of the House to that purpose ''[1] On the 15th of June the Lords proposed that the conference should take place the same afternoon, with the Committee already appointed to confer on the bill for abolition of hostile laws , which was agreed to and the result was reported to the House by Bacon on the 17th in the following speech,—as set down by himself

[1] 16 May, 1607 C J p 371

A Report made by Sir Francis Bacon, Knight, in the House of Commons, in Parliament, of a Speech delivered by the Earl of Salisbury and another Speech delivered by the Earl of Northampton, at a Conference concerning the Petition of the Merchants upon the Spanish Grievances. Parliament 5° Jacobi[1]

And it please you (Mr Speaker,) I do not find myself any ways bound to report that which passed at the last conference touching the Spanish grievances having been neither employed to speak nor appointed to report in that cause But because it is put upon me by a silent expectation, grounded upon nothing (that I know) more than that I was observed diligently to take notes, I am content (if that provision that I made for mine own remembrance may serve this house for a report) not to deny you that sheaf that I have in haste bound up It is true, that one of his Majesty's principal counsellors in causes of estate did use a speech that contained a world of matter, but how I shall be able to make a globe of that world therein I fear mine own strength

His Lordship took the occasion of this which I shall now report, upon the answer which was by us made to the amendments propounded upon the bill of hostile laws, quitting that business with these few words, that he would discharge our expectation of reply, because their Lordships had no warrant to dispute Then continuing his speech he fell into this other cause, and said, that being now to make answer to a proposition of ours, as we had done to one of theirs, he wished it could be passed over with like brevity But he did foresee his way, that it would prove not only long, but likewise hard to find, and hard to keep, this cause being so to be carried, as above all no wrong be done to the King's sovereignty and authority, and in second place no misunderstanding do ensue between the two houses And therefore that he hoped his words should receive a benign interpretation, knowing well that pursuit and drift of speech, and multitude of matter, might breed words to pass from him beyond the compass of his intention, and therefore he placed more assurance and caution in the innocency of his own

[1] Hal MSS 6797, fo 162, a copy corrected by Bacon himself

meaning, and in the experience of our favours, than in any his wariness or watchfulness over his own speech.

This respective preface used, his Lordship descended to the matter itself, which he divided into three considerations : for he said he would consider of the petition,

> First as it proceeded from the merchants
>
> Secondly as from them it was offered to the lower house
>
> And thirdly as from the lower house it was recommended to the higher house

In the first of these considerations, there fell out naturally a subdivision into the persons of the petitioners, and the matter and parts of the petition   In the persons of the merchants his Lordship made (as I have collected them) in number eight observations, whereof the three first respected the general condition of merchants; and the five following were applied to the particular circumstances of the merchants now complaining

His Lordship's first general observation was, that merchants were of two sorts, the one sought their fortunes (as the verse saith), *per saxa, per ignes*, and, as it is said in the same place, *extremos currit Mercator ad Indos*, subjecting themselves to weather and tempest, to absence and as it were exile out of their native countries, to arrests in entrances of war, to foreign injustice and rigour in times of peace, and many other sufferances and adventures, but that there were others that took a more safe but a less generous course in raising their fortunes.   He taxed none, but did attribute much more respect to the former.

The second general observation which his Lordship made was, that the complaints of merchants were usually subject to much error, in regard that they spake (for the most part) but upon information, and that carried through many hands, and of matters done in remote parts   so as a false or factious factor mought oftentimes make great tragedies upon no great ground Whereof towards the end of his speech he brought an instance, of one trading the Levant[1], that complained of an arrest of his ship, and possessed the counsel-table with the same complaint in a vehement and bitter fashion; desiring and pressing some present expostulatory letters touching the same.   Whereupon some counsellors, well acquainted with the like heats and forwardness

---

[1] So MS

in complaints, happened to say to him, out of conjecture and not out of any intelligence, *What will you say if your ship, which you complain to be under arrest, be now under sail in way homewards?* Which fell out accordingly the same person confessing six days after to the Lords, that she was indeed in her way homewards

The third general observation which his Lordship made was this in effect, that although he granted that the wealth and welfare of the merchant was not without a sympathy with the general stock and state of a nation, especially an island, yet nevertheless it was a thing too familiar with the merchant to make the case of his particular profit the public case of the kingdom

There follow the particular observations, which have a reference and application to the merchants that trade to Spain and the Levant Wherein his Lordship did first honourably and tenderly acknowledge, that their grievances were great, that they did multiply, and that they do deserve compassion and help, but yet nevertheless that he must use that loving plainness to them as to tell them that in many things they were authors of their own miseries For since the dissolving of the company which was termed the Monopoly, and was set free by the special instance of this house, there hath followed such a confusion and relaxation in order and government amongst them, as they do not only incur many inconveniences, and commit many errors, but in the pursuit of their own remedies and suits they do it so impoliticly and after such a fashion, as, except leger ambassadors (which are the eyes of kings in foreign parts) should leave their centinel, and become merchants' factors and solicitors, their causes can hardly prosper And, which is more, such is now the confusion in the trade, as shop-keepers and handy-craftsmen become merchants there, who being bound to no orders, seek base means by gifts and bribery to procure favours at the hands of officers there so as the honest merchant, that trades like a substantial merchant and loves not to take servile courses to buy the right due to him by the amity of the princes, can have no justice without treading in his[1] steps.

Secondly, his Lordship did observe some improbability that

---

[1] So MS   a slip of the pen, or rather of the memory He forgot that he had left the shopkeeper merchants in the plural

the wrongs should be so great, considering trading into those parts was never greater, whereas if the wrongs and griefs were so intolerable and continual as they propound them and voice them, it would work rather a general discouragement and coldness of trade in fact, than an earnest and hot complaint in words.

Thirdly, his Lordship did observe, that it is a course (howsoever it may be with a good intent), yet of no small presumption, for merchants upon their particular grievances to urge things tending to a direct war, considering that nothing is more usual in treaties, than that such particular damages and molestations of subjects are left to a form of justice to be righted, and that the more high articles do retain nevertheless their vigour inviolably, and that the great bargain of the kingdom for war and peace may in no wise depend upon such petty forfeitures, no more than in common assurance between man and man it were fit that upon every breach of covenants there should be limited a re-entry.

Fourthly, his Lordship did observe, in the manner of preferring their petition they had inverted due order, addressing themselves to the foot and not to the head. For considering that they prayed no new law for their relief, and that it concerned matter of inducement to war or peace they ought to have begun with his Majesty, unto whose royal judgment, power, and office did properly belong the discerning of that which was desired, the putting in act of that which mought be granted, and the thanks for that which mought be obtained.

Fifthly, his Lordship did observe, that as they had not preferred their petition as it should be, so they had not pursued their own direction as it was. For having directed their petition to the King, the Lords spiritual and temporal, and the Commons in Parliament assembled, it imported as if they had offered the like petition to the Lords, which they never did contrary not only to their own direction, but likewise to our conceit, who pre-supposed (as it should seem by some speech that passed from us at a former conference) that they had offered several petitions of like tenour to both houses. So have you now those eight observations, part general, part special, which his Lordship made touching the persons of those which exhibited the petition, and the circumstances of the same

For the matter of the petition itself, his Lordship made this division, that it consisteth of three parts

First of the complaints of the wrongs in fact

Secondly of the complaint of the wrongs in law, as they may be truly termed, that is of the inequality of laws which do regulate the trade   And

Thirdly, the remedy desired by letters of mart

The wrongs in fact receive a local distribution of three in the trade to Spain, in the trade to the West Indies, and in the trade to the Levant

Concerning the trade to Spain, although his Lordship did use much signification of compassion of the injuries which the merchants received, and attributed so much to their profession and estate, as from such a mouth in such a presence they ought to receive for a great deal of honour and comfort, (which kind of demonstration he did interlace throughout his whole speech, as proceeding *ex abundantia cordis*) yet nevertheless he did remember four excusations, or rather extenuations of these wrongs

The first was, that the injustices complained of were not in the highest degree, because they were delays and hard proceedings, and not unjust sentences, or definitive condemnations Wherein I called to mind what I had heard a great Bishop say, that Courts of Justice, though they did not turn justice into wormwood by corruption, yet they turned it into vinegar, by delays which soured it   Such a difference did his Lordship make, which no question is a difference *secundum magis*[1] *et minus*.

Secondly, his Lordship ascribed these delays, not so much to malice or alienation of mind towards us as to the nature of the people and nation, which is proud and therefore dilatory (for all proud men are full of delays and must be waited on), and specially to the multitudes and diversities of tribunals and places of justice, and the number of the king's councils, full of referrings which ever prove of necessity to be deferrings, besides the great distance of territories   All which have made the delays of Spain to come into a by-word through the world   wherein I think his Lordship mought allude to the proverb of Italy, *Mi venga la morte di Spagna*, let my death come from Spain, for then it is sure to be long a coming

Thirdly, his Lordship did use an extenuation of these wrongs,

[1] So MS

drawn from the nature of man, (*nemo subito fingitur*), for that we must make an account, that though the fire of enmity be out between Spain and us, yet it vapoureth the utter extincting whereof must be the work of time.

But lastly, his Lordship did fall upon that extenuation which of all the rest was most forcible, which was, that many of these wrongs were not sustained without some aspersion of the merchants' own fault in ministering the occasion , which grew chiefly in this manner

There is contained an article in the treaty between Spain and us, that we shall not transport any native commodities of the Low Countries into Spain, nay more, that we shall not transport any *opificia*, manufactures of the same countries   So that if an English cloth take but a dye in the Low Countries, it may not be transported by the English   And the reason is, because even those manufactures, although the material come from other places, do yield unto them a profit and sustentation, in regard their people are set on work by them. They have a gain likewise in the price, and they have a custom in the transporting   All which the policy of Spain is to debar them of , being no less desirous to suffocate the trade of the Low Countries, than to reduce their obedience[1]   This article the English merchant either doth not or will not understand   but being drawn with this threefold cord of love hate and gain, they do adventure to transport the Low Country commodities of these natures, and so draw upon themselves those arrests and troubles

For the trade to the Indies, his Lordship did discover unto us the state of it to be thus   The policy of Spain doth keep that treasury of theirs under such lock and key, as both confederates, yea and subjects, are excluded of trade into those countries, insomuch as the French king, who hath reason to stand upon equal terms with Spain, yet nevertheless is by express capitulation debarred   The subjects of Portugal, whom the state of Spain hath studied by all means to content, are likewise debarred , such a vigilant dragon is there that keepeth this golden fleece   Yet nevertheless such was his Majesty's magnanimity in the debate and conclusion of the last treaty, as he would never condescend to any article, importing the exclusion of his

---

[1] So corrected in the MS in Bacon's hand   The clause originally stood thus " is being no less directed to suffocate their trade than to subdue their territories '

subjects from that trade as a prince that would not acknowledge that any such right could grow to the crown of Spain by the donative of the Pope, whose authority he disclaimeth, or by the title of a dispersed and punctual occupation of certain territories in the name of the rest; but stood firm to reserve that point in full question to further times and occasions So as it is left by the treaty in suspense, neither debarred nor permitted. The tenderness and point of honour whereof was such, as they that went thither must run their own peril Nay further his Lordship affirmed, that if yet at this time his Majesty would descend to a course of intreaty for the release of the arrests in those parts, and so confess an exclusion, and quit the point of honour, his Majesty mought have them forthwith released And yet his Lordship added, that the offences and scandals of some had made this point worse than it was, in regard that this very last voyage to Virginia, intended for trade and plantation where the Spaniard hath no people nor possession, is already become infamed for piracy Witness Bingley, who first insinuating his purpose to be an actor in that worthy action of enlarging trades and plantation, is become a pirate, and hath been so pursued as his ship is taken in Ireland, though his person is not yet in hold

For the trade to the Levant, his Lordship opened unto us that the complaint consisted in effect but of two particulars the one touching the arrest of a ship called the *Trial*, in Sicily, the other of a ship called the *Vineyard*, in Sardinia The first of which arrests was upon pretence of piracy, the second, upon pretence of carrying ordnance and powder to the Turk That process concerning the *Trial* had been at the merchants' instance drawn to a review in Spain, which is a favour of exceeding rare precedent, being directly against the liberties and privileges of Sicilia. That of the *Vineyard*, notwithstanding it be of that nature, as (if it should be true) tendeth to the great dishonour of our nation, whereof hold hath been already taken by the French ambassador residing at Constantinople, who entered into a scandalous expostulation with his Majesty's ambassadors there, upon that and the like transportations of munition to the Turk, yet nevertheless there is an answer given by letters from the king's ambassador leger in Spain, that there shall be some course taken to give reasonable contentment in that cause, as far as may be in both which ships, to speak truly the greatest mass of loss may be included, for the rest are mean, in respect of the value of those two vessels And thus much his Lordship's speech comprehended concerning the wrongs in fact

Concerning the wrongs in law, that is to say, the rigour of the Spanish laws extended upon his Majesty's subjects that traffic thither, his Lordship gave this answer that they were no new statutes or edicts devised for our people or our times; but were the ancient laws of that kingdom *suus cuique mos* and there fore as travellers must endure the extremities of the climate and temper of the air where they travel, so merchants must bear with the extremities of the laws and temper of the estate where they trade Whereunto his Lordship added, that even our own laws here in England were not exempted from the like complaints in foreign parts, especially in point of marine causes and depredations, and that same swift alteration of property, which is claimed by the Admiralty in case of goods taken in pirates' hands But yet that we were to understand thus much of the king of Spain's care and regard of our nation, that he had written his letters to all corregidors, officers of ports, and other his ministers, declaring his will and pleasure to have his Majesty's subjects used with all freedom and favour, and with this addition, that they should have moe favours, where it might be shewed, than any other Which words, howsoever the effects prove, are not suddenly to be requited with peremptory reso lutions, till time declare the direct issue

For the third part of the matter of the petition, which was the remedy sought by letters of Mart, his Lordship seemed desirous to make us capable of the inconvenience of that which was de- sired, by setting before us two notable exceptions thereunto the one, that the remedy was utterly incompetent and vain, the other, that it was dangerous and pernicious to our merchants, and in consequence to the whole state

For the weakness of the remedy, his Lordship wished us to enter into consideration what the remedy was which the statute of Henry the fifth (which was now sought to be put in execution) gave in this case which was thus, That the party grieved should first complain to the keeper of the privy seal, and from him should take letters unto the party that had committed the spoil, for restitution, and in default of restitution to be made upon such letters served then to obtain of the Chancellor letters of

Mart or reprisal Which circuit of remedy promised nothing
but endless and fruitless delay, in regard that the first degree
prescribed was never likely to be effected it being so wild a
chase, as to serve process upon the wrong doer in foreign parts.
Wherefore his Lordship said that it must be the remedy of state,
and not the remedy of statute, that must do good in this case,
which useth to proceed by certificates, attestations, and other
means of information; not depending upon a privy seal to be
served upon the party, whom haply they must seek out in the
West Indies

For the danger of the remedy, his Lordship directed our considerations to take notice of the proportions of the merchants'
goods in either kingdom as that the stock of goods of the
Spaniard which is within his Majesty's power and distress, is a
trifle, whereas the stock of English goods in Spain is a mass of
mighty value So as if this course of letters of Mart should be
taken to satisfy a few hot pursuitors here, all the goods of the
English subjects in Spain shall be exposed to seizure and arrest,
and we have little or nothing in our hands on this side to mend
ourselves upon And thus much (Mr. Speaker) is that which
I have collected out of that excellent speech, concerning the first
main part, which was, *the consideration of the petition as it proceeded from the merchants*

There followeth the second part, considering *the petition as
it was offered in this house* Wherein his Lordship, after an
affectionate commemoration of the gravity, capacity, and duty,
which he generally found in the proceedings of this house, desired us nevertheless to consider with him, how it was possible
that the entertaining of petitions concerning private injuries, and
of this nature, could avoid these three inconveniences the first,
of injustice, the second, of derogation from his Majesty's supreme and absolute power of concluding war or peace, and the
third, of some prejudice in reason of estate

For injustice, it is plain, and cannot be denied, that we hear
but the one part whereas the rule, *Audi alteram partem*, is not
of the formality, but of the essence of justice, which is therefore figured with both eyes shut, and both ears open, because
she should hear both sides, and respect neither. So that if we
should hap to give a right judgment, it mought be *justum*, but
not *juste*, without hearing both parties

2 A 2

For the point of derogation, his Lordship said he knew well we were no less ready to acknowledge than himself, that the crown of England was ever invested, amongst other prerogatives not disputable, of an absolute determination and power of concluding and making war and peace · which that it was no new dotation but of an ancient foundation in the crown, he would recite unto us a number of precedents in the reigns of several kings, and chiefly of those kings which come nearest his Majesty's own worthiness wherein he said that he would not put his credit upon cyphers and dates, because it was easy to mistake the year of a reign, or number of a roll, but he would avouch them in substance to be perfect and true, as they are taken out of the records By which precedents it will appear, that petitions made in parliament to kings of this realm his Majesty's progenitors, intermeddling with matter of war or peace, or inducement thereunto, received small allowance or success; but were always put off with dilatory answers; sometimes referring the matter to their counsel, sometimes to their letters, sometimes to their further pleasure and advice, and such other forms; expressing plainly that the kings meant to reserve matter of that nature entirely to their own power and pleasure

In the eighteenth year of King Edward the first, complaint was made by the Commons, against the subjects of the Earl of Flanders, with petition of redress The King's answer was, *Rex nil aliud potest, quam eodem modo petere* that is, that the King could do no more but make request to the Earl of Flanders, as request had been made to him , and yet nobody will imagine but King Edward the first was potent enough to have had his reason of a Count of Flanders by a war , and yet his answer was, *nihil aliud potest* , as giving them to understand that the entering into a war was a matter transcendent, that must not depend upon such controversies

In the fourteenth year of King Edward the third, the Commons petitioned, that the King would enter into certain covenants and capitulations with the duke of Brabant , in which petition there was also inserted somewhat touching a money matter The king's answer was, that for that that concerned the money, they mought handle it and examine it, but touching the peace he would do as to himself seemed good

In the eighteenth year of King Edward the third, the Com

mons petitioned that they might have the trial and proceeding with
certain merchants strangers as enemies to the state   The King's
answer was, It should remain as it did till the King had taken
further order.

In the forty-fifth year of King Edward the third the Commons
complained that their trade with the Easterlings was not upon
equal terms, (which is one of the points insisted upon in the present petition,) and prayed an alteration and reducement   The
King's answer was, It shall so be as occasion shall require.

In the fiftieth year of the same King, the Commons petitioned
to the King for remedy against the subjects of Spain, as they
now do   The King's answer was, that he would write his letter
for remedy   Here is letters of request, no letters of mart
Nihil potest nisi eodem modo petere

In the same year, the merchants of York petitioned in parliament against the Hollanders, and desired their ships mought be
stayed both in England and at Calais   The King's answer was,
let it be declared to the King's Counsel, and they shall have
such remedy as is according to reason

In the second year of King Richard II the merchants of the
sea-coast did complain of divers spoils upon their ships and
goods by the Spaniard.   The King's answer was, that with the
advice of his counsel he would procure remedy.

His Lordship cited two other precedents, the one in the second
year of King Henry IV of a petition against the merchants of
Genoua; the other, in the eleventh year of King Henry VI of a
petition against the merchants of the Still-yard, which I omit,
because they contain no variety of answer

His Lordship further cited two precedents concerning other
points of prerogative, which are likewise flowers of the crown,
the one, touching the King's supremacy ecclesiastical, the other
touching the order of weights and measures.   The former of
them was in the time of King Richard II at what time the Commons complained against certain encroachments and usurpations
of the Pope, and the King's answer was, the King hath given
order to his Counsel to treat with the bishops thereof   The other
was in the eighteenth year of King Edward the first, at which
time complaint was made against uneven weights. and the
king's answer was, *Vocentur partes ad placita regis, et fiat
justitia*, whereby it appeared that the Kings of this realm still

used to refer causes petitioned in parliament to the proper places of cognizance and decision   But for matter of war and peace, as appears in all the former precedents, the Kings ever kept it *in scrinio pectoris*, in the shrines of their own breast, assisted and advised by their Counsel of estate   inasmuch as his Lordship did conclude his enumeration of precedents with a notable precedent in the seventeenth year of King Richard II a prince of no such glory nor strength, and yet when he made offer to the Commons in Parliament that they should take into their considerations matter of war and peace then in hand, the Commons in modesty excused themselves, and answered, the Commons will not presume to treat of so high a charge   Out of all which precedents his Lordship made this inference, that as *dies diem docet*, so by these examples wise men will be admonished to forbear those petitions to princes, which are not likely to have either a welcome hearing, or an effectual answer.

And for prejudice that might come of handling and debating matter of war and peace in parliament, he doubted not but that the wisdom of this house did conceive upon what secret considerations and motives that point did depend   For that there is no King which will providently and maturely enter into a war, but will first balance his own forces   seek to anticipate confederacies and alliances, revoke his merchants, find an opportunity of the first breach, and many other points, which, if they once do but take wind, will prove vain and frustrate   And therefore that this matter, which is *arcanum imperii*, one of the highest, must be suffered to be kept within the veil, his Lordship adding, that he knew not well whether in that which he had already said out of an extreme desire to give us satisfaction, he had not communicated more particulars than perhaps was requisite   Nevertheless he confessed that sometimes parliaments had been made acquainted with matter of war and peace in a generality, but it was upon one of these two motives, when the King and Counsel conceived that either it was material to have some declaration of the zeal and affection of the people, or else when the King needed to demand moneys and aids for the charge of the wars   Wherein if things did sort to war, we were sure enough to hear of it   his Lordship hoping that his Majesty should find in us no less readiness to support it than to persuade it

Now (Mr. Speaker) for the last part, wherein his Lordship

considered the petition *as it was recommended from us to the upper house*, his Lordship delivered thus much from their Lordships, that they would make a good construction of our desires, as those which they conceived did rather spring out of a feeling of the King's strength and out of a feeling of the subjects' wrongs, nay more out of a wisdom and depth to declare our forwardness, if need were, to assist his Majesty's future resolutions (which declaration might be of good use for his Majesty's service, when it should be blown abroad), rather, I say, than that we did in any sort determine by this our[1] overture, to do that wrong to his highness' supreme power, which haply might be inferred by those that were rather apt to make evil than good illations of our proceedings   And yet that their Lordships, for the reasons before made, must plainly tell us, that they neither could nor would concur with us, nor approve the course; and therefore concluded that it would not be amiss for us, for our better contentment, to behold the conditions of the last peace with Spain, which were of a strange nature to him that duly observes them, no forces recalled out of the Low Countries, no new forces (as to voluntaries) restrained to go thither   so as the King may be in peace, and never a subject in England but may be in war   and then to think thus with ourselves, that that King, which would give no ground in making his peace, will not lose any ground upon just provocation to enter into an honourable war   And then in the mean time we should know thus much, that there could not be more forcible negociation on the King's part, but blows, to procure remedy of these wrongs; nor more fair promises of the king of Spain's part, to give contentment concerning the same, and therefore that the event must be expected

And thus (Mr Speaker) have I passed over the speech of this worthy Lord, whose speeches, as I have often said, in regard of his place and judgment, are extraordinary lights to this house, and have both the properties of light, that is, conducting and comforting   And although (Mr Speaker) a man would have thought nothing had been left to be said, yet I shall now give you account of another speech, full of excellent matter and ornaments, and without iteration.   Which nevertheless I shall report more compendiously, because I will not offer the speech

[1] The MS has *then*   But *they* has been corrected into *we* in the line before, and *then* into *our*, three lines further on

that wrong as to report it at large, when your minds percase and attentions are already wearied

The other Earl, who usually doth bear a principal part upon all important occasions, used a speech, first of preface, then of argument   In his preface he did deliver, that he was persuaded that both houses did differ rather in credulity and belief, than in intention and desire   for it mought be their Lordships did not believe the information so far, but yet desired the reformation as much

His Lordship said further, that the merchant was a state and degree of persons, not only to be respected, but to be prayed for, and graced them with these additions, that they were the convoys of our supplies, the vents of our abundance, Neptune's almsmen, and fortune's adventurers   His Lordship proceeded and said, this question was new to us, but ancient to them, assuring us that the King did not bear in vain the device of the Thistle, with the word, *Nemo me lacessit impune* , and that as the multiplying of his kingdoms maketh him feel his own power, so the multiplying of our loves and affections made him to feel our griefs.

For the arguments or reasons, they were five in number, which his Lordship used for satisfying us why their Lordships mought not concur with us in this petition   The first was the composition of our house, which he took in the first foundation thereof to be merely *democratical,* consisting of knights of shires and burgesses of towns, and intended to be of those that have their residence, vocation, and employment in the places for which they serve   and therefore to have a private and local wisdom according to that compass, and so not fit to examine or determine secrets of estate, which depend upon such variety of circumstances ; and therefore added to the precedent formerly vouched, of the seventeenth of King Richard 2d when the Commons disclaimed to intermeddle in matter of war and peace, that their answer was that they would not presume to treat of so high and variable a matter   And although his Lordship acknowledged that there be divers gentlemen in the mixture of our house, that are of good capacity and insight in matters of estate, yet that was the accident of the person, and not the intention of the place, and things were to be taken in the institution   not in the practice

His Lordship's second reason was, that both by philosophy and civil law, *ordinatio belli et pacis est absoluti imperii,* a prin

cipal flower of the crown   Which flowers ought to be so dear
unto us, as we ought if need were to water them with our blood
For if those flowers should by neglect, or upon facility and good
affection, wither and fall, the garland would not be worth the
wearing

His Lordship's third reason was, that kings did so love to
imitate *primum mobile*, as that they do not like to move in borrowed motions   so that in those things that they do most willingly intend, yet they endure not to be prevented by request
Whereof he did allege a notable example in King Edward 3d,
who would not hearken to the petition of his Commons, that besought him to make the black prince prince of Wales . but yet
after that repulse of their petition, out of his own mere motion
he created him.

His Lordship's fourth reason was, that it mought be some
scandal to step between the King and his own virtue, and that
it was the duty of subjects rather to take honours from kings'
servants and give them to kings, than to take honours from kings
and give them to their servants   which he did very elegantly set
forth in the example of Joab, who, lying at the siege of Rabbah,
and finding it could not hold out, writ to David to come and
take the honour of taking the town

His Lordship's last reason was, that it may cast some aspersion upon his Majesty, implying as if the King slept out the
the sobs of his subjects, until he was awaked with the thunderbolt of a parliament

But his Lordship's conclusion was very noble, which was with
a protestation, that what civil threats, contestation, art, and argument can do, hath been used already to procure remedy in this
cause and a promise that if reason of state did permit, as their
Lordships were ready to spend their breath in the persuading of
that we desire, so they would be ready to spend their bloods in
the execution thereof

This is the substance of that which passed

This report appears to have been received without any remark,
nor was anything more heard of the matter during the remainder of
the session which closed on the 4th of July, and in which little
else passed that retains any interest for us,—nothing in which
Bacon was a conspicuous actor

For his own personal fortunes, the most important event of the session was his promotion at last to the Solicitorship, which took place silently on the 25th of June   Croke, who was King's serjeant, was made a Puisne Judge of the King's Bench.   Doderidge became King's Serjeant in his place, and Bacon succeeded as Solicitor,—an office which he reckoned to be worth £1000 a year[1]

[1] Commentarius Solutus, vol ii p 86

CHAPTER IX.

A.D. 1607.   ÆTAT 47

1.

It was probably about this time that Bacon finally settled the plan of his "Great Instauration," and began to call it by that name   In 1605, he had (as I have already mentioned) digested the subject in his head into two parts   1st, the art of experimenting, that is of following an investigation with intelligence from one experiment to another—which is in fact the art that Science has been practising ever since, and by means of which she has achieved all her successes; and 2dly, the art of what he called "Interpretation of Nature," which was to furnish the key of the cipher, and in revealing the secret of all natural operations to give command of all natural forces

This last, as he came to look into it more closely, he proposed to distribute into three books   the first to prepare the way for the reception of the new method by removing the impediments which he anticipated in the state of opinion and the errors of the mind ; the second, to expound the method itself ; the third, to exhibit the results of the method applied [1]

Further consideration (with reference however not merely to the exposition of the argument, but also to the better preservation of his own various philosophical writings) led him to enlarge the plan still further   A review of the existing stock of human knowledge,—of which the Advancement of Learning was a sketch, and the *Descriptio Globi Intellectualis*[2] was meant, I think, for the beginning,—was to form the first part   The second was to include a complete exposition of the new method or *organum*, together with all the preliminary matter designed to prepare the way for it   The third

---

[1] Temporis Partus Masculus   sive de Interpretatione Naturæ, libri 3
   1 Perpolitio et applicatio mentis
   2 Lumen Natura, seu formula Interpretationis
   3 Natura illuminata, sive Veritas Rerum
[2] See Philosoph. Works, Vol III p 713

was appropriated to the collection of natural and experimental history, —*Phenomena Universi*,—the observed and ascertained facts of nature, upon which the new method was to work   A fourth was to exhibit examples of the application of the new method in certain selected subjects,—examples of a true induction carried through all its processes, from the observation of the facts to the discovery of the "form"   A fifth was to contain certain provisional speculations, suggested by the way, on subjects to which, for want of completer knowledge, the true method could not yet be applied   The sixth and last was to set forth the new philosophy itself,—the book of Nature laid open and explained,—*Natura illuminata, sive Veritas Rerum*

How much of this he expected to execute or see executed, it would be vain to conjecture   But though the accomplishment of the last part seemed to him, even in his most sanguine moods, remote beyond all definite anticipation,—a thing reserved for " the fortune of the human race" to achieve in some future century,[1]—there is no doubt that (given workmen enough and time enough) he believed the whole to be practicable by human means, and himself to be capable of making a beginning which would lead in due course to the accomplishment of the whole   The difficulty was to find the workmen, the first step towards which was to find hearers and believers   And upon this point the taste he had taken of men's opinions during the last year or two appears to have given him some new light   It had shown him that besides the "fallacies or false appearances" enumerated in the Advancement of Learning—illusions inseparable from our mental condition, and afterwards distinguished as Idols of the Tribe, the Cave, and the Market-place—there was another class of idols to be dealt with, which, though not inherent in the constitution of the mind itself, nor inseparable from the condition of man's life, were nevertheless extant and potent in fact, and stood more obstinately in the way   These were the received systems, in the belief of which men had been brought up, the doctrines taught in the schools, the *orthodoxies*, in short, of philosophy   To clear the way for the reception of his own views, it was requisite in the first place to shake men's faith in these   and it was at this time that the "*pars destruens*" was designated for the foremost place in the great argument, and the *redargutio philosophiarum* (afterwards called the caution against the Idols of the Theatre) for the foremost place in the

---

[1] " Hanc vero postremam partem perficere et ad exitum perducere, res est et supra vires et ultra spes nostras collocat   Nos ei initia (ut speramus) non contemnenda, exitum generi humani fortuna dabit, qualem forte homines in hoc rerum et animorum statu haud facile animo capere aut metiri queant " Works, I p 144

pars destruens.[1] Of this he made two or three different sketches, in different forms and styles, experiments, I think, as to the most effective manner of treating the subject; the dates and even the order of which we have no means of ascertaining with precision. But there is one which I am inclined to regard as representing at once the earliest and the latest form in which this part of the argument was set forth, the form in which, as being most natural to him, he probably began, and in which for the same reason, after making trial of the others, he certainly rested although the copy in which it has been preserved may be very different from the first draft, which would naturally be altered and enlarged in successive revisions This however is only a guess What we know is, that some time before February, 1607-8, he had shown to Sir Thomas Bodley a treatise entitled *Cogitata et Visa*, containing (according to Sir Thomas) "many rare and noble speculations," and "abounding with choice conceits of the present state of learning and worthy contemplations of the means to procure it," the general purport of which was to "condemn our present knowledge of doubts and uncertitudes," to recommend the "disclaiming of all our axioms and maxims, and general assertions, that are left by tradition from our elders unto us," "and lastly to devise, being now become again as it were *abecedarii*, by the frequent spelling of particulars to come to the notice of the true generals, and so afresh to create new principles of sciences," and "a knowledge more excellent than now is among us"—(I quote Bodley's own expressions, though not the aptest that might be devised)—and that among the pieces published by Gruter in 1653, there is one entitled *Cogitata et Visa de Interpretatione Naturæ, sive de Inventione Rerum et Operum*, consisting of a series of meditations upon the various causes which had hindered man in acquiring the command of nature, among which the incompetency of the received systems of philosophy and the received methods of demonstration and enquiry, hold a prominent place —a treatise to which all Bodley's remarks apply well enough, as far as they go

The letter which contains them, and which was printed in the 'Remains' (1618), is dated February 19, 1607, that is 1607-8; and helps to date the following letter from Bacon to Bodley, which being evidently written before he had heard from him, and at the beginning of a vacation, must be referred either to July or December, 1607 It does not much matter which, for the inference on either supposition must be that the *Cogitata et Visa* represents sub-

---

[1] "Itaque primus imponitur labor, ut omnis ista militia theoriarum, quæ tantas dedit pugnas, mutatur ac relegetur " —Philos Works, III p 518

stantially the state of his philosophical enterprise in the summer of
that year, and the part of the task upon which he was then at work
I say substantially because the allusion to "the lodgings chalked
up, whereof I speak in my preface," implies either that the treatise
was not then exactly in the shape in which it has been preserved,—
for it has no preface nor is there anything in it about the chalked
lodgings,—or that it had been accompanied with other papers on the
same subject. which indeed seems very probable and that one of
them was the *Partis Instaurationis Secundæ Delineatio et Argu-
mentum*, in which (as printed by Gruter) such a passage does occur [1]

A Letter to Sir Tho Bodley, after he had imparted
       to Sir Tho   a writing entituled Cogitata et Visa [2]

Sir,

In respect of my going down to my house in the country, I
shall have miss of my papers, which I pray you therefore to return unto me. You are, I bear you witness, slothful, and you help
me nothing; so as I am half in conceit that you affect not the
argument, for myself I know well you love and affect I can say
no more to you, but *non canimus surdis, respondent omnia sylvæ*
If you be not of the lodgings chalked up (whereof I speak in my
preface) I am but to pass by your door   But if I had you but a
fortnight at Gorhambury, I would make you tell me another
tale, or else I would add a Cogitation against Libraries, and be
revenged on you that way.   I pray send me some good news of
Sir Thomas Smith, and commend me very kindly to him   So
I rest

Bodley might help Bacon with supply of books, but, for ideas,
it must have been manifest from the moment his answer came that
no light could be looked for from that quarter, not even the
light which is given by intelligent opposition   Nothing can be
weaker or more confused than his reasons for dissent, unless it be
his apprehension of the question at issue

[1] "Atque quod Borgia facete de Caroli octavi expeditione in Galliam dixit,
Gallos venisse in manibus cretam tenentes qua diversoria notarent, non arma
quibus perrumperent, similem quoque inventorum nostrorum et rationem et suc-
cessum nobis præcipimus, nimirum ut potius animos hominum capaces et idoneos
seponere et subire possint quam contra sentientibus molestæ sint."—Works, III
p 558
[2] Add MSS 5503, f 32 b

2

Bacon had the more leisure for the prosecution of these studies at this time, because Salisbury, though he had consented at last to help him to the Solicitorship, showed no disposition to use him (as he would no doubt have been very willing to be used) in higher matters than those immediately belonging to his office It might have been supposed that as his services in the House of Commons had been found so valuable to the government, his advice and assistance in all measures which were likely to come under discussion in the House of Commons would have been sought and prized But whether it was that Salisbury preferred the service of men who could not be suspected of being more than servants; or that he knew Bacon's modes of proceeding (and his ends, perhaps, likewise) to be different from his own, or that he feared to admit such an eye too near the secrets of his purposes and policy (for he was at this time privately receiving an annual pension from the King of Spain)[1]—certain it is that no traces of confidential consultation on matters of general policy are to be found among the papers of either,—no memorials or letters of advice addressed by Bacon to Salisbury, like those " Considerations touching the Queen's service in Ireland" which he volunteered in 1601; but only a few letters and drafts on matters falling directly within the duty of the Solicitor-General

Among these however there are two drafts of Proclamations, which though not included in Bacon's own collection, or otherwise acknowledged as compositions of his own, have marks of his hand upon them, sufficient, I think, to entitle them to a place here They are preserved among the State Papers now at the Rolls House, where, if they were drafts submitted to Salisbury for consideration, they would naturally be They are both written in the hand of a scribe known to have been in Bacon's employment about this time [2] both are corrected here and there, and both are docketed, in his own hand, and one of them is largely corrected in the hand of Salisbury The presumption therefore is that the papers in their original form were of Bacon's own composition Whether of his own suggestion also, or drawn up by direction of the government, it is not possible to say

The first bears upon a question of considerable interest in the history of the struggle between the Royal Prerogative and the

[1] Gardiner ii p 356
[2] Compare them with the manuscript of the "Filum Labyrinthi "—Harl MSS 6797, f 139

Courts of Law,—the question as to the Jurisdiction of the Provincial Council in Wales , of which an account will be found in Mr Heath's preface to Bacon's legal arguments on the " Jurisdiction of the Marches "[1] It will be best introduced here by two other papers, both of which are referred to by Mr Heath in connexion with it— one, as " bearing evident marks of having been of Bacon's drawing or settling," the other " as substantially embodying Bacon's advice to his clients and to Salisbury " both of which therefore may be thought to have a title to insertion, even independently of their connexion with the draft Proclamation,—of which the title is less disputable.

That Bacon was engaged in the dispute professionally both before and after, and also that it was one of the subjects which he had under consideration with a view to offer advice upon it as upon a question of state, we have positive evidence   And though it was probably as counsel for one of the parties interested that he drew up these memorials, I see no reason to doubt that they represent his own personal opinion upon the merits of the controversy.   At all events they represent very clearly the grounds upon which the government proceeded in a matter which became important afterwards, as bearing upon the relation between the Crown and the Commons at a time when Bac 's advice was more in request, as well as the view then taken of the constitutional relation between Prerogative and Law —a view which, whether judged right or wrong now, was certainly believed by Bacon to be the sound constitutional view , and ought to be always recognized and remembered as underlying all his opinions and proceedings in matters affecting it

They are both very fair transcripts, without any corrections, and though they bear no date, either on face or back, the allusions which they both contain to Sir Edward Coke, under the title of " Mr Attorney," may be taken as evidence that they were not drawn up later than June 1606, when he was promoted to the Bench.[2]

A VIEW OF THE DIFFERENCES IN QUESTION BETWIXT THE KING'S BENCH AND THE COUNCIL IN THE MARCHES [3]

A poor widow sued one Farlie for a copyhold which she

[1] Literary and Professional Works, ii pp 569-585
[2] Between them is inserted another paper in a different hand, with the following heading —
"Upon divers conferences had between his M Attorney General on the one part, and Sir John Crook one of the King's Serjeants, and Sir Francis Bacon, Knight, of his M Counsel Learned on the other part, concerning the matters in question between the King's Bench and the L President and Counsel of the Marches, in some points they have agreed and in some they differ, as followeth "
[3] Domestic, James I x 86

claimed by the custom of a manor; and upon judicial hearing before the Lord President and Council in the Marches, Farlie being ordered to suffer her to have possession till the Court of that manor (where the customs were known) had tried their right, was for contempts and breach of that order committed to prison. Thereupon he complained to the King's Bench and thence got a writ to remove his body and cause. This writ (for that none of that nature had ever taken place at the Council) was not obeyed. But the Lord President, considering the inconvenience that might grow by contentions of Courts, and that it properly belonged to the wisdom of his Majesty, as a point of government and not of law, to compose such differences as may fall out, even by the honest and dutiful care of his ministers to improve the reputation and authority of their places, referred the whole cause to the judgment of the state.

The King in his princely and tender care of unity and justice, first commanded the Judges to proceed no further till his pleasure were known, and then in person vouchsafed to hear the reasons of both parts: and finding no just exception (as it seemed) against the Lord President's proceedings, only referred to his Council the examination of particulars for reconciling and maintaining both Courts in their rights.

To this purpose when their Lordships gave hearing, it was not denied by the reverend Judges that the order of the Council in the Marches, whereupon this question grew, was just, nor that their instructions gave them warrant for it. besides it was granted that the Council there was an absolute Court, and to be controlled by none save the high Court of Parliament, for matters within the jurisdiction thereof.

Thus their former grounds being left, a new and collateral exception was taken by them to justify their writ, namely that the four shires of Salop, Hereford, Worcester, and Gloucester, were not contained in the Act of Parliament by which that Council was established; and howsoever they were expressed in the Commissions of our Kings, yet the legal Prerogative by law did not extend so far as to erect a Court of Equity for trial of suits, and therefore the causes of those shires must return to Westminster and the course of Common Law. Upon this assumption, though contrary (for aught appeareth) to the King's commandment and without formal judgment or other order from the Lords, the King's Bench (upon reasons to them known) thought good to proceed. And first they awarded one writ to the Sheriff of Shropshire to attach the Porter that had Farlie in ward, and another writ of assistance for raising the Country to fetch him out by force. And though Farlie were delivered before, yet such was the rigour of the Sheriff, that the Porter was arrested even in the place of his public service, to more disgrace of that Court, and not only brought to London, there imprisoned and fined, but also prosecuted with an action of wrongful imprisonment to his great affliction and charge. Secondly they also imprisoned the Counsellor at law that followed the widow's cause. Thirdly, they sent more writs to remove other prisoners, and a multitude of prohibitions to stop all the suits for these shires in that Court. And hereupon it came to pass (though doubtless against the purpose of those honourable persons) that without any crime or justifiable complaint, and at the suit of one clamorous person, the Lord President of Wales, a Peer of the Realm and Counsellor of Estate, was publicly disgraced, the Court of the Marches, being the King's Council, was brought in contempt, and his Majesty's Prerogative (the chief jewel of his Crown) was laid open to more exception than in former times it had been.

And this being the plain and true progress of this business, it may be considered, first whether Farlie were a worthy Sampson to shake at once so many pillars of this state: then whether the exemption of the shires was not brought in question only for supply to maintain the writ, seeing it was confessed at the first engagement, that point was not known: and lastly whether it will not be a great derogation both to the King and Council to have the sovereignty of his government either cried down with the strong voice of law, or referred to Parliament and there made subject to popular dispute.

But seeing these questions (which both parties in their zeal and duty to his Majesty and the public peace wish had never been moved) are now by mischance proceeded in so far, it will be necessary to examine more at large the material grounds and proofs which are in dispute.

And these are three:

1   The power of the King.

2   The authority of the Law.

3. The reason of both

For the King's power it is alleged: that the Council of the Marches had a royal foundation, and was first established by Edward the 4th to govern by his instructions and commission both the counties of Wales and the shires adjoining, and that it hath continued King after King to this present day, as by divers records and infinite precedents testifying the continued practice thereof, and by nothing to the contrary that can be produced, shall hereafter appear

To this answer is made First in general, that the Prerogatives of our Kings are only given them by law, and then in particular, that by the law they have no power to establish a Court of equity, and therefore neither the Council-board of right can decide any matter between party and party, neither any other Court or Council that hath not a proper establishment by law

But it is replied, first to the general, that the King holdeth not his prerogatives of this kind mediately from the law, but immediately from God, as he holdeth his Crown, and though other prerogatives by which he claimeth any matter of revenue, or other right pleadable in his ordinary courts of Justice, may be there disputed, yet his sovereign power, which no Judge can censure, is not of that nature, and therefore whatsoever partaketh or dependeth thereon, being matter of government and not of law, must be left to his managing by his Council of State And that this is necessary to the end of all government, which is preservation of the public, may in this particular appear. For no doubt but these grave and worthy ministers of justice have in all this proceeding no respect but their oaths and the duties of their places, as they have often and deeply protested, and in truth it belongeth not to them to look any higher, because they have charge but of particular rights But the State, whose proper duty and eye is to the general good, and in that regard to the balancing of all degrees[1]   will happily consider this point above law That Monarchies in name do often degenerate into Aristocraties or rather Oligarchies in nature by two insensible degrees The first is when prerogatives are made envious or subject to the constructions of laws, the second

[1] Two or three words worn away in MS

2 B 2

when law as an oracle is affixed to place   For by the one the King is made accomptable and brought under the law , and by the other the law is over-ruled and inspired by the Judge , and by both all tenures of favour, privy Counsel, nobility and personal dependances (the mysteries that keep up states in the person of the Prince) are quite abolished, and magistracy enabled to stand by itself   The states of Venice and Poland might be examples hereof   And the *Maires du Palais* in France, by making the Law great and themselves masters thereof, supplanted the whole line of their ancienst[1] Kings   And what greater strength had the League there of late than the exorbitant greatness of the Parliament of Paris ?   And from hence also in the time of Henry the 3rd, our Parliament challenged power to elect and depose the Lord Chancellor, Treasurer, and Chief Justice of England, as officers of the State and not of the King   Whether then these popular titles of limiting prerogatives for subjects' birthrights and laws may not unawares, without any design or thought of the authors, open a gap unto new Barons' wars, or other alteration and inconvenience in government, the wisdom of the state is best able to discern   And therefore all I conclude is this, that the ordering of these matters doth belong thereunto.   Yet God forbid (as one said) that we should be governed by men's discretions and not by the law   *For certainly a King that governs not thereby can neither be comptable to God for his administration, nor have a happy and established reign* [2]

But God forbid also upon pretence of liberties or laws government should have any head but the King   For then as the Popes of Rome, by making their seat the only oracle of God's religion, advanced themselves first above religion and then above God, so we may fear what may in time become of our laws, when these reverend fathers, in whose breasts they are safe, shall leave them to others perchance of more ambition and less faith.   But because I assure myself that no soul living will charge his Majesty with any manner of encroachment upon the subjects' rights, I confess I marvel, and some perchance may doubt, why we should be so curious to wrest that right from his hand which all his progenitors have enjoyed heretofore.

Again to the particular of his power to establish Courts of equity it is further said   That by the ordinance of God it pro-

[1] So MS   This is an extract from King James's "True law of free monarchies"

perly belongeth to a King *To administer justice and judgment to his people, and to be a hiding place from the wind and a refuge from the tempest, to open his mouth for the dumb   To judge righteously the poor and afflicted, and to establish his throne with mercy   To provide among the people men of courage and truth, and appoint them rulers over thousands, over hundreds, over fifties, and over tens; that they may judge the people at all seasons in their smaller matters, and reserve their greatest causes to be heard by himself*   And our own law giveth no less power to our Kings, for as Bracton saith *Rex habet ordinariam potestatem et omnia jura in manu sua*.   And their practice in all times doth confirm as much   For King Alfred first divided the land into shires and provincial law days.   William the Conqueror brought in the Exchequer, and kept the Chancery and Common Pleas at his Court.   Henry the 3rd settled the Common Pleas at Westminster.   Edward the 3rd erected the Admiralty and Duchy   Edward the 4th the Councils of Star chamber and the Marches   Henry the 8th set up the Courts of Requests, of Wards and Liveries, and the Council at York.   And though some of these were since approved by Statute Law, yet the author and life giver of them all was the prerogative of our Kings, which must of necessity be impeached in all, if denied in any.

Besides we say that in the King's prerogative there is a double power   One which is delegate to his ordinary judges in Chancery or Common Law, another which is inherent in his own person, whereby he is the supreme judge both in Parliament and all other Courts; and hath power to stay suits at the common law, yea *pro bono publico* to temper, change, and control the same   as Edward the 3ᵈ did when for increase of traffic he granted juries to strangers *de medietate linguæ*, against the common law.   Nay our acts of Parliament by his sole authority may be mitigated or suspended upon causes to him known   And this inherent power of his, and what participateth thereof, is therefore exempt from controlment by any Court of Law   For saith Britton lib 1 *We will that our jurisdiction be above all jurisdictions in our realm   so as we have power to give or cause judgments to be given as shall seem to us good, without other form of process, where we may know the true right as judge*   Now this free jurisdiction the King exerciseth by his Councils, which are not delegations of power, but assistances thereof inherent in himself

Esay 32
1, 2, 3

Prov xxxi
8, xx 28

Exod
xviii 21

Varner's
case Sᵣ
Ed Coke
in Mr
Darcio's
case

And upon this ground the Council Table judgeth matters in equity when they are referred unto them. And the same sufficient warrant have these Councils in the Marches and the North for all their proceedings, though they had no other law. For that this is also a Council of Estate, and not a bare Court of Law, may appear, First by the style thereof both in the instructions and statute itself. Secondly by the institution, which was to assist the Prince of Wales as well in matters of government as law · Thirdly, by their oath, which is the same with the oath of a Councillor of State. Fourthly, by their authority to make proclamations. and fifthly by the attendance of their Pursuivants and Sergeant at Arms. So by all this it may appear both that this Council was duly established by the King's prerogative, if it had no other right, and that therefore it ought to be subject to no controlment but his.

And thus much for the first point.

The point of law.

For the law it is alleged that this Council of the Marches is not only built upon the firm rock of the Prerogative Royal, but also confirmed and strengthened by an Act of Parliament made in 34 Hen. 8.

But they answer that this act establisheth a President and Council, only in the dominion and Principality of Wales, and the Marches of the same. And that these four shires are not intended to be Marches of Wales, they prove by former statutes, writs, and records, whereof some term those the Marches of Wales where the King's writs do not run, and others call certain Lordships Marchers by that name, and these shires the Counties adjoining to the marches of Wales.

But to these inferences rather than our[1] authorities we say. First that these statutes which shew there were outward Marches where the writs do not run, do rather affirm than deny that there were inward marches where the writs do run. Secondly, we deny not that there were Lordships Marchers, nor that some statutes are restrained to them; but that these counties wherein many of them lay, not as parts but contents, should not also be the Marches of Wales, though not subject to those disorders which the Statutes repress, is not concluded thereby, considering that in all lands not only places but whole provinces adjoining are called Marches, and thereof Marquesses, as here the Earls of March, that is *limitis Walliæ Comites*, have had their honours and names   Thirdly, where these shires are called the shires adjoining to the Marches of Wales, it proveth indeed that those outward marches at that time were in a peculiar manner called by that name, as hereafter shall be shewed, yet that these English shires should not then in a more large denomination be also called Marches belonging to the King, as the other to private Lords, doth not follow thereupon.   But to clear this point we must [search] [1] a little into the differences of times

Our stories agree that the river of Severn was the ancient bound of Wales, and then all beyond it of Herefordshire, Shropshire, Worcestershire and Gloucestershire being the body of Wales, the rest on this side must be the marches thereof   And this is also confirmed by three ancient charters of the Town of Hereford, wherein it is called *Herefordia in Wallia*   So Ludlow is called a chief city in Wales   Shrewsbury the chief seat of the Princes of Wales   Gloucester and Worcester joining upon Wales   And we have records to shew of orders from Henry the 3d at several times for the fortifying of Shrewsbury, Hereford, Bridgnorth, and Worcester, as special frontiers against the Welsh.   For after that William Rufus and Henry the first had driven the Welshmen into narrower room, specially after the conquest of Wales by Edward the first, and his new division thereof into shires, these countries beyond Severn also were no more called Wales, but the Marches thereof   And even from that time, for the better union of the Welsh, these shires may seem to have been joined to the government of Wales.   For there is a commission extant of 6 Ed I for the hearing and determining of causes in Wales and the Marches thereof, wherein by name the sheriffs of Hereford and Salop are appointed to attend for juries   And so all this while no doubt but these shires were called the Marches of Wales   But when the continual rebellions of the Welsh had caused our Kings to erect certain signories or martial colonies to keep them in awe, and to that end had endowed them with many regalities and exempt jurisdiction, then in process

Marginal notes:
Camden

Walliæ nomen universam quondam transabrinam regionem complectebatur
Camden
1 Rich 1
17 Joh
11 Hen 3

Polidor
Camden
Wigorniens

Comitatus Salopiensis limitanea regio
Camden

[1] This word worn away in the MS

of time, because the English shires under their protection lived long in peace, and because they had carried their own frontiers and the war beyond these shires up into Wales, and because they lived like marchers continually in arms, therefore were they called *terra guerra in Wallia*, and in a peculiar manner the Marches of Wales   And these shires then began in statutes and records to be named the English shires adjoining to the Marches of Wales, not that they ceased to be marches, but to distinguish them as belonging to the King, and of another nature from the foresaid marches of proprietary Lords.   For that all this while they still retained the name and reputation of the King's Marches we have many records of sundry times to witness

First, inquisitions of the manor of Caldecot 10 Ed. 3, said to be in Gloucestershire in the Marches of Wales: and of the castle of Goodridge 16 Ed 3, said to be in Herefordshire, in the Marches of Wales   Then patents of land for the said Goodrich, and the great manor of Urchenfield, 1 Ed. 4, and for the manor of Kilpeck, 5 Ed 4 all *in Comitatu Hereford in Marchia Wallie*   Also patents of Escheatorships of 4 Hen. 6 for Gloucestershire, Herefordshire, and Shropshire, all entitled *in Marchia Wallie*   And that the government of these shires was also continued with the government of Wales, may appear by a patent of Lieutenancy granted 11 Hen. 4 to Henry Prince of Wales, the words whereof are these   *Constituimus ipsum primogenitum nostrum locum tenentem in partibus South-wallie et Northwallie, ac Marchiis regni nostri Angliæ eisdem partibus adjacentibus*   and these marches must needs be the English shires, both because the Lordships Marchers are nowhere also called the Marches of England, and also for that the King's eldest son in no probability could have a narrower scope, specially being sent *tam ad rebelles partium et marchiarum prædictarum guerrandum quam pro regimine et gubernatione earundem juxta sanam discretionem suam*, etc   But Ed. 4 for aught appeareth was the first establisher of that form of [government[1]] which continueth to this day, when he sent Edward Prince of Wales, and under him the Earl Rivers his uncle, the first Lord President (as I suppose) and a select Council, as well to govern as to minister justice in Wales and the marches thereof   And that the marches [thereof[2]] comprehended the four shires may

[1] om MS   [2] A word worn off in MS

be gathered, first because the ordinary residence both of the said Lord Rivers and the Bishop of Worcester his successor was in Shrewsbury, but more clearly by the continuance of the same government in the time of Hen 7th under Prince Arthur, when the Bishop of Lincoln was Lord President of his Council, for then they had not only their abode in their shires, but were assisted with knights and esquires of the Marches of Wales, which are particularly named; of Herefordshire 7, of Shropshire 9, of Worcestershire 2   And the fees are also set down which every of them received from the King   So in the time of Henry 8th, from his 1th to his 16th year, the Bishop of Lichfield was President, and from the 17th to the 25th, when the Princess Mary was sent thither, the Bishop of Exeter succeeded   by the copy of whose instructions, ready to be shewed, it is plain that not only these shires were within his commission as Marches of Wales, but that his authority and jurisdiction was in all points as absolute and large as it is at this present   And the patents for the office of Clerk of the Council and signet first made to Henric Knighte in the 3d of Hen 8th, and then to Tho Hacklewit in the 18th, do plainly establish them *tam infra principalitatem nostram Southwalliæ et Northwalliæ quam infra comitatus nostros Salop, Hereford, Gloucester, Wigorn,* etc   Howsoever then the Lordships Marchers might still restrictively be called the Marches of Wales, it is plain enough that these shires also in a more large sense were ever reputed as the King's Marches and Counties Marchers of Wales   But after the statute of 27th of Hen 8th, by which the country and dominion of Wales was *de novo* reestablished, and distinguished into shires, these Lordships Marchers being then quite abolished and incorporated part into Wales and part into England, can no more be such marches as they were before, when (as the Statute saith) they lay between the shires of England and Wales, and where parcels of none; but needs henceforth as parts follow the nature of the whole, and have no more being or subsistence of themselves.

So then (to apply all that hath been spoken to the purpose in hand) if these four English shires from the beginning were partly Wales itself and the rest marches, and if in those middle times of the Lordships Marchers these shires never lost the name nor reputation of marches, and if when they are called the shires adjoining to the marches they are intended to be Counties

Marchers, or the King's free marches adjoining to the restrictive
and proprietary marches of the Lords; and lastly if after the
extinguishing of the Lordships Marchers no other marches can
be found but these, I say that the Statute of 34 Hen 8th must
of necessity be understood of them

Moreover howsoever the power of our lawyers may wrest the
ambiguity of the word marches, yet in that statute other clauses
may be found of equal or more force to include these shires.
The words are these *There shall be and remain a President and
Council in the said dominion and principality of Wales and the
marches of the same, with all officers, clerks, and incidents to the
same, in manner and form as hath been heretofore used and accustomed, which President and Council shall have power and authority to hear and determine by their wisdoms and discretions such
causes and matters as be or hereafter shall be assigned to them
by the King's Majesty, as heretofore hath been accustomed and used*

This establishment consisteth plainly of two distinct parts
The first part appointeth only the place of residence for the
President and Council namely within *Wales or the Marches
thereof* The second giveth it jurisdiction and power *to hear
and determine all matters assigned by the King, and accustomed
to be there heard,* without other limitation either to person or
place. So that if the causes of these shires were then usually
heard there, and are now assigned by the King, then by this
statute they must be continued whether they be marches or no
marches of Wales And for the usage, besides all that hath
been alleged, it is further confirmed, first by the precedents and
registers of the practice of that Council from time to time ready
to be vouched Secondly by the continual residence thereof at
Bendhe, Ludlow, Ticknell, Gloucester, Salop, Hereford, Worcester, and never in any Lordship Marcher or in Wales. Thirdly
by the instructions of Henry the 8th under his own hand to the
Bishop of Coventry and Lichfield, who was President there from
the making of this statute to the second year of Edward the 6th,
wherein these counties are called the King's Marches, and expressly distinguished from the Lordships Marchers: Fourthly by
the instructions and commissions of other Presidents in succession to this day, or at least by so many of them as may be
gotten And lastly by formal decrees of the Privy Council of
the late Queen, made upon the mature examination of the same

question namely, one dated 13 May 1574 against Robert Wilde, who sought to exempt the county and city of Gloucester; and another dated 25th January 1581 against the Mayor of Hereford for refusing to submit to the authority of that Court. And lastly by an Act of Parliament of 18 of Elizabeth, which in confirmation of this usage appointeth the penalties incurred by the justices of Gloucestershire for not repairing Chepstow bridge to be recovered only before the Council in the Marches, before whom at this instant that suit doth depend, which was a motive why they laboured to exempt themselves, that they might retain those great sums which they have levied to this use

> But here it is objected that in the same Queen's time Cheshire was exempted from this jurisdiction, which in former time had been also carried under the same title

Hereunto may be answered · first, that Cheshire had a peculiar reason, because it was a County Palatine, and had both Chancery and Common Law in itself   Besides that if the power of the Earl of Leicester had not swayed that cause, the reasons happily might then have been stronger to have kept in that shire, than now to put out these.   And lastly that the same authority which exempted that one concluded all the rest   for *exceptio firmat legem in casibus non exceptis,* as the Law saith   and yet besides all this no order or judgment can be shewed by which that shire was formerly exempt, but by sufferance of time   Then to finish this point   If the statute refer to usage, and the usage be confirmed for an hundred years at the least without interruption, and if usage be so potent that it prevaileth against law, as Mr Attorney hath shewed in the case of Checker Seals,[1] I may strongly conclude that these shires by good right should continue in the Marches

And thus much for Law.

The reasons of convenience or inconvenience

The third and last point is the reason of this change, containing the conveniences or inconveniences which follow   And if *salus populi* be *suprema lex,* then though law and usage and prerogative were all against us, yet *bonum publicum* should be always preferred.

[1] I suppose in *Lane's case   See Rep pt ii p 17*

The consequents then of this renting and discountenancing the government in Wales may probably be these

1. It will be a dangerous beginning of innovation in the general government of the land For if the King's Prerogative, the ancient and main foundation upon which this jurisdiction was built, be thus questioned and shaken, then of necessity the Council at York must fall after this, which is not denied, and the Court of Requests must follow, and happily other Courts of equity, which may seem to be blemished in the handling of this cause. And what further way may be opened to Parliament or lawyers to dispute more liberties, may rather be feared than discovered at the first

2 It will be a blow to the established religion for it is well known that these marcher shires are overgrown with Papists, who were suppressed only by the justice of this Court and are since the disgrace thereof so multiplied and encouraged, that the state hath already been troubled with their disorders and routs

3. It will dissolve the union betwixt England and Wales, by breaking of their great traffic, then mutual alliances, and then equality of right For what Welshman will traffic with an Englishman when he must travel to London to recover his debt, and then try his action in the English shires? Or what Englishman will marry into Wales, when they are thus sequestered from us as a contemned people? And why should not both again spoil one another when they have no common justice to keep them in fear? Or when Welsh malefactors may find impunity in the marches, and the marchers in Wales?

4 The nature of these marchers is so notoriously prone to fighting and brawling, that notwithstanding the necessary severity of this Court in the greatest strength thereof, there have been ever more riots and misdemeanours in some one of these shires than any three of Wales and therefore the lessening of authority in what degree soever must needs increase disobedience and at length danger to the state

5 If by the wisdom of former ages these shires were added to the government of Wales, partly to sweeten and allay the harsh differences of laws, customs, languages, and affections betwixt Welsh and English, and partly with the ready strength of these shires to bridle the rebellious humour to which Wales by nature and situation is subject, then of necessity they must

return to their old condition of borderers and highlanders, when they are again cantonised the one from the other

6 As the establishment of this Council was also directed to suppress the insolencies and oppressions of the Marcher Lords, so the disabling thereof will again set them up, and restore the sword of violence to their hands   For all that know those parts must acknowledge that the power of the gentry is the chief fear and danger of the good subject there   and even this is the sum of all their heinous complaints against the President and Council, that for incontinency, striking, and every disorder, they are forth-with molested with process and fines

7. If it be the blessing of God to his chosen people to have justice administered in every city, it must follow as a curse upon these poor shires, when they shall be driven from home to seek justice at London where besides their travel, loss of time, and all charges of law, the very expense of their journey will come to more than at the Council the whole costs of their suit   And considering how the Courts at Westminster are already pestered, shall not all England suffer more for despatch, when the suits of these shires, which are half the business of the Council, are put to that heap ?

8 If by law it be concluded that the Council in the Marches never had power to hear the causes of these shires, then all the orders and judgments in their cases, whereby many men hold both their goods and lands, as given *sub non judice*, are quite overthrown   And his Majesty of right should repay all the fines levied there since the beginning of that Court   And then what confusion and what clamour will grow amongst the people ? And what new work for those troublesome Attorneys which have stirred all this mud to bring water to their mill?

Besides all these, many other inconveniences may be remembered ; as the acknowledgment of wrong and usurpation in the Crown time out of mind · The condemning of the acts and instructions of so many former kings The present disparagement and overthrow of a Council of Estate, and the depriving of all convenient places of abode: An addition of more scope and business to the potent ministers of the law   together with the scandal, trouble, and doubtful event of change, wherein all the mischiefs cannot possibly be foreseen

And besides all this, can it be denied that by means of this

Court, established as it now is, all those countries both of Wales and the Marches have been reduced from barbarism, poverty, and disorder, and thus long been maintained in civility and peace? or can any just and important exception be taken against their present proceedings? or is there any ground of all this ado to satisfy present or after times?   Why then, I demand with Cassian, *cui bono* do we hazard all this? specially considering that as that Council now standeth by his Majesty's instructions, whatsoever shall at any time be found inconvenient either in matter or form, may presently be redressed with one dash of a pen, whereas if it be once carried out of his royal hand he shall hardly or never recover like power· and what incongruity soever time shall discover the remedy will be past.

3.

Such being the state of the case upon which it seems that an appeal was made to the Government on the part of the President and Council of the Marches, the question was in what way the government should interfere   The next paper which appears to be by the same hand as the last, and must also have been written while Coke was still Attorney-General, gives what Mr Heath supposes to be the substance of Bacon's advice upon this point   It is a fair transcript in the same handwriting as the other, and without any corrections   The original docket was simply "Wales," in Salisbury's hand, over which a more modern pen has written, "Answer to the Judges' reasons justifying the proceedings in the Court of"   But its main object is to recommend a practical measure for determining the controversy , and it might be better described as a

SUGGESTION SUBMITTED TO THE EARL OF SALISBURY FOR THE SETTLING OF THE DISPUTE BETWEEN THE KING'S BENCH AND THE COURT OF WALES

The President and Council in the Marches of Wales have usually before the statute and ever since determined matters of *meum* and *tuum*, as well in the four shires as in Wales, without contradiction , as by precedents of that Court for every shire ready to be shewed may appear , and are warranted so to do by the 9th article of their instructions.

Against this practice the Judges object matter of law and matter of inconvenience

For Law, they deny that the four shires are within the

marches, and that being not included in the statute of
31 H 8, they must therefore follow the course of common
law, and have these matters determined at Westminster.
And that the Judges of the King's Bench, being sworn to
do justice to every subject that seeketh it at their hands,
cannot without perjury refuse to give prohibitions to any
that demand them in these cases

To the first point hereof we answer, that the Marches were
never limited by any written law, but by common reputation
only, and that diversely according to the times   And as the
Lordships Marchers were esteemed Marches before 27 H 8, at
what time they were extinct, so both before and ever since these
four shires in common reputation and also in usage have been
held for Marches ; as by the precedents of that Court ready to
be shewed may appear, which reputation and usage in other
cases hath made law, as by Mr Attorney's own reports may
plainly be proved

For the second point, as the reverend Judges, though sworn
to do justice to all according to law, yet many times in mercy
and conscience both reprieve prisoners, and stay judgments after
verdicts, and forbear prosecutions if cause so require, and that
justly   because *salus populi est suprema lex*, so no doubt they
may be sparing both in prohibitions and *habeas corpus* in this case,
wherein not only the good of all the people of those shires, but
also his Majesty's prerogative royal is so highly engaged.

For matter of inconvenience, Mr Attorney objecteth, that
God forbid men's inheritances should be tried by any Court
of equity, or by men's discretions only

To this we answer, that though the statute enables his Majesty
to authorize this Court to judge of men's inheritances, yet his
Majesty in his instructions never giveth them that power, further
than concerneth the installing of possessions, which Mr. Attorney
himself denieth not to be fit   The matters then of debt are the
chief which are here dealt in, and these are in like sort determined at York, as by their instructions doth appear   And if
these petty suits should be drawn to London, all the traffic betwixt the Welsh and English must of necessity decay, and Wales
must again grow wild and barbarous, as his Lordship (by whose
grave wisdom the last instructions were directed) did of his own

knowledge and experience well remember, and the Welshmen must be forced to seek foreign trades with the Irish and others, the inconveniences whereof are best known to your Honour, as also that these forgotten wisdoms of our ancestors, who by the union of these shires in traffic, alliances, and common justice reduced them first to civility and peace, should not without manifest and great necessity be changed

And whereas the freedom and birthright of the subject is so much urged, your Honour may be pleased to consider whether in all *Magna Charta* there be any greater benefit than this— to have near and cheap justice and whether the Attorneys of the Courts of Common Law inhabiting those shires, from whom all this business springeth, do seek their own or the people's good, when they would draw them an hundred miles and make them spend twenty nobles and a twelvemonth's time to recover forty shillings and whether as the administration of justice in particular men's causes is necessarily delegated to men of law, so the provincial and equal distribution thereof doth not in all countries belong unto men of state, as a chief branch of the King's prerogative, who as *Pater patriæ*, and the source of all laws, will ever be more wise for his people than they are for themselves, though in this case every one be sensible enough of his own interest and ease, and of the great difference of charge and expedition betwixt the Council there and the Courts above

But for the determining of all this controversy If his Majesty will be pleased for the preservation and strengthening of his prerogative in these shires, and for the continuance of the peace and good government thereof, but to grant such a commission unto the Lord President for them, as he granteth for York, and as former Kings granted for Wales and the Marches, before the statute was made, Then it may be hoped that the reverend Judges will give way to h [four or five words worn away here in the MS] alike, and the people of both places shall find equal care over them, and continue as they have done so many years under this government in unity and peace

The practical measure, therefore, recommended by Bacon at this time,—that is in 1605 or 1606,—for settling the difference, (assuming that Mr Heath is right in regarding this memorial as "substantially embodying his advice") amounts to this The interference of the

King's Bench having begun upon an assumption that it had authority to control the Provincial Court even in matters within its jurisdiction, and this assumption having been subsequently withdrawn, and the justification of the proceeding rested upon the assertion that the four shires were *not* within its jurisdiction; let them be now *brought* within its jurisdiction, and the dispute would cease   Now it was not denied that the Council of the North, which had a similar jurisdiction, derived its authority from the King's Commission only, without any Act of Parliament then or afterwards to warrant it,[1] and so did this very Council of Wales and the Marches, for several years before the passing of the statute by which it was confirmed.[2] If therefore it was doubted whether its jurisdiction extended to these four shires, let a new commission be issued conferring that jurisdiction upon it.

4

In the earlier stages of the dispute it is possible that such a measure would have answered the purpose   But I suppose that when the question came to be agitated in the House of Commons (as it was in the session of 1605-6) and threatened to take its place among the Grievances, the assumption of such an authority by the Crown (though not so great as that which had established the Council of the North, inasmuch as it would have rested on usage of long standing and till then unquestioned) was thought impolitic and hazardous   It was resolved therefore to let it rest upon the law as it stood, trusting that the appointment of a new President, with reformed instructions, would remove the causes of dissatisfaction   A new President was accordingly appointed in the summer of 1607, a new set of instructions issued, and the following Proclamation drawn up, apparently by Bacon, and with reference to them, though I cannot find that it was ever published.

PROCLAMATION TOUCHING THE MARCHES.[3]

R.

It hath well appeared since our coming to the Crown of this our Realm of England how little we affect change and innovation, having maintained and preserved the whole frame of the government, as we found the same, and all estates and degrees in their ancient dignities, liberties, and privileges, even to the

[1] Coke's Institutes, part iv c 49
[2] See Preamble of Subsidy Act, 32 Hen VIII c 50
[3] S P Dom James I vol xxxvii. no 55

continuing of particular persons in then services and places, with
very rare and sparing removes or alterations In respect whereof
as all our loving subjects are the more our debtors that none of
them on their part do offer or presume to make any innovation
upon us and our prerogatives and legal jurisdictions, so are
we ourselves the more engaged and obliged to make and retain
the like measure to our Crown and our posterity which we have
freely made and yielded unto our subjects

And although it is and ever hath been our princely resolution
to give unto our laws their full force, free course, and right use,
in all cases already adjudged, decided, and ruled, and in all
cases the nature whereof dependeth wholly upon a legal science
and interpretation, So on the other side, where we do find an
ancient possession in our Crown without interruption, and a
question or doubt newly stirred, and that the cause is likewise
mixed with consideration of estate, which cannot fall under the
ordinary and vulgar rule of law, we are also in ourselves resolved
not to lose or give over, but to continue and maintain, every
such ancient possession and practice of jurisdiction, and in no
sort to endure, under the pretence of any opinion of law, either
the acts of our predecessors to be blemished or questioned, or
the rights of our posterity to be diminished or prejudiced, except
such alteration should be introduced by the advice of our three
estates in Parliament, unto whose counsels we shall always be
ready to give a gracious hearing and respect

Whereas therefore it is come to our knowledge that certain
questions have been lately moved tending to the impeachment
and overthrow in great part of the jurisdictions of our two provincial Counsels established, the one in the Marches of Wales,
the other in the Northern parts, which our said Counsels have
had a continuance of their authority by the space of four regal
descents of this Crown, and the one of them much longer, and
were instituted and ordained as well for the ease and succour of
the poorer sort of our subjects, as for many other politic considerations, which we reserve to our own censure, and have since
from time to time had their authority warranted by instructions
under the signature of former Kings, and have had the places
of their Presidents supplied by principal persons of the Nobility,
and Bishops, and Counsellors of Estate, and the rest of the body
of the said Counsel compounded in part of divers great learned

men in our laws, some of them Judges, and have had their jurisdiction affirmed by continual references of causes from our Courts
at Westminster, and generally obeyed as well by our ministers
and officers as other our loving subjects of all degrees, Although
we have just cause to think those questions moved to be in derogation both of our power and honour, and thereby mought have
been provoked to a more severe and peremptory course herein, yet
nevertheless such is our inclination to clemency and moderation
as we are willing rather to correct the fault than to deal with
the persons whom it may concern, and in our proceeding with
the persons, first to warn before we punish, and further also
not so to be transported by dislike of the course taken, but that
we are content likewise to look into the occasions whence the
griefs may arise

First therefore to the end to remove all just ground or colourable pretence of complaint, we have by advice of our Privy
Council reviewed and reformed our instructions, reducing them
to those limits and restrictions which we thought fittest for the
times and the good of our people, and for the avoiding any occasion of abuse in the execution of them, and for the better correspondence and agreement of those jurisdictions with our principal
Courts of Justice, which our proceeding, as it cannot but give
great satisfaction to all that are dutiful and modest, so we intend
thereby to take away all excuse from such as are contemptuous
and turbulent, and to the end that the said limitations may be
publicly known, we have given charge to our Presidents severally
that those parts and articles of our instructions which concern
ordinary justice, they do no more keep private, but record them
in such convenient place and manner as every man may have
access to them, and sight and knowledge of them. And thus
having removed all colour and pretence of want of notice of the
authority by us given to our said Counsels, or of just exception
to the same, we do by these presents publish and declare to all
our loving subjects, and do ordain and establish and command,
that from henceforth the authority and proceedings of our said
Presidents and Counsels (keeping themselves within the compass
of our instructions) be duly and fully, without making further
questions or practising any manner of evasions, acknowledged
and obeyed   And for that purpose we do hereby straitly
charge and command as well all our Sheriffs, Under-sheriffs, Bai-

liffs, Serjeants, and all other inferior officers and ministers of Justice to whom it may appertain, that they serve, execute, and obey all precepts, process, or letters of Justice of our said Presidents or Counsels, and in all points be attendant to them as heretofore in the time of our late dear sister Queen Elizabeth and former times was used, as also all our loving subjects remaining or being within the precincts of the jurisdictions of the said Counsel, (as they shall be set down by our said instructions), that they yield their obedience and submit themselves in such manner and form as hath also heretofore been used; and that no parties that shall be sued before the said Counsel according to the tenor or warrant of our said instructions, or their servants, attorneys, or solicitors, or any other person for them, do take forth, procure, or serve any our writs of false imprisonment, prohibition, *Habeas Corpus*, or the like, which may directly or indirectly impeach or draw in question the said jurisdiction of our said Counsels as it standeth now limited and warranted by our said instructions   And we do hereby give to understand, as well to our said Presidents and Counsels as to all our said officers and ministers, that we shall always protect, maintain, and defend them from all manner of danger, peril, trouble, or molestation which may any ways grow unto them in the exercise of any jurisdiction or authority pursuing our said instructions, or in the observing and execution of this our Royal Commandment, as also to all persons whatsoever that shall willingly infringe, transgress, or neglect the same, that we shall hold them and proceed against them as contemners and resisters of our Royal power and authority, and opposers unto our proceedings, and disturbers of the quiet and peace of our government, and shall with such severity make examples of those that shall begin or attempt the same, as shall easily contain others within their bond of duty and make them find the effects of any[1] obstinate abusing of our former clemency[2]

What was done with this draft, and for what reasons it was judged inexpedient to publish a Proclamation to this effect,—which would apparently have been a very judicious measure, if the jurisdiction was to be maintained,—we are not informed   We know only that

---

[1] *and* in MS
[2] Docketed in Bacon's hand, 'Proclamat touching the Marches' Below (in another hand), 1607

the measures actually taken were not effectual in settling the dispute, of which we shall hear more in due time

5.

The other draft relates to a subject of more general interest, and looks to me very much like an original suggestion of Bacon's own, appreciated and acted on by the King, but (like many of his ideas) too far in advance to take effect upon popular opinion The 'British Jury' is one of our most venerated institutions, and has done and continues to do an incalculable amount of good service Yet it cannot be said that on a disputable question of fact the decision of a Jury carries much authority in men's opinions, or that our veneration for the institution protects it from ridicule, when the verdict is distasteful This could hardly be,—the gravity of the office considered,—if the capacity of the men to whom it is usually committed were not felt to be somewhat below the general level And it is very difficult to say why a business of such importance should be thought below the dignity of the best instructed classes, or entrusted to any below the best procurable The truth, I suppose, was simply that the service being troublesome and unattractive, the higher classes used their influence to be relieved from it, and fashion is too strong for kings and laws The following draft, written in a hand known to have been in Bacon's employment about this time, and corrected and docketed in his own, was an attempt to introduce a better fashion, which, had it succeeded, would have greatly raised the value of a Jury's verdict, and produced effects, direct and indirect, more than can be easily estimated, and certainly beneficial The form in which it was originally drawn being that which best represents Bacon's idea, (if I am right in supposing it to be of his composition), I print it from the manuscript as it stood before Salisbury touched it

A PROCLAMATION FOR JURORS [1]

As it is a principal part of our kingly office to administer justice to our people, by which also our throne and sceptre is established and confirmed, so we conceive that we may truly and justly thus far reap the fruit of a good conscience, as to be witness to ourselves, and likewise to report ourselves not only to our Privy Council, which are acquainted with our more secret

---

[1] This is the title of the printed Proclamation The draft (Dom Jas I xxviii 67) has no title, but is docketed in Bacon's hand, 'Jurors'

cares and cogitations, and our Judges and Learned Counsel, with whom we have had more frequent conference than princes formerly have used, but generally also to all others our loving subjects (in regard of some our public actions), whether in these few years of our reign (notwithstanding we could not be at our first entrance so well informed as now we are in the laws and customs of this our realm) we have not exercised and employed our princely care, power, and means for the furtherance and advancement of justice duly and speedily to be administered to all our loving subjects   For it appeareth that we have encreased the number of our Judges in our principal benches, to avoid the delay of the subject by equality of voices, and we have moderated and appeased some differences and contentions amongst our Courts in point of jurisdiction, to avoid double vexation of suits, and have from time to time in person given more strait charge to our Judges before their circuits and visitations, and received again from them more strait accounts and reports at their returns, than heretofore hath been accustomed   And as we have been thus careful of our Courts and Judges of the Law, so may we nowise omit to extend our princely care to another sort of judges (though they be termed by another name) upon whom lieth a principal part of judicature, which are the Judges of the fact, and by the custom of the realm called Jurors, which try and decide the issues and points of fact in all controversies and causes,—a matter no less important to the sum of justice than the true and judicious exposition of the laws themselves   For even that judgment which was given by a King in person, and is so much commended in the Scriptures, was not any learned exposition of the law, but a wise sifting and examination of the fact, where testimony was obscure and failed   unto which sort of Judges also the law of this our realm doth ascribe such trust and confidence, as it neither ties them to the evidence and proofs produced, neither disableth any witness (except in case of perjury) to be used, but leaveth both supply of testimony and the discerning and credit of testimony wholly to the Juries' consciences and understanding, yea to their private knowledge   But herewithal we consider with ourselves that this proceeding by Jury, which is one of the fundamental laws and customs of this our island of Brittany, and almost proper and singular unto it in regard of other nations, as it is an excellent institution in itself (as that

which supplieth infinite delays which grow upon exceptions to
witnesses, spareth rigorous examination by torture in cases capital, and doth not accumulate upon the same persons the trust
and confidence to be Judges both of law and fact,) so nevertheless it is then laudable and good when those persons which serve
upon the said Juries are men of such quality, credit, and understanding, as are worthy to be trusted with so great a charge as to
try men's lives, good names, lands and goods, and whatsoever
they hold dear in this world   Wherein we cannot but observe
and highly commend the wisdom of the laws of this our realm
(taking them in their own nature before abuses crept in) which
have in this point so well provided   For as in the trial of any
Peer of this realm, the law doth not admit any to pass upon him
but Peers, so in the trial of any of the Commons (which the law
beholdeth but as one body) there is no person whatsoever (were
he of our Counsel of Estate) by rule of law exempted, in respect
of his quality and degree only, from the service upon Juries,
whereas on the contrary part the law hath limited that none
serve except he have a certain proportion of freehold, and yet
notwithstanding time and abuse have so embased the estimation
of this service, and altered the use thereof, as sheriffs, under
sheriffs, and bailiffs do not only spare gentlemen of quality
in a kind of awe and respect, but do likewise for lucre,
gain, and reward, forbear to return many of the ablest and
fittest persons, so that the service oftentimes resteth upon such
as are either simple and ignorant, and almost at a gaze in any
cause of difficulty, or else so accustomed and inured to pass and
serve upon Juries, as they have almost lost that tenderness of
conscience which in such cases is to be wished, and make the
service as it were an occupation or practice   Upon these grounds
therefore, and upon advice taken with our Privy Counsel and
conference with our Judges and Counsel Learned, we have resolved to give remedy to these abuses, and to restore the trial of
this our realm of England to the ancient integrity and credit
And therefore we do hereby publish and declare to all our loving
subjects, that they take light from us of the greatness of this
service, and that the gentlemen of the best quality do put away
that vain and untrue conceit that they are any ways disgraced
or disesteemed, if they be called upon or used in this part of
Justice to be Judges of the fact, knowing that all judgment is

God's principally, and by him committed unto us within the precinct of our kingdoms as his minister upon earth, to whom likewise they are subordinate, and we do likewise charge and command all our Judges, Justices, Sheriffs, Undersheriffs, Bailiffs, and others to whom it may appertain, to take knowledge that it is our express will and pleasure that all persons which have freehold according to the law (other than such as we shall by our express letters patents privilege and discharge, which we mean to do moderately, and but upon special circumstances, and upon a reasonable fine as hath been used) shall be returned to serve upon Juries as occasion shall require, foreseeing also that they use a respect that the same persons be not too oft returned and troubled, but that the service may rest more equally and indifferently upon the whole body of freeholders in every county, the one to ease and relieve the other, wherein nevertheless our intention is not but that there be a discretion retained in returning the more principal persons upon the greatest causes.   And above all we do strictly admonish and prohibit our said sheriffs and the undersheriffs and bailiffs, that they presume not at their uttermost peril directly or indirectly to take any manner of reward profit or gratification whatsoever for sparing or forbearing any person whom the law doth allow to be returned upon the service aforesaid, upon pain to be punished with all severity according to our laws, and also as contemners of this our Royal prohibition.

The idea was approved by the Government, and the proposed Proclamation, with many additions, omissions, and alterations, chiefly by Salisbury, but without substantial variation, so far as I can see, was published by authority on the 5th of October, 1607 [1] The seed fell upon soil too hard trodden by custom to nourish and make it grow, and it is not likely that it will ever bear fruit in old England But reason does not die, and it may be that in some younger community the principle may yet be taken up by "the common sense of most," and the function of the petty Jury may come to be regarded as equal in dignity to any

---

[1] "A book of Proclamations, published since the beginning of his Majesty's most happy reign over England, etc, until the present month of Feb. 3, anno dom 1609"

INDEX TO VOLUME III.

☞ The small roman numerals refer to the Preface

— ·◆ —

A.

ADVANCEMENT

Advancement of Learning, design and commencement of, 88
Finished and published, 248
Letters with presentation copies, 252—256
Translation of into Latin, 300—302
See 363
Alexander the Great's retort to Parmenio, 308
Alfred the Great, divisions of the land instituted by, 373
Algiers, Spanish enterprise against, 45 17
Anderson, Sir Edmund, C J Common Pleas, death of, 257
Andrews, Dr Launcelot, Bishop of Chichester, why called by Bacon his "inquisitor" 256 *See* 55
Ante nati (Scottish subjects born before Elizabeth's death) Naturali-

BACON.

Ante nati—continued
zation of recommended, 211 306
Distinction between them and the *Post nati*, 333, 334 339—341
See Naturalization
Aquila, Don Juan d', his invasion of Ireland and Proclamation against Elizabeth, 76
Aragon, cause of a rebellion in, 96 320
Assurances, bill concerning, 34
Attainder, rule of inheritance how affected by, 341
Attorney General *See* Coke Hobart
Attorney of the Wards, 199
Atye, Sir Arthur, 199
Aubrey, John, on an alleged proposition by Ralegh relative to the succession to Q Eliz 72
On Ralegh s plot for entrapping Cobham and his friends, 135

B

Bacon, Ann Lady, her reason for objecting to her son Anthony's lodging in Essex House, 9 *note* *See* 10
Bacon, Anthony, death of, 5
His character, correspondence preserved at Lambeth, etc , 6
Cause of his excessive expenditure, 7
Letter to him from Walsingham, 8
Imputations against him, 9
Story told of him by Wotton examined and explained, 11
His character of Nicholas Trott, 40
His regard for Sir Thomas Challoner, 61
See 59 66 143
Bacon, Francis, portraits of, iii—v
His altercation with Coke in the Exchequer, 1—4
His letter of expostulation, 4

Bacon, Francis—*continued*
His opinion of Coke, 5
Sum assigned to him out of the fines imposed on Essex's associates, 11
His view of the true relation between Crown and Parliament, and the impolicy of calling Parliament ostensibly for money only, 17
His speech on bringing in Bill against abuses in weights and measures, 17, 18
His speech for repealing superfluous laws, 19
His speech on a point of privilege, 21 *note*
His speech on bringing up the report of Bill touching the Exchequer, 22
His speech against Bill declaring monopolies illegal, 26 28

Bacon Francis—*continued*

His speech in support of Townshend's motion, 29, 30, 31

His speech against motion for apologetic message, 33 *note*

Short notes of other speeches

On the Merchants Assurance Bill, 34

Against repealing the Statute of Tillage, 34

Against making a judicial exposition of a Statute part of a Statute, 36

Against committing to the Tower for an assault on a member's servant, 37

Against repeal of Act relating to Charitable Trusts, 37—39

His excitement on the occasion, *Ibid*

His pecuniary embarrassments, mortgage of Twickenham Park and account with Nicholas Trott, 10—14

His Letter to Cecil after the defeat of the Spaniards in Ireland, with " Considerations touching the Queen's Service " there, 45—51

His desire to be favourably regarded by the new king, 56

Letters in recommendation of his services

To Michael Hickes, 57

To the Earl of Northumberland, 57

To David Foulis, 59 61

To Bruce Abbott of Kinloss, (sent by Toby Matthew) 60, 61

To Sir Thomas Challoner, 63

To Mr Davys, 65

To Dr Morison, 66

His idea of the advice which should be given to the King, embodied in the draft of a Proclamation sent to the Earl of Northumberland, 66—71

Is continued in the office of Learned Counsel under the same conditions as before, 72 73

His letter to Toby Matthew concerning the first proceedings of the King, 73

His letter to Robert Kemp concerning the state of things on the death of the Queen, 74

His relations with the Earl of Southampton and letter to him upon his approaching liberation, 75, 76

His personal interview with the King, and letter to the Earl of Northumberland describing

Bacon, Francis,—*continued*

his first impressions of him, 76, 77

His official position and prospects 78

Receives help from Cecil in some difficulty about money, and writes a letter to him explaining the state of his private affairs, 79—81

His note of his debts, 82

Is knighted, *ibid*

Progress of his great philosophical work on the *Interpretation of Nature*, 82—84

Translation of the Preface intended for it 84—87

His probable motive in writing the *Advancement of Learning*, 88

His Discourse on the Union of Kingdoms, 89—99

His view of the dispute between the High Churchmen and the Puritans, 100—103

His " Considerations touching the better Purification and Edification of the Church of England addressed to the King, 103—127

His suggestions mostly adopted by the King, 129

Not employed in the investigation of the Priests' plot, or the trial of Ralegh, 133 136

His ' Apology in certain imputations concerning the late Earl of Essex ' occasion and object of the publication why addressed to Lord Mountjoy, 136—160

The vindication complete, if his statements are to be believed, 161

Reasons for believing them, 162

Part taken by him on the proceedings upon Sir F Goodwin's case, 164, 165

Advises the House to agree to a conference with the Judges, 166, 167

Is employed to deliver to the Lords reasons against such Conference, 167

Reports to the House what passed, 167, 168

Is appointed spokesman at conference with the Judges, and called upon for a report, 169—171

His proceeding approved 172

His suggestion of a course for terminating the dispute between the Commons and the Warden of the Fleet in the case of Sir Thomas Shirley, 173 and *note*

Bacon, Francis *continued*

Member of a subcommittee to report upon the new edition of the Book of Common Prayer, 177

Reports resolutions of Committee concerning Wardship, 178

Reports conference with the Lords concerning the same, 179, 180

Chosen by the House to present to the king their petition touching Purveyors, 181

His speech on the occasion, 181—187

His report of the King's answer, 187, 188

His report of conference with the Lords on the same subject, 189

His advice to the House, 190

His speech on the Union of the two Kingdoms in name, 191

His speech on preparations for conference with the Lords, 192

His report of the King's speech to the Committees of both Houses, 193

His enumeration of the sorts of objections to be avoided, 195, 196

His reports from the Committee, of objections to be urged at conference with the Lords against the change of name, 196 197—200

His speech at the conference, and report of same, 20 202

His report subsequent conferences,)4

Delivers draft of an Act for the au g of Commissioners, etc , 204—206

Chosen by the Commons for one of the Commissioners,

Deprecates proposed address of satisfaction to the King, 208 *note*

Reports conference touching the Bishop of Bristol's book, 208, 209

Reports conference concerning the Bill of Subsidy of Tonnage and Poundage, 211

Supports motion for Committee to consider of some gratuity to be offered to the King, 215 *note*

Letter to Toby Matthew, desiring his help in preparing some report, 216

Receives a grant by patent of the office of Learned Counsel; also a pension for life of 60*l*, 217

Desires a conference with Sir Robert Cotton about the Union, *ibid*

"Certain Articles or Considera-

Bacon, Francis *continued*

tions touching the Union of the Kingdoms" written for the king's service, 218 -231

Prepares draft of "Proclamation touching his Majesty's style" 235—239

His employments as one of the Commissioners of the Union, 240, 241

Prepares a preface to the report, which was not adopted its value, 242 -245

Passed over on a vacancy in the Solicitor Generalship, 247

Publishes the "Advancement of Learning," 248

Recommends the Lord Chancellor to take measures for getting a history of Great Britain compiled, 248—252

Letters to Northampton, Bodley, Salisbury, Buckhurst, the Lord Chancellor, and Toby Matthew, with copies of the "Advancement of Learning," 252—256

His relations with Bishop Andrews, 256

Again passed over on a legal vacancy occurring, 257

Examination of a man who had heard another express sympathy for the Gunpowder Plot, 257, 258

A Letter to Sir Michael Hickes, 259

Not prominent in Parliament during the session of 1605—6, 260

His supplementary report of the conference touching Recusants, 261—263

His report of conference concerning   astical grievances, 265

Is select others to conduct the argument on behalf the Commons in a conference concerning Purveyors, 267

Reports the proceedings 267—268

Speaks in favour of composition, 269, 270

Cries up the Bill against Purveyors, 271

His approval of the proceedings of the House with regard to the Subsidy Bill, 273

Letters to Salisbury on the subject, 275 277

Report from the Committee, 276

Appointed to read the collection of grievances to the King, 282

His report of the King's speech in reply *ibid*

His reply to an objection that

Bacon, Francis *continued*
  members of the House being of
    the Learned Counsel, could not
    be witnesses for the Crown, 283
  His objections to a bill for the re-
    gulation of fees, 285—287
  Letter to Salisbury upon a rumour
    of the intended promotion of the
    Attorney General, 288—290
  His marriage, 290—292
  His letters to the King, the Lord
    Chancellor, and the Earl of
    Salisbury on occasion of Sir H
    Hobart being made Attorney
    General, 293—297
  His letter to Sir T Hobby on the
    death of his friend Bettenham,
    297—299
  His memorial and inscription to
    Bettenham in Gray's Inn Gar-
    dens, 299
  Proposes to Dr Playfere to trans-
    late the *Advancement of Learning*
    into Latin, 299—302
  His advice to the House how to
    proceed with the Instrument of
    Union, 303, 304
  His Speech in favour of general
    Naturalization, 307—325
  His reports of conferences on the
    question of Law as affecting
    Naturalization, 327—332
  His speech against the motion for
    Union of Laws, 335—341
  Chairman of Committee upon the
    Bill for abolishing hostile laws,
    343
  His difficulties in getting the pre-
    amble accepted, 344
  His report of the speeches of
    Salisbury and Northampton on
    the Merchants petition for re-
    dress of wrongs from Spain,
    347—361
  Made Solicitor-General 362
  Final settlement of his plan of the
    Great Instauration, 363—365
  Correspondence with Bodley on
    the subject, 365 366
  Relations with Salisbury, 367
  Part taken by him upon the ques-
    tion of the Jurisdiction of the
    Council of Wales, 368
  His ' View of the Differences in
    question betwixt the King's
    Bench and the Council in the
    Marches," 368—381
  Suggestion for settling the dispute,
    384, 385
  Draft of Proclamation touching
    the Marches, 386—388
  Draft of Proclamation for James,
    389—392
Bacon Finn 153

Barker, Mr Serjeant, 5
Barkley, Sir Maurice   *See* Berkely
Barnham Alderman father of Bacon's
  wife, 290
Barnham, Alice, married to Bacon,
  290
  Her character and conditions, 291
Beard, one, " suspected for a papist and
  practiser, 257
  Examination of his bootmaker's
  servant, 258
Bedford Earl of, fine imposed on, for
  complicity in Essex's plot, 14
Beeston, Sir Hugh, a guest at Bacon's
  wedding feast 291 *note* A
Berkely Barklay Barkley, Sir Mau-
  rice, part taken in the conference
  on the Scottish union by, 192,
  200 311
  Seconds a motion for a Committee
  of Supply, 274
Berwick ' endued with the liberty of
  a Staple ' for commerce between
  English and Scottish traders,
  220
  Question of creating there a court
  of justice for the Borders, 221
Bettenham, Jeremiah Reader of Gray's
  Inn death of 297
  His claim on Sir T Hobby, 298
  Inscription to his memory by
  Bacon 299
Bingley, a colonist turned pirate, 353
Birch, Editor of Bacon's works 2 4 79
  His treatment of Anthony Bacon's
  correspondence, 6
Bishops, circumstances in the govern-
  ment of, 108—111
  King James's Conference with
  them at Hampton Court, 127—
  129
  See 210 261 265 Bristol Bishop
  of Church Convocation
Black, Mr John, " a beardless boy,'
  his views of conformity 127
Blackbourn, Editor of Bacon, 320 *note*
  323 *note*
Board of Green Cloth, 270 272 273
Bodley, Sir Thomas letter to him from
  Bacon, with copy of the " Ad-
  vancement of Learning 253
  His correspondence with Bacon
  respecting the " Cogitata et
  Visa," 365, 366
Bowyer, Mr, "my L Treasurers
  man," in Committee on Hostile
  Laws, 314
Brabant, Duke of answer of Edw III
  to a petition of the Common
  concerning him, 350
Bracton on the power of kings, 373
Breach of Privilege, cases of
  Arrest of a member's solicitor, at
  the suit of a tailor, 24, 25

Breach of Privilege—*continued*
　　Assault on a member's servant, 36, 37
　　Sir F. Goodwin's case, 163—172 See Goodwin
　　Arrest of Sir Thomas Shirley, at the suit of a goldsmith, and detention of him by the Warden of the Fleet 173—176
Bristol (Bristowe), Bishop of, complaint of the Commons against his book, 200
　　Bacon's report of a conference thereon, 208, 209
　　Submission and apology of the Bishop, 209 *note*
Britain or Great Britany, discussion as to application of the name to England and Scotland united, 191 195 197—200, 225 237
Britton on the king's jurisdiction, 373
Bruce, Edward, Abbot of Kinloss, a friend of Anthony Bacon 59

Bruce—*continued*
　　Letter from Francis Bacon to him, 60, 61
　　Made Master of the Rolls, 78
Buccleuch, Duke of, owner of the original of the engraving prefixed to this volume, iii
Buckhurst, Thomas Sackville Lord, Lord Treasurer, pecuniary dispute of Bacon's referred to, 41 43 44
　　Letter to him from Bacon with copy of his "Advancement of Learning,' 251
Bucks county, member for expelled from the House for an invective against the Scotch, 306, 307 *note*
Burgundy, duchy of, how lost to its duke, 321
Burstone manor money paid to Mr Nott on sale of, 12
Butlerage and Prisage 270

C

Calais, 318
Caldecot manor in the marches of Wales, 376
Canon law not adopted by England 311 *note*
Canterbury, Archbishop of at Q. Eliz death bed 55
　　Heads of his speech in the conference on ecclesiastical grievances, 265
　　Report from Committee on question of composition for Purveyors, 271
Canterbury, Dean of, on Q Eliz last illness, 55
Carew, Sir George, 45 *note* 75 *note*
Carey, Sir George, Master of Chancery, 200
Carleton, Dudley, on the character of Sir Henry Wotton, 10
　　Reference to his paper on the Scottish Union conference, 190 *note*
　　His notes and abstracts of Bacon's speeches and reports, and also of the King's speech thereon, 191 192 193 195 201 326 327 329
　　On the Ecclesiastical conference, 265 *note*
　　On the Bill of Purveyors, 271 *note*
　　His account of Bacon's marriage, 291
　　His note of Sir Edwin Sandys' "conclusion' in the Conference concerning the *ante-nati* and *post-nati*, 333 *note*

Carlisle question of erecting there a Court of Justice for the Border, 221
Cartakers See Purveyors
Carey, Sir Robert, Queen Elizabeth's death announced to king James by, 60
Castlehaven harbour destruction of Spanish ships in, 44
Catesby fined for his complicity in Essex's plot, and a share of the fine allotted to Bacon, 14 41
Cecil, Sir Robert afterwards Lord Cecil, Viscount Cranbourne, and Earl of Salisbury (Mr Secretary) letter from Bacon to, concerning his altercation with Coke, 2, 3
　　Explains to the Commons the causes of their meeting 17
　　Speaks for government on Subsidy Bill 21
　　His proceedings on the monopoly question, 23 24 26 28 30—33
　　Leading man at the English Council board 44
　　Letter to him from Bacon on the state of Ireland, 45
　　His instructions to Montjoy with regard to Tyrone, 53
　　Courted by Bacon as a means of introduction to the King, 56 57
　　Origin of his secret correspondence with k James 59
　　Keeps his lead in Council 78
　　Helps Bacon in some difficulty, 79 290

Cecil—*continued*

Letters of thanks from Bacon, with account of his private affairs, 79 81

His advice to Bacon in reference to Essex, 148

His account of the dispute concerning the election of Sir Francis Goodwin, 163 *note*

On the opinion of the Judges as to the effect of changing the name of the kingdom, 200

Project from the King produced by him, 202

His speech at the conference touching the Bishop of Bristol's book, 208, 209

Created Baron Essendon and Viscount Cranbourne, 241 *note*

His share in the preamble to the articles of Union, 242

Letter to him from Bacon, with a copy of the "Advancement of Learning," 253

Letter from the same with an examination bearing on the Gunpowder Plot, 257

His hint about Supply in conference, concerning Recusants, 262

Warns the Commons of the fate of the Purveyance Bill, 268

His huckstering system, 270

His endeavour to keep back the Purveyance Bill, 271

Letters to him from Bacon about the Subsidy Bill, 275 277

Shows an interest in Bacon's fortunes letter from Bacon upon a rumour of the promotion of Coke, 288, 289

Reason for doubting the sincerity of his professed desire to advance Bacon, 292

Letter from Bacon "touching the Solicitor's place," 296

Suspected of secretly furthering the dispute about Escuage, 305

Avoids an inconvenient debate by advising the Speaker to be too ill to go to the House, 334 and *note*

His speech on the merchants' petition upon Spanish Grievances, 347

Why he did not employ Bacon more confidentially, 367

Receives an annual pension from Spain, *ibid*

Suggestion submitted to him for settling the dispute between the King's Bench and the Court of Wales, 382 384

See 13 *note* 16 *note* 75 *note* 163 202 *note* 259 292

Chidderton, Mr., one in the Hampton Court conference, 129

Challoner, Sir Thomas, 61

Letter to from Bacon, bespeaking his services with the King, 63

Chamberlain John Dudley Carleton's correspondent

On Barker being made Sergeant, 5

On the death of Anthony Bacon, *ibid*

On the character of Sir Henry Wotton, 10

On the fines laid on Essex's associates, 14

On the Spaniards at Kinsale 20

On the progress of Parliament mess 21

On Queen Elizabeth's last illness, 31

Notice of the publication of the "Advancement of Learning," 255

On Lady Packington, 290

See 291 *note*

Chancellor of England, never made a deputy, 111

Despatches the suits in Equity of the whole kingdom, 122

See 230 Ellesmere

Chancery, Court of, 35 38

Jurisdiction of, in matter of Election returns, 164 165 171

Charitable Trusts Act alteration in the Commons about the, 37—39

Chepstow bridge, question as to jurisdiction concerning, 379

Chichester Bishop of See Andrews

Chichester Dean of 55

Church, bill against pluralities of benefices, 21

Bill against wilful absence from, 25

Diversity of rites in 97, 337

Dispute between High Churchmen and Puritans, 98—102

Considerations touching pacification and edification of, 103—127

Conference at Hampton Court, 128—132

Protest from the Convocation House against the pretensions of the House of Commons to deal in matters of religion, 210

Proceedings and conferences relative to heresies and popish recusants and ecclesiastical grievances 262—265

Cicero, of Crassu, 251

Clergy See Church

Cobham, Lord, his plot, Ralegh's connexion with it, 134, 135

Cogitata et Visa Correspondence with Bodley concerning 563 566

Coke, Sir Edward, Attorney General,
his altercation with Bacon, 1—3
Bacon's letter of expostulation, 4
Bacon's opinion of him as a
lawyer 5
The Queen entertained by him at
Stoke, 11
His responsibility for the manner
in which Ralegh's trial was con-
ducted, 133
Part taken by him in the annul-
ling of Sir F. Goodwin's election
for Bucks, 164 *note*
Not raised to the Bench on the
death of Chief Justice Ander-
son 257
Called in to assist the Lords in
maintaining the Prerogative
touching Purveyance, 268
Explains to the Conference Com-
mittee the defects of the Bill of
Purveyors, '71
Gives evidence on behalf of the
Crown against the Gunpowder
Plotters, 284
Wishes an end of the Parliament,
287 *note*
Rumoured promotion of, 288 290
Made Chief Justice of the Com-
mon Pleas on the death of
Gawdy, 292
See it, 78 138 *note* 164 165
217 261 303 368 382
Collier John Payne F S A, Letter of
Bacon's first printed by, 249
Commentarius Solutus, by Bacon, how
dealt with in this work *See*
Index to Vol IV
Common Prayer Book and Liturgy,
Remarks of Bacon on the, 111—
117
Same considered in conference
with the King, 128—131
New edition of, referred to Select
Committee, 177
Commons, House of their message of
thanks to the Queen for her pro-
ceedings with regard to mono-
polies, 15
Their eagerness to vote supplies
for the expulsion of the Spa-
niards from Ireland, and indis-
position to interpose other busi-
ness 17—20
Their grant of four Subsidies, 20
Their proceedings against abuses
on the Exchequer, 21
Their proceedings against Mono-
polies, 23—33
Their proceedings on Sir Francis
Goodwin's case, 163—172
Their proceedings on Sir Thomas
Shirley's case, 172—176
Their proceedings against the

Commons, House of—*continued*
Bishop of Bristol and his book,
208, 209
Their proceedings against the Convocation House for impeaching
their privileges, 210
Their proceedings upon Church
reform, *ibid*
Their proceedings on liberation of
trade, *ibid*
Their dispute with the Lords about
Wardship and Tenures, 211
Their expeditious proceeding with
the Union act, 212
Their interchange of explanations
with the King and preparation
of an 'Apology,' 211—214
Their discouraging reception of a
motion for a Committee to consider of some gratuity to be
offered to the King, 215
Their altered temper after the discovery of the Gunpowder Plot,
and agreement to grant a double
subsidy, 259, 260
Their proceedings against papists
and recusants 260 263
Their proceedings upon ecclesiastical grievances 263—266
Their proceedings upon Purveyance 267—271
Their proceedings upon the Subsidy bill, 273—278
Their proceedings in the collection
and presenting of grievances,
278—283 [*See* Grievances]
Their proceedings upon the "Instrument of Union," 303—345
Their proceedings upon the petition of the merchants for relief
of wrongs from Spain, 347—361
See Breach of Privilege Grievances Naturalization Par-
liament Patents Purveyors
Scotland Subsidies Ward-
ships
Convocation *See* Church
Cooke, Bacon's cousin and one of his
sureties, 12
Cope, Sir Walter, one of the three
knights present at Bacon's
wedding, 291 *See* note on same
page
Coppin, Sir George, his part in the
proceedings *in re* Sir Francis
Goodwin, 164 *note*
Cotton, Sir Robert, letter from Bacon
to, desiring a conference about
the Union 217
See 172 *note* 303
Cowell's, Interpreter, definitions from
Reuser, 2
King's Serjeants, 293 *note*
Cranbourne Viscount *See* Cecil

Crew, Mr, M P, 200
Croesus, Solon's rebuke to, 323
Crofts, Sir Herbert, M P, 200
Croke, or Crook, Sir John, King's Serjeant, made a puisne Judge, 362
See 368 note

Cromwell Edward Lord, implicated in the Essex conspiracy, fine imposed on 11
Cuffe, Henry 117

D

Darby, Lady, wife of Lord Ellesmere, 291
David, King, 98 361
Davies, Mr, afterwards Sir John, letter from Bacon to bespeaking his good word at Court, 65 and note
Demosthenes, his request to the Athenians when voting on great questions, 308
Descriptio Globi Intellectualis, beginning of a projected work by Bacon 363
Devonshire, Earl of See Montjoy
D Ewes, Sir Simonds, 18
 Passage of a debate omitted in his Journals, 24
Dissenters See Puritans
Dixon, Hepworth, F S A, reference to his "Personal History of Lord Bacon 11 note 257 277 note 284 291 note
Doderidge, Serjeant, appointed Solicitor General, 217
 Principal representative of the

Doderidge—continued
 government in the Lower House, 259
 Opposes retrospective law against the "miners," ibid
 Reports Conferences on Bill against Recusants 262 263
 Change of office suggested for him, 292 293
 Appointed King's Serjeant, 362
 See 199 257 261 290 297
Donne, Dr, 61 note
Derrington, Master, how he broke his neck 157
Dorset, Earl of, 194
Downhall, George ('Mr Downalde') the Lord Keeper's secretary, calls for the Bill against Patents, 21
Drake, Jh, examination of, in regard to treasonable words uttered by one Beard, 258
Dublin College, 19
Dyott, Mr, Bill against Patents introduced by 23

E

Eastlake Sir Charles, on the practice of Portrait painters in James, time, iv
Edward I, his replies to petitions from the Commons on matters concerning the Prerogative, 356 357
Edward III, his treatment of similar petitions, 356, 357 361
 Courts erected by him, 373
Edward IV, Courts erected by, 373 376
Edward VI, power granted by parliament to, 178
Egerton, Sir Thomas, Lord Keeper See Ellesmere
Elizabeth, Queen, entertained by the Attorney - General (Coke) at Stoke, 14, 15
 Promises to continue the examination of monopoly-patents, 15
 Reasons for dilatory proceeding 16
 Suddenly summons a new Parliament, 17
 Her manner of meeting the attack upon monopolies, 24 26
 Her message of thank for the

Elizabeth, Queen — continued
 promised grant of subsidies with incidental notice of her intention to suspend certain abused patents, and refer them to the decision of the Common law, 31, 32
 Her last meeting with her Parliament, 33
 Her continual activity and prosperity in administration of affairs Her instructions to Montjoy with regard to the conditions to be offered to Tyrone, 52, 53
 Her last illness and death, 54, 55
 Her policy is to the succession, and its result, 55, 56
 Her manner of employing Bacon in business of the Learned Counsel, 78
 Her policy with regard to the parties in the Church, 99
 Stipendiary preacherships erected by her, 121
 Bacon frequently admitted to speech with her 137

Elizabeth, Queen—continued
    Her connivance at Montjoy's implication in Essex's treason, 138
    Difference between Bacon and Essex as to the mode of dealing with her, 144, 145
    Bacon's account of his conversation with her about Essex, 147, 149—160
    Erection of a tomb to her memory, 219
    See 17 22 23 26 47 58 67 71 74 80 106 112 177
Ellesmere, Thomas Egerton Lord, Lord Keeper and Lord Chancellor
    Delivers the Queen's answer to the Commons concerning monopolies 15
    In collision with the Commons on a point of privilege, 21 note 25
    Offers to take the lower end of the Council table during the interregnum 71, 72 note
    The four unions named by him, 191 note
    Declares the King's wishes as to the new name proposed for the United Kingdom, 200
    Letters to him from Bacon "touching the History of Britain" 249 With a copy of the "Advancement of Learning, 251 Touching the Solicitor's place, 295
    His wish for the advancement of Bacon, 293
    The merchants "roundly shaken" by him, 305
    See 163 168 190 202 247
England, its greatness in forces truly esteemed, 323
    Canon law never adopted here, 341 note

England—continued
    Proceedings on proposed union with Scotland See Scotland
Erskine, Sir Thomas, 77
    Made Captain of the Guard, vice Ralegh, 78
Escuage peculiarity of the service so called, proposed to be abolished, difficulty in the way, 304, 305 311
Essex, Robert Devereux Earl of, relations of Anthony Bacon with, 9
    Story told by Sir Henry Wotton, 11—13
    Ransoms paid by the participators in the earl's conspiracy, 14
    Letters and devices written in his name by Francis Bacon, 65 note
    His correspondent Dr Morison, 66
    Origin of the imputation against Bacon of falsehood and ingratitude towards him, 136, 137
    Implication of Montjoy in his treasonable projects, 137, 138
    Fynes Moryson's account, ibid notes
    Bacon's Apology in certain imputations concerning him, 143—160 [See Bacon]
Exchequer, Bill concerning the, 22—26
Exchequer Court, Fleming, Solicitor General, appointed Chief Baron of the, 217
Excommunication, remarks by Bacon on the abuse of, 121
    Lords' Bill for restraint thereof rejected by the Commons, 264
Experientia Literata, scope of a projected work by Bacon so called, 82 See 300

F.

Fabritio, Signor See Wotton, Sir Henry
Farhe's case dispute upon, between the King's Bench and the Council in the Marches, 365—370
Fez, King of, a partner with Spain in an enterprise upon Algiers 45 note
Field, Dr, one in the Hampton Court conference 129
Fivye (or Fite), Lord, President of the Council in Scotland, one of the Union Commissioners, 241
Flanders, Earl of, complaint of the Commons against 386
Fleet Warden of the, proceedings of

Fleet, Warden of the—continued
    the Commons against, for the detention of a member, 173—176 See 208
Fleetwood, Mr, MP, case of breach of privilege concerning, 36, 37
Fleming, Solicitor-General, 4
    Queen's order for enquiry into monopoly-patents given to him and Coke 16
    Made Chief Baron of the Exchequer, 217
Florence and Pisa united, without naturalization the consequence thereof, 320
Fortescue Sir John, elected for Bucks, vice Goodwin, 161

Fortescue, Sir John — continued
  Proceedings preliminary thereto, ibid note
  Compromise suggested by the King 171
  Foulis, or Foules David formerly resident ambassador in London from the Scotch Court, 5.
  Letters from Bacon to him on James's accession, 59 61
  See 61 73
  France whether to be placed last in the enumeration of the titles of the English crown 226 259
  Grand Council of, 233

France—continued
  Powers of the King of, "when our King here was King of France" 331
  See 92 239 note 311 321 322 323 337
Fuller, Nicholas, on the Judges' doctrine touching purveyance, 269 note
  Speaks against the Naturalization Bill leader of the Opposition, 307
  See 343
Fuller's Worthies, notice of Dr Playfere in 302

G

Gansford, Sir John, inoperative Statute against the Will of, 29
Gardiner S R, author of "History of England from 1603 to 1616," passage in the Commons Journals misunderstood by, 190
  Misled as to a date by Mr Dixon, 277 note
  His suggestion relative to the delay on promoting Doddridge to be King's serjeant, 293
Garnett Father, 277
Gawdy, Sir Francis puisne judge K B made Chief Justice of the Common Pleas, 287 290
  Changes consequent on his death, 292
Genoa merchants (temp Hen IV) petition against, cited as a precedent, 357
Gloucestershire, parts of, anciently held as being a portion of Wales, 375
  See 369 376 379
Goodman's "Own Times," references to, 52 53, notes
Goodrich, or Goodridge, Castle 376
Goodwin Sir Francis, ousted from his seat on the ground of outlawry, 163
  Collision of the House with the Court of Chancery thereon also with the Lords and the King 164, 165
  Advice given by Bacon Con-

Goodwin, Sir Francis—continued
  ference with the Judges, 166—169
  Proceedings in the Council Compromise suggested by the King and acceded to, 170—172
Great Britain, letter from Bacon recommending the compilation of a History of, 249—252
Greece, advantage of union of provinces under the name of, 97
Green, Mrs Everett, date of Bacon's marriage first published by, 291
Grey, Lord, puritan, a participator in the "Priests' plot" 133
Grievances, course of proceeding adopted by the Commons with respect to and Message from the King thereon 278 280
  Collection of Grievances presented King's Speech in reply, 281—283
  See 303 303 note 385 Patents Purveyors Wardships
Gruter Bacon's Cogitata et Visa published by, 369
Guernsey, 318 330
Guise duke of, why called the greatest usurer in France 111
Gunpowder Plot discovery of the, 246 255 257
  Effect of same on the proceedings of the Commons 259
  Attainder of the Offenders course taken on the Bill for same, 283, 284

H

Hacklewit, Thomas, office granted by Patent to, 377
Hall, Arthur, committed to the Tower by the House of Commons for defamatory word, 57

Hamilton, Sir T Lord Advocate of Scotland Commissioner for the Union, 211
Hampton Court Conferences on Church matters See Church

Hare, M.P. selected as spokesman at a Conference about Purveyors, 267 note

Hastings, Sir Francis, altercation in the House between him and Bacon 38, 39
Moves for a Committee to consider of some sort of gratuity to be offered to the King, 215
See 200

Hatfield Collection, Bacon letters from the, 2, 79

Heath, Mr., Editor of Bacon's professional works 368, 382, 384

Henry I, limits of Wales narrowed by, 375

Henry III, Court of Common Pleas settled by, 373
Places fortified by him 375

Henry VIII, Power to dissolve the Court of Wards granted to him by Parliament, 178
Courts set up by, 373, 377, 378

Henry IV of France negotiates a separate treaty of peace with Spain, 15
In secret correspondence with Q. Eliz. about his 'Great Design," 52

Heptarchy, the, 321

Heraclitus "the obscure," 90

Herbert, Mr. Secretary, messages delivered and bills carried up by, 25, 203, 278, 282

Herefordshire, parts of anciently portions of Wales, 369, 375, 379

Hickes, Mr. afterwards Sir Michael, a friendly creditor of Bacon's, 14, 41, 258
Office held by him under Burghley and Cecil, 57
Letters from Bacon to him, 14, 57, 258, 302
At Bacon's wedding, 291

Hide, or Hyde, Laurence, moves the reading of an Act touching "Patents, commonly called monopolies, 23, 24, 25
See 31, 200, 267 note

Hiero, Simonides' answer to, 96

Hippocrates, maxims of, 106, 221

Hobart (or Hubbard), Sir Henry, Serjeant, chosen Attorney of Wards, 292
Made Attorney General, 293
See 199, 264, 294

Hobby, Sir Thomas Posthumus, Letter to him from Bacon as executor of Jeremiah Bettenham, concerning a debt due to the testator's estate, 297—299

Hoby, Sir Edward, moves for a Committee to consider of a gratuity to be offered to the King, 215
Refuses to sign the Report on the Union of England and Scotland, 245
See 200, 264 note, 267 note

Holland, a scrivener, his quarrel with a member's servant, 36
Penalty inflicted on him by the House, 37

Hollanders, petition of the York merchants against the, 357

Hollis, Sir John, 199

Hostile laws, proposed abolition of, 304, 305, 343, 344
Bill passed 343

Houbraken's engraved portrait of Bacon probably taken from Oliver's miniature, iv

House of Commons See Commons

Howard, Charles See Nottingham

Howard, Henry See Northampton

Hubbard See Hobart

Huntington, Lord, 38

Hyde See Hide

I.

Interpretatio Naturæ, Design of an intended work by Bacon so called, preface to some translated etc., 82—87 See 363

Ireland, alarming condition of, 15
Landing of Spanish forces, the Pope's Proclamation 16, 17
Tyrone and his Spanish allies decisively defeated 44
Letter from Bacon to Cecil on the state of the country and the policy to be pursued, 15—51, 99
Submission of Tyrone terms made with him, 52—54

Ireland—continued
The King's resolution propounded at the Hampton Court Conference, 129
Bacon's advice to Essex upon the offer of the Irish service, and upon his return, 116—118
Financial items annual charge, exchange etc. 189, 214
Place, privileges, etc., under the proposed Union and Naturalization schemes, 225, 226, 230, 239, 318, 323

Israel and Judah, example drawn from the union of, 98

J.

James I proclaimed King 66
  "Offer of service" from Bacon 62
  "Proclamation drawn for his first
    coming in," by Bacon 67 71
  Course taken for carrying on the
    government pending his arrival
    in England, 71 72
  Bacon's report on his first acts and
    of his subsequent interview with
    him, 73 76
  Makes a new Master of the Rolls,
    and dispossesses Ralegh of the
    Captaincy of the Guard, 78
  Literary work in which he would
    be likely to take an interest his
    learning, 88
  "Discourse touching the Union of
    England and Scotland, dedicated
    in private" to him, by Bacon,
    90-99
  His qualification for dealing with
    the dispute between the High
    Churchmen and the Puritans,
    99, 100
  Considerations on the subject ad-
    dressed to him by Bacon, 101 -
    127
  His conferences with the Bishops
    and others at Hampton Court,
    and their result 128 - 132
  Alleged plot to dispossess him of
    his crown, 131
  His speech on opening his first
    Parliament 163
  Involved in dispute concerning Sir
    F. Goodwin's election argu-
    ments and conferences thereon
    compromise suggested by him
    and accepted by the Commons
    165—172
  Course pursued by him in the dis-
    pute between the Commons and
    the Warden of the Fleet, in the
    case of Sir T. Shirley 174 176
  His anxiety for settling the Union
    of England and Scotland 176
  His proclamation in reference to
    monopoly licenses 177
  Parliamentary discussions relative
    to his Prerogative of Wardship,
    178—180
  Petitions of the Commons touching
    Purveyors, Bacon's Speech to
    him on presenting same and re-
    port of his reply, 181—189
  His proposition as to the order of
    proceeding in regard to the
    Union, 190
  Substance of his speech thereon as
    reported by Bacon, 193 —195
  His "project of an act," and its
    effect upon the House his mes-

James I —continued
  sage to them thereon, 195,
    196
  Objections by the Judges to his
    proposition for changing the
    name of the Kingdom by Act of
    Parliament 200
  Act for authorizing Commissioners
    on the Union presented to him,
    201- 206
  His letter to the Commons, im-
    plying dissatisfaction and nearly
    provoking a formal remon-
    strance, 207, 208
  His speech to them, with similar
    effect, 211 212
  His apologetic message, 212
  His forbearance to ask for a grant
    of money unsatisfactory issue
    of an attempt by his friends to
    obtain one for him and with-
    drawal of the motion by his own
    desire 213 - 215
  Office and pension conferred by
    him on Bacon 217
  Analysis of the several questions
    involved in the Union of Eng-
    land and Scotland drawn up by
    Bacon for his information, 218-
    231
  Proposed Proclamation touching
    his style, by Bacon 235- 239
  Evidence of his earnestness in the
    matter of Purveyors 267 272
    271
  False alarm of his assassination,
    276
  His attitude and intentions with
    regard to Grievances explained
    in a public declaration to the
    Commons through the Speaker,
    279 280
  His answer to Bacon after hearing
    the collection of grievances read,
    282 See also 303
  His speech on the Naturalization
    question before the Latter recess
    311 312
  Proclamation "touching the
    Marches," drawn for him by
    Bacon 385—388
  A like Proclamation for Jurors,
    389 - 392
  See 60 65 66 202 note 209 210
    259 266 293 331 note
Jansen, Cornelius, x
Jardine Mr, fact in Bacon's history
  discovered by 11
Jesuits 266 See Papists
Johnson Mr, of Gray's Inn surety for
  money due by Bacon 12
Jones, Edward the like 12

Judah and Israel, union of, the lesser trying to draw the greater, 98

Julius Cæsar, obtained naturalization for a city in Gaul, 96
   See 182

James Petty, attempt to improve the constitution of, draft of a Proclamation concerning same, 389—392

K.

Kempe, Robert, Bacon's cousin, one of his sureties, 12
   Letter to him from Bacon on Elizabeth's death and James's accession, 71

Kilpeck Manor, 376

King, Dr, participator in the Hampton Court Conference, 129

"Kingdom of Man," meaning of the expression as used by Bacon, 83

Kinsale invaded and occupied by Spaniards, 16, 20. The Spaniards forced to capitulate, 41

Knewstubbs, Mr, participator in the Hampton Court Conference, 129

Knighte, Henry, office granted by Patent to, 377

L.

Lake, Mr, afterwards Sir Thomas, messenger from the Council to Scotland, 61, 64
   Letter from Coke to 287 *note*

Lambeth, extent and character of Anthony Bacon's correspondence at, 6

Lascelles, Edmund, on James's order for tombs to Elizabeth and his mother 219 *note*

Laws, Union of, Bacon's Speech against, 335—341

Leicester, Robert Dudley Earl of, 147, 379

Levant, references to arrests of ships trading to the 348, 349, 351, 353

Leveson, Sir Richard, destruction of Spanish ships in Castlehaven harbour by, 44

Lewis XII part of his dominions how lost to, 321

Lewknor, Sir Lewys, 200

Lichfield, Bishop of (temp Hen VII) President of the Council of Wales, 377

Lincoln, Bishop of (temp Hen VIII) President of the Council of Wales, 377

Livy on the union of the Romans and Sabines, 95

London, popular manifestations in, at James's accession 56
   Debt due to the City from the Crown, 214
   Pestered with new buildings 307

London, Bishop of, argues for the maintenance of Ceremonies at the Hampton Court Conference, 129
   His declaration on the question between the Commons and the House of Convocation, 210

Lord Keeper *See* Egerton, Sir Thomas

Lord Treasurer *See* Buckhurst

Lords, House of, the parts of the body nearest the head, 166
   Their sympathy with the Commons as to Purveyors, 189
   Propose an annual payment by way of composition, 190, 266
   Their proceeding in regard to the Bishop of Bristol's Book, 209 *note*
   In Conference with the Commons on divers subjects *See* 178, 179, 200, 201, 208, 211, 267, 268, 273

Low Countries, trade restriction on the, 352
   Policy of the Spaniards towards them, *ibid*

M.

Macaulay, Lord on Bacon's defence of his conduct towards Essex, 162

Machiavel on the causes of the increase of the Roman Empire, 96
   On the true sinews of war, 323, 324

Magna Charta, 331

Man, the Kingdom of, meaning of the expression as used by Bacon 83

Manningham, on the last hours of Queen Elizabeth, 55
   On the popular manifestations at James's accession, 56

Mar, Earl of, 59

Marcellus Consul a naturalized citizen beaten with rods by 96

Much Tails of, origin of their title, 67

Marches on Welsh Borders, a View of the Differences in question betwixt the King's Bench and the Council in the, 368–282

  "Suggestions for the settling of the Dispute" 382–384

  Persons for taking a different course, 385

  Draft of Proclamation, 385–388

  See 221 229 233

Marque on Mart Letters of occasion of Henry the fifth's Statute respecting, 316

  Policy of a like proceeding (temp James I) discussed, 354, 355

Martin Mr, in Committee upon the Bill for abolishing hostile laws, 313

Mary, Queen, 178 577

Mary, Queen of Scots commencement of a tomb to 249 note

Matthew Toby, son of the Bishop of Durham, Bacon's friendship for 61 64

  Charged with a letter from him to the King ibid

  His collection of letters published with dedicatory letter by Dr Donne plan on which they are edited 62 72 215

  Letters to him from Bacon 73 216 255

  See 61 note

Maynard Henry, negotiates between Bacon and Trott 41

Merchants Assurance Bill, 34, 35

Merchants Petition for redress of wrongs from Spain and for letters of Marque 345–361

Monck ... was, on the satisfaction of the Commons at the Queen's dealing with Monopolies, 33, not 3

Money the news of war, 324

Monopolies See Patents

Montague, Basil 11 297

Montague, Dr his memoranda of the proceedings at the Hampton Court Conference 128–132

Montague Sir Edward, his motion for subsidies 273 274

Montjoy, Charles Blount Lord, afterwards Earl of Devonshire, Tyrone and the Irish rebels defeated by 11

  Receives the submission of Tyrone, 52 51

  His implication in Essex's intrigues the Queen's bold conduct therein 137, 138 note

  See 73 note 99 159 141

Moore, Francis MP for Reading, moves thanks to the Queen for her Proclamation respecting Patents 52

Moore, George, recusant Bacon's motion relative to, and altercation with Coke which grew out of it, 3

Moore Sir George MP 200

Morison, Dr friend of Essex and Bacon letter from Bacon to him, 66

Moryson Fynes, 53 note

  His account of Montjoy's proceedings upon news of the insurrection and apprehension of Essex, 137 note

Moses appointment of elders and judges cited as a precedent, 112

Mounteagle Lord sum paid as fine by for his implication in Essex's insurrection 11

Munster, Bacon's comments on "the last plot for the population of," 51

Murdin, Bacon letters found at Hatfield by 2 79

Muscovy and Turkey merchants, 233

N.

Napier, Mr Macvey, on Raleigh's connexion with Cobham's plot 134, 135 note

Naturalization in England of the natives of Scotland Ante note and Post note, 211 304

  Scheme opposed in the Commons, 306

  Speech in its favour by Bacon 307–325

  Objection of the Commons to admit any to the benefit of naturalization except upon conditions their resolution that the

Naturalization continued

  Post nati were not naturalized de jure Committees and Conferences, 325 341

  Speech of the King, its character and object, 341, 342

  The subject indefinitely postponed 342

Neville Sir Henry, 199

  On rumoured promotions in the Law 288

Nicholas, Reynold, purchaser of the land Essex gave to Bacon, 143

Nonconformists See Puritans

Northampton Lord Henry Howard, afterwards Earl of relations of Anthony Bacon with, 11, 12
A confidential correspondent with James before his accession 56
Letter from Bacon requesting him to present his book to the King 292
His speech in answer to the Merchants, 360
See 194
Northumberland H. Percy Earl of, a confidential correspondent with James before his accession, 56

Northumberland—continued
Letter to him from Bacon with an offer of his services, 58
Another from same, with draft of Proclamation on James's accession, 67
Said to have disputed the right of the Council to act during the interregnum 71
Left in the shadow by Cecil, 79
See 79 note 76
Nottingham Charles Howard, Earl of, an interceder for the Earl of Southampton, 79 note

O.

Oliver, Peter and Isaac, miniature portrait painters, v
Osborne Mr, Treasurer's Remembrancer in the Exchequer, com-

Osborne Mr—continued
plaint of abuses in the office of, 21 22
Owen, Sir Roger, 329 note 341

P

Packington, Lady, mother of Bacon's wife, 290
Packington, Sir John, Bacon's wedding dinner at the lodgings of, 291
Papists and Recusants 'much watching and searching for' 258
The Commons in a humour of great severity against them, 259
Laws passed against them, 260—263
Parliament, Elizabeth's dislike of dependence upon for money 16
Relation between the Crown and 17
Bills brought in by Bacon, and why 17—19
King James's first Parliament, 163
Prorogations, 215 287
See Commons Lords
Parry, committed for a seditious and contemptuous speech, 37
Parry, Dr on the last days of Queen Elizabeth, 55
Pass, Simon, engraving of Bacon by, v
Patents and Monopolies, Elizabeth's promise to the last Parliament to enquire into them, 15
Use made of those by her 16
Her action on the matter interrupted by Essex's insurrection, ibid
Feeling of the new Parliament on the subject, 20, 21
Proceedings against them 23—32
Proclamation issued, suspending the execution of them and refer-

Patents and Monopolies—continued
ring them to the decision of the common law, 33 34
see 33 note 177 210 Grievances
Peccum, Mr bonds deposited by Bacon with, 298
Penal Statutes bill drawn respecting, 177
Perkins, Sir Chro, 200
Persia, 321
Persian magic, Bacon's idea and definition of 89 90
Phelipps, Sir Richard, on the procedure of the Commons relative to grievances, 281 note
Philip of Spain negotiating a treaty with Henry IV of France 15
Hopes inspired in France by his death, 52 note
Phillips, Mr, opposition of Bacon to a bill introduced by, 38
Philosophia Prima 89
Pickering the late Mr, publisher, letter of Bacon's communicated to the Author by, 297, 298
Plato's notion on the education of the Persian Princes, 89
Playfere, Dr, requested by Bacon to translate his Advancement of Learning into Latin 300
Probable causes of his failure to complete the translation, his ill health and death 302
Pluralities and non-residence 122 129
See Church
Polonia, multiplication of Scotchmen in 311

Polydore Virgile, a defacer of MSS., 251

Post nati Scottish subjects born after Elizabeth's death their naturalization recommended, 244 306
  Adverse feeling of the legislature, 325, 332
  Distinction between their case and that of the ante nati, 358 359 340
  See Naturalization

Preaching Bacon on the art of, 118—120

Prerogative in relation to monopolies, 15
  Proceedings in the Commons touching, or touching upon it 24 27 29 30
  In collision with privilege, 165
  King James's sentiments concerning it, 170 172
  Its oppressiveness in the matter of Wardship, 179 208
  Coke ceases to be its champion, 292
  See 166 268 269 367 Patents Purveyors Wardship

Priests' plot discovery of the, and disposal of the chief delinquents, 133

Privilege See Breach of Privilege

Profuence and Advancement of Learning See Advancement of Learning

Puritans, unsettled dispute between High Churchmen and 99
  Nature of King James's objection to them 100

Purveyors and Cart-takers, abusers of their authority, 177
  Committee charged to draw a bill to restrain such abuses, ibid
  Petition to the King touching same 181 187
  His answer, 158, 189
  Conference with the Lords concerning composition proposed, 189
  Committee collecting evidence, 208
  Matter to sleep till next Session, 212
  Resolution to proceed by Bill, 260 261
  Consideration of subject resumed discordant views of Lords and Commons, 266
  Message from the King Conference between the two Houses, 267 268
  Debate on report, 269, 270
  Composition put aside bill passed in the Commons and thrown out in the Lords, 271
  Proclamation against abuses published its provisions, 272
  Second Bill passed by the Commons reasons of the Lords for not proceeding with it, 273
  See 274 282

R.

Raleigh, Sir Walter leads the discussion on a Subsidy Grant, 20
  Answers Bacon's speech in favour of the 'Statute of Tillage, 36
  His proposition to the Council during the interregnum, 72
  Removed from the Captaincy of the Guard, but receives compensation, 78
  Tried for treason effect of his defence, Mr Napier's theory of his connection with the plot, 133–135
  Conduct of his trial by Coke, 136

Rawley Dr, Editor of the Resuscitatio, notes on papers of Bacon printed by, 3 4 5 16 note 58 59 102 218
  See 201

Reynolds, Dr, at the Hampton Court Conference, 129 130

Reynolds Th Shoemaker, his deposition relative to Bead the Papist, 258

Richard II, his answer to the merchants' complaints, 357
  His offer to the Commons and their reply, 358

Ridgway, Sir Thomas, purport of his motion touching Wardships and Tenures, 211
  Moves for Committee of Supply, 274

Rivers, Earl, First Lord President of the Marches, 376
  His place of residence, 377

Roman Catholics See Papists

Rome, illustrative references to the laws and government of, 95–27, 312 319

Russell, Lady, mother of S F Hobby 298 note

Rutland, Earl of, fine imposed on, for complicity in Essex's plot, 14

S

Sabines and Romans, their perfect mixture, 95 99

Saint Albans, Lady (Bacon's wife) 291

Saint John, Sir Oliver, 200

Saint Paul's double nationality, 95, 96
On the Duty of providing for a man's family, 322
On the difference between Neophytes and born Christians 340

Salisbury, Earl of See Cecil

Sands, Lord, fine imposed on, for his complicity in Essex's plot, 14

Sandys, Sir Edwin, takes charge of the question of Wardships his position in the House, 180 210
Part assigned to him in the conference on the Union, 197 199 201
His report of the conference on Wardships, 211
'Bill for the better establishing of true Religion,' brought in by him, 264
His books burned by order of the High Commission, ibid
His argument on the Naturalization question, 328
His refusal on the part of the Commons to allow the cases of Ante-nati and the Post-nati to be treated as distinct, 333 note
His suggestion of a perfect union, 331

Savile, Sir John, 200
Objections to the Bill of Purveyors collected by him, 271 note

Scotland, union of, with England, 89
'Brief Discourse' thereon, by Bacon, 90 99
Commencement of proceedings in Parliament relative to the Union, 190— 191
Objections to change of name, 195—202
Appointment of a mixed Commission to consider the other questions, 202—207
Time fixed for the meeting of the Commissioners, 217
Articles or considerations touching 'the Union,' drawn up by Bacon, 218—234
Draught of proclamation of the King's style, prepared by Bacon, but not used, 235—239
Proceedings of the Commissioners presentation of the articles, 240—242
Preface to the report, prepared by Bacon but altered, 242—245
Debates and Proceedings on the

Scotland—continued
Naturalization of Scotsmen in England, 211 304 306 307— 325 327—345
See Ante-nati Naturalization Post-nati

Seward's "Anecdotes," Monumental Inscription printed in, 299

Shirley, Sir Thomas, M P, arrested for debt and sent to the Fleet, proceedings in the Commons thereon, 173—176

Shrewsbury, Earl of, on the altered temper of the Commons after the discovery of the Gunpowder Plot, 260

Shropshire and the Marches, 369 370 375

Sicily, arrest of an English ship in, 353

Simonides, anecdote of, 196

Smith, Sir Thomas, charged with implication in Essex's treason, 159
Another of the name, 366

Solicitor General See Doderidge Fleming

Solon's reply to Crœsus, 323

Southampton, Henry, Earl of, expects release by the next despatch Bacon's relations with him, and letter on the occasion, 74, 75
Released from the Tower, 76
See 137

Southampton Thomas, Earl of, Lord Treasurer, Story respecting Ralegh told by him, 135

Spain, landing on the Irish coast of, troops from, 16 20
Landing and defeat of additional troops, 14
Union of the kingdoms of, 92 97 320, 321
Relations of Ralegh with, 134
Impositions in, 189
Complaints of English merchants relative to wrongs done to them by Spaniards, 345—361
Salisbury in receipt of pension from King of Spain, 357
See 15 15 note 47 214 222

Sparke, Dr, at the Hampton Court Conference, 129

Speaker of the House of Commons See Commons

Spencer, Sir Richard, 199

Stansby, Major, his account of Ralegh's connexion with Cobham's treason, 135

Star Chamber, 281 285 note

Starkey Ralph, MS relating to the Goodwin case, in his handwriting, 172 note

Stuart, Lady Arabella, plot in favour of, abetted by Ralegh, 134

Subsidies and Supplies, 15
    Impolicy of calling a Parliament for supply only, 17
    Hurry of the Commons to vote Supplies pending the Spanish invasion of Ireland, large amount granted, 20, 21
    Queens thanks for same, and reception of the members, 31—33
    Report of Conference on Tonnage and Poundage Subsidy, 214
    Failure of an effort to procure money for James, 215
    Double Subsidy agreed on, 260 264
    Order of proceeding on the occasion 273, 274

Subsidies and Supplies—continued
    An additional Subsidy voted, and Bill for 3 subsidies passed and sent to the Lords, 275—278 281
    See Patents

Sully on the death of Philip of Spain and Elizabeth of England, 52 note
    On the fashion in James's Court of depreciating the memory of Elizabeth, 67

Superfluous Laws, Committee for repeal of, moved by Bacon, 18, 19

Sympson, a goldsmith, committed for arresting a member of the house, proceedings thereon, and penalty imposed on him, 173—176

T.

Tanfield, Serjeant, 199

Tenison, Archbishop, on Dr Playfere s translation of the Advancement of Learning, 302

Tenures See Wardship

Tillage, Statute of, Bacon s Speech against its repeal, 35

Tonnage and Poundage Bill, Conference on, reported by Bacon, 213, 214
    See 270

Tower, Lieutenant of the, proposed fine on him, 174

Townshend s Notes of Debates in Elizabeth s Parliaments, citations from or references to, 17 19 19 note 20 21 23—56 30 37—39
    His motion touching monopolies, 20

Treasurer s Remembrancer in the Exchequer, proceedings relative to abuses in the office of, 21, 22

Trial, The, pretext of the Spaniards for arresting a ship so named, 353

Trott, Nicholas, statement of account between him and Bacon, 40—44

Twickenham Park mortgaged by Bacon to Nicholas Trott, 40
    Amount offered by Bacon for its redemption, 43, 44

Tyrone, Earl of, in arms in Ireland against Elizabeth, 20
    Defeat of himself and his Spanish confederates, 44
    His offer of submission Montjoy s politic dealing with him and its result, 52 54

U

Union of England and Scotland See Scotland

Union of Laws, Bacon s Speech against a motion for, 335—341

V

Valerius Terminus, 89

Van Somer s portrait of Bacon at Gorhambury, iii, iv

Vineyard, The, pretext of the Spaniards for arresting a ship so named, 353

W.

Wales, proposal for uniformity of its weights and measures with those of England, 18
    Differences betwixt the King's Bench and the Council in the Marches, 368 et seq See Marches

Walsingham, Sir Francis, Letter from him concerning the services of Anthony Bacon, Francis Bacon s brother, 8

Walsingham, Lady, redeems Essex House, 11

Wardship and Tenures, origin of
Wardship beginning to be felt
as a burden and grievance, 176
Referred to a conference Bacon's
reports of proceedings therein,
177—180
Composition for this Prerogative
still under discussion, 208
Change of temper in the Lords
and report of conference by
Sir Edwin Sandys, 210, 211
Connection of Escuage with the
Question, 305
Salisbury suspected of secretly
furthering the dispute, *ibid*, *note*
Weights and Measures, Bill against
abuses in, 17—19
West Indies, interference of Spain
with English traders to the,
351 352
Wilde, Robert, Privy Council decree
against, 379
William the Conqueror, Exchequer
Court founded by, 373

William Rufus, and the Welsh Marches,
375
Wilson, Sir Thomas, on the proceed-
ings of Wardship, 305 *note* 2 3
See 343
Winchester, Bishop of, at the Hamp-
ton Court Conference, 129
Windsor, Dean of, on Elizabeth's last
illness, 55
Wingfield, Sir Rob, 200
Winwood, Secretary, his opinion of
Sir Henry Wotton 11
Woolmer, amount of Bacon's debt to,
82
Worcester, Bishop of, Lord President
of the Marches, 377
Worcester, City and County of, and
the Marches of Wales, 369 375
Worcester, Lord, 188
Wotton, Sir Henry, his story about
Anthony Bacon and the Earl of
Essex, 9—11
Wroth, Sir Robert, 178 200

Y.

Yelverton, Henry, M P, his proceedings in the Goodwin case, 169
See 200 267

York provincial council, 229 233 384
Petition of York merchants against
the Hollanders, 357

END OF VOL III

PRINTED BY J E TAYLOR AND CO,
LITTLE QUEEN STREET, LINCOLN'S INN FIELDS